SAMUEL AND THE
DEUTERONOMIST

Indiana Studies in Biblical Literature

Herbert Marks and Robert Polzin,

general editors

SAMUEL AND THE DEUTERONOMIST

A Literary Study of the Deuteronomic History

Part Two
1 SAMUEL

ROBERT POLZIN

INDIANA UNIVERSITY PRESS
BLOOMINGTON & INDIANAPOLIS

Manufactured in the United States of America

Grateful acknowledgment is given for the use of the following material:

Unless otherwise noted, the Scripture quotations are from the Revised Standard
Version Bible, copyright 1946, 1952, 1971 by the Division of Christian Education
of the National Council of the Churches of Christ in the U.S.A., and
are used by permission.

The quotations of M. M. Bakhtin are from the *Dialogic Imagination: Four Essays*
by M. M. Bakhtin. Edited by Michael Holquist. Translated by Carole Emerson
and Michael Holquist. Copyright © by the University of Texas Press.
Used by permission of the publisher.

An earlier version of my reading of 1 Sam. 1, found in chapter one, appeared
as "The Speaking Person and His Voice in 1 Samuel," *Supplements to Vetus
Testamentum* XXXVI. Edited by J. A. Emerton. (Leiden 1985).
Copyright © by E. J. Brill. Used by permission of the publisher.

Library of Congress Cataloging-in-Publication Data
Polzin, Robert.
    Samuel and the Deuteronomist : a literary study of the
Deuteronomic history: part two: 1 Samuel / Robert Polzin. — 1st
Indiana University Press ed.
        p.   cm. — (Indiana studies in biblical literature)
    Originally published: San Francisco : Harper & Row, c1989.
    Includes bibliographical references and indexes.
    ISBN 0-253-34552-9 (cloth : alk. paper). — ISBN 0-253-20849-1
(pbk. : alk. paper)
    1. Bible.   O.T.   Samuel, 1st—Criticism, interpretation, etc.
    I. Title.   II. Series.
    [BS1325.2.P65   1993]
    222'.43066—dc20   92-43856

    1 2 3 4 5   97 96 95 94 93

For
Joan
and
Shirley

CONTENTS

ACKNOWLEDGMENTS

Two scholars, Frank Cross and the late G. Ernest Wright, first taught me the importance of high standards. I have been grateful to them ever since. Over the years, the writings of Mikhail Bakhtin and his school have influenced me profoundly; I only hope that my own reflections, which try to capture the spirit of Bakhtin's work, accurately convey something of the enigmatic power of his genius. Meir Sternberg, a genial friend and brilliant guide, has helped me, in countless ways and with unfailing generosity, to sustain my commitment to an ancient treasure. Other scholars have been a source of insight and inspiration along the way. The following study documents much of their help. Finally, Herbert Marks and Priscilla Stuckey-Kauffman, a wonderful copy-editor, have helped me purge the manuscript of many embarrassments; I am responsible for any that remain.

I dedicate this book with love to my wife and to my sister.

SAMUEL AND THE DEUTERONOMIST

INTRODUCTION

Both read the Bible day and night, But thou read'st black where I read white.
(William Blake, "The Everlasting Gospel")

For his hand is heavy upon us. (Men of Ashdod, 1 Samuel 5:7)

On Matters Black and White

The reader will find precious little in the way of textual criticism or history in the following pages; this activity, so necessary in itself, tends to become addictive and can divert one's efforts all out of proportion to the preliminary task of getting a global picture of what a "book" even as textually corrupt as 1 or 2 Samuel is driving at. Whatever textual differences are represented by all the ancient witnesses to 1 Samuel, and whichever established text modern translators use as the starting point for their interpretive activities, the similarities between one witness and another are so overwhelmingly greater than their often important differences that a law of diminishing returns takes effect the further one proceeds. The more time and effort one puts into establishing the text, the less crucial successive effort will be for matters of global interpretation.[1]

Even more to the point, the kind of close attention to the text that many biblical scholars' criticism represents turns out to be little more than textual in the narrow sense; the almost exclusive attention to *real texts* exhibited in their writings is attention to establishing a kind of *physical* text as a starting point for getting beyond it historically. Other meanings for a text-as-real do not occupy or hold their interest. Take Kyle McCarter's commentaries on 1 and 2 Samuel in the Anchor Bible. No one would deny his contribution to the text criticism and textual history of 1 and 2 Samuel or the judicious way he establishes a specific ancient text as the basis for his translation and interpretation. But having accomplished his task of translation, McCarter spends the rest of the over one thousand pages at his disposal mostly attending to matters of literary or cultural history. That is to say, the text that he establishes and translates so competently simply becomes a pretext for reconstructing either the prior stages in the formation of that text, or else those stages in the history of the religion of Israel that are exemplified in the textual strata he has "discovered." Anyone wanting to know how specific parts of 1 or 2 Samuel fit together or cohere in their final form finds amazingly little that does justice to the very text that McCarter so long and arduously establishes as a basis for his translation and so-called interpretation.

A commentary like McCarter's—and his is typical—moves from establishing the text to translation to matters of literary and cultural history, proceeding with a profound lack of attention to what the entire text might mean in its final shape. This is simply not an important interest of biblical scholarship since the nineteenth century. It is true that the Anchor Bible, for example, does contain holistic commentaries like Moshe Greenberg on Ezekiel or Anderson and Freedman on Hosea, and that for all their novelty the first is impressive rather than clumsy and the second vice versa. Yet no scholars belonging to either the fragmenting or holistic camps of biblical scholarship have succeeded in conversing easily or productively with their counterparts. More importantly, few scholars I know do both kinds well. The scholarship of those who do try to do both tends to be bifurcated or schizophrenic. Their poetic sides apologize for the "flawed" composition of the final text they are trying to make good sense of, while their genetic sides are working hard to portray a supposed earlier stage as more coherent or clear before those inept redactors got their damned hands on it.

This attitude toward final redactors and the quality of the text they are supposed to have produced brings me to a discussion of exemplary works which, I hope, will illustrate the reasons why I have not done in the following pages some of the "necessary" things scholars are wont to do. After offering a detailed illustration of how scholars tend to approach a specific portion of 1 Samuel, the Ark Narrative, I will provide some general background for such tendencies by discussing broader issues involving the Deuteronomic History.

The Heavy Hand of the Redactor

In many respects *The Hand of the Lord: A Reassessment of the "Ark Narrative" of 1 Samuel* by P. D. Miller and J. J. M. Roberts is an improvement over previous treatments of the ark narrative.[2] Its judicious discussion of extrabiblical parallels and its obvious desire to recognize within chapters 1–6 of 1 Samuel as many intertextual connections as its basic assumptions will allow are praiseworthy. Nevertheless, its view that the final hand at work on 1 Samuel 1–7 is a "redactor" makes it impossible for its authors to recognize the many signs of the highly artistic composition that they worked on so assiduously as they reconstructed the prebiblical narrative (1 Sam. 2:12–17, 22–25, 27–36; 4:1b–7:1) that is the subject of their monograph.

The Hand of the Lord provokes a basic question all biblical scholars ought to ask themselves: What has brought us to the present situation in which we on one hand recognize in theory and practice the necessity of *establishing the text*, but on the other simply use it to do the kind of excavative scholarship that has dominated our field for well over a century? Why have we chosen to apply our not inconsiderable skills to reconstructing a supposed prior text and to determining its theological intention and probable date of composition, without employing as much sympathetic care and effort in determining the global meaning of the very text that has helped shape Western civilization and the Judeo-Christian culture at its core? Why do we typically choose to do what we do, even as we avoid what we choose not to do?

These questions, I must point out, do not take the unfair tack of criticizing a book for not doing what its authors did not intend it to do in the first place. Rather, the issue here is something else: what in *The Hand of the Lord* indicates the position of its authors about what they chose not to do? What is their opinion of the nature and value of *the real text* of 1 Samuel 1–6, on which they chose not to write a monograph? My suggestion throughout this introduction will be that Miller and Roberts, like many of our colleagues, are heirs of a scholarly tradition that, by dint of effort and direction, denigrates the Bible in many of its esthetic, historiographic, and ideological dimensions, however loudly and often scholars claim the contrary.

One has only to read *The Hand of the Lord* to see the tortuous path we scholars prefer to pursue. Having established and exegeted their "pre-text", Miller and Roberts pose a fundamental question that pre-text raises: if "the narrative at no point proposes such an interpretation [the anger of Yahweh] of this seemingly catastrophic event [the capture of the ark]," what could be the point of it all? They give their answer on the following page: the ark narrative emphasizes "the manifestation of Yahweh's power over Israel's historical enemies in the earlier period." Thus, in analyzing their reconstructed ark narrative (1 Sam. 2:12–17, 22–25, 27–36; 4:1b–7:1), they are able to assert that its turning point "is found in 1 Sam. 5:1–5 [Yahweh's victory over Dagon], and the rest of the narrative (after the death of the Elides) centers around the meaning of the capture and return of the divine 'representation,' the ark." The theological aim of the account is a theodicy "answering the question, who is supreme, who is God, Yahweh or Dagon?" The turning point of the account is the loss of the ark.[3]

If we compare the aim and the turning point of their reconstructed text with the "obvious" or "apparent" aim and turning point of the real text before their eyes, somehow everything is turned upside down: the supremacy of Yahweh is never a real concern of the story at this point;

he is always portrayed in full control of all situations, be it Hannah's lack of progeny, the sins of the Elides or communication with them, the loss of the ark, the fairly comical struggles of the Philistines to rid themselves of their plague-filled Israelite booty, or the destructive return of the ark to the people of Beth-shemesh by means of a pair of leaderless milch-cows. Nothing is clearer in the final form of the text than Yahweh's utter mastery of the situation, whatever it may be. Far from being a turning point in the final form of the story, Yahweh's defeat of Dagon in 1 Samuel 5:1–5 is the least problematic incident in the entire account. Nothing is less surprising in the story than that Yahweh defeats Dagon. As for puzzling out why all this could have happened—the double defeat at Ebenezer, the deaths of Eli and his sons, and the loss of the ark—the biblical account could not be clearer: these events are the result not only of Elide leadership but also of the foreign gods and Ashtaroth that Samuel commands the Israelites to put away if they are finally to deserve victory over their enemies, the Philistines (1 Sam. 7:3–5).

If, then, we were to ask Miller and Roberts to explain how this reversal of theological aim between reconstructed and actual ark narrative could have come about, the answer is obvious from their monograph: between the composition of this early theodicy and the present biblical account in 1 Samuel 1–6 lies, finally, the hand of a redactor with crude literary skills of integration if not also ideological perspectives, who beclouds the whole point of the ark story with narrow or dim-witted purposes.

It is true that Miller and Roberts have salvaged as "original" much more of the material in 1 Samuel 1–6 than many biblical scholars—most of chapter 2 and all of 4:1b–7:1. However, what is secondary for them, that is, not completely integrated into the real text, is the Samuel material in chapters 1–3, which, like the Samuel material in 7:3ff., is part of a later someone's subverting plan. Whether author or redactor, it is this individual who inserted the Samuel material rather violently into the already existing ark narrative to satisfy personal desires.

Why, according to Miller and Roberts, is much of the material in chapters 4–6 originally unified? Favorably quoting Willis's indications of the symmetry and interconnectedness of these three chapters,[4] and indeed pointing to other indications they themselves adduce in the body of their monograph, Miller and Roberts argue a persuasive case for unity.

But what of those connections between 4:1b–7:1 and 7:2–17, "original" connections for Willis,[5] but whose originality Miller and Roberts insistently deny? Well, they assert, these offer no conclusive argument for "original unity" because, in contrast to the symmetries within chapters 4–6, these "can be adequately explained by assuming that the redactor responsible for introducing this material had 2:12–17, 22–25, 27–36; 4:1b–7:1 [that is, Miller and Roberts's original ark narrative] before him, and thus, as with the birth and childhood stories, could shape his material to create links."[6]

The problem here is not with the recognition of "interconnections and symmetries" in the text—to use Miller and Roberts's terminology. These features can be pointed to and their plausibility assessed in scholarly debate. Dialogue between those who disagree whether this or that feature of a text is a "connection" or a "symmetry" is not only possible, it is expected—part of what interpreters do. But Miller and Roberts go a step further, and they employ a double standard in the process. Not only do they recognize interconnections and symmetries (for example, just as the Beth-shemites are "smitten" [*hikkāh*] in 6:19, with the root occurring three times there, so also were the Philistines [5:6, 9, 12]), they further distinguish between interconnections and symmetries that are "original" (for example, those within chapters 4–6) and those that are "redactional" (features in chapters 4–6, for example, found also in chap. 7ff.). Yet nowhere do they discuss how one can distinguish the two kinds of symmetries.

Anyone who reads chapter 7 carefully will notice many striking interconnections between it and the preceding chapters. As my reading of 1 Samuel 1–7 will bring out, Samuel's reference to Israel's "foreign gods" in 7:3 has profoundly ironic interconnections with the supposedly erroneous belief of the Philistines expressed in 4:8: "Woe is us! Who can deliver us from the power of these mighty gods?" If the Philistines and Israelites alike are "smitten" in chapters 4–6 (an original interconnection for Miller and Roberts), so also the soon-to-be-victorious Israelites "are afraid" in 7:7, just as the soon-to-be-victorious Philistines were in 4:7 (a redactional interconnection, according to Miller and Roberts). The "who can deliver us?" of the Philistines in 4:8 is answered by Samuel's "he will deliver you" in 7:3 and the narrator's remark in 7:14, "And Israel delivered their territory." Samuel's victorious setting up of the stone called Ebenezer, in 7:12 correlates with Israel's double defeat at Ebenezer in chapter 4; chapter 4 ends with an etymology of defeat, chapter 7 with one of victory.

When Miller and Roberts characterize these kinds of interconnections between chapters 4–6 on one hand and chapter 7 on the other, they believe they are able to distinguish them as redactional and secondary, whereas the similar and often less striking symmetries within chapters 4–6 appear to them as assuredly original. They give no reasons why one series of interconnections is original, another redactional. What, to them, indicates a redactor's secondary connection, as opposed to an original story's embodied connection? Miller and Roberts never say, and I suspect that they would have difficulty justifying their ability to distinguish such supposed differences in the chapters under consideration. They employ such a distinction without justification or explanation.

Another example of their use of a double standard involves their determination of original and secondary material within chapters 1–6. On one hand, an indication for them—and for many others—that the Samuel material does not originally belong to the ark narrative is that Samuel is nowhere mentioned in 4:1b–7:1. On the other hand, when the account of the wickedness of Eli's sons in 2:12–36 contains or is bracketed by numerous references to Samuel (vv. 11, 18–21, 26), this chapter "would read quite smoothly if the intervening vss. [referring to Samuel] were simply deleted."[7] However, in view both of the many references to him in chapter 2 and of the abiding and complex manner in which Samuel is present in all the sections in chapter 2 that do *not* refer to him,[8] it simply will not do to state categorically that (1) *no reference to Samuel* is a sign of his original separation from the ark story; and (2) *frequent reference to him* is a sign of redactional inclusion. With such double-barreled artillery Miller and Roberts can always hit their target.

Certainly when Miller and Roberts approach the text, their emphasis is on *genetic* composition, whereas mine will be on *poetic* composition. Meir Sternberg's discussion of source-oriented and discourse-oriented analysis is relevant here.[9] Miller and Roberts confront the real text to get behind or beyond it; a discourse-oriented reading such as mine is concerned rather with the meaning of the text itself. This distinction is largely a matter of emphasis, so that our objects will overlap in key respects. Nevertheless, our conflicting opinion on one's ability to distinguish between "original" and "redactional" interconnections is itself a good example of an overlapping of object and my central reason for emphasizing our differences. I want to suggest here that the ability to distinguish so-called genetic from poetic features of a text must begin by treating the poetic dimensions of the text—here the discovery and description of interconnections and symmetries between parts of a text—much more carefully and fairly than is usually done in source-oriented inquiries like *The Hand of the Lord*.

My reading of 1 Samuel will rarely, if ever, claim to distinguish authorial from redactional, or original from secondary, interconnections and symmetries. (When I do use the adjective *authorial* in the following pages, it will generally be my code word for *artful* and will point to some aspect of the crafting of the text, whether by author or redactor.) Lacking the discovery of an ancient manuscript containing an approximation of Miller and Roberts's original ark narrative, I find their analyses, like those of the scholars I will shortly discuss, highly speculative and ultimately disappointing. However laudable the historical impulse behind them, such analyses profoundly neutralize the power for good or ill that the Bible has exerted on people down through the ages. It is to begin redressing this unfortunate neglect of the real text that my preliminary reading of 1 Samuel avoids the pre-texts once violated, in Miller and Roberts's view, by the heavy hand of the redactor.

Near Eastern Contexts

I employ little textual criticism or genetic reconstruction in the following pages; yet another ingredient is missing in my reading of 1 Samuel, which Miller and Roberts's monograph underlines by its presence. They suggest that "openness to the broader cultural context in which Israel's faith developed could freshen up a scholarly discussion grown stale within the narrow confines of internal biblical exegesis." Indeed, their monograph is strong on analysis and application of comparative ancient Near Eastern material relating the ark narrative to sources about the capture and return of divine images. Their final conclusion, "perhaps most important of all," addresses their sources' ability to provide background for the theological interpretation of history—the ideology—behind the ark narrative. They suggest that the account was written—after the ark's capture but before David's imperial expansion—as a theological counterattack on views equating loss of ark to defeat of Yahweh: "The very few theological treatments of the past originating in such periods of uncertainty reflect, by their very insistence on the native god's absolute control of events, the underlying doubt against which such accounts were written."[10]

There is little doubt that we biblical scholars can use every bit of historical background we can muster as we encounter an ancient text. However, what my example illustrates once again is the unfortunate tendency of scholars to lavish their comparative insights upon an imagined text, a pre-text, while ignoring the obvious relevance of these same insights to the real text. If we suppose for the moment that Miller and Roberts's suggestions about theological aim and historical dating of their pre-text are plausible, even probable, we end up with an interesting way to describe what *The Hand of the Lord,* as exemplar, is all about.

Two biblical scholars of the twentieth century, using their impressive command of ancient Near Eastern literature, reconstruct a pretextual ark narrative whose main purpose, they suggest, was to counteract the ancient Israelite's doubts of Yahweh's power during the few years between the defeats at Ebenezer and David's victories. The narrative's answer to such doubts is that capture of the ark does not equal defeat of Yahweh. In short, Miller and Roberts use comparative material to reconstruct the putative setting of a putative text, all the while ignoring the rather obvious relevance of their material for the real text. What is the putative doubt of Israelites during a putative few years in Israel's history counteracted by a putative document, in comparison with the relevant background everywhere apparent in the real text? The monarchic history introduced in 1 Samuel 1–7 will culminate not in the ark's temporary capture, but in its puzzling disappearance from history. North and south will be defeated, the temple destroyed, and Judah sent into exile.

Miller and Roberts never see the possible relevance of their comparative material for the real text. The Israelite doubts that Miller and Roberts imagine as the catalyst for their pre-text are shades of the doubts set up and responded to by the Deuteronomic History itself, especially in its climax. If Miller and Roberts's perceptive comparisons have any relevance for a few years' interlude in premonarchic times, how much more for monarchy's climactic end? The supposed doubts motivating Miller and Roberts's supposed story supposedly ended with David's victories. The actual History's doubts end and begin with Israel's violent destruction and exile; these doubts have had real relevance for millennia, persisting even to plague Israel's heirs as they contemplate the holocaust in this century.

Why, once more, have Miller and Roberts chosen not to use comparative material to provide historical background for the real text, if it is not because they consider the real text's answer to its disaster, the exile, not worth lavishing their insights upon? Perhaps it is because they believe that this real text's theology of history is unbelievably naive in its droning insistence of the obvious: defeat of Israel equals anger of Yahweh. At any rate, according to Miller and Roberts we have a text already violated by the heavy hand of a pragmatic but nearsighted redactor, who subverted the original ideology of their pretextual ark story for purposes of his own.

What biblical scholars typically choose not to do, therefore, seems to me more revealing than what they choose to do. If the historical problematic motivating their pre-text ended with David's victories, it nevertheless remains the main problematic of the entire history leading up to the exile, and it continues on, even to the hour Miller and Roberts first set pen to paper. It is this problematic that keeps the biblical pages alive today; it is this connection that Miller and Roberts nowhere make in their use of contemporaneous comparative material—a lack that is widespread in much modern biblical scholarship.

Lavish attention to pre-texts and their background makes it difficult to give equally lavish attention to real texts and their interpretation. Insofar as the Deuteronomic History is concerned, the physical corruption of the texts we have of 1 and 2 Samuel is symbolic of modern scholarship's view of the larger history's ideological limitations. If we find ourselves necessarily married to such an ancient document, whatever care is lavished upon correcting its physical defects sadly corresponds to a fatal ignoring of that text's ideological and esthetic brilliance, or even, in some cases, to a profound denial thereof. The search for antecedants, for pre-texts, has itself turned into a pretext. It may be helpful to see all this from a wider perspective.

The Mechanical Author

In his foreward to the English translation of the first half of Martin Noth's *Überlieferungsgeschichtliche Studien*, E. W. Nicholson accurately and succinctly assesses its importance for subsequent study of Deuteronomy– 2 Kings: "This is a 'classic' work in the sense that it still remains the fundamental study of the corpus of literature with which it is concerned, and still provides, as far as the majority of scholars are concerned, the basis and framework for further investigation of the composition and nature of this corpus."[11] Nicholson's assessment, written thirty-eight years after Noth's study first appeared, testifies to the central value of this ground-breaking work for further research on the so-called Deuteronomistic History. Indeed, here, as is often the case elsewhere, a work that spawns whole generations of further research contains within it scholarly genes whose strengths and weaknesses are transmitted—often in magnified form—to its progeny. We cannot understand the attitudes of present-day scholars toward 1 Samuel without understanding what Noth accomplished so many years ago.

In discussing Noth's work, I will largely ignore the methodology by which the text is separated into sections composed by Dtr, the author of the History, earlier sources used by Dtr, and later editorial supplements.[12] Noth himself generally accepted most of the previous literary-critical conclusions about these matters and therefore concentrated his efforts on seeing such results in a new light, that is, as forming the basis for viewing the Deuteronomistic History as "an independent and united work."[13] What interests me is Noth's description and evaluation of the History as a unified work and of Dtr as its artful author.

Dtr organized traditional material, Noth explains, by systematically inserting speeches of anticipation and retrospection, delivered by key characters such as Joshua (Josh. 23), Samuel (1 Sam. 12), and Solomon (1 Kings 8), as well as by itself as narrator. The traditions it selected, compiled, and arranged were highly diverse and existed already in written form. Dtr mostly reproduced sources and only occasionally corrected or changed them.

What does the History look like, then, according to Noth's descriptions of its process of composition? Noth tells us, on one hand, that "Dtr's method of composition is very lucid. The closest parallels are those Hellenistic and Roman historians who use older accounts, mostly unacknowledged, to write a history not of their own time but of the more or less distant past." Noth's basic evaluation of Dtr's end product is unequivocal: "When we have learned to regard his work as a self-contained whole, we shall find that he has crafted a work of art which merits our respect."[14]

On the other hand, however much Noth praises Dtr for his work, and however strongly he insists that Dtr is more than an editor or compiler, that he is an author in the strict sense of the term, Noth's detailed reconstruction of what Dtr has done to produce "this great work" gives us a picture of an individual whose mode of composition is mostly editorial compilation and arrangement of the most mechanical kind. As a compiler of traditions, Dtr simply reproduced his sources, arranging them in a carefully conceived chronological framework that is partly received, partly invented. Like Qoheleth with his proverbs, we might say, Noth believes that Dtr "being wise, taught the people knowledge, weighing and studying and arranging [his traditions] with great care" (Qoheleth 12:9). Dtr had such respect for his sources that he hardly ever corrected them according to his own lights. In such rare cases when he did alter his sources, he "tried to eliminate inconsistencies between them because he wanted to construct a complete self-contained work." Moreover, as a compiler, he unintentionally "often gave [the different traditions] a meaning and significance at variance with the material really contained in them."[15]

Even as an author, that is, as writer of the passages of the History that Noth attributes directly to the individual who produced this work, Dtr left much to be desired. Noth writes of the "repetitive monotony of his judgments" and the "monotonous repetition of the same simple expressions and the continual references to divine law, the necessity of obeying it and the disastrous consequences of disobedience . . ." Moreover, in spite of his overriding concern to show how disastrous kingship was for Israel, Dtr, as author, still muddied the water by allowing reverence for sources to produce a story of Saul's accession to the throne that in Noth's view "made for a very disconnected narrative."[16]

If we try to assess Noth's achievements in this influential work, we are struck first by the discrepancy between his evaluation of Dtr's compositional techniques ("this great work," "Dtr's very lucid method of composition," "a work of art that merits our respect") and his accompanying description of this author at work (Dtr mostly arranged a collage of traditions, very rarely changing them to remove inconsistencies but often unintentionally altering their meaning; he wrote in a dully repetitive style, making the same point over and over again). With respect to 1 Samuel, which in Noth's view straddles the end of the judicial period (up to 1 Sam. 12) and the beginning of the monarchic period (1 Sam. 13ff.), we are asked to believe that Dtr, who did all his direct writing before chapter 12 precisely in order to give the reader a correct view of the evil of kingship's establishment—*in Noth's view the prime cause of Israel's destruction*[17]—still produced a muddled account that contains old traditions sympathetic to kingship.[18]

Noth's picture of how the history came to be written—its process of composition—mostly fails to account for its artful construction because, second, it unduly concentrates on superficial aspects of the composition (like its recognizable chronological framework and its periodically didactic sermons), and therefore completely neglects the many artful features of the text that I will be at pains in the following chapters to describe. The result of Noth's work is a learned analysis that claims more than it delivers: Noth's detailed description of the process of composition does not form a credible basis for his glowing encomiums about the product composed. Anyone who has even a beginning awareness of literary criticism—in its broad humanistic context rather than in narrow biblical studies terms—should feel uncomfortable by all the accounts of the History generated by Noth's influential work. One senses that Noth and his progeny are right when they praise the History for its greatness. Nevertheless, one has to admit that such source-oriented scholarship has failed to justify its extravagant praise of the History and its author. By concentrating on the pre-text more than the real text, scholars have ignored many of the features of the History that account for its proper place in the treasury of world literature.

Noth's ground-breaking work does indeed form the "basis and framework" for subsequent studies of the History, which, whether they agree with or react against his views, continue to ignore the many artful features of the real text. Many of these studies share their progenitor's tendency toward extravagant praise of the History, even as their descriptions of its process of formation imply much the opposite.

The Double Edition

In an important and influential revision of Noth's thesis of a unified Deuteronomistic history encompassing Deuteronomy through 2 Kings, Frank Cross has eloquently argued "that there were two editions of the Deuteronomistic history, one written in the era of Josiah as a programmatic document of his reform and of his revival of the Davidic state. . . . The second edition . . . updated the history . . . It also attempted to transform the work into a sermon on history addressed to Judean exiles."[19] Since the retouching of the second edition was light, Cross emphasizes, its conforming of "Judah's fate to that of Samaria, and Manasseh's role to that of Jeroboam" did not wholly obscure the earlier framework.[20] Although Cross is in "broad agreement with Noth's description of the primary Deuteronomistic historian (Noth's Dtr, our Dtr[1]) as a creative author and historian,"[21] his fundamental disagreement with Noth centers on Cross's arguments that the first, preexilic, edition of the history[22] contained and contrasted two themes—one of hope, the other of punishment—built around "the old Deuteronomic covenant theology . . . and the eternal promises to David," whereas in the second, exilic, edition "the original theme of hope is overwritten and contradicted . . ." Besides this basic disagreement over the themes of hope and punishment, Cross also believes that the stance of his Dtr[1] (Noth's Dtr) toward the monarchy was "overwhelmingly positive,"[23] while Noth maintained, as we have seen, that Dtr wrote his history precisely to show how the monarchy had led Israel into final disaster.[24]

How can it be that two such influential source-oriented scholars, agreeing on the literary unity of most of Deuteronomy–2 Kings, can differ so fundamentally on such basic issues as overarching theme(s) and ideological position of their respective "authors" toward the monarchy? Such disparity of views is possible, it seems to me, precisely because these scholars, as most source-oriented scholars before and after them, consider the real text to be obviously multilayered from a literary-historical point of view. Thus whenever they cite specific passages within the History to support their respective views, *the meaning of these pericopes within their present literary context never needs in principle to be determined,* since one's literary-historical reconstruction constantly juggles three layers of passages: pre-Dtr, Dtr, and post-Dtr texts. Thus, if Cross wants to maintain, against Noth, that the words of Samuel in 1 Samuel 12—a chapter recognized by both as crucially Deuteronomistic (Noth's Dtr, Cross's Dtr[1])—contain no hint of final destruction, Cross simply asserts, according to his reconstruction, that 12:25 ("But if you do wickedly, you shall be swept away, both you and your king") comes from the hand of Dtr[2], while Noth would firmly maintain that it is basic to Dtr's ideology.

Cross's theory of a double edition of the History is both an undoubted advance and an unfortunate retreat. By recovering the History's theme of hope, Cross has certainly corrected one of the most serious deficiencies in Noth's position. Cross has simply, elegantly, and powerfully recaptured a central ideological feature of the story. Nevertheless, Cross has also inadvertantly compounded Noth's inability to give an adequate account of Dtr as one who "has crafted a work of art that merits our respect."[25] For in Cross's scenario, the final form of the History now represents a crude and obvious attempt to twist a basically hopeful history into a sermon that would explain to Judean exiles *why such high hopes were not fulfilled.* Cross's double edition theory makes the real text something that is now seriously flawed in a double sense, ancient testimony to an ideological statement betrayed by a later editor who tries to pick up the pieces after history itself had shattered the original form of that statement. Two factors, first history and then an individual called Dtr[2], betray Dtr[1], with both "authors" finally rediscovered by a modern source-oriented reader.

In Cross's account, therefore, the original edition of the History was a failed sermon, one whose basic ideology was shown to be deficient by subsequent events of history, and the second edition was a slapdash attempt to alter the first. But the alteration was an unsuccessful salvage operation because it proceeded from "a less articulate Exilic editor."

Thus, within Cross's theory, in whichever edition one wants to look, there appears to me to be too little ideological or historiographic value—and even less esthetic value.[26]

This basic evaluative position of the double edition theory is in my opinion unfortunate; it implies a view of the final text, the real text, as the product of a well-intentioned hack who was even less perspicacious than overly optimistic and dully didactic predecessors. No matter, then, that for Cross (as well as for Noth in his way) Dtr is seen as "a creative author and historian."[27] Such an individual did not succeed in combining threat and promise within a credibly lasting history. It is not surprising that typical scholars like Miller and Roberts will lose no time in initiating additional source-oriented efforts *to get as far behind the first edition of the History as possible.* They seem to be trying to recover or reconstruct sources or documents that may contain more obviously coherent ideological values than those they believe to exist in the real text.[28]

The First Historian

In a recent comparative study, John Van Seters has addressed many of the shortcomings inherent in previous treatments of the History. Prefacing his analysis of the History with informative surveys on the present state of research in early Greek, Mesopotamian, Hittite, Egyptian, Levantine, and Israelite historiography, Van Seters argues, against Noth and all his followers, that "it is wrong to view Dtr as one who simply added pious and didactic phrases to pre-existing units." Van Seters shares Noth's and Cross's high estimation of the History yet rightly emphasizes a central weakness in Noth's theoretical account:

> Given the level of prose development for its time, the Dtr history is a literary work of superb accomplishment. . . . Dtr's unfortunate fate was that . . . he remained anonymous, so that his work . . . has been hopelessly dissected by modern scholars into numerous collections and redactions. Noth's recovery of this author is commendable, but Noth did not go far enough. He still attributed too little of the work to the author himself and too much to his sources and "traditions."[29]

Van Seters decries the tendency of scholars "to analyze a history by taking it apart in order to discern the original function of the various elements" and believes that such methods "will never yield the meaning of the whole." One of the best parts of Van Seters's work is his survey of Herodotean studies illustrating how biblical scholars might learn much from the more holistic efforts of their classicist colleagues: "In fact a rather strong tendency exists in Herodotean studies to pay less attention to, or even discount, the efforts of *Entwicklungstheorien,* and to focus on the high literary quality of the *Histories* and the masterful unity that

Herodotus has created out of the diversity of his material." Van Seters deplores those directions in biblical studies "in which the whole notion of an author may be dispensed with." Borrowing from Henry Immerwahr the concept of "paratactic composition" in Herodotus, Van Seters believes that "on the basis of narrative style and techniques alone, the Old Testament and Herodotus share a great deal in common and ought to be studied together." Van Seters believes that once such comparative work is carried out responsibly, Israelite historiography will be seen to be the result of truly literary and authorial activity, and of conscious compositional techniques. Any labeling of such techniques as "redactional" would "destroy completely the compositional work of the biblical authors." Van Seters ends his survey of comparative literatures and his analysis of the Deuteronomistic History with a sweeping conclusion in the final sentence of his book: "Nevertheless, I hope I have demonstrated that the first Israelite historian, and the first known historian in Western civilization truly to deserve this designation, was the Deuteronomistic historian."[30]

It would be hard to conceive of a scholarly clarion call more congenial to the kind of reading of the History I am advocating than that sounded by Van Seters's much needed statements. And yet, nothing could be further from the case than Van Seters's actual discussions of Deuteronomistic historiography in chapters 8–10 of his book. For in spite of his stated program of studying the "narrative style and techniques" of the History, it turns out that Van Seters's analyses conceive of literary analysis as nothing more nor less than the detailed description of the *literary history* behind the present text of Joshua–2 Kings. Van Seters spends over a hundred pages on the Deuteronomistic History, doing little more than adding to the mountain of speculative opinion on how the History got composed and spelling out for us such a history of the History's composition as he is able to determine, attempting to provide "evidence" concerning what belongs to Dtr's history (much more than previously thought), what predates it (much less than originally maintained), and what was later added to it (much more than anyone had realized).[31]

This Herculean, if largely traditional, effort of Van Seters is obviously necessary to his purposes because, in spite of all his high-sounding words about previous scholarship's deplorable tendency "to analyze a history by taking it apart" instead of looking for "the meaning of the whole," Van Seters is obsessed by the same desire as bedeviled his predecessors, that is, to establish a coherent pre-text out of what he believes is the ideological mess of the real text. The starting point of all Van Seters's literary-historical reconstructions is that the present form of the History suffers from a bad case of ideological and esthetic incoherence, and the result of his analysis claims to have discovered the causes of such a malady. For one thing, the present form of the History has been damaged by the artless efforts of some post-Dtr hands, which have severely disrupted its once fairly unified pages, most notably by inserting the Court History (2 Sam. 9–20, 1 Kings 1–2) into the larger story line, a move that produces, in Van Seters's view, a hopelessly confused picture of David in the final form of the story.

Like Noth, Cross, and others before him, Van Seters combines a high estimation of the History with an emphasis on its mode of composition as authorial rather than redactional. It turns out, however, that the Deuteronomistic History that Van Seters so highly praises is a reconstructed pre-text of his, based upon a veritable jungle of his own literary-historical considerations, and necessitated by a commonly held view of the present text of Deuteronomy–2 Kings as ideologically, esthetically, and historiographically flawed by later extensive additions to its pristine form. For Van Seters, the Court History's violent attack upon David is in strong and incoherent contrast to Dtr's view of him: "It is therefore inconceivable to me that Dtr would have included such a work virtually unedited in his history when his whole perspective was exactly the opposite." No matter, then, that Van Seters chides Noth for attributing too little of the work to Dtr.[32] Van Seters will himself remove the entire fourteen chapters of the Court History—believed central to the History by most scholars—from "this great work," thus robbing Noth's Dtr to pay Van Seters's redactor.

It is not difficult to understand the basis for the type of analyses found in chapters 8–10 of *In Search of History;* they are basically uninformed of literary-critical theory and practice both outside and within biblical studies, and they take for granted that the literary-historical questions they ask of the text are the only ones by which one can or should analyze "narrative style and techniques."[33] Apart from scattered statements showing some awareness of the complicated literary functions involved in aspects of repetition,[34] prolepsis, literary invention, or ring patterns, little of these matters and practically nothing of others inform this book's discussions of Joshua–2 Kings until *after*—methodologically speaking—it has isolated the pristine form of the Dtr history, which alone is then shown to contain all the necessary characteristics and concomitants of unified history writing as Van Seters defines it.

Perhaps it is unfair to criticize this book for its lack of a sophisticated understanding of literary-critical theory and practice outside the confines of biblical studies. Nevertheless, its remarks about the differences between Herodotean and biblical studies indicate little awareness of developments within the biblical field itself:

> But in Herodotean studies the new literary approach is not incompatible with the form critical or the developmental approach, whereas in biblical studies all three are for the most part completely at odds. This is because many of the literary analyses in biblical studies give little regard to the integrity of separate literary works, and the structuralism they employ is

often imposed from without. . . . In Herodotean studies an effort is
made to elucidate the form and structure from within the work itself and
as a quality of that particular author as distinct from others.[35]

Nothing is clearer from the book's thorough discussions establishing a
division of Joshua–2 Kings into pre-, post-, and Dtr passages than that
its "regard for the integrity of separate literary works" is not only much
less than the Herodotean scholars it quotes,[36] but also immeasurably less
than the many biblical scholars it fails to quote. Where is there reference
in Van Seters's book to Fokkelman on the Court History[37] or to Charles
Conroy on 2 Samuel 13–20?[38] It is true that the discussion shows
awareness of, even as it mostly disagrees with, David Gunn, a noted
literary interpreter of biblical narrative, but such disagreement is
certainly not because of any disregard on Gunn's part for "the text's
integrity."[39]

A central feature of *In Search of History* is that it shares with all the
source-oriented work upon which it generally builds, or with which it
specifically disagrees, a high regard for the integrity of the pre-text it
reconstructs and a high disregard for the integrity of the real text it
fragments for literary-historical reasons. The book tends to discuss
pre-texts—be they J's or P's or Dtr's—as if they enjoyed the same reality
status as real texts. Van Seters mentions "the Priestly writer," "the
Yahwist," or "Dtr" with the same confident accents and implying the
same level of abstractive existence as when he refers to "Herodotus" or
"the author of Chronicles."[40] It is as if for Van Seters "the Yahwist,"
whose theoretical existence was once acknowledged as secure in the
nineteenth century, has not in fact become today even more of a shade
than his former hypothetical self.[41]

In line with my discussion of Noth's and Cross's theories, my intention
is not to disagree with any of Van Seters's specific literary-historical views
on the formation of the Dtr history—however much I do in fact disagree
with them. Rather, it is to emphasize the destructive implications of such
views: whatever literary unity the books of Samuel may have enjoyed
through the genius of Dtr was destroyed, in Van Seters's view, by later
redactor(s), whose clumsy insertions of texts like 1 Samuel 15:1–16:13
and especially the Court History have damaged the integrity and
coherence of a once pristine text. Van Seters is surely right and clearly
eloquent in stating a case for the importance of the text's integrity and of
narrative style and technique, but in the end he is sensitive to these
matters only with respect to a theoretical reconstruction of his. The price
he has to pay for calling his pre-text "a literary work of superb
accomplishment"[42] is his corresponding contention that the real text,
the present form of the Deuteronomistic History in general and the
books of Samuel in particular, is in fundamental ways and strategic
places an incoherent mess.

The present book presumes the text of 1 Samuel makes sense, however worked-over the text is scribally and hermeneutically, and however deficient it is text-critically. Perhaps this sympathetic attitude will gloss over or excuse a number of textual warts or obvious genetic defects, but such mistakes are, in my opinion, a fair price to pay for trying to redress a lamentable neglect of an ancient treasure. That-which-is is certainly as valuable as all the valuable might-have-beens upon which biblical scholars continue to focus their attention. Many who have read the Bible down through the ages have understood this.[44]

One

HANNAH AND HER SON: A PARABLE (1:1–4:1a)

At any given moment of its historical existence, language is heteroglot from top to bottom: it represents the co-existence of socio-ideological contradictions between the present and the past, between differing epochs of the past, between different socio-ideological groups in the present, between tendencies, schools, circles and so forth, all given a bodily form. These "languages" of heteroglossia intersect each other in a variety of ways, forming new socially typifying "languages." (Mikhail Bakhtin, *The Dialogic Imagination*)

Hannah, why do you weep? And why do you not eat? And why is your heart sad? Am I not worth more to you than ten sons? (Elkanah, 1 Samuel 1:8)

Speaking Persons and Their Voices in 1 Samuel 1

The story of the birth and consecration of Samuel is a type scene of annunciation, as Robert Alter would say.[1] At the same time, its location at the start of 1 Samuel gives its meaning added dimensions, and it is this sense of a beginning that will largely occupy our interest. On one hand, the birth story signals the central role Samuel will play as kingmaker in Israel. On the other, if the patterning of the Deuteronomic History in previous books is assumed to continue in 1 Samuel, then the story of Samuel's birth may be more than this.[2] Just as the beginning of Joshua gave us a preview of major themes to be worked out within that book, and as the beginning of the book of Judges was a synopsis of what was to come there, so also we may suspect that the story of Samuel's birth contains within its texture threads that extend throughout the life and death of Samuel, well into the lives of Saul and David, and beyond. In other words, the opening scene of Samuel's birth may be a prospective statement about the entire book, and the answers that the book itself provides—indeed the entire complex of Samuel/Kings—could be answers to a set of questions that begin to be voiced in chapter 1.

Whom do we hear speaking? Obviously the narrator's voice not only conveys to us what the characters say out loud but even what they vow or think within their own hearts. The characters quoted by the narrator are only three: Elkanah, his wife Hannah, and old Eli, the priest of Shiloh. No other obvious voices are heard in the story. It should be a simple matter, then, to listen to only four voices and puzzle out the function of the story for the rest of the book. But we have only to look more closely at what each voice says, in itself and in relation to the other voices, to discover that surrounding these obvious voices are a number of others from within and without this chapter. The utterance of each voice speaking in the story provides a focal point for the intersecting words of others. The point of view represented by a single utterance of a single voice resonates with the words of others either in agreement or in opposition, with either emotive similarity or contrast. Loudly or faintly, we can perceive a cross-section of voices even when only a single person speaks in the text.

What is the voice of the narrator like, and what accents characterize it? The narrator's words, which at first glance appear to be one-dimensional and ideologically unified, contain a variety of hidden voices and competing viewpoints. Here, as in any artfully constructed narrative, is found a profound speech diversity that in fact is the determining factor of its prose style.[3]

The narrator, as one would expect, is omniscient, knowing what has happened in the past and what is happening in the story's "here and now." Moreover, the narrator understands behavior and describes it "from the point of view of the person himself or from the point of view of an omniscient observer who is permitted to penetrate the consciousness of that person."[4] This is a narrator's speech, which from a psychological point of view is internal to the characters being described for us. For example, the narrator can repeat word for word Hannah's vow to God in verse 11, even though we know (from v. 13) that "only her lips were moving and her voice was not being heard." Again, the narrator is able to penetrate Elkanah's consciousness because, even though this husband gives many portions to Peninnah but only one portion to Hannah, the narrator is able to tell us that Elkanah nevertheless loved Hannah (v. 5).

It is because of the convention of omniscience normally belonging to a narrator's voice that we have the distinction in narration between exposition and the story proper.[5] Exposition gives the reader the background information that is necessary for an adequate understanding of the story itself. Chapter 1 divides up neatly into verses 1–8 as preparatory exposition and verses 9–28 as story proper. The narrator's voice fundamentally shifts in tone between these two sections: in verses 1–8 that which is habitual over a long period of time is emphasized; in verses 9–28 three main events are described: Hannah's meeting with Eli, Samuel's birth, and finally his consecration at Shiloh. In the expository overview of verses 1–8, information is packed and condensed through the description of repetitious or habitual behavior indicated by imperfective verb forms: "he would give (*w*^e*nātan*)" (v. 4); "he would give (*yittēn*)" (v. 5); "so it went on (*ya*^{ca}*seh*)" (v. 7); "she would provoke her (*tak*^c*isennāh*)" (v. 7); "she would not eat (*to'kal*)" (v. 7). So, we are told, these things went on year by year, Peninnah habitually provoking the barren Hannah so that the latter would weep and refuse to eat. And Elkanah would habitually respond to Hannah's behavior with words of attempted consolation. Year by year Peninnah taunted Hannah, and year by year Elkanah tried to console her.

Then the narrator's voice shifts to the singular events of the story itself, and to signal such a move we encounter once more a piling on of imperfective verb forms like those encountered earlier, but here having a different function: Eli "was sitting (*yōšēb*)" (1:9), "was observing (*šōmēr*)" (1:12); Hannah "was crying (*tibkeh*)" (1:10), "was speaking (*m*^e*dabberet*)" (1:13), "only her lips were moving (*nā*^c*ot*) and her voice was not being heard (*yiššāmēa*^c)" (1:13). It is largely by means of these imperfective verb forms that we are able to enter the here and now or synchronic perspective of the story.[6]

So far we have introduced a number of literary categories that might be said normally and obviously to concern a narrator's omniscience: retrospective versus synchronic perspective, expository versus narrative point of view. These categories are well known and easily applied to the narrator's voice in chapter 1. But a number of voice characteristics are not so well recognized, and chapter 1 offers some examples of these as well.

A primary function of a narrator is to report to readers the words of a story's characters. Thus in chapter 1 the narrator directly quotes Elkanah's words in 1:8, 23; Hannah's words in 1:11, 15–16, 18, 22, 26; and Eli's words in 1:14, 17. A little less obvious, but still quite clearly recognized, is the narrator's direct quoting of Hannah's words without using the expected introduction: "She called his name Samuel, for [she said] 'I have asked him of the LORD'" (1:20). The "she said" is not in the Hebrew text, but is, for example, in the RSV translation because of the context. We are to understand that "I have asked him of the LORD" are the very words of Hannah, directly reported to us by the narrator but not signaled as such in the normal manner.

Other voices speak in this chapter, but the narrator introduces these in not so obvious a fashion as in the preceding cases. For example, when the narrator tells us in verse 6 that Peninnah, Hannah's rival, "used to provoke her sorely, to irritate her, *because the LORD had closed her womb*," the question arises whether this characterization of Hannah's barrenness ("the LORD had closed her womb") proceeds in fact from the narrator's convictions, from Peninnah's convictions, or from a combination of both. Again, when the narrator tells us in the preceding verse (1:5) that Elkanah gave Hannah one portion,[7] for "the LORD had closed her womb," the same type of question arises: is this the narrator's or

Elkanah's view or both? If one contends, as I do, that these two verses report at least the motivation of Elkanah in verse 5 and of Peninnah in verse 6, then we have in the words "for the LORD had closed her womb" the concealed reported speech of Elkanah and Peninnah in response to, and in explanation of, Hannah's continued barrenness. The inner speech, as it were, of Elkanah and Peninnah—if not of a portion of the Israelite populace—is represented by these words, and it remains to be seen whether the narrator as well as the implied author who controls narrator's speech share this view in the same way and with the same emotive accents as do Elkanah and Peninnah.[8]

Another example of concealed reported speech occurs in verse 13 where the narrator tells us that "Eli took [Hannah] to be a drunken woman." Here we can generalize by stating that whenever the narrator through omniscience invades the consciousness of characters to reveal in the narrator's own words their thoughts or convictions, or when the narrator anticipates their words, which are about to be quoted, we are meant thereby to hear the voice of these characters. Thus in verse 13 the narrator's words indicate to us that Eli has said to himself, or is about to say out loud, something like, "This woman is drunk!" just as his direct speech in 1:14 indicates.

Another kind of concealed reported speech occurs when the very words of a character, directly quoted by the narrator, show up elsewhere in the same or a similar context as words belonging to the narrator. When, for example, the narrator tells us in verse 19 that "the LORD *remembered* [Hannah]" in the conception and birth of Samuel, we are meant to recall Hannah's words in verse 11: "O LORD of hosts . . . *remember me* . . . and give to thy maidservant a son . . ." The narrator, speaking the very words of a character, once more calls attention to the character's speech. When we hear the narrator's voice in verse 11, there is concealed within it Hannah's voice also.

The most important aspect of the narrator's voice, as of any voice we encounter in the text, is its ideological perspective. By ideology or ideological perspective I mean, in Bakhtin's words, "a specific point of view on the world," a specific belief system or form "for conceptualizing the world in words, specific world views, each characterized by its own object, meanings and values." The voices we hear in 1 Samuel do not simply express individual ideologies in relation to one another; they represent social points of view that intersect each other in a variety of ways, forming what I call the implied author's story, the meaning (or meanings) of which is certainly a major task of the reader to discover or, as some would say, to invent. As Bakhtin writes, in a slightly different context but fully relevant here: "Behind the narrator's story we read a second story, the author's story; he is the one who tells us how the narrator tells stories, and also tells us about the narrator himself."[9]

The Matter of Kingship

We can look more closely at the opening chapter of 1 Samuel and concentrate primarily on its ideological dimensions, building upon our observations about the narrator's voice—its omniscience, its retrospective or synchronic emphasis, its expository or narrative tacks, and the obvious or concealed ways it reports the speech of others. In this way we should be able to begin saying something about what the author's story means. The voices we hear will intersect with voices previously heard in the Deuteronomic History and foreshadow what will not be finished until long after Saul is killed in chapter 31.

The first character to speak directly in the story is Elkanah. We hear his words at the intersection between the exposition (vv. 1–8) and the story proper (vv. 9–28). It is not clear whether his words here represent one of those habitual, repeated actions of the exposition emphasized above, or simply a statement opening up for us the singular events now recounted by the narrator. Elkanah's words float in a textual area that is both past and present with respect to the story. They sum up the expository material and at the same time get the story moving:

> Hannah, why do you weep? And why do you not eat? And why is your heart sad? Am I not worth more to you than ten sons? (1:8)

The area occupied by Elkanah's voice is much broader than his "actual" words in this chapter. Using Bakhtin's terminology, we can call such an area a *character zone* and attempt to describe what Elkanah's is like.

Listen first to the emotive accents that surround Elkanah's words. These are words of consolation certainly; after all, the narrator told us in verse 5 of Elkanah's love for Hannah. But listen again, and you will hear an aggrieved tone, a bitterness more plaintive than Hannah's but a bitterness nonetheless, in resonance with her own. Is there not a mild reproach here? For Hannah to be so disconsolate is to exhibit insufficient appreciation of her husband. If Hannah really understood the worth of Elkanah, she would know that ten children could not replace him in her heart. There is present in Elkanah's words to Hannah—spoken once or often we do not know—feelings of being slighted, undervalued or -appreciated, the first step perhaps toward feeling rejected. These words of Elkanah push him in two directions: he loves Hannah and understands her desire to have children; at the same time Hannah's bitterness says something to him about her attitude toward him.

The situation surrounding these words is immediately understandable at the individual level. A woman lacks what her rival has in abundance—children—and she desires greatly to receive what she does not have. Her husband has some understanding of her plight, yet he cannot help feeling to some degree slighted, even a bit rejected. The emotional overtones within Elkanah's character zone bespeak loving understanding mixed in with feelings of hurt. They interpret Hannah's desire for children as an undervaluation of Elkanah. Is there some political or ideological significance to this simple familial situation, to this intersection of conflicting emotions?

The meeting between Hannah and Eli during the yearly sacrifice in verses 9–18 will provide ideological and emotive accents of its own and will help us begin to sort out in what ways Elkanah's words in verse 8 form an epigraph for a story that will not conclude until the final words of 2 Kings.[10]

When the story begins in verse 9, we are immediately introduced to Eli, who is "sitting on the seat" in the temple. The narrator uses words here that are "double voiced" and give us our first indication of the character zone surrounding Eli: he is presented to us as a *royal figure* as well as a priest. The shift here to the imperfective verb *yōšēb* emphasizes the centrality of the image before us. Eli "is sitting on the throne" (*'al hakkissē'*); he is in the *heykal*. This key description of the place or position that Eli occupies when he overhears Hannah involves both of them in a zone of royalty: the word *kissē'* is first and foremost a royal seat, the throne, a metonymn for royal power and authority. "To sit upon the throne" carries with it associations of taking one's seat as king, of becoming a king, as, say, in 1 Kings 16:11. Also, Eli is sitting in the *heykal*, another word whose meaning oscillates between the priest's temple and the king's palace. This initial meeting, ostensibly between Hannah the would-be mother and Eli the has-been priest, has royal overtones that look forward in a number of interlocking ways to the central matter of kingship which forms the subject matter of the entire history. At the same time, this meeting is described primarily through the words of Hannah, in a manner that turns our attention backward toward the book of Judges. The intimate connection between judgeship and kingship is the appropriate ideological zone for this first chapter which forges a link between the subject matter of the book of Judges and that of Samuel/Kings.

How does what has gone before find itself made present in Hannah's words in verse 11 spoken silently to the LORD? Hannah is bitter of soul and weeping; she vows a vow. We are here reminded of Jephthah in the Book of Judges, who also vowed a vow (*wayyiddar neder laYHWH*) to ensure the success of his efforts against the Ammonites: he will devote (his daughter) to the LORD and will offer (her) up for a burnt offering (Judg. 11:30–31). Hannah, likewise, is so intent on getting her way that she also vows a vow (*wattiddor neder*): "Oh LORD of hosts, if you will grant my request for a son I will give him to you all the days of his life." She will knowingly sacrifice her son to the LORD as Jephthah is unknowingly willing to sacrifice his daughter. The issue here is one of ensuring that YHWH answer one's prayers. Like Jephthah, Hannah wants to make a deal with God to ensure success in obtaining her request. How does one go about getting one's way with YHWH? Vow to give him something if he gives you your something? Here we have the depiction of a *quid pro quo* belief system, whereby bargaining with the LORD is employed as a means of achieving one's ends.

Moreover, Hannah's promise, "and no razor shall touch his head," brings us back to the annunciation scene of the barren wife of Manoah in Judges 13. There the angel of the LORD promises her a son concerning whom "no razor shall touch his head." Later, Samson tells Delilah that he is different from other men because "no razor has come upon my head. If I be shaved, I shall be like any other man" (Judg. 16:17). "No razor" in the Samson story means a judge's distinctiveness in strength; here with Hannah, the idea of a razorless Samuel involves her solemn promise that he will not be like other "sons"; he will be the LORD's all the days of his life. He will be a different son as Samson was a different judge. Samson's lack of (in)sight about his role as deliverer of Israel permeates this account of Hannah's request for a son and speaks to the quality of her insight about being childless. This evocation of one judge who was physically and ideologically blind and another who felt that YHWH could be won over with arguments of reciprocity surrounds the silent prayer of Hannah in verse 11. In contrast to Manoah's wife, who was never quite sure whose messenger had given her the good news of a son,[11] Hannah may be characterized as one who indeed has a clear-cut idea of the LORD to whom she speaks. She is also convinced, as mothers are wont, that her son will be different. However, Samson's repeated failures to understand what went on around him cast a certain light on Hannah's self-awareness and certitude about what it is she is requesting.

The meeting between Hannah and Eli, we have suggested, looks forward as well as backward. What does having children or not have to do with the enterprise that concerns the entire book of 1 Samuel, the establishment of kingship in Israel? What evaluative social accents accompany Hannah's desire to have a child, sanctioned unknowingly or prophetically by Eli, but somewhat opposed by Elkanah who expresses a loving conviction that he is indeed worth more to Hannah than ten sons? Is the implied author of this opening story introducing us solely to Samuel the judge, or is he in addition giving us a thematic overture to the entire book of 1 Samuel and beyond?

The prophetic or supplicatory words of Eli in verse 17 echo similar words both inside and outside the chapter and, together with the narrator's evocation of Eli as a royal figure, provide us with further hints toward an answer. Eli says, "The God of Israel will grant the request you made to him (*šēlātēk . . . šā'alt*)" (1:17). Then, when her son is born, Hannah names him, saying, "For I requested him (*šᵉ'iltîw*) from the LORD" (1:20). Hannah, in her meeting with Eli after Samuel's birth, once again refers to "the request I made (*šᵉ'ēlātî . . . šā'altî*) to him"

(1:27). Finally, Eli refers later on to further progeny as "in place of the request [he?] asked of the LORD (*haššᵉ'ēlāh. . . šā'al*)" (2:20). In all these cases Samuel her son personifies Hannah's request itself.[12]

Another request receives as much prominence in the opening chapters of 1 Samuel, and it is no great step to make a connection between the two. In chapter 8 we hear the narrator's voice characterizing the people as those "who were requesting a king from him (*haššoᵃ'lîm*)" (8:10). Then later in the story Samuel introduces Saul to the people as "the king whom you requested (*šᵉ'eltem*)" (12:13) and speaks of the people's wickedness "in requesting (*liš'ol*) a king for yourselves" (12:17). The people respond by referring to this evil as "to ask (*liš'ol*) for ourselves a king" (12:19). No other specific requests are made of the LORD in these chapters, so that there is a solid basis in the text for suggesting that the story of Hannah's request for a son is intended to introduce, foreshadow, and ideologically comment upon the story of Israel's request for a king.

Confirmation of this close literary connection is found in Hannah's directly quoted words to Eli that conclude the chapter: "It is for this child I prayed; and the LORD has granted me my petition which I made to him. Therefore I have lent him to the LORD; as long as he lives he is lent to the LORD [that is, he is 'Saul!' (*hû' šā'ûl*)]" (1:27–28). These words of Hannah are to be understood together with her concealed speech of 1:20 where the narrator has her naming her son Samuel "for I asked him (*šᵉ'iltîw*) of the LORD." In both these pericopes (1:20, 28) commentators have grappled with the wordplay whereby Hannah speaks of Samuel, or refers to his name, using a puzzling etymology that appears more appropriately to explain the name of Saul. Is there an accidental or haphazard mixture here of two traditions, a hybrid, a *tebel*, which confusingly "explains" Samuel's name by offering an etymology for Saul's?[13] This common literary-historical solution turns out to be premature, as is often the case; it certainly casts no light on the story itself and simply causes these verses to intrude awkwardly in their present context. Can these "confused" etymologies be intregrated into the story by taking them at face value?

One attempt at integration would be to imbue the details of the story of Samuel's birth, a familial story, with sociopolitical overtones, that is, to assume that the implied author is foreshadowing and putting into context a complex account of the LORD's decision to give Israel a king by prefacing that account with an account of the LORD's decision to give Hannah a son. The birth of Samuel, in all its complex detail, introduces and foreshadows the birth of kingship in Israel.

"The having of sons" is the image chosen by the author to convey the complicated story of how Israel came to have kings. In chapter 8 it is Samuel's evil sons who give the elders of Israel a pretext for requesting from him a king "to govern us like all the nations," but Samuel considers this request with displeasure. When he prays to the LORD about it, he is told to hearken to the people's request; kingship is a rejection not of Samuel but of Yahweh himself. The words of the LORD to Samuel, "They have not rejected you, but they have rejected me" (8:7), are very close in their emotive register and ideological accent to Elkanah's words to Hannah quoted above (1:8). All one has to do is have God say to Israel what Elkanah says to Hannah:

> Israel, why do you weep? And why do you not eat? And why is your heart sad? Am I not worth more to you than ten kings?

In other words, the story in chapter 1 about how and why God agreed to give Hannah a son, Samuel, is an artistic prefiguring of the larger story in 1 Samuel about how and why God agreed to give Israel a king. It is in the light of these and other thematic, emotive, and ideological connections within the larger story line that the etymology spoken by Hannah makes artistic sense; the story of Samuel's birth *is* the story of Saul's birth as king of Israel. Saul's destiny, like his name, explains Samuel's. When Hannah says, "For I asked for him (*š^e'iltîw*) from the LORD," she speaks also about Saul (*hû' šā'ûl*) and the royal history his reign inaugurates.

Ideology Backward and Forward

Seen in this way, the voices we hear in chapter 1, those of the narrator and the characters, take on a dual accent that reverberates backward and forward on the question of kingship in Israel. The expository material in verses 1–8 deepens in significance both as a depiction of Israel before the establishment of monarchy and as background material about Elkanah's family life before the birth of Samuel. "Peninnah had children but Hannah had no children . . . The LORD had closed her womb" (1:2, 5, 6). Peninnah is described as Hannah's "adversary or foe (*ṣārāh*)," an uncommon familial designation until we remember that Israel's enemies, its neighbors, had kings, but Israel had no king because the LORD had not allowed it. The taunting and provocation of monarchic neighbors provide the motivating background for Israel's desire to have a king. This dimension of the text helps to answer the question raised above about the narrator's depiction of Hannah's childlessness as "the LORD had closed her womb." In the matter of the kingship at least, the narrator's voice is indeed clear; it speaks with its own evaluative accent.

Then the story proper, as it works itself out principally in the dialogues between Hannah and Eli on one hand and Hannah and Elkanah on the other, becomes a programmatic inner dialogue in which the Deuteronomist[14] expresses many of the conflicting ideological issues involved in the establishment of kingship in Israel.

At the beginning of Hannah's meeting with Eli, the piling on of imperfectives in verse 13—Hannah is speaking inwardly, only her lips are moving, her voice is not being heard—brings us into the very center of the question about the meaning of her actions. At first, Eli misunderstands and thinks her drunk. This conjunction of the themes of misunderstanding and drunkenness goes to the heart of the matter about kingship. Hannah is speaking in her heart. Her words go to the heart of the matter, whereas Eli, like Hannah a royal figure in this encounter, "looks on the outward appearance," as the LORD will later say to Hannah's son once Saul is rejected and David is about to be chosen (16:7). Is kingship in Israel a matter of drunken desire, a mistake, or is it a proper matter of the heart?[15] On one hand, Hannah appears drunk but is not; kingship appears ungodly but is not. On the other hand, this encounter's backward glance at the book of Judges casts a suspicious shadow on the sobriety of Hannah's request. Was it a wise thing to have asked for? Which is more real in this detail of 1 Samuel's initial event, the literal drunkenness of Hannah that is not, or her metaphorical drunkenness that very well might be?

It is not only that she appears drunk to Eli; the theme of strong drink once more hearkens back to the annunciation scene involving Samson's mother. When the angel of the LORD commands Samson's mother, "You shall conceive and bear a son; therefore beware and drink no wine or strong drink" (Judg. 13:4), the "divine" connection is already made between having a son—in this case also, a future judge—and avoiding wine or strong drink. This theme is taken up here and reprocessed with many of the emotive accents that surround the paradoxical life of Samson, the unknowing judge, remaining. "Do not drink wine and strong drink," the angel of the LORD commands Samson's mother; "Wine and strong drink I have not drunk!" protests a royal Hannah to Eli, the priest of the LORD. It only appears a drunken deed to ask for a king. What is it really?

Moreover, to be accused of drunkenness is equivalent, in Hannah's eyes, to accusations of worthlessness: "Do not regard your maidservant as a base woman (*bat bᵉliyyāᶜal*)" (1:16). In my longing for a son, she claims, I am not a worthless woman, a good-for-nothing. We are here asked to consider and evaluate, through the most judgmental of Deuteronomic terms, *bᵉliyyāᶜal*, this matter of Israel requesting a king. Was it a base or worthless desire for Hannah-Israel to have requested a king? Is Hannah-Israel in this matter like those "base fellows" in Deuteronomy 13:13–17, who draw away Israelites to serve other gods, an abominable thing to do and punishable by the law of *ḥerem*? Is Hannah's inward heart (*ᶜal libbāh*) like the worthless heart that shuts the hand against one's poor brother (Deut. 15:9)? Is Hannah-Israel like the base fellows of Gibeah (Judg. 19–20), who lived in the time of the Judges when "there was no king in Israel and every man did what was right in his own eyes"? Is Hannah like Eli's own worthless sons (2:12)? Is she worthless like those who will be *against* King Saul (10:27) and even against David, such as Nabal (25:17) and Sheba (2 Sam. 20:1), or *for* King Ahab, such as the two base fellows dragooned by Jezebel to bring a charge against poor Naboth, who, they claimed, "cursed God and the king" (1 Kings 21:10–13)? As this last reference suggests, the question opened up by Hannah's protestation in 1:16 is this: Is there any connection between the establishment of kingship in Israel and the cursing of God? Is Hannah's prayer drunken, as Eli mistakenly assumes, or worthless, as Hannah vehemently denies? Or is it a devout and worthwhile thing to desire a king? However complicated and nuanced the answer—and our reading of the Deuteronomic History so far should lead us to expect complexity—Eli's final words to Hannah foreshadow God's decision to Hannah-Israel to grant the petition they request of him.

If Hannah's and Eli's character zones involve a meditation on the theme of mistaken drunkenness, that is, a meeting in which both the subject and the object of the mistake are disoriented without knowing it, another kind of "mistake" in this encounter involves being more right than one realizes; this is a central feature of Eli's characterization here. Without knowing what it was Hannah was praying for (until she tells him later on, in v. 27), Eli identifies himself with her request: "Go in peace; (for) the God of Israel will grant your petition which you have made to him" (or "may the God of Israel grant . . .") (1:17). Israel, Eli says, will (or should) have a king. Was Eli in this sense "mistaken" even after Hannah corrected him about her drunken condition? The questions over kingship raised in the meeting between Hannah and Eli in terms of appearance and reality, drunkenness and prayer, conscious and unconscious error or truth, will find their complex answers in the ensuing history of kingship in Israel.

Significant details worked into the Deuteronomist's account of Hannah and Elkanah's interchange in verses 21–23 provide further insight into this matter of the kingship as it will be developed in subsequent chapters of the story. A key question has to do with kingship and delay, and this in a dual sense. First, given the fact of kingship in Israel, why did the LORD wait so long in establishing it? Second, once having decided to allow Israel a king, why did the LORD repent and switch from Saul's house to David's? Both senses of delay, that is, of providential design and improvident false start, are beautifully integrated in the image of the weaning of Samuel.

Consider, for example, Elkanah's response to Hannah's plans for bringing Samuel to Shiloh after weaning him: "Do what seems best to you, wait until you have weaned him; only may the LORD establish his word" (1:23). This statement, "only may the LORD establish his word," seems anomalous and strangely intrusive until we put it in the context of the larger story line as we have been developing it; the central problem of the kingship is not simply in what senses it is good or evil for Israel. Rather more central to its beginnings is an additional problem: Given Israel's rejection of the LORD for a king, and given the LORD's mysterious acceptance of their request, why in fact was Saul's kingship aborted so soon after it had been established? How can the LORD be seen to have established his word when he rejects Saul? In Hannah's words, Samuel-Saul is to appear in the presence of the LORD and abide there *forever* (1:22): "I will give him [Samuel-Saul] to the LORD *all the days of his life*" (1:11). That Samuel stands for or prefigures Saul is made explicit, as we have seen, in Hannah's final words of the chapter, "As long as he lives he is lent to the LORD, he is 'Saul!'" Elkanah's statement in 1:23 sets up a central puzzle of the book: Once having selected Saul, how then can the LORD have rejected him? How can the LORD be seen as establishing his word (*yāqēm dᵉbārô*) when he has Samuel say to Saul, "But now your kingdom shall not be established (*lo' tāqûm*)" (13:14)? The reason given in 15:11 is that Saul has not established God's word (*dᵉbāray lo' hēqîm*). Israel had remained in existence for over two hundred years during the period of the judges even though the people were consistently disobedient to the LORD. And after Saul, kingship in Israel remained for hundreds of years in spite of a long series of evil kings. Why then did Saul's line, indeed Saul's rule itself, not last, given the LORD's choice of him? The false start of Saul's reign is a central ideological puzzle of 1 Samuel.

The other sense of kingship's delay—as providential design—is featured and foreshadowed in Hannah's words to her husband: "As soon as the child is weaned, I will bring him, that he may appear in the presence of the LORD, and abide there *forever* (*ᶜad ᶜôlām*)" (1:22). Earlier, in her silent prayer, Hannah proposed only to give her son to the LORD "all the days of his life" (1:11). Both phrases are obviously equivalent within the narrow confines of Samuel's life and destiny, but Hannah's switch to the phrase *ᶜad ᶜôlām* is especially appropriate if there is a question here of the duration not only of an individual life but also of a house, be it priestly (as in 2:30 when the LORD says to Eli, "I promised that your house and the house of your father should go in and out before me forever") or monarchic (as in 2 Sam. 7:16 when the LORD tells David through Nathan, "And your house and your kingdom shall be made sure forever before me"). Was this *forever* of kingship worth waiting for with respect to the delay embodied in Israel's long history of judgeship? This sense of providential delay looks backward just as the delay-as-false-start looks forward.

Such a backward glance is even verbalized by Elkanah when he connects up Hannah's decision to wait until Samuel is weaned with doing what is best in one's eyes: "Do what seems best to you (*haṭṭôb bᵉᶜênayik*), wait until you have weaned him . . ." (1:23). Tying together the delay in presenting his son/king to the LORD with the striving of humans to do

the right thing, Elkanah's words reverberate with the narrator's characterization of Israel in the premonarchic period: "In those days there was
no king in Israel; every man did what was right in his own eyes (*hayyāšār
bᵉᶜênāyw*)" (Judg. 21:25). Once again we see how profoundly double
voiced biblical discourse can be. The narrator's words in Judges 21:25
and Elkanah's in 1 Samuel 1:23 mutually contaminate each other. The
question about kingship reraised here in 1 Samuel will be looked at in
magnificent detail and with shifting perspectives in the coming books:
was the weaning worth it?

Finally, one other issue featured in the various dialogues of this
opening chapter needs to be emphasized. The emotive and ideological
accents present in the various character zones of Elkanah, Hannah, and
Eli set up a profound contrast between the God-centered perspective of
Elkanah, on one hand, and the human-centered perspective of Hannah
and Eli on the other. Whatever the specific concerns about kingship that
will form the subject matter of the coming chapters, at many points in
the narrative the line seems drawn between that which establishes God's
word (Elkanah) and that which fulfills human desires (Hannah and Eli).
In what respects will Israel's experiment with kingship display a concur-
rence of divine word and human desire, in what respects their mutual
alienation? It is this conjunction of and tension between the "forever" of
human desires and the "forever" of God's promises that forms the
central drama of Samuel/Kings.

The Song of Hannah (1 Samuel 2:1–10)

The presence of "inserted" poetry throughout the prose narrative of the
Bible is well known. What is not always so clearly seen is with what care
these poems are placed within their literary context. If the Deuteronomic History's high degree of artistic composition is largely what this
present reading illustrates, then surely the heightened language that is
an essential feature of the Song of Hannah ought to serve key esthetic
and ideological purposes in the Deuteronomist's plans. Appearing as it
does at the beginning of the account of the establishment of kingship in
Israel, the Song of Hannah does not disappoint. We hear in the song not
one but at least three voices, each with its own perspectives and
multivoiced accents, each cooperating with the other two to form, in
Bakhtin's terms, a "polyphonic composition" that is both harmonious
and dissonant, transparent yet opaque, looking backward and forward,
full of thematic variations on themes already met or soon to be
encountered. The "chorus" performing this song forms a trio of voices:
(1) Hannah, the rejoicing mother; (2) a persona of the exultant king;
and (3) the Deuteronomist, the "author" of the song in its present setting
at least. This final voice subtly but powerfully casts a melancholy tone
over what is at first glance a psalm of personal and national thanksgiving.

The poem can be understood at its most superficial level as the grateful maternal cry of a once-barren woman. Within it, obvious references to Hannah's immediate situation are easy to enumerate. When Hannah states, "My mouth is open wide against my enemies (*'ôyᵉbay*)" (2:1), we recall how the taunting Peninnah was described earlier as Hannah's opponent or enemy (*ṣārātāh*) in 1:6. Hannah's words, "But those who were hungry have ceased to hunger" (2:5), can be seen as referring back to the narrator's words, "Therefore Hannah wept and would not eat" (1:7) . . . "Then the woman [Hannah] went her way and ate" (1:18). And when we read, "The barren has borne seven, but she who has many children is forlorn" (2:5), the barren Hannah and the fertile Peninnah with "all her sons and daughters" (1:4) come to mind.

Moreover, the royal undertones present in chapter 1 are now explicit in the song; the LORD makes the poor "sit with princes and inherit a throne of honor" (2:8), and "He will give strength to his king, and exalt the power of his anointed" (2:10). The royal climax of Hannah's song appears out of the blue, completely irrelevant to Hannah and her situation until we understand the story of Samuel's birth as a finely orchestrated overture on the birth of kingship in Israel. In short, apparently appropriate to its context primarily by its tone of joyful thanksgiving and by the brief reference to birth following barrenness (2:5), the poem can be seen as closely allied with preceding events in its use of royal imagery in verses 8 and 10. Both aspects of Hannah's situation, the maternal and the monarchic, are present.

But the poem's allusions to kingship are not simply a matter of the references to throne, king, and anointed in verses 8 and 10; Hannah's song reads like many of the psalter's hymns of thanksgiving in which composition in the first person singular and concluding references to God's anointed king specify them as royal psalms of thanksgiving. If we search through the psalter for a psalm that best duplicates this song's triumphant tone, its major themes, its precise vocabulary, and its deictic conclusion pointing to the kingship of David, Psalm 18 turns out to be amazingly similar.[16] Introduced as "A psalm of David . . . who addressed this song to the LORD on the day when the LORD delivered him from the hand of all his enemies and from the hand of Saul," Psalm 18 is itself "duplicated" in the concluding hymn of praise that David sings to the LORD toward the end of his life in 2 Samuel 22. In fact, the Song of Hannah could easily serve as an abbreviated version of 2 Samuel 22, so that when the reader of the exploits of Saul and David comes upon David's hymn at the end of 2 Samuel, it will be no accident to hear within it echoes of that shorter hymn with which the story of Israel's move to kingship is inaugurated. Hannah's initial song and David's final hymn of praise form a poetic *inclusio* for the history contained within the books of Samuel. Just as 2 Samuel 22 is meant by its introduction to evoke in song the preceding exploits of David and Saul from the triumphant king's point of view, so also the song of 1 Samuel 2 foreshadows and prefigures in a striking manner this same account and perspective. That the Deuteronomist's artistic and ideological purposes merge in the songs coming at the beginning and toward the end of the books of Samuel seems to me particularly suggestive, especially when one considers that the Song of Hannah is preceded by a prose account that similarly evokes concerns about royalty in ways both subtle and provocative.

If David is king *par excellence* in the books of Samuel, and if his hymn of praise in 2 Samuel 22 recalls his rise to power in the face of Saul's opposition, then perhaps we may be justified in hearing the prefiguring voice of a victorious king in the Song of Hannah, in concise harmony and counterpoint with its longer version at the end of 2 Samuel. The emotive and ideological features present in the character zones of both Hannah and David through the songs placed in their mouths unite their voices in a striking way.

Take the matter of vocabulary. The Song of Hannah is filled with the words of 2 Samuel 22. Take also the matters of triumphant tone, of similar themes, and so forth. Assume that all these similarities are present simply because both songs somehow rehearse their subject matter with similar emotive and ideological perspectives. Assume, moreover, that there is no genetic compositional relationship between the longer poem and its more concise counterpart. Assume all this, and it is still necessary to explain what this song is doing in Hannah's mouth in 1 Samuel 2 if it is not to prefigure the matter of kingship that forms the stuff and substance of 1 and 2 Samuel, and more precisely the conflict between Saul and David during the inauguration of kingship in Israel. If in 1 Samuel 1 we have seen a number of examples of how deeply multivoiced that narrative could be in the service of a royal ideology, here in the Song of Hannah we see how multivoiced a poem can be toward the same purpose—multivoiced because a poem, placed in the mouth of this or that character, takes on the variable accents of its speaker.

The expressive features of David's hymn of praise in 2 Samuel 22 are easily summarized: an impassioned, breathless staccato about the LORD as the speaker's savior; a cosmogonic description of the LORD's thundering power; deep satisfaction over the defeat of one's enemies; the speaker's belief that his own filial obedience merited such deliverance; an overwhelming confidence that one so blessed can do all things in the God who strengthens him; an immense exaltation both of God and self; exultant praise and thanksgiving for past victories; and a royal statement of certitude about future triumphs both personal and dynastic.

Although the Song of Hannah is only one-fifth the size of David's song, it contains many of these same emotive elements. Hannah exults in the LORD her rock; she derides her enemies and identifies herself with all the downtrodden of the earth who have risen up to defeat their foes. She sings of a knowledgeable God who weighs all actions and repays her faithfulness with victory. She concludes her song with an unexpected exclamation about the strength and exaltation of God's king and anointed.

Despite the many differences between the two poems, it would not be off the mark to characterize the Song of Hannah as a proleptic summary of David's final hymn, nicely duplicating its triumphant tone. David's poem is in praise of kingship, human as well as divine, his as well as his descendants'; it rehearses nothing less than the victory of kingship in Israel. Hannah's poem, at the level of her own discourse, is a prophetic song looking forward to that same victory. Hannah's arrogant enemies now include all those within Israel who oppose kingship for whatever reason. The monarchy will be established by a "God of knowledge." The poor and downtrodden who rise up to "sit with princes and inherit a throne of honor" are all Israel's kings who will take their place in the arena of international politics. "For the pillars of the earth are the LORD's and on them he has set the world" (1 Sam. 2:8) immediately follows upon Hannah's reference to prince and throne. (2 Sam. 22:44–46 similarly revels in David's rise to international prominence.) God's faithful ones (v. 9) are his kings, whose enemies both national and international "shall be broken to pieces." Against them God "will thunder in heaven" (v. 10) just as "the LORD thundered from heaven" (2 Sam. 22:14) against David's enemies.

In this way the voice of a triumphant king merges with that of an exultant mother. Such an understanding helps to explain why, in their respective contexts, the emotive and ideological accents of Hannah's song and David's psalm are so similar:

1 SAMUEL 2:1–10	2 SAMUEL 22
1. My mouth opens wide against my enemies. I rejoice in thy salvation [O LORD]; my horn is exalted in the LORD.	4. I am saved from my enemies. 3. The LORD is . . . the horn of my salvation.
2. There is no rock like our God.	32. Who is a rock except our God.
4. But those who stumble have put on strength.	40. For thou didst gird me with strength for the battle.
6. The LORD brings down to Sheol.	6. The cords of Sheol entangled me. 48. God brought down people under me.
7. The LORD who brings low also exalts.	28. Your eyes [O LORD] are on the exalted to bring them down.

1 SAMUEL 2:1–10	2 SAMUEL 22
8. He raises up the poor from the dust.	43. I beat [my enemies] fine as the dust of the earth.
9. The feet of his faithful ones he will guard.	26. With the faithful one thou dost show thyself faithful.
	34. He made my feet like hind's feet.
	39. [My enemies] fell under my feet.
The wicked shall be made silent in darkness.	29. My God lightens my darkness.
10. The LORD will thunder from heaven.	14. The LORD thundered from heaven.
The LORD shall be made silent in darkness.	29. My God lightens my darkness.
The LORD will thunder from heaven.	14. The LORD thundered from heaven.
[The LORD] will exalt the horn of his anointed.	51. The LORD shows steadfast love to his anointed.
He will give strength to his king.	51. Great triumphs he gives to his king.

David, of course, is the triumphant king of the books of Samuel. If we continue along these same lines, other connections between the royal voice of chapter 2 and those heard further on in the text seem appropriate.

"Do not multiply your words, 'Tall! Tall!'" (2:3), Hannah says to her "enemies." We are reminded that Saul will be introduced as one who "was taller than any of the people" (9:2); "When he stood among the people, he was taller than any of the people from his shoulders upward" (10:23). Like Saul, David's other archenemy, Goliath, was unusually tall: "His height was six cubits and a span" (17:4). On the other hand, when he sends Samuel to anoint David, the LORD speaks disparagingly of Eliab's—perhaps indirectly of Saul's—height: "Do not look on his appearance or on the height of his stature, because I have rejected him; for the LORD sees not as man sees; man looks on the outward appearance but the LORD looks on the heart" (16:7). (Samuel, it seems, is not to make the same mistake about David that Eli made about Samuel's "drunken" mother, that is, judging by appearance only.) If one narrative contrast between David the triumphant and Saul the rejected be physical height, then one may wonder if the sad affair of Saul's aborted kingship is not here being prospectively alluded to from David's point of view.

"My horn is exalted in the LORD" (2:1). Does this "horn" of strength have anything to do with the "horn of oil" with which Samuel anoints David (16:1, 13) and Zadok Solomon (1 Kings 1:39)? Is there any significance to the fact that Samuel uses, by contrast, a vial (*pak*) of oil to anoint Saul (10:1) and Elisha Jehu (2 Kings 9:1, 3)?[17]

"The bow of the mighty (*gibborîm*) are shattered . . . for not by power shall a man be mighty (*yigbar*)" (2:4, 9). In the books of Kings, *g⁽ᵉ⁾burāh* refers exclusively to royal power or might, almost always in formulaic expressions.[18] Closer to home in Samuel, both David and Saul are referred to as *gibborîm*, "mighty men," who themselves lead mighty men. But what draws our special attention to the royal tones surrounding Hannah's rejoicing over the defeat of mighty men is another song of David, his lament over Saul and Jonathan after the death of Saul. Here David's elegy to the defeated Saul returns again and again to the might (*gbr*) of Saul and his line:

2 SAMUEL 1

19. How are the mighty fallen!
21. For there the shield of the mighty was defiled, the shield of Saul.
22. From the fat of the mighty . . . the sword of Saul returned not empty.
23. Saul and Jonathan . . . were stronger (*gāberû*) than lions.
25. How are the mighty fallen!
27. How are the mighty fallen!

It is true, of course, that in Samuel/Kings *gibborîm* can refer to kings or commoners, Israelite or Philistine, the victorious or defeated, and, like much of the language of Hannah's song, is readily applicable to any number of variant referents in the story to follow. Nevertheless, what is interesting about the series of royal applications we have been pursuing is the underlying assumption that enables this line of interpretation: if the beginning story of Hannah has been fashioned as an artful introduction to the history of kingship in Israel, and if this history proceeds with the same careful attention to detail that a fine jeweler exhibits while fashioning an appropriate setting for a precious gem, then one ought to look for and expect to find many examples of that artful use of language that makes for great literature.

Why not read the Song of Hannah as something more than a song "not wholly unsuited to its secondary context . . . fitting enough on Hannah's lips"?[19] Why not avoid that tone of timid defensiveness with which the Song of Hannah is so often made part of its literary setting? It seems clear that if a royal voice is now being heard singing its own song in harmony with Hannah's, then it is singing of the mighty Saul to come, as well as of the mighty king who defeats him. If the biblical text is read with as much careful attention to detail as one assumes its author(s) possessed when it was fashioned, then the question is, simply, how much artful contrivance can the text bear? Immeasurably more, I am suggesting, than is usually allowed it.

"He raises up the weak from the dust . . . to make them sit with princes and inherit a throne of honor" (2:8). Read in the narrow context of Hannah's improved maternal situation, these lines do convey something of the hyperbolic joy experienced by a new mother who was once barren. At the same time, they form one of the few explicit references in the song to kingly matters, so that it is but a short step to find Hannah's words echoed in the coming words of Yahweh to Jehu against King Baasha, "Since I exalted you out of the dust and made you leader over my people, Israel . . ." (1 Kings 16:2). Not only from Hannah/David's point of view but also from God's, this matter of kingship was an affair in which the weak (*dal*) are raised up "to sit with princes." But this connecting up of weakness with the rise of kings is counterbalanced by its use in reference to their downfall also: "There was a long war between the House of Saul and the House of David; and David grew stronger and stronger, while the House of Saul became weaker and weaker (*dallîm*)" (2 Sam. 3:1).

In hidden accents such as these, then, the Song of Hannah is sung by other voices besides hers, ones that sing of the story to come with joy as well as sadness, feelings much like David will express in his lament of 2 Samuel 1 and his jubilation of 2 Samuel 22. This little hymn at the beginning of our story is far from an "all-purpose poem" appropriate wherever a pragmatic redactor would need to have a character turn a tune for poetic relief within a monotonous sea of prose. Highlighted within its seemingly anonymous and formulaic expressions are literary glimpses of what will be, word pictures painted with a texture that is profoundly multivoiced, speaking of many things at once, often with mutually conflicting accents.

The Deuteronomist's Preview

Besides this regal voice, we hear, finally, the refracted voice of the Deuteronomist who, in ways both positive and negative as well as mysterious, comments on and foreshadows the stuff of the story to come. Much of the author's evaluative accents here will take the form of questions raised for the reader. If the voice of kingship—be it David's, Saul's, or any of their successors'—sounds a predominantly triumphant note within Hannah's song, the voice of the author casts an air of ironic melancholy (much like the feelings expressed by Elkanah in 1:8) over the entire affair.

The song, for example, rejoices in various reversals of (mis)fortune—the feeble become strong, the hungry cease hungering, the lowly are exalted, and so forth. As a poetic preview of the hopes and dreams surrounding kingship in Israel, images of the hungry finally being fed and the poor raised from the dust to inherit a throne of honor strike a triumphant note here at the beginning of Israel's romance with kingship; there is much in the coming history to justify the jubilant use of these images. However, the author's prescient voice puts these upswings into ideological and historical perspective. For the climax of Israel's affair, described in 2 Kings 24–25, uses these same images to temper their triumphal tones and comment upon the final meaning of Israel's regal entrance into the world arena.

When Nebuchadnezzar besieges Jerusalem a second time, the narrator tells us that "the famine was so severe in the land that there was no food (*lehem*) for the people of the land" (2 Kings 25:3). Famine caused by threats both internal (for example, the Gibeonite affair in the time of David, 2 Sam. 21) and external (Ben-hadad's siege of Samaria in Elisha's time, 2 Kings 6–7) were not new to Israel, but this final famine undergoes an ironic reversal at the very end of the story. Thirty-seven years into his exile, Jehoiachin, king of Judah, put off his chains and was given by Evil-Merodach, king of Babylon, "a throne above all the thrones of the kings who were with him in Babylon . . . And all the days of his life *he ate bread* before [the king of Babylon]" (2 Kings 25:27–29). Here we have the final king's final reversal of fortune: "The hungry are fattened on food" (McCarter's translation); "He raises the poor from the dust to make them sit with nobles and inherit a throne of honor" (2:5, 8). The throne of honor and the fattening food spoken of by Hannah may point to the glories of David and Solomon, but they also force us to contemplate the final table and throne of honor accorded the final Israelite king, now luxuriantly subjugated to the king of Babylon. Here is a move to fortune that is at the same time an ultimate misfortune, a bittersweet fate that reminds one, perhaps as it is meant to, of the melancholy fate of another king. Defeated by the Israelites who cut off his thumbs and great toes (as the Babylonians would later put out the eyes of Zedekiah), Adonibezek said, "Seventy kings with their thumbs and their great toes cut off used to pick up scraps under my table; as I have done, so God has requited me! So they brought him to Jerusalem and he died there" (Judg. 1:7). In light of the Babylonian king's table and his own throne of honor, Jehoiachin's fate seems preferable to Adonibezek's. Nevertheless, the prophetic words of Moses show the relationship between their two fates: "Like the nations that the LORD makes to perish before you, so shall you perish, because you would not obey the voice of the Lord your God" (Deut. 8:20).

The Deuteronomist's voice contains other evaluative accents affecting the meaning of Hannah's song in the light of what is to come. When Hannah sings, "The bows of the mighty (*gibborîm*) are broken, but the feeble gird on strength . . . [The LORD] raises the poor (*dal*) from the dust" (2:4, 8), we hear the voice of a jubilant mother who contrasts the once mighty position of Peninnah with her own previously barren state and revels in their reversal of fortune. At the same time, we have indicated how one can hear in these words the voice of the triumphant king of Israel who looks forward in general to monarchic Israel's victories over other nations, but more specifically to David's victorious occupation of Saul's throne. Kingship, paradoxically, belongs, after all, to the poor whom the LORD raises up out of the dust. Even the mighty Saul, so tall in stature, is reminded by Samuel, "Though you are little (*qāṭon*) in your own eyes, are you not the head of the tribes of Israel?" (15:16).

The Deuteronomic history concludes with a final reversal on the royal topic of the weak and the strong. For the last chapters of 2 Kings make crystal clear that the fate of those Israelites who requested and received from Yahweh royal power and a throne of honor was exile in a strange land. "He carried away all Jerusalem, and all the princes, and all the mighty men of valor, ten thousand captives. . . . And the king of Babylon brought captive to Babylon all the men of valour, seven thousand . . . all of them mighty men fit for war" (2 Kings 24:14, 16). Indeed, the personification of all this power, Jehoiachin, finally does inherit a place of honor, but he is nonetheless subjugated to the king of Babylon and exiled, forced to receive from his master "every day a portion, as long as he lived" (2 Kings 25:30)—so like the barren Hannah who got the whole affair started in the first place and who, year after year, received a portion from Elkanah. The circle is finally closed.

In contrast to the mighty men of Israel, now barren figures in exile, the only Israelites in the story who remain in Jerusalem at the end are the poor. The Deuteronomist makes this point not once but twice, as if to reinforce the final message. After the first siege of Jerusalem we are told, "He carried away all Jerusalem . . . None remained except the poorest people of the land (*dallat ʿam hāʾāreṣ*)" (2 Kings 24:14), and after the second siege, "But the captain of the guard left some of the poorest of the land (*dallat hāʾāreṣ*) to be vinedressers and plowmen" (2 Kings 25:12). The only heirs left in the fertile land that the LORD swore to give to their forebears are the poor (*dal*).

Finally, that careful attention to detail of which this history gives us so many examples provides us with a reverse image that casts a final poignant shadow over Israel's high hopes for kingship as portrayed in the story of Hannah. She had vowed that, once granted the son she wanted, she "would give him to the LORD *all the days of his life*" (1:11). She promises Elkanah that her son "will appear *before the LORD* and abide there forever" (1:21). And to Eli she proclaims proudly, "*All the days that he lives* he is lent to the LORD" (1:28). With all these words, the Deuteronomist depicts the solemn promise of Israel that its requested king would "serve the LORD" (2:11) all the days of his life. Then the author, in describing the final action of the final king, summarizes, as it were, what Israel's desire to have a king like all the nations finally had come down to: in place of the picture of Israel's king "serving before the LORD all the days of his life," the Deuteronomist gives us a subservient

Jehoiachin, who "ate bread before [the king of Babylon] all the days of his life" (2 Kings 25:29). Oh, how the mighty have fallen!

The Ever-present Figure of Samuel (2:11–36)

Instead of Hannah, who only denied being worthless (1:16), we now meet Eli's two sons, who indeed "were worthless men" (2:12). The narrator's black-and-white judgment sets the tone for the rest of the chapter. Narrative language had been largely neutral in chapter 1, leaving us to infer the types of evaluative issues raised in the story; there were no obvious villains in Samuel's birth story. Here in chapter 2, after the Song of Hannah, the stories about the fall of the House of Eli and the rise of Samuel begin, and the narrator's definitive judgments are spelled out for us from the start. We know right off that the sons of Eli and their servants are as bad ("Now the sons of Eli were worthless men; they had no regard for the LORD [2:12]; . . . thus the sin of the young men was very great in the sight of the LORD," 2:17) as Samuel is good ("Now the boy Samuel continued to grow in stature and in favor with the LORD and with men," 2:26). We immediately learn, before any of the characters involved, that the LORD will kill Eli's sons for their sins (2:25). So that there will be no doubt in our minds about the sinfulness or fate of Eli's house, we are told about these things by the narrator (2:12, 17, 22, 25), by Eli, who hears it by way of the people (2:23–25), by a man of God (2:27–36), and finally by the LORD himself (1 Sam. 3). All this evaluative and descriptive overkill allows us no surprise when Eli and his two sons finally die their violent deaths in chapter 4.

If nothing is overtly surprising about the reasons for the fall of the House of Eli, neither are we kept in the dark about the rise of Samuel, who is never far from the narrator's lips even when speaking of others. For one thing, there is a continual contrastive pairing of Samuel and Eli's sons in chapters two and three:[20]

2:11. And the *boy* ministered to the LORD.
　12. [But] *the sons of Eli* were worthless men.
2:17. Thus the sin of *the young men* was very great in the sight of the LORD for the men treated the offering of the LORD with contempt.
　18. [But] *Samuel* was ministering before the LORD.
2:21b. And *the boy Samuel* grew in the presence of the LORD.
　22. [But] Eli heard all that *his sons* were doing to all Israel.
2:25b. For it was the will of the LORD to slay *them* [the sons of Eli].
　26. [But] *the boy Samuel* continued to grow . . . in favor with the LORD.
2:36. And *everyone who is left in [Eli's] house* shall come to implore
　　　　him . . .
　3:1. [But] *the boy Samuel* was ministering to the LORD under Eli.

All one has to do to see the compositional strategy of this chapter is to make explicit, as I have done, the implied *but* or *however* that hovers before the second statement in every one of the above instances: the house of Eli shall fall, *but* Samuel's is on the rise. There is good reason to suggest, as we shall see, that these statements about Samuel are much more tightly woven into the fabric of the chapter than many scholars believe.[21] If we use this central feature of repeated contrastive composition as an indicator of authorial intention rather than redactional intrusion, we can come to some conclusions about what is not so clearly expressed in the text.

Take the matter of redundancy referred to above. We are told in four different ways about the sins of the house of Eli: by the narrator in expository material (2:11–21), by Eli (2:23–25), and the man of God (2:27–36) in two separate events,[22] and finally by a fourth account in chapter three. The redundancy is functional in the structure of chapter 2, in which the material distributes itself into past, present, and future perspectives on the topic.[23]

First, the narrator describes the sins of Eli's house from the point of view of the condensed past actions of the sons of Eli (vv. 11–21). Having chosen to summarize the habitual actions leading up to the events of chapter 1 ("So it went on year by year when she went up to the house of the LORD," 1:7), the narrator now does the same on a larger scale in chapter 2 ("So they did at Shiloh to all the Israelites who came there," 2:14). The text is filled with at least thirty-three imperfective verb forms, many of which function to represent the habitual, repeated, or condensed action that makes up the exposition proper. In order to make the following story of Eli's disintegrating house immediately understandable, the narrator summarizes actions—or their omission—that took place over a long period of time. Moreover, the narrator concludes this telling with an explicit judgment (2:17), allowing the reader to have no doubt at all about the past sins of Eli's house.

Second, the narrator, in verses 22–25, recounts an incident in which Eli himself confronts his sons with their sins ("Why do you do such things?") and follows this up with their reaction ("But they would not listen to the voice of their father"). What is obvious from this second telling of the sins of the Elides is the overwhelming feeling of *presentness* that confronts the reader: Eli [is] very old; he *hears* all that his sons *are doing:* they *are laying with* certain women who *are serving* at the entrance to the tent of meeting; so (he said), why *are you doing* such things as I *am hearing?*; it is no good report I *am hearing* from those who *are spreading it abroad;* if a man *sins* . . . God *will mediate,* but if a man *sins* . . . who *can intercede?*[24] but the sons *do not listen* to their father.

In this piling up of twelve imperfective verb forms in only four verses, the narrator, Eli, and the people bring us into the very presence of the situation, just as we were brought into the very presence of Hannah's meeting with Eli through the use of the synchronic imperfectives found in the narrative events of the first chapter.[25] It is not only what the sons of Eli *continually did* in the preceding exposition, it is what they *are now doing* that needs to be dealt with. Moreover, just as the narrator concluded the past section with an evaluation (2:17), so now the present section concludes with another evaluation (2:25b). The matter is made more and more explicit. We see the Elides going to their destruction; we are with Eli as he confronts his sons; we find out how they respond, even as the narrator divulges to us what none of the participants yet knows: "For the LORD had decided to kill them."[26] Which is meant to lead us into the third telling of the story.

The oracle of the LORD (vv. 27–36), as befits its genre, proceeds from the dominant perspective of *the future*.[27] Since it points to the consequences of the sins of the Elides, and since this house's fateful descent involves Samuel's ascent, it is appropriate that we find explicit references to Samuel that bracket this account also (2:26; 3:1). There is no need to end this third section of the chapter with the narrator's evaluative conclusion, as was the case in the previous two (vv. 17, 25b), because the content of the LORD's words in the oracle centrally addresses the issue of judgment. This oracle also contains a sixth instance within the chapter wherein the sons of Eli are contrastively paired with Samuel; as I will suggest below, the individual prophesied in verses 33 and 35 is Samuel himself, and reference to the deaths of Hophni and Phinehas is found sandwiched between the verses in verse 34. It is as though the chapter may not mention the sons of Eli without referring to their opposite.

With respect to the identification of the individual(s) mentioned in verses 33 and 35, there is obviously good cause to point to Abiathar (1 Sam. 22:18–23; 1 Kings 2:26–27) and Zadok (2 Sam. 8:17; 1 Kings 2:35) respectively, as is normally done.[28] Nevertheless, the multivoiced potential of biblical discourse ought not to be ignored in this prophetic word. Whoever the *long-range* referents of the LORD's prophecy may be, these words have an *immediate* referent in their present context, many aspects of which point in diverse ways to Samuel.

The obvious feature of chapter 2, in which Samuel is made continuously present by numerous explicit references to him[29] waiting in the wings, as it were, until such time as he starts to take an active part in the story in chapter 3, is reinforced by a number of verbal echoes in each of the three sections of the chapter—echoes that are less explicit certainly, but all the more effective in the subtle artistry with which the Deuteronomist keeps Samuel before our eyes and close to our ears, even while ostensibly talking of others.

In the exposition of verses 12–17, it is not enough to begin and end the account with a reference to Samuel: "And the *boy* was ministering to the LORD before Eli *the priest*" (2:11); "Samuel was ministering before the LORD, a *boy girded with a linen ephod*" (2:18). The very word used to refer to Samuel, *na‘ar*, is also introduced into the account under the guise of "the priest's servant (*na‘ar hakkohēn*)" in verses 14 and 15, so that the contrast between the actions of the sons of Eli and those of Samuel echoes throughout. There is a servant of the priests, Hophni and Phinehas, but there is also a servant of the priest, Eli. All the while that one lad was serving the LORD, the other was sinning greatly in his eyes. With this apparently gratuitous introduction of the servant of the priest, an authorial voice rather than a redactional intruder keeps Samuel before us even when it describes other things.

A second feature about Samuel in the exposition, one that will have special relevance below in the oracle, is his priestly aura: he serves the priest Eli in an ephod of white linen (*bad,* v. 18), a material worn only by priests, angels, and David.[30] Samuel's mother was continually bringing him little robes when she came to Shiloh for the yearly sacrifices (v. 19). Of course Samuel will turn out to be more than a priest in the stories to come; he is to be also a prophet of the LORD (3:20) and a judge who will judge Israel all the days of his life (7:15). Here, however, although never actually called a priest, Samuel is characterized throughout as a priestly figure, one who would eventually come to judge Israel even as Eli, the priest, judged Israel (4:18).

Concerning the "present" telling of the sins of Eli's sons (vv. 22–25), the mention once more of Samuel functions as a personal *inclusio:* "And the boy Samuel grew in the presence of the LORD" (v. 21); "And the boy Samuel continued to grow. . . ." (v. 26). In addition, his name echoes within the words of Eli and the narrator through the similarity of the sounds, *šin-mem,* in the root *šmᶜ,* "to hear, obey," which is repeated five times in this section: *wᵉšāmaᶜ* (v. 22), *šōmēᵃᶜ* (v. 23), *haššᵉmuᶜāh, šōmēᵃᶜ* (v. 24), *yišmᵉᶜû* (v. 25). It is clear that the "pronounced" repetition of this root serves some special function in the text (and more than one, as we shall see). The suggestion here that its sound recalls for us the sound of Samuel's name is yet another way in which the narrator echoes Samuel in the midst of words about his counterparts, the sons of Eli. This echo literally strikes one's ear. In the *šᵉmuᶜāh* that Eli *šōmēᵃᶜ,* we hear the name *šᵉmû'ēl,* about whom the narrator is speaking.

Concerning the "future" fate of Eli's house (vv. 27–36), again the figure Samuel both brackets the oracle (2:26 and 3:1) and echoes throughout it. Earlier in our discussion of 1 Samuel 1 we pointed out an example of concealed reported speech in which the "remember me" of Hannah's prayer (1:11) is echoed by the narrator's words, "And the LORD remembered her" (1:19). This phenomenon, discussed at length and brilliantly by Bakhtin throughout his writings, is much more common in literary discourse than usually recognized and is exemplified in some pertinent examples within the oracle of the anonymous "man of God." When he reports the LORD as saying, "I revealed myself (*nigloh niglêtî*) to your father's house" (2:27), these introductory words in the divine rejection of Eli's house are carefully chosen to reverberate with the successive words of the narrator describing Samuel as the successor to this same house: "And the LORD appeared again at Shiloh, for the LORD revealed himself (*niglāh*) to Samuel at Shiloh by the word of the LORD" (3:21). The LORD tells Eli that he had revealed himself to Eli's father's house in Egypt; then the narrator tells the reader that the LORD reveals himself to Samuel at Shiloh. In addition, the oracle culminates in a prediction: "And I will raise up for myself a faithful (*neʾemān*) priest . . . and I will build for him a sure (*neʾemān*) house. . . .'" (2:35); we have only to wait until the end of the account of Samuel's visions for the narrator to tell us that "all Israel knew that Samuel was established (*neʾemān*) as a prophet of the LORD" (3:20). Finally, Eli's successor, like Eli's predecessors, will "go in and out (*wehithallēk*) before [the LORD's] anointed (*mesîhî*) forever" (2:35). Granted the appropriateness of these words to future priests during the reigns of David and Solomon, Samuel's more immediate association with the anointed of the LORD brings him immediately to mind.

Seeing, therefore, that this "futuristic" account of the Elide sins in verses 27–36, like the two treatments before it, also refers to Samuel in a number of ways both direct and oblique, we can summarize this chapter's constellation of statements—and echoes of statements—about Samuel even before he takes an active role in the Deuteronomist's stories. Whereas Eli and his house is associated with old age (2:31; see 4:18), Samuel is only a youth, *naʿar* (vv. 11, 18, 21, 26), pointedly contrasted with the *naʿar* of the wicked priest(s) in verses 14 and 15, Eli's sons; Samuel's name is echoed in the words of Eli to his two sons: *šemûʾāh - šemûʾēl; šmʿ* in this passage (vv. 22–25) means both "to hear" (vv. 22, 23, 24 [twice]) and "to obey" (v. 25). Samuel shall go in and out before the LORD's anointed (*wehithallēk, mesîhî*, 2:35).

If we take all this language as somehow representing the character zone surrounding the beginning of Samuel's career, then it is interesting to find many of these same terms clustering around his character zone as represented in his farewell speech toward the end of his career:

> And Samuel said to all Israel, "Behold I have hearkened to (*šāmaʿtî*) your voice in all that you have said to me, and have made a king over you. And now behold the king goes in and out (*mithallēk*) before you; and I am old (*zāqantî*) and gray; and behold *my sons* are with you; and I have gone in and out (*hithallaktî*) before you from my youth (*minneʿuray*) until this day. Here I am; testify against me before the LORD and before his anointed (*mesîhô*). (1 Sam. 12:1–3)

The language is reprocessed: then it was a case of Eli's sons, now it is a case of Samuel's; Eli's sons did not listen to their father, but now Samuel listens to the people; what was Eli's old age and Samuel's youth is now gathered up in the youth and old age of Samuel; those who go in and out were priests—one of whom was Samuel—but now they are Samuel and the king; the referents before whom one goes in and out were the LORD and his anointed, but now they are the people; and then as now Samuel is intimately connected with the LORD's anointed.

The Ever-present Figure of the King (2:11–36)

The range of voices we hear throughout 2:11–36 extends far beyond the priestly concerns we have been discussing up to now. Just as the story of Samuel's birth turned out to be an introductory meditation on the rise of kingship in Israel, so also the material in 2:11–36, on the surface an introduction to the rise of Samuel, itself turns out to continue this same meditation.

What principles of selection guide the Deuteronomist in the stories chosen to tell of Samuel's rise and in the details invested in them? One answer keeps reappearing as we probe the text for indications: the particular manner in which the opening stories are told allows the author to invest the stories with a number of royal voices, all subordinated to the author's own voice, which itself is continually working out the various relationships between Israel's fate and God's reluctant decision to grant its request for a king. The strategy that the implied author employs here at the beginning of 1 Samuel is similar to Nathan's strategy in 2 Samuel 12, who when sent by the LORD to address the problem of David's murder of Uriah chooses a parable to introduce God's judgment. When David misinterprets the parable by taking it literally, Nathan points to its real meaning with the words "you are the man" (2 Sam. 12:7).

In a similar fashion the Deuteronomist introduces us to the central problem of the ensuing history, kingship in Israel with all its messy and complicated details, and does this by means of a selection of stories that take place on the threshold of kingship's appearance—stories whose details prepare us for the main topic by providing us with anticipatory perspectives on Israel under the monarchy. I am suggesting, therefore, that these early stories about the fall of the House of Eli and the rise of Samuel, in addition to having inherent interest in themselves, form a kind of parabolic introduction to the Deuteronomic history of kingship. Both Eli's house and its successor, Samuel's house, like the rich man in Nathan's parable, are stand-ins for royalty, especially David's.[31]

Take the detail in Samuel's birth story where we encountered Eli "sitting on a seat/throne in the temple/palace" (1:9). It is no accident that we will find Eli in a similar position at the end: "Behold Eli was sitting upon the seat/throne" (4:13). From first to last Eli is a royal figure, so that the triple treatment of the evil practices of Eli's house in 2:11–36 reverberates with royal implications.

More than royal, Eli is also "very old" (2:22). In fact, "Eli was ninety-eight years old and his eyes were set so that he could not see" (4:15). There is an aura of ultimacy about him; he is a figure of royalty at the end of the line, old and blind, so that the oracle of the LORD reads very well not only as an introductory parable on the coming reigns of various kings throughout Israel's history, but especially as a parable about the ultimate fate of the monarchy itself. Indeed, at its deepest level, we hear within the text the Deuteronomic voice once again foreshadowing the bittersweet finale of Israel's king as the History will portray him. The "you" being addressed in the oracle is kingship on its last legs, after the experiment has run its course and failed.

A concluding image centers on the eating of bread and the receiving of an allowance: "And everyone who is left in your house shall come to implore him [your successor] for a piece of silver or a loaf of bread, and shall say, 'Put me I pray you in one of the priest's places, that I may eat a morsel of bread'" (2:36). The fate of Eli's house shimmers with reflections of the sardonic picture of Jehoiachin in chains in 2 Kings 25, who finally "put off his prison garments. And every day of his life he ate bread at the king's table, and for his allowance a regular allowance was given him by the king, every day a portion, as long as he lived" (2 Kings 25:29–30). Eli's "descendants" will beg to be put "in one of the priest's [= king's] places," and indeed will get more, and less, than they request: Jehoiachin is given "a seat above the seats of the kings who were with him in Babylon" (2 Kings 25:28). At the same time, the irony is that, however improved his situation after prison, Jehoiachin—like Israel— ate the bread of bondage as long as he lived.

Besides the royal figure Eli, other details about the fall of his house carry on the images of kingship begun in chapter 1; the most obvious of these, as we have seen, involves sonship. What ties together the triple account of Eli's evil house in 2:11–36 with the story of Samuel's birth in chapter 1 is chapter 2's emphasis on the actions of Eli's sons rather than those of Eli. If it were not for Eli's sons, his house would not have been condemned. Just as the birth story of Samuel revolved around the implications of Hannah's request for a son, and of her receiving what she had asked for, so this story revolves around the evil practices of Eli's sons and the fate that such practices will bring upon his house. Eli is condemned, the LORD says, because "you honor your sons above me" (2:29). Like Hannah, Eli stands for a royal Israel, and his sons, like Samuel, stand for Israel's kings. Even more to the point, Samuel in this chapter is "a boy girded with a linen ephod" (2:18) and will be followed in the history by only one other nonpriest who is similarly garbed: "And David was girded with a linen ephod" (2 Sam. 6:14).

If we take such royal indicators seriously, then in spite of the many difficulties surrounding the text's meaning—especially obvious in the oracle's unintelligibility in places—the general lines of the Deuter- onomist's opening "parable" can be established. We have a guide through an ideological maze that makes up what Bakhtin would call "the ultimate conceptual authority of the text"; this authority sets up parabolic echoes between the specific discourse found here, when kingship is not yet directly addressed, and the discourse that soon will be concerned about, indeed obsessed with, kingly matters. Some preliminary examples of the multivoiced language within chapter 2 will indicate how it echoes forth other language to follow. Not only the fact of kingship's failure but the how and why of it are addressed in a number of provocative ways that put the matter into proper perspective. Three words seem especially appropriate in this regard: *kābēd*, *ne'ºmān*, and *šāmaᶜ*.

Kābēd is the most graphic of the three and provides an especially clear picture of how the Deuteronomist inserts complicated evaluative positions on kingship into these opening stories. The entire range of this "word" is used in this chapter to paint a remarkable inner portrait of the nature of kingship and its accompanying dangers. From its physical meaning of being heavy to its more abstract meanings of being dull, insensitive, or burdensome, *kābēd* has a whole range of negative connotations. At the same time, it possesses an equally wide range of positive meanings. It exemplifies the best in human experience—to be weighty in riches, honor, or glory; God himself is *kābōd* personified. It is no wonder, then, that the Deuteronomist chooses this word to illustrate both the positive hopes and negative outcome of Israel's experiment with kingship; the paradox of the story is that this institution will embody the best and the worst in principle and in practice.

Eli's house will fall because, God says, "you honor (*wattᵉkabbēd*) your sons more than me . . . Those who honor me I will honor (*mᵉkabbᵉday*, *ªkabbēd*), but those who despise me shall be lightly esteemed" (2:29–30). Since Eli stands for monarchic Israel in this oracle, it is no wonder that the LORD hearkens all the way back to when "I revealed myself to the house of your father when you were in Egypt subject to the house of Pharaoh" (2:27). Israel's sin in the land is to have honored its kings more than the LORD by "letting [your sons] eat from the first part of all the offerings of Israel before me."[32]

If Eli is a royal figure, that is, if he stands for Israel who demanded a king, our last clear image of him in 1 Samuel is especially revealing. Old and blind, he hears of the ark's capture by the Philistines and of his sons' deaths and "fell over backward from his 'throne' . . . And his neck was broken and he died, for he was an old man and heavy (*kābēd*)" (4:18). Israel's fate will be defeat and disaster because its monarchy, so full of honor and glory, is ultimately (in a fundamental as well as a chronological sense) heavy, burdensome, a central cause of that defeat. Monarchic Israel fell because it was heavy with the fat of the LORD's offerings.

The Deuteronomist's play on the various meanings of *kbd* and its connections with kingship does not end here. "The Glory" (*kābōd*) designates God himself in many biblical passages outside the Deuteronomic History, but it plays a special role within it. After our oracle predicts the fall of the house of Eli because of its failure to honor (*l^ekabbēd*) the LORD (2:29–30), and after the sign of that fall is stated as the death of Hophni and Phinehas on the same day (2:34), the fulfillment of that sign is itself "signed" by Phinehas's wife giving birth to a son on the day of her husband's death: "And she named the child Ichabod, saying, 'The Glory (*kābōd*) has gone into exile from Israel!' because of . . . her father-in-law and her husband" (4:21). With the death of Eli's sons—these deaths being a sign of God's rejection of Eli's house—"the glory" departs from Israel, and this departure is signified by the birth and naming of Ichabod. Once again the birth of a son and the explanation of his name by his mother have a definite connection with the making and breaking of royal figures in the story: in both cases—the naming of Samuel and the naming of Ichabod—the kingship of Saul comes particularly to mind.

It is not simply that Saul, like his priestly stand-ins in this chapter, dies with his sons "on the same day together" (1 Sam. 31:6). It is not only that the narrator signals Saul's serious wounding and imminent death with the words "And the battle pressed heavy (*wattikbad*) upon Saul" (1 Sam. 31:3). More to the point is Saul's response to Samuel's informing him of God's decision: "And the LORD has rejected you from being king over Israel . . . the Glory (*nēṣah*) of Israel will not lie or repent" (1 Sam. 15:26, 29). Saul responds, saying, "I have sinned; yet honor me (*kabb^edēnî*) before the elders of my people and before Israel" (1 Sam. 15:30).

As I indicated above concerning 1 Samuel 1, the kingship of Saul, like the rise of Samuel, is paradigmatic of the establishment of kingship itself. How can Israel honor its king and still honor God? How could God, having chosen Saul "forever," have rejected him? How can God be seen as repenting, yet not repenting, of having given Israel the monarchy? God " 'will not lie or repent; for he is not a man that he should repent.' . . . [But] the LORD repented that he had made Saul king over Israel" (1 Sam. 15:29, 35).

The ensuing struggle between Saul and David exemplifies this problem. Long into this struggle, Ahimelech says to Saul about David, "Who amongst your servants is as faithful (*ne^{'e}mān*) and honored (*w^enikbad*) in your house as David?" (1 Sam. 22:14). This characterization of the victorious king over his rejected counterpart leads us to the second royal "word" involved in this section on Eli's sons, *ne^{'e}mān*.

The meaning of *ne^{'e}mān* ranges from the faithfulness of God and humans to the lasting nature of divine word (for example, 1 Kings 8:26) or human house, be it royal or priestly, material or generational. As used in the oracle against Eli's house, both extremes are addressed in the "faithful priest" and the "lasting house" of 2:35. What is especially clear from the oracle is that this promise of a stable house for the faithful priest who is Eli's successor follows upon and mirrors God's similar promise to Eli's father's house, made long before the oracle: "I promised that your house and the house of your father should go in and out before me *forever*" (2:30). No matter how sure the LORD's word is, sin can intervene and the LORD is forced to make another promise to Eli's successor.

This rise, fall, and rise of priestly houses foreshadows exactly the repetitious rise and fall of kingly houses in the history to follow. First Saul would have been given an everlasting promise (1 Sam. 13:13), but his sins intervene and he is rejected (1 Sam. 13:14). Then David is given this very promise, "And your house and your kingdom shall be made sure (*ne'man*) forever before me" (2 Sam. 7:16) with an added proviso that the LORD will not "take my steadfast love from [Solomon] as I took it from Saul, whom I put away from before you" (2 Sam. 7:15).[33] Nevertheless, sin intervenes and, in spite of God's strengthened promise to David, most of Solomon's kingdom is torn away. Once again the LORD is constrained to promise Jeroboam, "And I will build you a sure house (*bayit ne'emān*) as I built for David" (1 Kings 11:38). Israel falls to the Assyrians nonetheless, and none is left but the tribe of Judah (2 Kings 17:18). Finally, the fate of this remaining tribe fares no better (2 Kings 17:19–20 and to the end).

The royal implications of the oracle of the LORD incline, therefore, toward the instability of the "sure house" of Eli's successor, whoever he may be, and foreshadow his unfaithfulness as certainly as the sins of Eli's sons disrupted and destroyed their father's house. It is as though hope must spring eternal in the divine breast. Given the dishonor, the burden, the heaviness that will characterize Israel and its kings to the very end, how can the Glory keep on promising all his "forevers"? And given the royal scraps finally bestowed upon Jehoiachin "as long as he lived," the triumphant side of the oracle seems betrayed by a history too burdened to end the cycle with any conclusive certainty.

Central to this burden is our third royal "word," *šāmac*, and the immense gulf between the "listening," or "hearing" at one extreme of its semantic range and the "listening to" or "obeying" at the other. These extremes are programmatically portrayed in the "present" account of chapter 2 (vv. 21–25), where, as we have seen, Eli confronts his sons with their sins through the use of *šmc* four times in three verses, all with the simple meaning of "to hear." The narrator then indicates the sons' response, "But they would not listen to (*yišmecû*) the voice of their father" (2:25).

This play of meaning within *šāmac* echoes throughout the Deuteronomist's account of the establishment of kingship and provides us with a central theme on the nature and failure of kingship. In 1 Samuel 3, Samuel is not able to receive God's thrice-attempted revelation to him until Eli gives him the response that will open things up: "Speak LORD for thy servant hears/obeys (*šōmēac*)" (3:9). Further on, Samuel is commanded by God to "hearken to the voice of the people (*šāmac bᵉqol*)" requesting a king (8:7, 9). When he counsels them against kingship, "the people refused to listen to (*lišmo*^{ac}) the voice of Samuel" (8:19), just as Eli's sons would not listen to their father's voice. Then, after Samuel hears the words of the people (8:21), the LORD again commands him, "Hearken (*š²ma²*) to their voice" (8:22). Samuel recalls all this at the beginning of his farewell address: "Behold, I have hearkened (*šāma²tî*) to your voice . . . and have made a king over you" (12:1). Later, when he refers again to the king, he commands them to "hearken to the voice [of the LORD] . . ." and threatens them, "if you do not hearken to the voice of the LORD . . ." (12:14, 15). But Saul's kingship, once established, is soon aborted. Samuel confronts Saul, "Why did you not obey (*šāma²tā*) the voice of the LORD?" (1 Sam. 15:19). Saul responds, "I have obeyed (*šāma²tî*) the voice of the LORD" (1 Sam. 15:20). Samuel says, "Has the LORD as great delight in burnt offerings and sacrifices as in obeying (*kišmo*^{ac}) the voice of the LORD? Behold, to obey (*š²mo*^{ac}) is better than sacrifice" (1 Sam. 15:22).

The problem and paradox of the kingship is bound up with this play on *šāma²* in these dialogues between Eli and his sons, Samuel and Eli, Samuel and the LORD, Samuel and the people, Samuel and Saul. In one sense, to hearken to the voice of the LORD means not to desire a king, "for they have not rejected you, but they have rejected me from being king over them," as God tells Samuel (8:7). On the other hand, Samuel must hearken to the voice of the LORD who commands him to hearken to the people's voice by giving them a king; kingship paradoxically results from both obeying and not obeying the LORD.

The implications of the LORD thrice commanding Samuel to make Israel a king (8:7, 9, 22)—and thereby commanding him to cooperate with and *enable their rejection of him*—fill the first two chapters of 1 Samuel with ominous tones concerning the history to come. The voices commingle: " 'Am I not worth more to you than ten sons?' (1:8) . . . But they would not listen to the voice of their father; for the LORD wanted to slay them" (2:25).

Sight and Insight (1 Samuel 3:1–4:1a)

After the ever-present statements about an absent Samuel in chapter 2, he finally appears in chapter 3, entering the scene a boy (v. 1) and exiting a prophet (v. 20). The opening exposition is full of language about the diminution of sight and light—no frequent vision, eyesight growing dim, not being able to see, a lamp not yet extinguished—metaphoric language pointing to a conspicuous lack of insight exhibited largely, but not exclusively, by Samuel. Throughout the story, the narrator makes it clear that the lad does not know what to make of it all. Samuel is first puzzled by the strange voice, for he "did not yet know the LORD, and the word of the LORD had not yet been revealed to him" (v. 7). Only after recounting the entire event does the narrator accompany a reference to Samuel's growth with a notice about his establishment as a prophet when the LORD "continued to appear at Shiloh and revealed himself to Samuel at Shiloh" (v. 21). In the story itself, the apprentice understandably looks to Eli to provide him with the appropriate response that will allow the LORD's revelation to occur: "Speak LORD for thy servant hears" (v. 9). When Samuel fearfully recounts his experience to Eli, the old priest remarks, "It is the LORD" (v. 18), intimating that however precise was Samuel's description to Eli of his vision (we are not given his exact words in v. 18), reference to the LORD was not part of it. From first to last in this story Samuel remains in the dark even though "the lamp of God had not yet gone out" (v. 3).

This impression of an imperceptive and mostly passive prophet is strengthened by another image, that of the LORD standing before an ever-reclining Samuel who is not yet able to stand on his own two feet. Before the vision occurs, the narrative is strewn with references to Samuel's typical position: "Samuel was *lying down*" (v. 3); "*Lie down* again. So he went and *lay down*" (v. 5); "*Lie down* again" (v. 6). The LORD's appearance itself is bracketed by more references to Samuel flat on his back: "So Samuel went and *lay down* in his place. And the LORD came and stood forth. . . . Samuel *lay* until morning" (3:9–10, 15). Samuel in a horizontal position and needing an almost blind priest to identify the LORD for him may tell us something about the Deuteronomist's first reference to a prophet since the time of Gideon (Judg. 6:8).

Is Samuel's inability to get beyond appearances a personal feature not confined to the immature stages of his career? When the omniscient narrator tells us that "Samuel was afraid to tell the vision to Eli" (v. 15), the word *mar'āh* is used, not the *ḥāzôn* of verse 1. Like Eli in chapter 1 and unlike him here in chapter 3, Samuel will continue to be bedeviled by "appearances (*mar'āh/mar'eh*)" that deceive. Later on when Saul is rejected, the LORD will have to turn Samuel away from the impressive Eliab: "Do not look on his appearance (*mar'ēhû*) . . . Man looks on the outward appearance, but the LORD looks on the heart" (16:7). After chapter 2's "hearing but not obeying," "being heavy but not honored," and "faithful but not stable," chapter 3 confronts us with "seeing but not understanding." Throughout the history, no matter how often the narrator and God thunder forth their apodictic statements and apparently clear-cut evaluations, the Deuteronomist continually confronts and even thematizes the complexity of situations. Despite centuries of criticism to the contrary, the Deuteronomic History is anything but didactic in its ideology; its introduction to monarchy fits this profile.

These initial features of Samuel's character zone are important. Although he will be absent from explicit reference during the coming accounts involving the ark of the covenant, Samuel's reappearance in chapter 7 and his subsequent role in the Deuteronomist's story of the

establishment of kingship are foreshadowed by this preliminary characterization. Samuel's hesitation, fear, and occasional insensitivity do not
cease with his coming of age and establishment as prophet and judge of
all Israel; he will continue to stand for, as he now lays down for, human
puzzlement over the LORD's designs.

God's revelation to Samuel about the fall of Eli's house seems
superfluous from Eli's point of view. The oracle of God given the priest
by a man of God in chapter 2 could not have been clearer on this point.
What is to be gained by a second revelation? The answer lies in the
narrator's gradual revelation of what is involved in the LORD's rejection
of Eli. For one thing, we were not told in chapter 2 what Eli's reaction
had been to the devastating oracle, whereas here in chapter 3 Eli's
resignation to God's decision voices a seemly end to the account: "And
[Eli] said, 'It is the LORD; let him do what seems good to him' " (v. 18).
As with Elkanah's response to Hannah's plans for "presenting her son to
the LORD forever" (1:23), so with Eli's response to God's plans for
"punishing his house forever" (3:13): both Hannah and God are to do
what seems best in their eyes. We will return to these words below as we
listen for the royal accents contained in them. For now it is significant
that from first to last all Eli's words about the LORD and his designs are
knowingly (2:23–25; 3:18) or unknowingly (1:17) exemplary. Equally
exemplary will be the final action of Eli's life when he falls over backward
off his "throne," a movement embodying, as it were, God's designs.

As before, the narrator continues to bring the reader into the center
of the action by piling up imperfective verb forms. Here, however, this
practice is intensified by the repeated use of *hinnēh* in verses 4, 5, 6, 9, 11,
and 16. The narrator speaks in the present in verses 1, 2 (twice), 3
(twice), and 8; so also, the LORD speaks predominantly and appropriately in the present or future in verses 11 (3 times), 12, 13 (twice), and
14 (twice). It is as if this story from Israel's past has special meaning for
the author's present audience. The rise of Samuel and the fall of the
house of Eli are relevant far beyond their original context; they have a
deeper significance for the Deuteronomist's contemporaries who hear
the LORD state, "I *am doing* a thing in Israel, at which the two ears of
every one that *hears* it *will tingle*" (v. 11). Because these opening chapters
form a parabolic introduction to the Deuteronomist's history about the
rise and fall of monarchic Israel, the voices within them, speaking of
events that happened long before the text's composition, are made
continually to speak in the present to a fallen Israel bereft of the
kingship it had so insistently demanded. Here at the beginning the
Deuteronomist confronts each (exiled?) Israelite with Nathan's words,
"You are the man."

By chapter 3, a feature of these opening chapters that sets them apart
from the history itself has become apparent: in contrast to later stories in
which certain characters are described as carrying on conversations with

the LORD, for example, Samuel 8:21–22, here in the beginning human characters do not converse with the LORD. Two-way discourse between a privileged person and the LORD does not occur. It is as if we are in a time when it is both *not yet* and *no longer* possible for humans directly to converse with the LORD. Word *from* the LORD is abundant; directly responsive word *to* the LORD does not exist. The situation of a partially absent LORD, one who hears humans and whom humans hear but do not—or cannot—respond to directly, is indicative of these opening chapters, but expressed in a special way in chapter 3: precisely where Samuel has an opportunity directly to speak to the LORD, he is commanded by Eli to express a willingness simply to listen—and even then Samuel unaccountably omits the LORD's name. Eli's "Speak O LORD . . ." (v. 9) becomes Samuel's "Speak . . ." (v. 10). Direct dialogue with an explicit LORD is not part of the picture. Are there hints here of a postexilic situation?

These considerations prepare us to understand how chapter 3 reverberates with that "royal" voice we have been hearing continually since the beginning of the book. The narrator's voice embeds this chapter with concealed reported speech—its own and others'—containing premonitions of the royal tragedy to follow and even alluding to royal language already used or soon to be employed. We can now consider some of these allusions.

The narrator, as we have said, begins the account with language about sight and light:

> There was no frequent *vision*. At that time Eli whose *eyesight* had begun *to grow dim,* so that he *could not see.* . . . The *lamp of God* had not yet gone out. (Vv. 1–3)

These images cluster around sight as an obvious metaphor for insight, but they do more: they carefully indicate a royal object in view and "the lamp of God" is this object's brightest image.

It is true that David will call the LORD "my lamp (*nîrî*) who lightens my darkness" (2 Sam. 22:29) and that the parallel in Psalm 18:29 uses the alternate spelling (*nēr*) as here in verse 3. However, what is crucial for our understanding of this guiding metaphor, and its precise object here, is the History's use of *nîr* to refer to David's kingship. When Ahijah confronts Jeroboam with the word of the LORD he refers to David's dynasty by using this word: "Yet to his son I will give one tribe that David my servant may always have a *nîr* before me in Jerusalem . . ." (1 Kings 11:36). That the *nîr* here mentioned is a symbol of the Davidic dynasty has long been recognized by scholars.[34] If Ahijah the prophet will use this language to refer to David's house, so also will the narrator, who later refers to the sinful Abijam of Judah: "Nevertheless, for David's sake the LORD his God gave him a *nîr* in Jerusalem, setting up his son after him . . ." (1 Kings 15:4). And in reference to the unfaithful

Jehoram of Judah, the narrator will write, "Yet the LORD would not destroy Judah, for the sake of David his servant, since he promised to give a lamp (*nîr*) to him and to his sons forever" (2 Kings 8:19).

The *nîr* about which Ahijah and the narrator speak in these passages is being alluded to here in 1 Samuel 3:3. "The lamp of God (*nēr 'elohîm*) had not yet gone out (*yikbeh*)" is a royal reference—either metaphorical or paronomastic—that precedes the LORD's word about the dynastic darkness to come; word about the fall of a priestly house is at the same time word about the fall of the last remaining royal house in Israel. Thus David's men will adjure him, "You shall no more go out with us in battle, lest you quench (*tekabbeh*) the lamp (*nēr*) of Israel" (2 Sam. 21:17). The effective "quenching of the lamp," which David and his descendants long avoided—sometimes through cautious obedience but most often in spite of their sins—will finally be described in the closing battles of 2 Kings 24 and 25. We last see a referent of the lamp of Israel at the table of the king of Babylon.

Another visual allusion to David is apparently accomplished by the narrator's ironic description of the situation preceding the prophecy. It is a time when "the word (*dābār*) of the LORD was rare . . . There was no frequent vision (*ḥāzôn*)" (3:1). Rare word of God and infrequent vision preface this parabolic prophecy of the fall of houses in a manner that is in striking contrast to the way the narrator will conclude Nathan's triumphant prophecy about David's dynasty: "In accordance with *all these words* (*debārîm*), and in accordance with *all this vision* (*ḥizzāyôn*), Nathan spoke to David" (2 Sam. 7:17). Since the climax of the history justifies Samuel's parabolic prophecy rather than Nathan's literal one, it is significant that prophecy and history concur precisely where the word of God is described as spare and sparse, as in Samuel's time, rather than frequent and expansive, as in Nathan's. This seems to correspond with our earlier observation about the partially absent LORD in these opening chapters. At any rate, it is suggestive that the word chosen to describe the presence of the LORD's word here in 3:1 is *yāqār*, which means "rare" but also "precious" or "valuable"; we are in a narrative time when there was "no frequent vision," in contrast to "all this vision" in the time of Nathan.

There is other concealed speech in this chapter involving sight and light, speech that looks backward rather than forward on the matter of kingship. God says to Samuel about Eli's house, "On that day *I shall establish* (*'āqîm*) against Eli *all that I have spoken* (*dibbartî*) concerning his house from beginning to end" (3:12). Eli responded to Samuel's report with, "It is the LORD; let him do *what seems good in his eyes*" (3:18). We hear concealed within these words of God and Eli the words of Elkanah. In response to Hannah's plans, after weaning Samuel, "to bring him that he may appear in the presence of the LORD and abide there forever" (1:22), Elkanah said, "Do what seems good in your eyes . . . only may the LORD establish (*yāqēm*) his word (*dᵉbārô*)" (1:23). In both cases the figure Samuel "conveys" Hannah-Israel's request: he embodies the request for kingship itself (1:17, 20, 27; 2:20) and is the intermediary who brings to Eli notice of a dynastic house's coming destruction (3:18). Samuel "represents" kingship ascendant and descendant. Paradoxically, both royal phases are depicted by the Deuteronomist as "good in the eyes of the LORD" because both somehow "establish his word."[35]

Finally, not only does the account of God's revelation to Samuel end with a reference to the LORD's eyes (v. 18), it also begins with a reference to Eli's eyes, which had begun to grow dim (*kēhôt*). In what way does this description of Eli's weakening sight stand for Israel's diminishing insight about kingship? If the parabolic prophecy of kingship's coming destruction is described as uttered at a time when "the lamp of God had not yet gone out," how may this matter of dimming eyesight have royal implications? What had Eli/Israel lost sight of? As D. N. Freedman has already suggested,[36] the weakening (*kēhôt*) of Eli's sight in verse 2 may somehow be related to Eli's failure to "weaken (*kihāh*)" his sons in verse 13. We can go further: the middle term connecting these two words is Eli's knowledge that "his sons were blaspheming God" (v. 13), so that Eli's weakening sight stands for his knowing failure to extinguish his sons' blaspheming. The theme of sons as stand-ins for kings continues in this chapter. At the same time, the LORD's references in verse 13 to Eli's sons' blaspheming (*mᵉqalᵉlîm*) recalls the LORD's words about their fate in the previous chapter: "Those who despise me shall be accursed (*yeqallû*)" (2:30). For Eli, his failure to weaken his sons (*lo' kihāh*) weakens his eyesight (→ *kēhôt*); for his sons, their blaspheming of God (*mᵉqalᵉlîm*) results in God cursing them (→ *yeqallû*).[37] In our introduction to kingship, Eli's sons are predominantly active—as Eli himself is a continually passive—pretender(s) to the throne.

Two

ARK IN EXILE: THE PARABLE CONTINUES (4:1b–7:17)

Philistine must have originally meant, in the mind of those who invented the nickname, a strong, dogged, unenlightened opponent of the chosen people, of the children of the light. (Matthew Arnold, *Essays in Criticism*)

The lamp of God had not yet gone out. (1 Samuel 3:3)

General Comments on 4:1b–7:2

The ark narrative divides up roughly into two sections: the story about the initial loss of the ark as an effective symbol of the fall of Eli's house (chap. 4), and the story of the ark's sojourn in Philistine country with its eventual return to Israel (chaps. 5 and 6).

In recent years, scholars have written many words about the ark narratives.[1] Much of the energy expended on these texts—as on most others in the Bible—has been in the arena of excavative scholarship, especially compositional history.[2] What is not generally apparent in the secondary literature is a dedicated effort to work out how the stories about the loss and eventual return of the ark fit into the overall story line of the books of Samuel. What factors—ideological, esthetic, or historiographic—may account for the selection and combination of these stories about the ark and the specific details subsequently worked into them? What are the compositional relationships (*compositional* in the poetic not genetic sense) between these stories of the ark and their immediate and remote context in the Deuteronomic History? Do the earlier ark narratives really interrupt material about Samuel's life and career, or vice versa? Or do they fit in with their immediate context in ways that make plausible suggestions of literary artistry and careful attention to detail? Questions of this type will fuel the discussion.

A general feature of the ark stories is their deliberate and abiding emphasis on similar circumstances and language affecting Israelite and Philistine. The ark in and out of battle entails defeat and disaster for both communities—the death of thirty thousand men on the side of the

Israelites and widespread physical ailments on the side of the Philistines. To reinforce similarities between Israel and Philistia and to minimize their obvious differences, the narrator fills the account with language applying to both camps, often in similar ways. If the LORD is said to defeat or afflict (*nāgap*) the Israelites (4:3) with a great slaughter (*maggēpāh gᵉdôlāh*, 4:17), so also does he afflict the Philistines: "For the same affliction (*maggēpāh 'aḥat*) was upon all of you and your lords" (6:4). The LORD evenhandedly strikes (*hîkkāh*) Israelite (6:19) and Philistine (5:6, 9, 12). Tumult accompanies the ark or news thereof wherever it goes, whether it be a great panic of death among the Philistines (5:9, 11) or the Israelites' ironically unjustified shouts of joy causing the earth to resound (4:5), followed by the uproar in Shiloh at the news of the ark's capture (4:14). If it is made abundantly clear that the Philistines' mistake was to have seized (*lāqaḥ*) the ark (4:11, 17, 21, 22; 5:1) in the first place, an even earlier mistake was the Israelites' carrying out of their elders' decision: "Let us seize for ourselves (*niqᵉḥāh 'ēlênû*) from Shiloh the ark of the covenant of the LORD" (4:3). Also, the play on *KBD* that began in earlier chapters continues on in the ark stories with all its ideological implications; the capture of the ark negatively signifies the departure of the Glory (*kābôd*) for the Israelites in 4:21, 22, for the Philistines the heavy hand of God (*kābēd*) upon them (5:6, 7, 9, 11), in remedy of which the Philistine sorcerers offer a way out—the making of golden images to give glory or tribute (*kābôd*) to the Israelite God who might then lighten (*yāqēl*) his heavy hand. Why should the Philistines continue to make their hearts heavy (*tᵉkabbᵉdû*), just as the Egyptians of old made heavy (*kibbᵉdû*) their hearts (6:5–6)?

Another characteristic of the speech of the narrator and the characters in these stories is a tendency toward hyperbole. Thirty-four thousand Israelites are killed at the beginning and fifty thousand are killed at the end. In between, shouts, slaughter, defeat, tumult, and stone are all "great" (4:5, 6, 17; 6:14, 19) and sometimes "very great" (4:10; 5:9), just as the LORD's hand can be "very heavy" (5:11).

Finally, the figure Samuel is never mentioned within 4:1b–7:2. Since this account is preceded by "And the word of Samuel came to all Israel" (4:1a), and followed by "Then Samuel said to all the house of Israel . . ." (7:3), it is tempting to view the ark narrative as an independent tradition more or less skillfully combined with the story of Samuel at this point. (The first account of Abraham's sojourn in Egypt in Gen. 12:10–13:1 and the speeches of Elihu in Job 31–37 exhibit a similar kind of "intrusiveness" within their literary contexts.) However, whatever this section's compositional history, the care with which the ark narrative fits into its present context will be the main focus of our attention. What the Philistine sorcerers say about God's "heavy hand" is relevant as the reader ponders the nature of the intricate compositional connections between chapters 4–6 and their literary context. The text offers two alternatives: the intricacy happened "by chance" or "it is *his* hand that strikes us" (6:9). Is the narrative hand "crude"—what critics usually mean when they write *redactional*—or "careful"—what I mean when I write *authorial?*

That the Deuteronomist's careful hand is indeed striking throughout the ark narratives is first seen in the intricate manner in which the absent Samuel, and everything he stands for, is made present in the account of the lost ark and the end of Eli's house in chapter 4.

The Glory Departs from Israel (4:1b–22)

The general story line of chapter 4 is clear. The Israelites' initial defeat at the hands of the Philistines, who slay four thousand of their enemy on the field of battle, occasions the Israelites' decision to take out the ark from Shiloh in order to bring about a change of fortune. Israel is nevertheless defeated again, this time with thirty thousand dead, the ark captured, and Eli's two sons killed. News of all this occasions the death of Eli and the birth of his grandson Ichabod. The previous prophecies about the fall of the house of Eli are now fulfilled.

Superficial plot motivation is also obvious. Israel's first defeat is necessary to help explain why the ark and its two priestly carriers were put in peril. Then Israel's second defeat sounds the death knell for Eli's house and establishes the ark in alien territory, two occurrences that symbolize the Glory in exile and prepare for the story to follow in chapters 5 and 6. If the plot is clear, it is the intricate stitching together of the narrative themes that amazes.

The paradoxical picture of a blind Eli keeping watch (*mᵉsappēh*) by the road is emblematic of the entire chapter. Emphasis on the diminution of sight and light, found throughout chapter 3, continues in chapter 4, but in a different fashion. The language here revolves more around sound than sight. The Philistines do not see the ark coming into the Israelite camp; rather, they hear the noise of shouting when "all Israel gave a mighty shout so that the earth resounded" (v. 5). "What does this great shouting mean?" (v. 6), they ask. When the Israelites are told the news of the ark's capture, "all the city cried out" (v. 13). When the messenger brings tidings (v. 17), Eli dies (v. 18). When his daughter-in-law hears the news, she gives birth and also dies (v. 19). Both the aural emphasis of this chapter and the figure of a blind Eli comment upon the events contained therein. Eli and the Israelites are blind to affairs, but so are the Philistines. Neither camp is said to understand, through any insightful sighting, what is happening to them, until chapter 5 when "the men of Ashdod saw how things were" (5:6) and chapter 6 where emphasis on sight becomes ideologically significant.

In contrast to the narrator's previous inclination to use imperfective verb forms either to condense expository action or "make present" the narrative events themselves, in chapter 4 the narrator is sparing in the depiction of synchronic perspectives.[3] As for spatial perspective, the narrator's point of view continually shifts from descriptions from within the Israelite camp (vv. 3–5) to those from within the Philistine camp (vv. 6ff.) or in the vicinity of Shiloh (vv. 12–16). In verses 6b and 7b–8, the external psychological perspective of the narrator shifts to the internal life of the Philistines and presents their generalized thoughts and fears.

This chapter's emphasis on sound without sight coincides with the complete lack of insight, indeed the utter confusion, that surrounds both camps. The Israelites' noisy confusion soon becomes obvious; under the Elides and without Samuel, they mistakenly believe that they can reverse the disaster of an initial defeat by seizing the ark and bringing it with them in battle. This strategy results in a greater defeat, the loss of the ark, and the death of Eli's sons. Israel unwittingly effects the fulfillment of God's prophecies narrated in chapters 2 and 3.

The Philistines themselves are depicted as misguidedly ignorant, a characterization that will make their coming victories especially hard to take for an Israelite reader. This almost playful picture of Philistines preparing for battle on the basis of obvious misinformation is accomplished by the narrator's incorporating into the few words they speak (in vv. 7b–8) an unusual number of what Israelites would view as factual errors. "Woe to us for nothing like this has happened before!" (v. 7). If the Philistines mean that they have never faced Israel when the latter is accompanied by the ark of the covenant, perhaps this is so. But if they are suggesting that Israel never went into battle so accompanied, then as every Israelite knew—and the history we are reading has made abundantly clear—they are woefully in error. They say, "Who can deliver us from the power of *these mighty gods?*" (v. 8). How ignorant to believe that the Yahwists worshiped many gods and that the ark of the LORD housed their presence![4] Finally, the Philistine belief that Israel's gods had "smote the Egyptians with every sort of plague *in the wilderness*" (v. 8b) is another error that must have struck the Deuteronomist's reader with some force. We might even suggest that specific passages in the Deuteronomic History are being playfully evoked here, such as Deuteronomy 11:4–5 or Joshua 24:5, in which statements about what the LORD did to Egypt are immediately followed by reference to the Israelites *in the wilderness*. The Israelite, knowing well such traditional depictions of the mighty acts of God, would have taken special pleasure in recognizing how the Philistines had misheard or misread their opponent's sacred traditions.

The manner in which the absent Samuel is everywhere present in chapter 4 is striking. Just as the narrator managed to evoke the presence of Samuel in chapter 2 even when speaking only of Eli and his sons,[5] so also here in chapter 4 the narrator's account of Israel's humiliating defeats without Samuel is constructed in a number of interlocking ways that link it up with the account in chapter 7 of Israel's triumphant victories over Philistia under Samuel's leadership. These connections concerning the *poetic* composition of chapters 4 and 7 are especially relevant when one puzzles over the genetic composition of these chapters and the supposed redaction of the ark material (chapters 4–6) within the Samuel story of chapters 1–3 and 7ff. If chapter 4 contains examples of what I have termed "concealed reported speech" along with other signs of deliberate artistic construction, then present theories about the redactional relationship of the ark stories and the Samuel-complex of traditions will need to be reevaluated. Take the "erroneous" statements of the Philistines, reported in 4:7–8, about Israel's mighty gods. Having manipulated the reader into experiencing smug pleasure at the Philistines' ignorance of Yahwism, the Deuteronomist springs a surprise. Once the plague-filled ark is returned to Israel, Samuel's first order of business is to strike at the cause of Israel's defeats at the hands of the Philistines: "Then Samuel said to all the house of Israel, 'If you are returning to the LORD with all your heart, *then put away* the foreign gods and the Ashtoroth from among you . . .'" (7:3). What the narrator had earlier failed to mention and now abruptly reveals is the presence of the "mighty gods" within Israel's midst to whom, it turns out, the Philistines are made to refer, but of whom they were unjustifiably afraid. As in previous chapters, the narrator quotes a character whom the reader will later discover to be more right than either the character or the reader could be expected to know earlier.[6]

Take also the narrator's statement that the soon-to-be-victorious Philistines "were afraid" when they heard of the ark's arrival in the Israelites' camp (4:7), and compare it to the statement that the about-to-be-victorious Israelites were afraid when they heard of the Philistines marshaling their troops (7:7). In both cases, the victorious combatant does the initial fearing, and not vice versa.

Take also the fearful question of the Philistines, "Who can deliver us (*yaṣṣîlēnû* from the hand of these mighty gods?" and compare it to Samuel's statement to the Israelites, "Direct your heart to the LORD, and serve him only, and he will deliver you (*wᵉyaṣṣēl*) out of the hand of the Philistines" (7:3). Consider also the narrator's concluding remark, "And Israel delivered (*hiṣṣîl*) their territory from the hands of the Philistines" (7:14). These verses in chapter 7 contain echoes of the Philistine question in 4:8.

Take Samuel's victorious setting up of the stone, Ebenezer, (7:12) and compare it to Israel's double defeat at Ebenezer in chapter 4. And finally, take the end of both stories: the etymological conclusion of chapter 4, wherein the birth of Ichabod signifies that "the Glory has departed from Israel," is balanced with the etymology toward the end of chapter 7, wherein the stone signifies that "up to now the LORD has helped us."

In all these cases, the sorry fate of Israel under the Elides and without Samuel (chapter 4) is evidently contrasted with Israel's triumphant fate under Samuel (chapter 7). It seems clear that chapter 4 is more tightly linked to the Samuel material than many scholars believe.[7] When we add to these close connections with chapter 7 the clear profile of chapter 4 as fulfillment of the prophecies in chapters 2 and 3 in all their dimensions, the case for unity is even stronger. The voice that all along has been contrasting the fall of Eli with the rise of Samuel continues to be heard in chapter 4. Samuel, as the direct successor to Eli in terms of prophetic, judicial, and priestly leadership over Israel, is central to chapter 4, notwithstanding the absence of any reference to the figure Samuel throughout the chapter.

The Royal Voice in the Lost Ark

Other reasons also suggest that chapter 4 is of the same literary cloth as the chapters that precede and follow it. Most importantly, the matter of kingship continues to occupy a central place in the details of how the ark came to be lost.

In spite of all the tumult and commotion surrounding the ark's movement, the blind Eli, sitting upon his "throne" by the road watching, is this chapter's central image. The scene in verses 12–17 of the man from Benjamin bringing Eli news of the battle and thus occasioning the old priest's death is sharply focused and bristling with details that make of Eli not just a royal figure but, more specifically, a Davidic one at that. The details of this central denouement of the story beginning in 2:12 form a carefully crafted montage of incidents, themes, and graphic details from the coming account of the establishment of the Davidic dynasty, with special emphasis on the death of Saul and the revolt of Absalom.

McCarter is correct when he states, "The structural parallel between the present episode [vv. 12–17] and the report to David of Saul's death in II Sam. 1.2ff is quite striking," but he is far from the mark, in my opinion, in believing that "this is an example of the common use of a literary motif by different writers."[8] Details show 4:12–18 to be a parabolic overture to the coming conflict between Saul and David on one hand, and David and his son Absalom on the other. Compressed within these few verses is a foreshadowing of royal intrigues to come, culminating in the Deuteronomist's image of how it all turns out in the end: Eli falls off his throne and breaks his neck.

The account of the man of Benjamin bringing news to Eli certainly parallels 2 Samuel 1:2ff., as McCarter suggests, but it also brings to mind 2 Samuel 15ff., the account of Absalom's threat to David's kingship. Opposition to David from his "father" Saul on one hand (Saul will persist in calling David "my son" in coming chapters) and his son Absalom on the other is bound up in this story of the blindly watchful Eli. Besides the voice that tells of Samuel's triumphant succession to the priestly, prophetic, and judicial position of Eli, we hear in these verses a royal voice previewing David's coming consolidation as king over Israel in the face of threats from previous and succeeding generations.

Notice how the Benjaminite messenger is described: "His clothes were rent and earth was upon his head" (4:12). It is no accident that language like this occurs only two other times in the entire Deuteronomic History (in the entire Bible, for that matter); in each case a messenger brings news to David concerning somone threatening his kingship—first Saul, then Absalom:

> Behold a man came from Saul's camp with his clothes rent
> and earth upon his head. (2 Sam. 1:2)
> And behold, Hushai, the Archite came to meet [David], his
> coat rent and earth upon his head. (2 Sam. 15:32)

Notice also that the messenger is described as "he who brought the tidings (*mᵉbasser*)" to Eli (4:17). What is significant about *BSR* wherever else it is used in the Deuteronomic History is that it always refers (1) to *good* news[9] (2) concerning the welfare of a royal house (1 Sam. 31:9; 2 Sam. 1:20; 4:10 (twice); 18:19, 20 (twice), 26, 31; 1 Kings 1:42; 2 Kings 7:9). In all cases but the last, it is to David's house alone that the news can be termed "good" or "glad." The good news almost always involves the death of someone threatening David's kingship: Saul in 1 Samuel 31:9; 2 Samuel 1:20; 4:10 (twice), and Absalom in 2 Samuel 18:19, 20 (twice), 26, 31. Indeed, the conflicting nature of this news—good and bad at the same time—is thematized in both cases. With reference to Saul's death, David says, "When one told me, 'Behold, Saul is dead,' and thought he was bringing good news, I seized him and slew him at Ziklag, which was the reward I gave him for his news" (2 Sam. 4:10). And in reference to Absalom, the entire section in 2 Samuel 18:19–19:1 revolves around the contradiction inherent in notice of his death: it is glad tidings for the king, but terrible news for the father: "Oh my son, Absalom, my son my son, Absalom! Would I had died instead of you, O Absalom my son, my son!" (2 Sam. 19:1).

As we have been noticing all along in this parabolic introduction to the history of kingship that will begin in earnest in 8:1, time and time again the contradictory nature of Israel's romance with kingship is emphasized through the semantic play of central terms such as *kābôd, ne'emān,* and *šāmaᶜ*. We now have *bāsar*. The crashing death of Eli in 4:18 foreshadows and embodies the Deuteronomist's graphic evaluation of the institution that Israel at first thought would bring good news and glad tidings; the news results mostly in death and destruction.

When we combine these literary connections between chapter 4 and passages concerning Saul's threat to David's kingship with the inclusive detail of Eli sitting upon his "throne" in 1:9 and 4:13 and with all the royal details in between, we begin to see how intricately the figure of Eli is tied into the coming account of kingship in the books of Samuel and beyond.

These connections are made even tighter when we consider how chapters 4–6 bind together the fates of Eli and the ark. If Eli's news can be seen as foreshadowing the news that comes to David concerning the final dissolution of the threat from Saul, then the weaving together of the fall of Eli's house with the loss of the ark points strongly to Absalom's revolt recounted in 2 Samuel 15. When one compares the discursive and thematic material in 1 Samuel 4–6 with that in 2 Samuel 15, the similarities as well as the differences are striking; both are significant in determining the ideological perspectives of 1 Samuel 4.

Once again we find a similarly described messenger. Like the earlier messenger to David in 2 Samuel 1, Hushai in 2 Samuel 15 has "a torn coat and earth upon his head" (v. 32) corresponding to the condition of the Benjaminite in 1 Samuel 4:12. 2 Samuel 15 begins with Absalom standing "before the way of the gate" (*ʿal yad derek haššaʿar*, v. 2); 1 Samuel 4 has Eli sitting "*yad derek*" (v. 13) and "*bᵉʿad yad haššaʿar*" (v. 18). Absalom, the royal pretender, states, "O that I were judge in the land" (2 Sam. 15:4) and revolts after forty(!) years (2 Sam. 15:7); Eli, the royal stand-in, "had judged Israel forty years" (1 Sam. 4:18). In 2 Samuel 15:26 David, in reference to the threat to his house, states, "Behold, here I am, let [the LORD] do to me what seems good in his eyes"; in 1 Samuel 3:18 Eli is a bit more certain about who threatens him: "It is the LORD; let him do what seems good in his eyes." If David "went forth" with all his household and all his people after him to escape Absalom (2 Sam. 15:16, 17), 1 Samuel 4 begins with Israel "going forth" to battle the Philistines (1 Sam. 4:1). For those who might be tempted to consider these "interconnections and symmetries" simply as recurrences of similar language because of similar situations of threat, additional thematic elements tie the two disparate accounts together in significant ways.

Is it a coincidence that 2 Samuel 15, like 1 Samuel 4:1–7:2, involves the leaving and returning of the ark from and to its rightful place? Or that two priests and their two sons accompany the ark in 2 Samuel 15, while Eli's two sons accompany the ark in 1 Samuel 4? Why, of all David's household and of all the people following him out of Jerusalem, does the account in 2 Samuel 15 single out Ittai the Gittite, leader of six hundred Philistines, for a prominent dialogue with David, a conversation emphasizing the unity between them? (2 Sam. 15:18–23). Why the congruence in both accounts of dynastic threat, round-trip journey of ark, and prominent Philistine presence? Why, in other words, do both accounts emphasize the similarities between Israelite and Philistine in close proximity to the ark?[10] It is true that the account of David's processional crossing of the Kidron is strongly reminiscent of Joshua 3–5, especially with its ritual description of "crossing over" (*ʿābar* is used eight times in 2 Sam. 15:19–24). Nevertheless, what is also striking is the emphasis on *hāʿobᵉrîm* in 2 Samuel 15 and *hāʿibrîm* in 1 Samuel 4:6, 9.

In spite of these linguistic, discursive, and thematic similarities, the differences between the two accounts are perhaps more striking. Nothing symbolizes the tension-filled existence of these similarities and differences so well as the speech of the Philistines in each chapter:

> Take courage and acquit yourselves like men
> O Philistines, lest *you serve* the Hebrews as
> they have served you. (1 Sam. 4:9)
> But Ittai [the Gittite] answered the king,
> "Wherever my lord, the king shall be, whether
> for death or for life, there also will *your*
> *servant* be." (2 Sam. 15:21)

Its enemy, having feared servitude to Israel, now joyfully proclaims it.

Notice other differences as well. The similarly described messenger comes to the defeated Eli in 1 Samuel 4 on one hand but to the ultimately vindicated David in 2 Samuel 15 (and 2 Sam. 1) on the other. And, most important of all, David triumphs through the death of Absalom in 2 Samuel 18, but Eli falls off his throne and dies in 1 Samuel 4.

It would not be an easy thing to puzzle out the literary connections between 1 Samuel 4 and 2 Samuel 15 if it were not for the recurring pattern we have already seen in the previous chapters of 1 Samuel. All along we have heard a royal voice speaking of an absent king, just as an obvious voice could continually refer to Samuel even when mention of him was absent from the text. Hannah spoke of her son, but also of Israel's kings. She sang triumphantly of those kings, notably with David's voice, but she also sang for the Deuteronomist, who put the coming triumphs of Israel's kings in proper perspective by overturning their intermittent victories and recurrent claims of an enduring dynasty through the cruel and indisputable turn of history evoked in the closing chapters of the History. In chapter 2, the man of God spoke with a royal voice that claimed eternal victory for David's house, even as Samuel, "the faithful one," was to succeed Eli. Nevertheless, the doleful accents of David's ultimate defeat were contained within the very structure of the oracle itself: God's forever and that of humans rarely coincide. When the revelation to Samuel comes in chapter 3, blind Eli, symbol of a blind Israel seeking blindly to follow its kings, hears his fate from the mouth of his successor Samuel, one even less perceptive than he; the blind lead the blind. In this chapter, Samuel's and David's triumph, signified by God's prophecy of Eli's fall, is muted by the opening statement of the narrator; "The lamp of God had not yet gone out" is another way of saying that it finally would.

By the time we get to the events of chapter 4, the ideological perspectives of the royal voice we have been hearing have already taken on a distinctive accent. Of course Eli's death means the rise of Samuel. Of course Samuel signifies the glory that David's house will experience in the coming history. But the Deuteronomist is also foreshadowing all the royal triumphalism about to be recounted with such brilliant and evocative detail, and the shadows foreshadowed are unmistakable: Israel's romance with kingship was a tragedy of immense proportions.

The fundamental way in which the Deuteronomist outlines, prefigures, and foreshadows the mysterious lessons the coming history will provide is to rehearse at the outset the key elements of that history in a manner that can short-circuit all the emotional attachments to the hopes and past glories of kingship with which the exiled and defeated audience was burdened. The essence of the message is contained in an introductory typology of events that apparently predate Israel's request for a king and that supposedly have nothing at all to do with the matter of kingship. The opening chapters are filled with concealed reported speech about kingship—that of the narrator and characters uttered in chapter 8ff.—speech reworked and re-formed to give it its own prevenient authorial accents. In this opening parable of Samuel, the author of the History is Nathan to all the Davids who would read it and react as impulsively and unknowingly against themselves as their royal precursor did in 2 Samuel 12:5–6. Only when David thinks he is speaking of another can he dare to say, "As the LORD lives, the man who has done this deserves to die"; only when readers are freed of all the pomp and circumstance surrounding royalty are they open to the Deuteronomist's difficult message about it.

If chapters 1 to 7 form an overture to the entire monarchic history, the picture in 4:18 of Eli falling backward off his throne to his death is this overture's central event, the Deuteronomist's view of kingship in a nutshell. Eli represents all the burden and doom that kingship brought Israel. He had "judged" Israel for forty years; that is to say, in the fullness of time kingship in Israel would disappear.

The Ark Returns from Exile (5:1–7:2)

The story in chapters 5 and 6 is filled with details both bright and shadowy. That the ark of God can and does destroy its rival Dagon (5:1–5) is the least problematic feature of the entire account;[11] Israel may be defeated in spite of its possession of God's ark and the ark itself may be seized, but all this is not to imply that God has lost any of his power over other people's gods. As for shadows, both the narrator and the characters construct images of tumors and mice whose specific functions within each world—the narrator's or theirs—are not entirely clear.[12] If the uncomplimentary characterization of the misinformed

Philistines in chapter 4 is any indication of what is to follow, their struggles to free themselves from the ark's scourge may perhaps be understood as placing them in as humorously ridiculous a light as the narrator can devise. One has the impression, difficult to justify, that there is something of the "carnivalesque"[13] underlying some of the details within chapters 5 and 6. Yet in spite of some interesting and provocative suggestions on the historical and cultural background of certain features of the ark story,[14] it is likely that we have lost much of the background against which many aspects of the story specifically sounded and with which the story dialogically interacted. We must concentrate therefore on those textual details that exhibit some connection with the ideological and esthetic concerns already encountered in previous chapters.[15]

What remains clear throughout chapters 5 and 6 is the intimate association of ark with curse and destruction; this aspect has great import for the larger story line. In fact, the ark story's main problematic concerns God's heavy hand against Israelite and Philistine alike. When the Philistine sorcerers play with the glory/curse (*kbd/qll*) dichotomy ("You must give glory [*kābôd*] to the God of Israel; perhaps he will lighten [*yāqēl*] his hand from off you," 6:5), they are only rehearsing the same abiding tension inherent in the ark's relationship to Israel. It is precisely when the once exiled Glory returns to Israel that God "slew some of the men of Beth-shemesh . . . and made a great slaughter among the people" (1 Sam. 6:19). The similar fate of Israelite and Philistine vis-à-vis the ark of God is what the account in 1 Samuel 4–6 emphasizes at every point.

If sound and the sense of hearing functioned as the basis for mistaken or destroyed hope in chapter 4, in chapter 6 the emphasis is on seeing as the basis for the Israelite's ill-advised rejoicing. In chapter 4 the Israelites' joyful shout at the ark's approach turned out to be as much a mistake as the Philistines' fear of the cause of such shouting. By chapter 6 the Israelites' *lifting of their eyes to see* the advancing ark, and their rejoicing *at the sight* (v. 13) are the ironic prelude to some of them *looking into* the ark of the LORD (v. 19) and to the great slaughter that follows.

The superficial question of who takes care of the ark is also clear from each end of the story. The two sons of Eli are with the ark in 4:4; with their death and the fall of their house, and with the return of the ark to Israel, "they consecrated [Abinadab's] son Eleazar to have charge of the ark of the LORD" (7:1). The installation of the ark at Kiriath-jearim finally cancels the superficial meaning of Ichabod ("no glory"), who is the narrative remnant of Eli's house: the Glory is back. Nevertheless, Eli's house henceforth will lack political as well as priestly significance within the story. Israel under Eli's successor, Samuel, is now set to defeat the Philistines, and this will be described in chapter 7. On the surface, all these narrative features seem historiographically clear; their ideological function remains to be seen.

Most of chapters 5 and 6 is narrated from the Philistines' point of view, yet everything is motivated by the two Israelite questions at the end: "Who is able to stand before the LORD, this holy God? And to whom will he go away from us?" (6:20). We should understand the ark's sojourn in Philistia as analogous to Israel's prior exile in Egypt; the words of the Philistine sorcerers incline us in this direction: "Why should you harden your hearts as the Egyptians and Pharaoh hardened their hearts? After he made sport of them, *did they not send them off and they departed?* . . . *Send the ark off and let it depart*" (6:6,8). The story of the ark has something central to say, above and beyond the story of Eli and Samuel; it speaks about how exilic bondage comes about and under what conditions the captives will be able to return to their rightful place in the end: "Send away the ark of the God of Israel, and let it return *to its own place*" (5:11; see also 6:2).[16]

The ark has been chosen for a central role in this introduction to the monarchic history, not only because of its future place in the story of David, but also because of its ability to represent both the presence of the LORD within Israel and Israel itself; Israel is defined by the LORD present within the community. The ark is uniquely endowed to raise the primary question pervading the entire ark story: who is to be Israel's/the LORD's proper caretaker? The story of the ark not only looks backward in time to Israel's enslavement in Egypt, it also looks forward to Israel's exile from its proper place, the land. So a second question needs raising: to whom will it go away from us? (6:20). The questions of proper leadership and proper place are intimately related. How Israel will answer the question of leadership in the coming history—who can stand before the LORD?—will determine whether in fact the ark will once more depart from Israel. Even more pointedly from an exilic perspective, "To whom will it go away from us?" is a poignant reminder that the ark had simply dropped out of sight without a proper historical accounting, its present location unknown. And how in the world does one define an arkless Israel?

The space between the capture of the ark in 5:1 and its return in 6:21 contains many of the Deuteronomist's reflections on the nature of leadership in Israel. Improper leadership lost Israel the ark, and only a special kind of care on the part of its present custodians, the Philistines, will return it to its proper place. The Philistine experience with the ark contains programmatic reflections on Israel's hoped-for recovery of the land—and of the ark that had led them there in the first place. Key to understanding these reflections continues to be the Deuteronomist's employment of "the having of sons" as a metaphor for Israel's possessing a monarchy.

The issue of progeny remains central to plot motivation in chapters

4–6. Eli's two sons, and everything they stand for, accompany the loss of the ark. In fact, wherever Hophni and Phinehas are mentioned in chapter 4, the ark is also mentioned (4:4, 11, 17, 19, 21); Eli's sons are inseparable from the idea of the lost ark. On the other hand, when the Philistines seek a way out of their plague-filled dilemma, their sorcerers provide a formula that will successfully, even physically, drive the ark back to its proper place: two milch-cows with their "calves" (*bᵉnêhem*) taken away from them (6:7), with their "calves" (*bᵉnêhem*) shut up at home (6:10). That these two cows, who go straight to Beth-shemesh and "swerve neither to the right nor the left" (6:12), are central to the story's recipe for successful recovery of the ark is clear from this phrase, "to swerve neither to the right nor the left," which is always used figuratively in the History to signify straying from the path of obedience to Yahweh as, for example, in Joshua 1:7. Its use here in chapter 6 is no exception. How to get the people Israel and the lost ark back to the land of Israel after the disaster of the exile is central to the story's subject matter.

The cows' role is also seen in the extensive wordplay involving *ᶜālāh/ᶜûl/ᶜālal* that accompanies them throughout the story and connects them up to its final question. These cows are "milch-cows upon which there has never come a yoke (*pārôt ᶜolôt ᵃšer lo' ᶜālāh ᶜᵃlêhem ᶜol*)" (6:7); the Israelites then "offer the cows as a burnt offering to the LORD (*wᵉ'et happārôt heᶜᵉlû ᶜolāh laYHWH*)" (6:14). They seem, therefore, to be implicated somehow in the answer to the concluding question in 6:20: "To whom will it [the ark] go up away from us (*'el mî yaᶜᵃleh meᶜālênû*)?" [17] It is through "leaders" devoid of progeny that the ark and Israel eventually will be brought home. Dynastic leadership had lost Israel its proper place; nondynastic leadership will restore it.

If we take seriously the abiding metaphor of the having of sons as representing the having of kings in these opening chapters, we may be able to recover a small part of what is going on behind the mysterious details surrounding the ark in Philistine country. What kind of leadership is proper to the people of the ark? Where exactly does Israel's leader stand in relation to the ark? Who is able to stand before the LORD this holy God? It is in response to this first question about leadership at the end of the ark story that the account of the ark's sojourn in Philistia so obviously emphasizes the Philistine rulers, and the dependence of their people's fate upon them.

Notice first that although the lords of the Philistines are reported as speaking only in 5:8, the speech of "the men of Ekron" in 5:10, 11 is phrased as if it were spoken only by the lord of Ekron: "They have brought around to *me* the ark of the God of Israel to slay *me* and *my* people" (v. 10); "Let it return to its own place, that it may not slay *me* and my people" (v. 11). Then in chapter 6 the Philistine sorcerers explain that the five golden tumors and five golden mice are "according to the number of the lords of the Philistines: for the same plague was upon all of you and upon your lords" (6:5). Emphasized in these aspects of the story is the solidarity between fate of leader and fate of people, and the dependence of the second on the first.

Notice also that the story indicates the proper position of the lords of the Philistines in relation to the awesome ark. If the story ends by asking "Who can stand *before* (*lipnê*) the LORD, this holy God?" it also shows the five leaders of the Philistines *following behind* (*'aḥªrê*) the ark as far as Beth-shemesh (6:12). It would appear that the only leaders who finally escape the ark's wrath are those who, for narrative reasons that exceed concealment, follow rather than stand before the ark. Moreover, the only other leaders who are able to bring the ark to its proper place are those whose progeny are removed from the scene, that is, those for whom the dynastic status that kingship necessarily involves is irrelevant. That the milch-cows in the story are finally offered up to the LORD as burnt offerings says something ominous about the burdens of leadership.

The Davidic Voice in the Finding of the Ark

If one has any doubt that the ark material in 1 Samuel involves a meditation on the particular kind of leadership that is royal, the intimate connection between 1 Samuel 4–6 and 2 Samuel 6 may settle the question. Scholarship since Rost has continually been concerned with explaining the relationship between these two pericopes, but it has concentrated most of its efforts on genetic hypotheses.[18] What has not been attended to in any plausible way, in my opinion, is how these two ark stories are literarily related within the present text of 1 and 2 Samuel. Given our preceding analyses, it seems likely that the journey of the ark from Shiloh in 1 Samuel 4:4 to Kiriath-jearim in 1 Samuel 7:1 (signifying that the Glory once lost to Israel under the Elides returned to Israel under the leadership of Samuel) foreshadows and reinterprets the triumphant journey of the ark from Baale-judah to Jerusalem in 2 Samuel 6 (signifying here the victory of David over all his enemies).

The itinerary of the ark in 1 Samuel 4–6 is from Shiloh to the house of Abinadab on the hill, with a few months' stopover among the Philistines; its itinerary in 2 Samuel 6 is from the house of Abinadab on the hill to Jerusalem, with a few months' stopover among the Philistines.[19] Whatever one is to do with the urban discrepancy between the Kiriath-jearim of 1 Samuel 7:2 and the Baale-judah of 2 Samuel 6:1, and whatever one imagines the specific literary history behind these two ark narratives to be,[20] it is clear that each account in its present narrative shape and location is patterned to reflect the other in striking correlations—all orchestrated in a manner that serves the Deuteronomist's larger ideological purposes.

The similarities between 1 Samuel 4–6 and 2 Samuel 6 are suggestive in terms of structure, thematic detail, and language. We have already mentioned the similarly structured itinerary: the ark travels from one Israelite town to the other with a few months' stopover within Philistine territory. The ark makes its journey accompanied by the two sons of the priest in whose care it was placed: Eli in 1 Samuel 4 and Abinadab in 2 Samuel 6. Death accompanies the ark's chaperones in each story: both of Eli's sons are killed in 1 Samuel 4; Uzzah, one of Abinadab's sons, is killed in 2 Samuel 6. The ark is carried upon a "new cart" in both stories. Each cart is appropriately described as going toward its destination with rejoicing on the part of the Israelites. References to sacrifices before the LORD also accompany both journeys: at Bethshemesh in 1 Samuel 6:14–15, and every six paces from Obed-edom's house to Jerusalem in 2 Samuel 6.

All these similarities might be seen as details one would normally expect in the kind of ark story found throughout the history, whatever be the literary or ideological purposes for which it is used in each particular location within the final shape of the text. Could we not view these similarities simply as evidence of an original "ark narrative," as scholars since Rost have tended to emphasize? No matter what genetic considerations one may advance in this regard, it is significant that specific linguistic or thematic details appear in each story *in dialogic contrast* to apparent counterparts in the other, so that something more deliberately poetic may be presumed to be operative.

Thirty thousand Israelites are singled out to die at the beginning of the first story (1 Sam. 4:10); thirty thousand chosen men of Israel accompany the ark in glory at the beginning of the second story (2 Sam. 6:1). Panic, death, and destruction follow the first ark everywhere, even turning the brief rejoicing of the men of Beth-shemesh (1 Sam. 6:13) into mourning when the LORD makes a great slaughter among them (1 Sam. 6:19); there is hardly anything but rejoicing in 2 Samuel 6. We find mostly the language of curse in 1 Samuel 4–6, the language of blessing in 2 Samuel 6: the sound of Israel crying (*qôl hehāmôn*) in 1 Samuel 4:14 typically becomes the blessed Israelite multitude (*hāmôn*) of 2 Samuel 6:19. This language of curse affects Israel and Philistia alike in 1 Samuel 4–6, just as its blessed counterpart affects Israelite and Philistine alike in 2 Samuel 6: "And the LORD blessed Obed-edom [the Gittite] and all his household" (6:11); "And David blessed the people in the name of the LORD of hosts" (6:18).

2 Samuel 6 even incorporates a thematic play on the *kbd/qll* dichotomy in the dialogue between David and Michal (vv. 20–23), just as 1 Samuel 4–6 continues to do in the sorcerers' counsel to the Philistines (vv. 5–6). What unites these contrasts between honoring and cursing is the Deuteronomist's introductory meditation on kingship as honoring or cursing God:

> I promised that your house . . . shall go in and out
> before me forever . . . Those who honor me I will
> honor, and those who despise me shall be lightly
> esteemed (*yeqallû*). (1 Sam. 2:30)
> And I tell him that I am about to punish his house
> forever . . . because his sons were cursing (*mᵉqalᵉlîm*)
> God. (1 Sam. 3:13)
> Give glory to the God of Israel . . . Perhaps he will
> lighten (*yāqēl*) his hand from upon you. (6:5)
> I will make myself yet more contemptible (*ûnqallôtî*)
> than this [says David to Michal] . . . but by them
> [the maidens] I shall be held in honor
> (*'ikkabēdāh*). (2 Sam. 6:22)

Only the final statement is obviously spoken by a king in defense of his actions as king; the other statements never directly refer to royal performance, yet this is their main subject matter.

We see a final connection between the two pericopes in the first question that concludes 1 Samuel 4–6: Who is able *to stand before the LORD,* this holy God? (6:20). It is true, as McCarter remarks, that "standing before the LORD" is used here specifically of priestly attendance upon the ark,[21] and that texts such as Deuteronomy 10:8 and Judges 20:27–28 indicate the priestly connotations of this phraseology in connection with the ark. At this level the question looks to the solution narrated in 7:1 where a suitable priestly attendant for the ark is finally found. Nevertheless, more is at stake here than priestly concerns.

First, the question at the end of chapter 6 about who could *stand* before the LORD has an intrinsic connection with the beginning of the ark's sojourn in Philistia and the statement twice given there: "And behold, Dagon fallen (*nōpēl*) before the ark of the LORD" (5:3, 4). Who can stand before the LORD's ark? Certainly not a rival god.

Much more important than the intrinsic narrative contrast between "stand" and "fall" with its emphasis on divine power are details tying this account to monarchic themes. For one thing, reference to cherubim in connection with the ark such as we find in 4:4 is never found in the Deuteronomic History outside of a royal context.[22] More to the point, "standing before the ark" is a right not just of priests, but of kings also, as 1 Kings 3:15 shows concerning Solomon: "Then he came to Jerusalem and stood before the ark of the covenant of the LORD and offered up burnt offerings and peace offerings and made a feast for all his servants." Throughout the entire Bible, no one except priest or king "stands before the ark."

When we examine the ark story in 2 Samuel 6, we find that the ark is the one that is called by the name of *"the LORD of hosts who sits enthroned on the cherubim"* (v. 2), just as the ark is described in 1 Samuel 4:4. Who stands before this particular ark? Although 2 Samuel 6 never refers to David as standing before the LORD, his typical position throughout is "before the LORD": before the ark he makes merry (vv. 5, 21), dances (v. 14), leaps and dances (v. 16), and offers sacrifices (v. 17). And in response to the question, "To whom will it go away from us?" (1 Sam. 6:20), David, who is Israel's king par excellence, is made to respond with another question: "How can the ark of the LORD come to me?" (2 Sam. 6:9). 1 Samuel 4–6 looks to the triumphant David of 2 Samuel 6.

The Deuteronomist's Voice

What the Deuteronomic voice accomplishes in structuring the account of the lost and found ark is exactly what it has done in previous chapters: it conceals within the speech of its narrator and characters introductory statements and positions about the nature and significance of kingship within Israel. Specific discourse, repeated themes, even plot structures—all foreshadow selected sections of the monarchic history to come but are rearranged to present an opening meditation on the main ideological problems involved in the institution of kingship. This introduction rehearses both the triumphs and defeats the author is about to narrate, but in all cases these royal and national events are subjected to a profound and authoritative evaluation that underlines the complexity of the subject even as it avoids simplistic or simply didactic value judgments. The voice of critical traditionalism that we heard speaking throughout Deuteronomy–Judges continues to control the subsequent history as well.[23]

Typical of this voice, which speaks indirectly of kingship, is the perceptive and provocative asking of questions that ostensibly are directed to the narrative's characters but at the same time allow those readers to whom they are also directed to meditate upon the complex matter of kingship without having to struggle with the seductive trappings of royalty that so easily sway the emotions of those who want to be like other nations:

> Am I not worth more to you than ten sons? (1:8)
> If a man sins against a man, God will mediate for him;
> but if a man sins against the LORD, who can intercede
> for him? (2:25)
> Why honor your sons above me by fattening yourselves
> upon the choicest parts of every offering of my people
> Israel? (2:29)
> Why has the LORD put us to rout today before the
> Philistines? (4:3)
> Who is able to stand before the LORD this holy God?
> And to whom will [the ark] go away from us? (6:20)

The Parable Ends (7:3–17)

Last mentioned in 4:1, Samuel was already a prophet, priest, and royal stand-in; he returns in all these roles in chapter 7, but now garbed in judicial robes (vv. 6, 15, 16, 17) that signal the end of an era in a double sense, one proximate, the other remote.[24] Close to home, the narrator completes the transition from a rejected to a favored judgeship through Israel's victories under Samuel's leadership. At the same time, these events constitute the last occurrence of the cycle of judicial generations described earlier in Judges 2:11–3:6.

Chapter 7 also continues to speak with the triumphant voice of David—one we have been hearing in preceding chapters.

Finally, insofar as this chapter concludes the Deuteronomist's long parabolic introduction to the royal history of Samuel/Kings, it continues to concentrate on the ideological issues raised by an authorial voice in the preceding chapters; questions about kingship posed there will find definitive answers here. In order to accomplish its task of predisposing the reader toward the author's view of kingship as expressed in the coming history, the parable will have to set forth issues in the strongest possible way. The author's choice of language in this chapter leaves no doubt that its subject matter involves much more than the successful exploits of the last judge. In fact, the Deuteronomic voice will expose its very purpose in composing the history; the author writes to describe the causes of the exile and the conditions that will bring it to an end.

Turning to the LORD: Repentance and Immediate Reward

The narrator ties together certain short threads of the story by setting up verbal and thematic correspondences to preceding events. We have already discussed a number of these connections:[25] Israel's "foreign gods, the Baals and Ashtaroth" (7:3, 4), give an ironic twist to the supposedly erroneous reference of the Philistines to Israel's "mighty gods" in 4:8; the unjustified fear of the Israelites (7:7) corresponds to the unjustified fear of the Philistines (4:7); the Philistines' question, "Who can deliver us . . . ?" (4:8) receives Samuel's answer, "[The LORD] will deliver you" (7:3); Israel's two defeats at Ebenezer in chapter 4 are balanced by Samuel's setting up of the victory stone, Ebenezer, in 7:12; and the disastrous etymology of 4:21–22 is counterbalanced by the joyful one of 7:12. In short, the absence of Samuel signals Israel's defeat in chapter 4, his presence in chapter 7, Israel's victory.

In addition to these parallels, chapter 7 also contains an answer to the question raised by Eli in 2:25 when he confronted his sons on their evil ways. The narrator now presents Samuel as the person about whom Eli asked earlier.

But if a man sins against the LORD . . . who will intercede (*yitpallēl*) for him? (2:25)	They said, "We have sinned against the LORD." (7:6) Samuel said, "I will intercede to the LORD (*'etpallēl*) for you." (7:5)

Eli's sons did not listen to him and disaster followed, but the house of Israel listens to Samuel and its troubles end. Samuel's intercessory role will continue and even increase to such an extent that he will state in 12:23: "As for me, far be it from me that *I* should sin against the LORD *by ceasing to intercede* (*lᵉhitpallēl*) for [Israel]."

In addition, longer narrative threads leading all the way back to the beginning of the History's account of the period of the judges are now picked up to signal the end of an epoch.[26] The ideology behind this account of God's deliverance of Israel from the hands of the Philistines conforms in many ways to the cyclical theology of history in Judges 2:11–3:6. Here in chapter 7, as soon as the ark is safely lodged at Kiriath-jearim, Samuel reveals to the house of Israel—and the narrator to the reader as well—the reason for its prior defeats: Israelites have been serving "the foreign gods and Ashtoroth" (v. 3), "the Baals and the Ashtoroth" (v. 4) in their midst, just as Israel cyclically serves the Baals and Ashtoroth in Judges 2:13. The hand of the Philistines in 1 Samuel 7 corresponds to "the hand of all their enemies" in Judges 2. The emphasis in 1 Samuel 7 on Samuel as judge (vv. 6, 15, 16, 17) and on Israel's deliverance all the days that Samuel lived (v. 13) resumes the judicial pattern first described in Judges 2 and incorporated throughout that book.

At the same time, some significant differences appear between the judicial cycle described in Judges 2 and its culminating event here in 1 Samuel 7. Whereas the initial pattern includes no explicit reference to Israel's repentance—very probably no implicit reference either[27]—this last narrative instance of the cycle incorporates explicit statements of the narrator and Samuel about Israel's turning to the LORD and away from idolatry (7:3–4). The significance of the definitive element of repentance present here is underlined not only by its absence in Judges 2 but also by its rarity in the intervening history: explicit reference to Israel "returning (*šûb*) to the LORD" occurs only once in the entire book of Judges, in Judges 10:10–16, a passage that also has close affinities to 1 Samuel 7, as scholars have noted.[28] I have suggested elsewhere that the account in Judges 10 ought to be read as an instance of a superficial repentance on Israel's part, well understood by the LORD, who soon grew tired of Israel's hypocrisy.[29] Here, however, there is no hint of Israel's insincerity or lack of determination to put away the foreign gods, nor is there the smug confidence of a spoiled child so apparent in Israel's prayer to the LORD in the time of Jephthah: "We have sinned; do to us whatever seems good to thee; only deliver us, we pray thee, this day"

(Judg. 10:15). Israel under Samuel is much less confident of God's beneficence: "And the people of Israel said to Samuel, 'Do not cease to cry to the LORD for us, that he may save us from the hand of the Philistines'" (7:8).

As the preceding account of Israel's defeat and loss of the ark (in chaps. 4–6) makes abundantly clear, Israel's fear of its enemy and hesitancy about the LORD's will to save it is well founded. The practical confidence of Israel throughout most of the period of the Judges—more often than not delivered by the LORD in spite of continual dis-obedience—has dissipated; a catastrophe of immense proportions has intervened to provide an implicit background to chapter 7, as it does to the preceding six chapters.

This difference in tone between 1 Samuel 7 and its predecessors in the book of Judges is best seen in the growing emphasis on repentance as a key element in the practical solution to Israel's problems. In the cyclical pattern described in Judges 2, repentance occurs not at all—or at the most only implicitly. In Judges 10:10–16, the first and only reference to Israel's repentance in the book, the fly-by-night character of Israel's change of heart, in contrast to 1 Samuel 7, is symbolized by the differing strengths of the narrator's statements:

So they put away the foreign gods from among them and served the LORD. (Judg. 10:16)	So Israel put away the Baals and the Ashtoroth, and they served the LORD *only* (*lᵉbaddô*). (1 Sam. 7:4)

The addition of this one word, *lᵉbaddô*, "alone" or "only," is significant: if "to serve (*ᶜābad*) the LORD" occurs frequently in the Deuteronomic History,[30] it occurs in the strengthened form, "to serve the LORD *alone*," only here in 7:3, 4. Even when Samuel later recalls Israel's habitual promises to serve the LORD (12:10) and repeatedly admonishes the nation to do so (12:14, 20, 24), he never adds the exclusive term *lᵉbaddô*. The precise addition of this word in 7:3, 4 is important for our understanding of the Deuteronomist's ideological perspective in this conclusion to the author's programmatic parable.

The nature or necessity of repentance, that is, "returning to the LORD (with all one's heart)," plays a crucial role in our attempt to make sense of the entire "judicial" history that begins in Judges 2 and ends here in 1 Samuel 7. The pattern established in Judges 2 and exemplified through-out the book of Judges minimizes the necessity of repentance with respect to Israel's actual—as opposed to promised or requested—deliverance from the onslaughts of its enemies. 1 Samuel 7 now makes "returning to the LORD" central in Israel's subsequent victory over the Philistines. Certainly, "the hand of the LORD was against the Philistines all the days of Samuel" (7:13). Nevertheless, verses 3–12 make it clear that Israel's initial repentance at Samuel's command is a key factor in the

LORD's decision to deliver the people. The ideological perspective shifts from no repentance in Judges 2 to hypocritical or insincere repentance in Judges 10 to the actualization of necessary repentance here in 1 Samuel 7. It seems that Israel's actual deliverance from disaster is no longer to be expected without a thoroughgoing recognition and repudiation of the sin that brought disaster in the first place.

To see how the narrative emphasis on repentance changes as the Deuteronomic story develops, we can line up the various stages in five key pericopes: Judges 2, Judges 10, 1 Samuel 7, 1 Kings 8:33–34, and 46–50:[31]

Sin

Judg. 2:11, 13:	"They served the Baals and the Ashtoroth."
Judg. 10:13:	"You have forsaken me and served other gods."
1 Sam. 7:3:	"Put away the foreign gods and the Ashtoroth from among you."
1 Kings 8:33:	" . . . because they have sinned against thee."
1 Kings 8:46:	"If they sin against thee . . ."

Punishment

Judg. 2:14–15:	"So the anger of the LORD was kindled against Israel . . ."
Judg. 10:13:	"(Judg. 9:9: 'Israel was sorely distressed . . .') Therefore I will deliver you no more."
1 Sam. 7:3:	Israel finds itself in "the hand of the Philistines."
1 Kings 8:33:	"When thy people Israel are defeated before the enemy."
1 Kings 8:46:	"So that they take them away captive to the land of the enemy."

Repentance

Judg. 2:	*Missing.*[32]
Judg. 10:16:	"So they put away the foreign gods from among them and served the LORD."
1 Sam. 7:3, 4:	" 'If you are returning to the LORD' . . . So Israel put away the Baals and the Ashtoroth, and they served the LORD only."
1 Kings 8:33:	"If they turn again to thee . . ."
1 Kings 8:48:	"And if they repent with all their mind and all their heart . . ."

Deliverance

Judg 2:18:	"[The LORD] saved them from the hand of their enemies all the days of the judge."
Judg. 11:37:	"So the Ammonites were subdued before the people of Israel."

1 Sam. 7:13:	"So the Philistines were subdued . . . and the hand of the LORD was against the Philistines all the days of Samuel."
1 Kings 8:34:	"Then bring them back to the land . . ."
1 Kings 8:50:	"Then forgive thy people and grant them compassion."[33]

Given that "returning to the LORD (with all one's heart)" is now made a central element in Israel's actual avoidance of disaster and experience of success, such a requirement nevertheless remains only a necessary but insufficient condition for deliverance. We know, for example, that the repentance of King Josiah was unparalleled in its sweep and intensity: "Before him there was no king like him, who turned to the LORD with all his heart and with all his soul and with all his might, according to all the law of Moses; nor did any like him arise after him" (2 Kings 23:25). Yet Josiah's reform was insufficient: "Still the LORD did not turn from the fierceness of his great wrath by which his anger was kindled against Judah, because of all the provocations with which Manasseh had provoked him" (2 Kings 23:26). Repentance as thoroughgoing and fundamental as Josiah's was not enough to avoid the exile; what is the Deuteronomist's ideological position for ending it? The author's introduction here in 1 Samuel 1–7 centers around the institution of kingship and its role in Israel's turning (*šûb*) to the LORD and subsequent returning to the land that he had given them.

Samuel as Figure of the Triumphant King

The royal voice of a victorious David, first heard in chapter 2 with the Song of Hannah, continues to be heard in chapter 7. As K. McCarter has already recognized, there are distinctive parallels between this account of Samuel's success and later statements about David's early career, notably 2 Samuel 5:17–25 and 2 Samuel 8, *passim.*[34]

Before wondering which account is chicken to the other's egg, we need to treat each seriously in its present literary context. Following upon the previous chapter's many instances of a prefigurative royal voice proclaiming kingship's coming successes, chapter 7's depiction of Samuel as a figure of David should no longer be surprising nor its function enigmatic. The parallels are meant to foreshadow kingship's victories as well as its ultimate defeat. The multivoiced nature of a sophisticated history such as this recognizes a number of competing viewpoints all interrelated in a marvelous way—at times in harmony but often in conflict. The Deuteronomist's ultimate conceptual authority, to use Bakhtin's phrase, keeps everything in balance. Samuel is much more than a triumphant royal figure in chapter 7.

Turning to the LORD: Repentance and Ultimate Return

One aspect of Samuel's initial words to Israel is helpful in understanding the nature and object of the repentance described in 1 Samuel 7. Samuel's use of the imperfective verb form, "if you are turning (*šābîm*) to the LORD with all your heart" (v. 3), underlines the ever-present and ongoing nature of this repentance. In fact, we may even go so far as to state that reference to "turning to the LORD" is addressed as much to the Deuteronomist's apparently exilic reader as it is to Samuel's pre-monarchic audience. For whenever this phrase, "to return to the LORD (with all the heart)," occurs in the history, it occurs *in the explicit context of the central problem of the exile,* either in unsuccessful attempts to avoid this disaster (1 Kings 23:25, King Josiah) or in prophetic statements about how successfully to end it (Deut. 4:30; 30:2, 10, Moses' prophecies of exilic times; and 1 Kings 8:33, 48, Solomon's prophetic prayer for exilic times).

Moses had prophesied, "When you are in tribulation, and all these things come upon you in the latter days, you will return to the LORD your God and obey his voice" (Deut. 4:30). In Deuteronomy 30:2, 10 he repeats his exilic solution centered on turning to the LORD. Likewise, Solomon's great temple prayer refers to "turning to the LORD (1 Kings 8:33) with all their heart" (1 Kings 8:48) as the solution to Israel's coming exile. What the Deuteronomist does in 1 Samuel 7 is to address Josiah's exilic problem and Moses' and Solomon's exilic solution in an idealized way that creatively concludes the introductory meditation on kingship.

It is customary, following Frank Cross, to see most of these exilic references in the history as evidence of a "second Deuteronomist" or a "second edition."[35] Such literary-historical moves are, in my opinion, premature, given the haste with which most of the complex compositional relationships between parts of the history have been described or explained—if examined at all. The way in which Deuteronomic language such as "returning to the LORD (with all the heart)" interacts with its various literary contexts needs serious consideration on the level of discourse, before such sweeping source-oriented theories can be entertained. We need now to examine the nature of Israel's repentance in chapter 7 in relation to its literary context.

From Having Sons to Serving Foreign Gods

When Israel turns *to* the LORD in chapter 7, what is it to turn *from?* The answer is clear: it is to turn from serving (*ʿābad*) the foreign gods, the Baals and Ashtoroth. This service or worship of "other gods" or "foreign gods" is a key feature in the exilic prophecies of Moses (Deut. 4:28; 29:26), some of the other repentance texts we have been examining

(Judg. 2:11, 13, 19; 10:13), and countless other biblical passages. Israel's obligation to serve the LORD implies serving him *instead of* foreign gods. If this opposition between serving the LORD and serving other gods is obvious in most of the passages dealing with Israel's responsibilities of divine service, what is the significance of the phrase strengthened with *l*baddô, "to serve the LORD *only*," occurring here in 1 Samuel 7:3, 4 and nowhere else? Whom else might Israel serve and thereby incur the LORD's wrath?

In the book of Judges, a would-be king, Abimelech, seeks to receive royal service: "Who is Abimelech that we should *serve* him? . . . Why then should we *serve* him?" (Judg. 9:28, 38). Within the books of Samuel, it is possible for Israel, besides serving gods, to serve kings— either foreign upstarts like Nahash the Ammonite (1 Sam. 11:1) or fellow Israelites like Absalom (2 Sam. 16:19). In the books of Kings, foreign kingdoms serve Solomon (1 Kings 5:1) as Israel might serve its own or a foreign king, like Rehoboam (1 Kings 12:4) or the king of Babylon (2 Kings 25:24).

In 1 Samuel 7 "to serve God *alone*" means not only "not to serve foreign gods," it means also "not to serve kings." Just as the having of sons in chapters 1–6 is a surrogate for the having of kings, so in chapter 7 the serving of foreign gods is a surrogate for the serving of kings. Both forms of service are equated, and both are identified as central causes of Israel's problems. Removing *all* these "gods" from Israel's midst is the Deuteronomist's solution to the exile. Notice the contrast between the narrator's words in chapter 7 and Samuel's words in chapter 8:

And Samuel cried (*wayyiz'aq*) to the LORD for Israel and the LORD answered him (*wayya'anêhû*). (7:9)	And in that day you will cry out (*ûz'aqtem*) because of your king whom you have chosen for yourselves; but the LORD will not answer you (*lo' ya'aneh*) in that day. (8:18)

If we have any doubt that chapter 7 is to be read as an idealized account in which the service of foreign gods stands for the service of kings, the very next chapter, which begins the account of Israel's request for a king, fixes the equation within the authoritative word of God. When Samuel, displeased at the people's request for a king, relates the matter to the LORD, the LORD responds, "They have not rejected you, but they have rejected me from being king over them. *Just like* all the deeds which they have done, from the day I brought them up out of Egypt even to this day, *forsaking me and serving other gods, so they are doing to you*" (8:7–8). That is to say, the LORD himself in the very first chapter of the monarchic history is made to state that Israel's rejection of Samuel, the judge, for the proposed service of kings is like its forsaking the LORD for the service of other gods. After the parable about Israel's sad exilic state has been narrated, God points to the king—as Nathan will to David—and says, "You are the man."

Once we recognize that chapter 7 continues chapter 6's typological solution for recovery of ark and return to the land, it becomes clear why Samuel—heretofore characterized as prophet, priest, and royal stand-in—functions in chapter 7 in all these roles certainly, but as the judge par excellence. In order for Israel to turn to the LORD and thus to be able to return to the land, it must *remove* (*hāsîr*, vv. 3, 4) the "foreign" kings so alien to Israel's fundamental Yahwism and return to a pre-monarchic, judicial mode of leadership. The chapter describes a judge-ship that is to be free from the dynastic impulse to which even Samuel himself will fall prey; 8:1–3 makes Samuel's attempt at establishing a dynasty like Eli's the occasion for Israel's disastrous request for a king. Judgeship based on the LORD's choice rather than judicial genes is the programmatic model of chapter 7.

But the history will show that Israel did not succeed in removing "these foreign gods" from their midst. Consequently, when the northern kingdom "served Baal . . . the LORD *removed* them out of his sight" (2 Kings 17:16, 18). And in spite of Josiah's reforms—in the course of which he *removes* all the shrines of the Samaritan high places (2 Kings 23:19)—the LORD prophesied, "I *will remove* Judah also out of my sight, as I *have removed* Israel" (2 Kings 23:27).

In the light of all we have seen in chapters 1–7, to view the history as originally hopeful about kingship before a second edition put all the blame on Manasseh's shoulders, as many scholars following Cross have sought to do, is to ignore complex compositional relationships that tie together the introduction in 1 Samuel 1–7 with the succeeding monar-chic history. Such neglect makes the final form of the history much less coherent than it actually is in its thoroughgoing identification of kingship in general—not just Manasseh's in particular—as a fundamen-tal cause of Israel's captivity. Even if we were to grant Cross's genetic assumption that explicit references to Manasseh's role in causing the exile (in 2 Kings 21 and elsewhere) read easily as editorial additions, this, in my opinion, does not dissolve the clear picture, throughout the entire history and before such supposed revisions, of an Israel disastrously bent on monarchic aspirations. If Noth's solution to the genetic composi-tion of the History is now more than ever suspect, his depiction of its strongly antimonarchic ideology turns out to be poetically accurate.

The story of Israel's tragic romance with kingship is now set to begin.

Three

THE MONARCHY BEGINS
(8:1–12:25)

Heaven is above all yet; there sits a judge that no king can corrupt. (Shakespeare, *King Henry VIII*)

Do your duty bravely. Fear God. Honour the king. (Earl Kitchener, 1914)

This displeased Samuel. (1 Samuel 8)

Transitions

The previous chapters of 1 Samuel provided the reader with a parabolic preface to the story now set to begin. Chapters 8–12 are especially important, for they enjoy narrative primacy both chronologically and topically: they recount the first crucial decisions that led to the establishment of kingship in Israel.[1]

Between chapters 7 and 8, basic compositional shifts in the narrator's stance make the reader's task more challenging. For one thing, if in previous chapters we have grown accustomed to the narrator's explicit direction in matters of ideology or evaluation,[2] we now encounter a narrator who chooses to tell the story in a much more "objective" or at least less directive manner. In this new reportorial style, which will continue on for a number of chapters,[3] characters will directly speak for themselves and indirectly for the author as well. Readers' understanding of the narrator's or author's ideological perspectives will have to be inferred mostly from context, that is, through a whole range of means—sometimes formally marked, but often unmarked—whereby the author conveys personal ideological positions and accents.

This shift in narrative strategy makes some sense. The aim of predisposing readers for the subsequent history through a condensed, programmatic exposition helps to explain the explicitly evaluative qualities of the narrator in chapters 1–7. Having initially set readers upon certain paths, however, the author can afford to have the narrator now largely show what earlier the narrator had been allowed allegorically to tell. Along this new path, the mysterious forbearance of God and the continuing perfidy of God's people walk side by side.

A second narrative shift based upon the history's compositional structure—and complicated by the coming chapters' paucity of direct or explicit narratorial evaluations—is the move in chapter 8 toward characterizations that are more naturally complex or rounded.[4] Who Hannah, Elkanah, Samuel, Eli, or his sons were, and what evaluative accents surrounded the character zones of each in chapters 1–7, were determined to a large extent by what they additionally stood for; all do double duty in the introduction. Hannah was the mother of Samuel, but she also stood for Israel requesting a king. Elkanah was a slighted but loving husband, but he also introduced us to a God rejected by his people. Eli was the scion of a fallen priestly house, but in addition he was a royal figure falling to his death. Samuel himself was a priest, judge, and prophet certainly, but he also represented Saul (chap. 1), a victorious David (chap. 2–4), and an idealized judge who would succeed to leadership in exilic times (chap. 7). In chapter 8 these artificial complications to characterization cease and readers return to the more normal procedure of getting to know the story's characters as servants who serve the author still—if no longer parabolically.

Thus, for example, the allegorical situation in chapter 7, in which Israel's historiographic serving of foreign gods also stood for its serving of kings, is transformed into God's evaluative statement in chapter 8, wherein God tells Samuel that Israel's request for a king is tantamount to rejecting the LORD and serving other gods (8:8). Again, the idealized picture in chapter 7 of a postexilic Israel having thrown off its kings for a leader who cries to a LORD who answers him (7:9) gives way in chapter 8 to Samuel's quite literal prophecy about the burden of kingship: "And in that day you will cry out because of your king, whom you have chosen for yourselves; but the LORD will not answer you in that day" (8:18).[5]

The Rights and Duties of the King (8:1–22)

Chapter 8 introduces Israel's first request of Samuel for a king, the LORD's reluctant decision to grant its request, and his command to Samuel to solemnly warn Israel about the rights and duties (*mišpaṭ*) of the king who would reign over the people.

Dialogues between the elders of Israel and Samuel and between Samuel and the LORD comprise the events of this chapter. Its centerpiece is Samuel's long description of the king's *mišpaṭ* in verses 10–18. To discover how this solemn declaration of Samuel's relates to the chapter's obvious emphasis on God's command to him to hearken to the voice of the people requesting a king—repeated three times, in verses 7, 9, and 22—is the reader's main task. This responsibility should take account of the following compositional features of the chapter.

First, the narrator's use of imperfective verb forms highlights what is actually happening in the chapter and the author's evaluative position about these events: God describes to Samuel the people's continual idolatry as "so they are doing (*ʿosîm*) to you" (v. 8),[6] that is to say, the people "were asking (*haššoʾᵃlîm*) a king from him" (v. 10). These imperfective verb forms contrastively look back to the central action in the previous chapter highlighting the people's historiographic and idealized repentance: "If you are returning (*šābîm*) to the LORD . . ." (7:3). But given this fundamental picture expressing the narrator's basic perspective in chapter 8, what more can the reader provisionally learn about the text's ultimate conceptual authority—the implied author's fundamental ideological stance—concerning the events recounted in this chapter?[7]

Second, in the dialogue of this chapter, the reader encounters only a selective reporting of the direct words of its characters.[8] Thus, it is important to note that the words of God to Samuel and the words of Samuel to the people are highlighted both in quantity and in compositional terms through the use of direct discourse. On the other hand, what Samuel specifically says to God is not highlighted; he simply "prayed to the LORD" (v. 6) and after hearing all the words of the people "repeated them in the ears of the LORD" (v. 21).

At the same time, even though we are given the direct words of God to Samuel and Samuel to the people, the narrative is constructed in such a way as to keep the reader in the dark—or at least suspicious—about whether the directly quoted words of God in verses 7–9 and the directly reported words of Samuel in verses 11–18 are supposed to represent *all* that God and Samuel said on these occasions. That is to say, the words of God end with his command to Samuel to declare to the people the *mišpaṭ hammelek*, the rights and duties of the king (v. 9), and the words of Samuel begin with "This is the *mišpaṭ hammelek* . . ." (v. 11). In between these two verses the narrator states, "Samuel told all the words of the LORD to the people" (v. 10). The effect of these three verses, therefore, is to render it uncertain whether what Samuel says in detail about the *mišpaṭ* in verses 11–18 was itself part of what God had said to him previously or "really" only Samuel's own interpretation or adaptation of God's words to him or, finally, simply a matter already known to both of them—what "goes without saying" between a prophetic judge, who knows the law, and God.

Moreover, the dialogues are constructed in such a way as to make the reader uncertain about what else besides the *mišpaṭ* Samuel told the people as he related to them "all the words of the LORD" (v. 10). On one hand, this statement of the narrator in verse 10 implies that Samuel did in fact tell the people that their request for a king was in God's eye tantamount to idolatry, but that God nevertheless would grant them their request. On the other hand, if this be so, the reader quite naturally is struck by the fact that the narrator chooses not to directly report this part of Samuel's speech to the people, nor do the people, in their response in verses 19–20, appear to have heard it. Given the inherent importance of this divine evaluation of the request—its sinfulness and God's amazing decision to go along with it nonetheless—why does the narrator choose not to highlight this evaluation of the request for the people's benefit (the reader already knows about it from the narrator), but rather to have Samuel emphasize those aspects of the *mišpaṭ* that would limit the freedoms now enjoyed by the people under their present judicial government? A serious reading of this chapter ought to recognize and integrate this central problem of gaps in the reader's knowledge of who said what to whom.

Third, the narrator's new nondirective style is immediately signaled by the redundant nature of the two central expository facts in verses 1 and 3, followed by the words of the elders at the start of the "narrative event" in verse 4:[9]

EXPOSITION	BEGINNING OF EVENT
1 When Samuel became old . . .	4a "Behold you are old
3 Yet his sons did not walk	4b and your sons do not
in his ways.	walk in your ways."

This narrative situation—obvious from the elder's words alone—becomes the occasion for Israel's request of "a king to govern us like all the nations" (v. 5). All along, while stating how displeasing these words were to Samuel (v. 6), while reporting God's words about his (God's) attitude toward them, and while emphasizing God's command to Samuel to listen to the people's voice (vv. 7, 9, 22), the narrator reveals no personal viewpoint and chooses to use the reported words of God both to condemn the Israelites for their request and to authorize Samuel's later actions in granting it. In this way authorial evaluation is more thoroughly refracted than in previous chapters.

Characterization in Chapter 8

What does this chapter tell the reader about its characters and the zones surrounding them? In spite of the narrator's lack of explicit evaluation, God comes across as either magnanimous or pedagogic, whereas the imperceptive lad of chapter 3 now appears a stubborn, self-interested judge, who for his own reasons is slow to do the LORD's will. Finally, the people's request, however sinful, seems not entirely impractical. All these characterizations depend in large part upon the meaning of the king's *mišpaṭ* in verses 9 and 11 and Samuel's obvious delay in obeying the LORD's command.

To treat the last first, the narrative event that begins with the elders of

Israel gathering together at Ramah (v. 4) and ends with Samuel sending them off "each to his own city" (v. 22) is all talk and no action, even though the series of dialogues that comprise it has the people repeatedly requesting Samuel to give them a king and God repeatedly commanding him to do so. The narrative event ends without resolution, and we do not yet know how Samuel's delaying tactics will turn out. The inconclusive progression of the events is obvious: the story begins with the people's double request of Samuel to give them a king (vv. 5, 6), proceeds with God's double command to him to do so (vv. 7, 9), with Samuel's long speech to dissuade them (vv. 11–18), with the people's refusal to be dissuaded (vv. 19–20), and with the LORD's third and strengthened command—not just "listen to their voice," as in verses 7 and 9, but "listen to their voice *and make them a king*" (v. 22a)—and ends with Samuel doing nothing except sending the people away (v. 22b).

Seeing the chapter's obvious progression in this way, and primed by the narrator's reference to Samuel's initial displeasure at the people's request (v. 6), the reader develops a picture of a judge whose words and inaction show him to be obstructive in a self-interested way. As the event works itself out in this chapter, there is not a hint that the LORD himself intends to choose the king or that the people intend that this be so. The people say to Samuel, "Appoint for us a king" (v. 5), "Give us a king" (v. 6), and "We will have a king" (v. 19); God commands Samuel, "Hearken to the voice of the people *in all that they say to you*" (v. 7), "Hearken to their voice" (v. 9), and "Hearken to their voice and make them a king" (v. 22). The force of this progressive buildup of pressure on Samuel to act, with no reference yet to God's desire to do the choosing,[10] is in sharp contrast to Samuel's decision at the end of the chapter to do nothing but send the people home.

That Samuel's response to God's command is shown to be subversive as well as dilatory is clear from the people's response to Samuel's description of the king's *mišpaṭ* (in vv. 19–20) and Samuel's subsequent reaction. The people are reported by the narrator as understanding Samuel's words to be an attempt at dissuading them: "No! but we *will* have a king over us" (v. 19), and indeed this is the obvious import of Samuel's words to the reader as well. Nevertheless, dissuasion of the people is not at all what Samuel has been commanded by God to accomplish. Moreover, when his attempts to dissuade the people fail, Samuel returns and repeats the people's words "in the ears of the LORD" (v. 21), as if this superfluous act of telling God what he obviously already knows might, as a last resort, give God an opportunity to change *his* mind about allowing the monarchy. But when God issues his command yet a third time and in strengthened form, the narrator confirms the reader's suspicions about Samuel's inner motivation by having him send the people away, thus temporarily short-circuiting God's command.

Samuel's Speech to the People

Besides these progressive means by which the narrator gradually "shows up" Samuel without ever saying a word against him—surely a paradigmatic example of how even the purest kind of "objective reporting" can be filled through and through with the ideological and evaluative perspectives of the reporter—the narrator focuses in Samuel's speech on the *mišpaṭ hammelek,* "the rights and duties of the king." This tactic helps to expose Samuel's character and motivation in a particularly forceful way.

Samuel's words to the people in verses 11–18 are often interpreted as a thumbnail sketch of the "greedy abuse of power" reflecting Israel's "long and bitter experience with kingship."[11] Whatever the literary history behind this pericope—and its alleged counterpart in Deuteronomy 17:14–17—scholars have rarely examined the central function of Samuel's speech to the people within the context of chapter 8 itself.[12] To consider the royal practices listed here by Samuel as particularly abusive is, in my opinion, tendentious. Surely for ancient citizens—as even more so for modern readers—the king's predilection for tithing seems, for example, more responsible than corrupt; indeed the people's response in verses 19–20 recognizes this.[13]

What Samuel's words appear to exploit, as do the king's practices themselves, is the natural tendency of a king to make servants of his people (v. 17) rather than to serve them himself. This move on Samuel's part is precisely what has to be incorporated into a credible interpretation of the chapter. What is Samuel reported to be warning the people *about*? And how does this warning fit in with God's injunction to him in verse 9 to issue the people a solemn warning or testimony?

The phrase *heʿîd bᵉ* (v. 9), here strengthened by an infinitive, means "to testify against someone" or "to solemnly warn someone."[14] Does God enjoin Samuel to tell the people how sinful they are in requesting the king he will nevertheless grant them, or how abusive their kings will become, or to what standards the king must conform? Is Samuel's warning supposed to emphasize the evil that the people have already committed in requesting a king, or the evils that they and their kings are to avoid, but will not, in the future? The context does not make any of these questions especially easy to answer. Nevertheless, what is clear in the chapter is that Samuel's speech in verses 11–18 addresses none of these supposed responsibilities at all.

If, as we have suggested, abusive royal actions are not the issue in his speech, neither does anything Samuel says to the people convict them of the idolatrous implications of their request or deal adequately with the standards of conduct future kings must follow. Rather, Samuel is reported as concentrating solely on the monarchic rights and practices without which no king could effectively govern and that are, in fact, the normal baggage accompanying an ancient royal state. What is missing in the reported words of Samuel is precisely what the context clearly calls for—appropriate prophetic and judicial witness or admonition about past sins or future obligations, and the retributive implications of fulfilling such obligations or not. This is what all the occurrences of *he‘îd b‘* in the Bible are concerned with and what is significantly lacking in Samuel's words to the people. The only warning he gives them is about how restrictive their life will become under the monarchy. And this is the problem with his speech. It is hard to imagine that God's words to him in verses 7–9 enjoin the following: "Samuel, the people's request for a king is clearly idolatrous and tantamount to rejecting me. Nevertheless, give them what they ask for, but instead of emphasizing these points, tell them only how hard life will be for them under their king."

It seems much more likely that the LORD, whose forbearance permeates his plaintive words in verses 7–9—as Elkanah's does his in chapter 1—would not concentrate on having the people informed about how harsh their life will be under their new governors, but rather on having Samuel set down limits to the rights *and* duties of the king he is giving them.[15] However, Samuel is depicted by the narrator as concentrating solely on the future king's privileges—justified or unjustified as the case may be—and one can only conclude that his speech is to be understood as an attempt to delay, if not also to subvert, the LORD's decision. Samuel is not just worried about the new king's powers; his rhetoric is an attempt to block the institution itself.

Why Samuel's Mišpaṭ Is Only Half the Story

The meaning of *mišpaṭ* throughout the Bible extends from its very weak and rare use for something like "appearance" (2 Kings 1:7), to stronger legal usages like "custom or manner of acting" (for example, Judg. 18:7), up to its strongest sense of divinely decreed regulations involving, say, primogeniture (for example, Deut. 21:17) or the powers of judges (for example, Judg. 13:12), priests (for example, Deut. 18:3; 1 Sam. 2:13), or kings (as I am suggesting for 8:9, 11, and 10:25).[16] With respect to the monarchic contexts of this word in 1 Samuel (8:9, 11; 10:25), both the rights *and* duties of the king appear to be what Samuel would have "written in a book and laid before the LORD" (10:25); surely one without the other would have ill-served both God and the community.

If we concentrate upon this obvious feature of Samuel's speech on the king's *mišpaṭ*, then the narrative ambiguities of verses 9–11 mentioned earlier—the completeness or incompleteness of God's and Samuel's directly reported words—lose much of their relevance as the reader tries to understand the author's ideological perspectives in this chapter. Whether God is supposed to have told Samuel what specifically to say about the *mišpaṭ*, whether Samuel is understood to have recounted to the people God's characterization of their request as idolatry and his decision to grant it nevertheless, and whether Samuel is depicted as giving an expurgated version of the LORD's words to him—all these matters lose much of their hermeneutic relevance when we look at the chapter from the perspective of the narrator's principles of selection in reported speech and its effect on characterization: why does the narrator choose to directly report God's and Samuel's speech precisely as it appears in the chapter? Why do the directly quoted words of the LORD emphasize his decision to institute kingship in spite of its equation with idolatry and to the neglect of the *mišpaṭ's* details, whereas the directly quoted words of Samuel emphasize the *mišpaṭ's* details to the neglect of God's command and kingship's idolatrous nature? Why, moreover, does Samuel's description of the king's *mišpaṭ* concentrate on royalty's privileges, that is, on those matters that constitute an infringement of the people's freedom, to the neglect of corresponding royal obligations protecting God's and the people's interests— obligations that also must have been part of the decrees laid up before the LORD?

The answer to these questions seems to lie in the area of contrastive characterization. Given what God says in the chapter, his character zone with respect to Israel—as we have suggested above in chapter 1—is remarkably close in its emotive register to Elkanah's with respect to Hannah. The love of God for Israel comes across as predominantly disinterested and remarkably magnanimous: "Oh Israel, am I not worth more to you than ten kings? Your desires here are so like your previous idolatrous deeds. Nevertheless, I will grant your request, only there will be limits set." On the other hand, Samuel's words in verses 11–18 are full of self-interest, and this understanding of them corresponds both to the people's subsequent reaction and Samuel's own lack of action at the end of the chapter.

Certainly what Samuel says about the king's future actions is properly contained within the boundaries of *mišpaṭ*. Nevertheless, his speech is made to concentrate solely on the king's rights to the exclusion of his corresponding restrictions or obligations, because Samuel is being portrayed here as trying to delay or subvert the LORD's command even as he wants to appear fulfilling that command with a solemn warning. His motivation is clearly self-interested. God is either poignantly giving, like Elkanah, or reluctantly pedagogic ("I'll teach Israel a lesson about having kings like other nations!"). Samuel, on the other hand, seems shrewdly self-serving. God is not reported as describing the *mišpaṭ* in detail because his decision in response to action he characterizes as rejection of him is what the narrator highlights. Samuel is not shown as declaring to the people either kingship's idolatrous nature or God's amazing decision because neither serves his desire to dissuade the people; God's decision makes kingship's idolatrous nature *rhetorically irrelevant* for Samuel's dissuasive purposes. Thus the narrator paints the picture of a God who reveals his love in spite of being rejected, in contrast to a judge who fails to conceal his selfish reluctance to become the maker of kings.

At the same time, and by all these means, the narrator creates in the reader a curiosity about how God and Samuel will deal with the problems facing them. As this chapter indicates with respect to Samuel's reluctance, God will have to initiate the action.

The Rhetoric of Prophetic Persuasion (9:1–27)

Because of the ideological clarity of chapter 8, the reader is allowed no doubt about the intrinsic evil of kingship; throughout the entire history of the monarchy until the very end, this aspect of the royal institution forms the bedrock of the story. What now needs to be worked out in detail, therefore, is how kingship is to function. Given the LORD's decision to allow Israel its request, what are the divine ground rules according to which the king will rule? We have characterized Samuel's speech on the *mišpaṭ hammelek,* "the ways of the king," in chapter 8 as a lopsided, self-interested beginning of an answer. Chapters 9–12 now expand the discussion to include a fundamental constraint upon the king: the necessary role of the prophet (*nābî*) for the royal period of Israel's history. The end of Samuel's farewell address puts it succinctly: "Moreover, as for me, far be it from me that I should sin against the LORD by ceasing to pray for you; *and I will instruct you in the good and right way* . . . But if you do wickedly, both you and your king will be swept away (*tissāpû*)" (12:23, 25). Samuel, like Jeremiah after him, will carry out this obligation despite his personal inclinations and obstructive will. That his warning words in chapter 12 even express what will come true with respect to Saul, the very king before him there, is epitomized in the verb *sāpâh,* "to be swept away, destroyed (in the *nifal*)." David will later echo this warning of Samuel's with prophetic words about Saul near the end of the book: "As the LORD lives, the LORD will smite him; his day shall come to die; or he shall go down into battle and be swept away (*wᵉnispâh*)" (26:10). On the other hand, when David escapes to the land of the Philistines, it is to avoid what would surely happen if he remained: "I should now be swept away (*'essapeh*) by the hand of Saul" (27:1). Thus Samuel's prophetic words in 12:25 will come to pass concerning "your king" at the end of 1 Samuel with the death of Saul, and—even though *sāpâh* itself is not used—concerning "you" (that is Israel) at the end of 2 Kings with the destruction of Jerusalem and the exile.

What now appears to be addressed in the story are these questions: What is a prophet and how does he operate in relation to the king? Once Samuel dies, how will Israel distinguish the true from the false prophet?

Even during Samuel's life, which words of his are truly words of the LORD? The narrator, telling the story about Saul becoming Israel's first king, builds into the account an introductory portrait of that institutional and personal check meant by the LORD to keep the king on the good and right path: the prophet.

The ideological and narrative background to this portrait of the prophet in 1 Samuel 8–12 is Deuteronomy 13 and 18. In Deuteronomy 18 Moses himself details the main criterion by which Israel will be able to distinguish true from false prophecy once he, Moses, the greatest prophet of them all (Deuteronomy 34:10), dies and the prophet to come after him is on the scene: "And if you say in your heart, 'How may we know the word which the LORD has not spoken?'—when a prophet speaks in the name of the LORD, if the word does not come to pass or come true (*w⁽e⁾lo' yābô'*), that is a word which the LORD has not spoken" (Deut. 18:21–22). Deuteronomy 13 further qualifies this prophetic criterion by stipulating that not all prophetic signs that come true are necessarily from God; for example, those that lead to idolatry are not from God.

Chapters 9 and 10 of 1 Samuel are paradigmatic as they recount how God introduces Saul, Israel's first and future king, to the very prophet who, however reluctantly, is to keep his kingship in check. The story of Saul's journey to find his father's asses is meant to provide us with an outline of how God intends Israel's royal journey to proceed if it is indeed to remain "on the good and right path" (12:23). Saul's introduction to the LORD's prophet is the reader's introduction as well: chapter 9 begins a narrative instruction on the rhetoric of prophetic persuasion.[17]

Perspectives in Chapter 9

The story's shift from the well-known judge of chapter 8 to the unknown local seer of chapters 9 and 10 has often bothered scholars.[18] Typically for them, this "new" Samuel is symptomatic of chapter 9 as derived from a "source" different from that of the previous chapter. This supposed source is a necessary element in the text's literary history because of the very manner in which the source is considered to have been unsuccessfully integrated into the larger story line. The reader's journey between chapters 8 and 9, from the Samuel who is a popular and universally recognized judge of Israel to a Samuel who is but a local seer or man of God, and thus largely unknown even to people who matter like Saul, can only be literary-historical or genetic in nature if it is to remain coherent; so we have been taught. A heavy-handed redactor carved out a connecting path from one chapter to the next but did a rather clumsy job in the process—an ancient prototype of our modern "literary hack." The redactor's crudity, never so baldly stated, but implied nonetheless, should not scandalize us too much, we are usually counseled, since ancient Israelites were not so concerned about or bothered by historiographic, esthetic, or ideological "disintegration" as we orderly and right-thinking moderns are. Their standards of coherence were either less demanding than, or at least often different from, ours. Not to worry: this is the stuff of which many a literary history is ingeniously constructed.[19]

Apart from the patronizing and disdainful attitude hidden in such views, it is equally unfortunate that such literary-historical constructions do not seriously deal with the real text in its intricacy and literary sophistication. Such an attitude takes no account of many of the text's features because of an accompanying belief that such features are of little account.

How might the obvious shift in perspectives between chapters 8 and 9 fit from a nongenetic point of view? Why might this shift take place and how might it serve coherent ideological, historiographic, or esthetic purposes?

One answer has to do with the story's ability to generate curiosity, suspense, and surprise in the reader by the manner in which its narrator withholds relevant information—and thereby shapes the plot.[20] In chapter 9, the reader is kept in the dark concerning the identity of the nameless man of God or seer until verse 14, when the narrator has "Samuel" coming to meet Saul and his servant. If the reader comes to know this seer as Samuel, it is never clear when Saul recognizes him as a judge of Israel. Coupled with the narrator's temporary shielding of Samuel's identity is the permanent concealment from the reader of the city where Saul and Samuel first meet. From first to last, reference to it is anonymous (vv. 6, 10, 11, 12, 13, 14, 25, 27); all we are told is that the city is in the land of Zuph.[21] These varying degrees of ignorance and knowledge, discovery or the lack of it on the part of the reader and characters, work together to form the chapter's complex play of perspectives.

The narrator's manipulation of the reader's knowledge and ignorance seems bent on generating surprise and wonder even as the reader's curiosity is satisfied: given Samuel's subversive short-circuiting of the LORD's will in chapter 8, how will the LORD accomplish his purposes nonetheless? Briefly put, God is shown as having decided that if Samuel will not go to Saul, Saul will have to come to Samuel. But the narrator delays this expository information so that the reader encounters it simultaneously with Saul, who first encounters Samuel only in verse 14: "As they were entering the city, behold Samuel coming out toward them." This order of narration—first the encounter in verse 14, and then the reason for it in verse 15—generates surprise on the part of the reader; the story of the lost asses, which apparently had no relation to the preceding story, is now seen to be intimately connected to it. The

LORD controls all human words and actions: he makes plot, and the narrator, who can only shape it,[22] highlights the LORD's omnipotence by choosing to manipulate the reader toward the surprise encounter in verse 14.

If the reader's temporary ignorance of the identity of the seer or man of God in verses 1–13 can be plausibly viewed as ideologically and esthetically motivated, the reader's permanent ignorance concerning the identity of the city of encounter is not so easily explained. That the city's anonymity is relevant to the narrator's purposes seems clear; all voices in the chapter, narrator's and character's alike, consistently refer to a nameless city all eight times it is mentioned. What is not so clear is precisely what narrative purpose such anonymity serves.[23] The narrator's tendency elsewhere is toward urban specificity; what does the refusal to divulge the city's name here signify? Perhaps the secret anointing of Saul by Samuel in 10:1—Saul's servant is made to go on ahead so that Saul and Samuel will be alone, and later (10:16) Saul does not reveal to his uncle anything "about the matter of the kingdom"—is dramatized by the narrator's permanent concealment of the very city at the boundaries of which the anointing takes place. All this is in contrast to the later, slightly more open anointing of David by Samuel; the city, Bethlehem, is named, and the anointing takes place familially, "in the midst of [David's] brothers" (16:13).

This shift between chapters 8 and 9 from knowing to unknowing, from having a prophet to the unwitting search for one, serves, however, a much more generalized purpose than simply the creation of curiosity and surprise in the reader and the depiction of limited vision in the characters. At the beginning of chapter 9 Saul's servant says about the anonymous man of God, "Perhaps he will declare (*yāggîd*) to us about the path (*darkēnû*) on which we have set out" (9:6). The end of this section (chaps. 8–12) has Samuel say to Israel, "I will instruct you (*wehorētî*) on the good and right path (*derek*)" (12:23). Beginning in chapter 9, the manner in which Samuel declares what Saul's journey is all about is paradigmatic of how later prophets will instruct Israel in its journey along the king's road. Chapters 9 and 10 constitute the Deuteronomist's opening declaration of the *mišpaṭ hannābî*, "the ways of the prophet."

The Four Dialogues in Chapter 9

Chapter 9 tells the story of two men inquiring of the LORD (v. 9). When an Israelite went to a prophet to inquire (*lidrōš*) of the LORD, how could he or she distinguish the true from the false word of God? Deuteronomy 18 had provided the beginning of an answer: words that are not from God do not come true (*lo' yābô'*) (v. 22); conversely, it would seem, those that do come true are from God. The four dialogues in 1 Samuel

9—between Saul and his servant (vv. 5–10), between both of them and the young maidens (vv. 11–14), between God and Samuel (vv. 15–17), and between Samuel and Saul (vv. 18–21)—enlarge upon and refine this answer. Each encounter shows how a character's question generates a predictive response. Not only does each dialogue's response then come true, but each dialogue successively increases the magnitude of its predictive power, so that only the final two involving Samuel are seen to be truly prophetic: what God predicts in verses 15–17 and what Samuel promises in verses 19–20.[24]

When one inquires of another in normal circumstances, the response often correctly predicts what will come to pass. The prophet's word, however, is of a higher order. During the journey of Saul and his servant, the dialogues they engage in embody, as it were, a search for the prophetic word. Once the chapter makes clear both to Saul and the reader how the prophetic word operates and how it is to be distinguished from the "ordinary" predictions preceding it, Samuel is ready to say to Saul at its end, "Stop now, that I may make known to you the word of God" (9:27).

The first dialogue, a conversation between Saul and his servant, is a carefully crafted introduction to the chapter's main ideological concerns. It begins with the weakest of predictions: Saul's servant says about the man of God, "Perhaps (*'ûlay*) he will declare to us the path upon which we have set out" (v. 6). There is hope here, buttressed by the man of God's reputation as a seer: "All that he says is certain to come true (*bô' yābô'*)" (v. 6). The story indeed goes on to show how the servant's hope-filled statement comes to pass.[25]

The servant's speech contains elements often found in prophetic speech as the book and the history report it. First, "now, therefore (*ʿattāh*)" in verse 6 echoes forth with the prophetic accents of Samuel himself in 8:9; 10:19; 12:2, 7, 13, 16, and even of the Philistine sorcerers in 6:7.[26] Then the servant's use of *hinnēh*, "look" or "behold," in verses 6 and 8 also intones a rhetoric of persuasion superficially similar to a prophet's.[27]

Saul's servant, of course, is not speaking *as* a prophet, but *of* a prophet, and this is precisely the point: the lad is made to speak with faintly prophetic tones or accents so that the contrast between obviously nonprophetic predictions and the prophetic predictions to come will be highlighted. Authentic prophetic speech is, from this perspective, more than "perhaps," more even than "certainly will," as Deuteronomy 13:1–5 had already made clear.[28] Here, however, the emphasis is on a common experience; things that people say often come to pass. What makes a prophet's word—and the rhetoric surrounding it—different?

At this point in the first dialogue, the author signals to the reader the ideological perspective according to which the entire account has been constructed. The heart of this dialogue—as of the three dialogues to follow in the chapter—involves a question, an inquiry that requires a character to respond or answer (*ʿānāh*), just as a person inquires of God through a prophet and expects an answer. Here in the first dialogue, however, the Deuteronomist even goes so far as to artfully conceal the primary subject matter about which the entire series of dialogues ending in 10:16 has been structured. For when the servant suggests visiting the anonymous men of God in the anonymous city, Saul is reported as asking, "But if we go, *what can we bring the man? (mah nābîʾ lāʾîš)*" (v. 7).

What is most significant about this initial question in the initial dialogue of the chapter is its double meaning. Besides its obvious import in context, the phrase also expresses the main question of this and the following chapters: given that Israel is to have a king, what is the manner of the office that God has chosen to keep him in line? *Mah nābîʾ lᵉʾîš* also means in this context, "What is a prophet to man?"[29] With this opening question in verse 7, followed by the narrator's later statement in verse 9 that "he who is today called a prophet (*nābîʾ*) was formerly called a seer (*rôʾeh*)," the Deuteronomist calls attention to what Saul's journey to Samuel is all about: the *mišpaṭ hammelek*, the rights and duties of the king, will necessarily involve the *mišpaṭ hannābî*, the rights and duties of the prophet.[30]

The servant responds (*laʿᵃnot*) a second time in verse 8: "I will give [the money] to the man of God and he will declare (or "that he may declare") to us our path." Obviously this prediction is exactly what will happen later in the chapter, and just as obviously the servant's words in verses 6 and 8 are *not* prophetic in spite of their predictive value; what the servant purposes to accomplish comes to pass, but this fact in no way makes his words "prophetic."

This dialogue is followed by a second—between Saul and his servant, on one hand, and the young maidens they meet coming out to draw water, on the other (vv. 11–14). The meeting is a truncated "type-scene of annunciation," as Robert Alter has pointed out and therefore "in all likelihood a clue of meaning."[31] Its precise function here lies in the fact that it is constructed remarkably like the dialogues that precede and follow it. The encounter begins with a question, an inquiry, posed to the maidens by Saul and his servant: "Is the seer here?" (v. 11). As the servant before them (v. 8) and the LORD (v. 17), Samuel (v. 19), and Saul (v. 21) after them,

> They answered (*wattaʿᵃnênāh*), "Look (*hinnēh*) he is just ahead of you. Now therefore (*ʿattāh*) make haste for today (*hayyôm*) he has gone to the city. . . . As soon as you enter the city, you will find him . . . The people will not eat till he comes, for he will bless the sacrifice; afterwards the people invited will eat. Now therefore (*wᵉʿattāh*) go up, for this very day (*kᵉhayyôm*) you will meet him (Vv. 12–13)

This breathless, garrulous response to the two men's curt question gives them almost more than they care to know. It is packed with predictive information clothed in typical prophetic rhetoric; the narrator is quick to point out that these predictions immediately begin to happen:

MAIDENS	NARRATOR
As soon as you enter the city you will find him (V. 13)	As they were entering the city, they saw Samuel coming out toward them. (V. 14)

The Hebrew writer's "technique of contrastive dialogue," clearly described and emphasized by Robert Alter,[32] sets off the short/long contrast between the men's question and the maiden's response, but more importantly and generally it explains how the nonprophetic predictions of the servant and the maidens in the first two dialogues differ fundamentally from the authentically prophetic statements of God, the narrator, and Samuel found in the other dialogues in the chapter. Something more is necessary for a true prophet than simply predicting the future.

With the implicit dialogue between the LORD and Samuel in verses 15–17—I write *implicit* because verse 17 has God respond to Samuel (*ʿānāhû*), "Here is the man . . ." as if in reply to Samuel's prior but unreported question, "Is this the man?" in the space between verses 16 and 17—the narrator begins to represent authentic prophetic speech. Most notable here is a prophecy's origin in the LORD in response to human questioning or inquiring. The prophet or seer conveys or communicates the words of the "seer (*rô'eh*)" par excellence, God himself, who is made, therefore, to say in verse 16, "I have seen (*rā'îtî*) my people, indeed their cry has come to me." This dialogue between the LORD and Samuel is the expository basis for the prophetic promises and predictions Samuel makes to Saul in the dialogue to follow. The LORD's statement of what will happen, his "tomorrow" (v. 16), is intrinsically different from the human predictions of the preceding dialogues; the LORD's words "establish" the prophetic words of Samuel to Saul.

The content of God's words also sets out the boundaries of Saul's future actions and is in contrast to that of Samuel's previous words. For God, Saul is sent by the LORD and will save the people from the hands of the Philistines (v. 16); at the same time, God predicts that Saul—and his successors on the throne—will constrain, hinder, imprison (*yaʿṣor*) his people (v. 17). Whereas Samuel in 9:10–18 had subversively emphasized to the people only how the king would restrict their freedoms, God here balances these constraints with the office's advantages. This difference between the narrow, self-interested discourse of a prophet and the wider, more magnanimous vision of the God he is supposed to represent is not lost on the reader.

Because of the contrastive nature of the first three dialogues in the chapter (the first two in contrast to the third), the reader is prepared for the fourth dialogue, that between Samuel and Saul. This encounter concentrates on the miraculously predictive powers of Samuel as seen by fellow Israelites—but always and only to be understood by the reader against the background of the third dialogue's seer needing constantly to be led by God step by step, in an almost infantile way. God had told Samuel, "Make them a king," but Samuel had obstinantly sent the people home; Samuel needs to ask, "Is this the man?" and God answers, "This is the man."[33] The prophet's contemporaries see mostly his miraculous gifts, the Deuteronomist's contemporaries see even the prophet's flaws and weaknesses.[34]

The dialogue between Samuel and Saul (vv. 18–21) is structured like those preceding; it is fueled by a question that provokes a response (*wayya‘an*, v. 19). This response is also full of predictive information that the narrator is careful to fulfill. Nevertheless, the information and promises of information that Samuel gives Saul are mostly of a higher order than what is contained in the first two dialogues. If it is hardly remarkable that Samuel tells Saul he will eat with him that day and be sent off on the morrow, Samuel also claims nothing less than a participation in the omniscience of God at least on a par with that of the narrator: "I will declare to you all that is in your heart" (v. 19). And whereas the compact between the omniscient narrator and the less knowledgeable reader has the latter only able to believe or accept the narrator's information about what is "truly" in a character's heart, Saul, on the other hand, within the world of the narrative is in a position to know for sure how extraordinary the prophet's knowledge is, since it is *his* heart that the prophet probes and what is in it that he declares. Samuel reveals to Saul the very purpose for his journey and even declares the search no longer necessary: "As for your asses that were lost now three days, do not set your heart on them for they have been found" (v. 20). Samuel not only reveals human hearts; his knowledge, like that of the narrator, spans space and time.

Following this remarkable dialogue, verses 22–27 detail the rest of Saul's visit with Samuel and their leaving the city together on the next day, as Samuel had promised. The stage is now set for the secret anointing of Saul and a more detailed exposition of the *mišpaṭ hannābî* in chapter 10.

Chapter 9's Dialogue Between Author and Reader

Once we see this chapter as a carefully worked out meditation on prophetic declarations and the rhetoric by which they are conveyed, we are able to fit together many of its narrative elements to form a coherent picture; a number of significant features are conspicuously distributed throughout the chapter.

First, the narrator carefully speaks mostly in the narrative past, using imperfective verb forms only five times, either to bring the reader into the action of the story or to describe a scene from a character's perspective (vv. 11, 14, and 27). This emphasis of the narrator on past action is, of course, normally to be expected; it is distinctively accentuated nonetheless. The Deuteronomist wants to highlight by contrast the present and future perspectives of the characters' speech in the chapter and thus reports them speaking mostly in ways that are either prophetic or prophetlike.

Nevertheless, even here the narrator's voice is to be understood like the LORD's and Samuel's in its prophetic and omniscient powers, rather than like Saul's, his servant's, or the young maidens'. For just as the Deuteronomist had the narrator periodically "break frame" in the book of Deuteronomy to remind the reader of the narrator's prophetic and authoritative voice in describing the exploits of the prophet Moses,[35] so also here the narrator's voice breaks frame in 9:9 by switching from narrative past to narrator's present in order to underline its omniscient and prophetic qualities through the very contract between narrator and reader that makes up the Israelite narrative convention.[36] Here in 1 Samuel 9, as in the book of Deuteronomy generally, despite their enormous differences, the epistemological similarities between Israelite narrator and Israelite prophet are explicitly underlined: "He who is now (*hayyôm*) called a prophet was formerly (*lᵉpānîm*) called a seer" (v. 9). This relationship between "now" and "then" is essential to the narrative act; the narrator *now* reports what was the case *then*, and the reporting is obviously omniscient whenever the narrator chooses it to be so.

In fact, this omniscient power, belonging by right of convention and ideology to the Israelite narrator, is very much like a predictive power: the narrator brings about events by the very act of narration. As if, therefore, to make this point about the "prophetic" nature of the narrative act and to underline its similarity to the prophetic and predictive powers of the LORD and Samuel in this chapter, the narrator breaks the flow of the story, forces the reader to attend focally to the narrator's words rather than those of the characters, and then "brings his words about":

> Formerly in Israel when a man *went* to inquire of God
> he said, "*Come let us go* to the seer" (V. 9).
> And Saul said to his servant, "*Come let us go*," and
> they *went* (V. 10).

Narrative "postdiction" is simply prophetic prediction in reverse. Like the Israelite prophet's knowledge, the Israelite narrator's omniscience is always and everywhere constrained by the LORD's omnipotence. Concerning future events, the prophet can speak about only what the LORD will accomplish; concerning the past, the narrator can describe only what the LORD has accomplished. This commonly shared trait is why the narrator, as Sternberg has pointed out,[37] is the shaper rather than the maker of plot.

Second, therefore, we can now see one of the reasons why chapter 9 places its scenes in a permanently anonymous city—*ha'îr* in verses 6, 10, 11, 12, 13, 14, 25, and 27—and temporarily depicts Samuel as an anonymous man of God (vv. 6, 7, 8, 10) or seer (vv. 9, 11). The narrator all along knows him to be Samuel and so designates him in narrative discourse (vv. 14, 15, 17, 18, 19, 22, 23, 24, 26, 27). The reader, on the other hand, discovers the man of God to be Samuel only in verse 14, when the narrator chooses to disclose the fact. This epistemological symmetry between reader's and characters' ignorance up to at least verse 14 dramatizes the ideological perspective of the chapter—the quest to discover who is a prophet in Israel—by emphasizing the precariousness of identifying the true prophet and the true word of God. From verse 14 on, the dissymmetry between the reader's knowledge and Saul's ignorance of Samuel's position in the scheme of things allows the reader to learn how a true prophet operates, even as the reader is told the story—from verse 18 into the next chapter—of Samuel convincing Saul of his prophetic authority.

Far from necessitating the introduction of another source with a differing ideology, therefore, the shifts in perspective between chapters 8 and 9, on one hand, and within chapter 9 on the other, may simply suggest the varying play of perspectives (between narrator and reader, between reader and characters and between character and character) that forms the stuff of sophisticated narrative.[38] The challenge of any reading is to put these various shifts in perspective in the service of a plausible ideological, esthetic, and historiographic framework.

Third, if the reader sees chapter 9 as beginning a search for the authentically prophetic word—occasioned at this point, I might add, by the reader's immediately preceding experience in chapter 8 of a true prophet uttering words that are at least partially subversive to God's plans—it becomes clear why the narrator distributes upon the lips of *all the characters in the chapter who respond to questions* mostly predictive statements, all of which come true:[39]

SAUL'S SERVANT:	Perhaps he will tell us about the journey on which we have set out. (V. 6)
	I will give [the money] to the man of God and he will tell us our way. (V. 8)
SAUL:	Behold we will go. (V. 7)

THE MAIDENS

He is just ahead of you. (V. 12)
As soon as you enter the city you will
    find him before he goes up to
    the high place to eat. (V. 13)
The people will not eat till he comes.
    (V. 13)
Afterward they will eat who are
invited.
    (V. 13)
Go up, for you will meet him
immediately.
    (V. 13)

THE LORD:

Tomorrow about this time, I will
    send you a man from the land of
    Benjamin. (V. 16)
And you will anoint him . . . (V. 16)
He shall save my people . . . (V. 16)
He it is who shall constrain my
people.
    (V. 17)

SAMUEL:

Today you will eat with me . . .
And in the morning I will let
    you go
And tell you all that is on your mind.
    (V. 19)

Fourth, seeing this chapter as beginning the Deuteronomist's instruction on the human search for the prophetic word in the midst of normal human rhetoric about present meanings and future happenings helps to explain why the speech of all the characters uniformly concentrates on the present and future, not only with over thirty-five imperfective verb forms, but also with a noticeable distribution of words and phrases that rhetorically point to the present or future. In each character's answer (*ʿānāh*) to an interlocutor's prior question (vv. 8, 12, 17, 19, 21), the answer is made to point at least once to something present or future using *hinnēh*, "look, behold" (vv. 6, 7, 8, 12, 17, 24), and such speech is sprinkled with "now" words and phrases employing *ʿattāh*, "now therefore" (vv. 6, 12, 13) and *yôm*, "today, now" (vv. 12, 13, 19, 20, 27).

At the same time and in contrast to this chapter's declarations about the present and future, only Samuel's telling of affairs is referred to by the solemn term *higgîd*, "to announce, declare" (vv. 6, 8, 18, 19). Others may speak or answer, but only Samuel, like Moses before him, "declares" the LORD's "declared one (*nāgîd*)."[40]

The Power and Limits of Prophetic Persuasion (10:1–16)

Following the dialogues in chapter 9, which contrast humanly predictive with divinely prophetic discourse, the first part of chapter 10 (vv. 1–16) provides a fitting climax. First, the power of truly prophetic speech is emphasized by Samuel's control over even the smallest details of what will befall Saul after his anointing. Verses 2–8 are loaded down with geographic and circumstantial detail that is meant to overwhelm Saul, if not the reader, with its predictive power. Saul's three-staged itinerary, how many people meeting him at each stage, what precisely they will say to him, what they will be carrying and offering him, how he will respond and "be turned into another man," and what finally he will do at Gilgal—all this is spelled out with impressive prophetic authority. Second, after establishing that "all these signs came to pass that day" (v. 9), the narrator singles out for specific narrative fulfillment Samuel's prediction that Saul would prophesy among the prophets. There follows a second dialogue, one between the people and "a man of the place" questioning Saul's prophetic status (vv. 11–12), and finally a third dialogue, between Saul and his (unexpected) uncle (vv. 14–16).

The first "dialogue" in chapter 10 continues the predictive perspective outlined above in the dialogues of chapter 9, but everything is now raised to a higher power. Samuel's opening statement, "Has not (*hᵃlô'*) the LORD anointed you to be prince over his inheritance?" (v. 1), does double duty as both question and answer and therefore makes verses 1–8 an implicit dialogue. Although the form of verse 1 is a question, it is also a delayed response to Saul's previous question to Samuel in 9:21: "Why then have you spoken to me in this way?" In fact, since it introduces a question that requires a positive answer—"Yes, the LORD has anointed you to be prince"—the particle *hᵃlô'* functions here very much like *hinnēh*, "behold": "Behold, the LORD has anointed you to be prince." Thus chapter 10's opening "dialogue" begins with the series of questions that Saul addresses to Samuel in 9:21, to which it is an appropriate response.

This first dialogue introduces in an especially graphic way the central problem of the chapter, indeed of the entire section (chaps. 8–12): what is to be the precise relationship between prophet and king? If 10:1–8 shows the prophet in his predictive and commanding roles with reference to Israel's first king, it also immediately introduces a complicating question: may not Israel's king be Israel's prophet also? The conflict with which Samuel ends his opening speech in chapter 10—Saul is commanded on one hand to do whatever his hand finds to do (v. 7), yet he will (have to?) wait until Samuel shows him what to do (v. 8)—is simply representative of the entire section. How does God intend the rights and duties of Israel's king to be related to the rights and duties of the

LORD's prophet? How does the *mišpaṭ hammelek* relate to the *mišpaṭ hannābî*?

The narrator, introducing the second dialogue of chapter 10, that between the people and an anonymous individual (vv. 11–12), centers it around the fulfillment of Samuel's third prediction to Saul in verses 5–6: God *does* give Saul another heart and his spirit *does* come upon him, so that by prophesying he occasions the proverbial question, "Is Saul also among the prophets?" (v. 12). It is clear from verses 9 and 10 that if Samuel had foretold this turn of affairs, it is God who brings it about. The conflict in Saul between the freedom of verse 7 and the limitations of verse 8 is the result of the very action of God himself.

By verse 13, the *mišpaṭ hannābî* in conflict with the *mišpaṭ hammelek* has taken central stage in the story. If verses 1–8 show Samuel in prophetic action and verses 9–13 have Saul join him in this activity, thus causing the people's wonderment at this turn of affairs, verses 14–16 now surround Saul with a prophetic aura. For Saul is asked by his uncle to "please declare (*higgîd*)" what Samuel had said; and Saul responds by indicating—but only partially—what Samuel the prophet had himself declared. If it is Samuel's prophetic role to declare to Israel what God had said about the rights and duties of the king (8:9) but in fact gives them only a partial answer, here the fledgling prophet, Saul, tells his uncle what Samuel had said but does not declare to him anything about the matter of the kingship. This use of *higgîd* paronomastically clothes Saul with both royal and prophetic garb. It thematically compares his prophetic declarations with Samuel's and at the same time calls fresh attention to him as the newly anointed *nāgîd*, or "royal designate" of 9:16 and 10:1—the *nāgîd lo' higgîd*. In this way prophet and king are both etymologically and ideologically intertwined.

The remaining verses of chapter 10 (vv. 17–27) may be profitably discussed in conjunction with those aspects of characterization that are crucial for an understanding of this chapter's main ideological points of view.

The Characterization of Saul, Samuel, and God (10:1–27)

A coherent picture of the main characters in the drama of Israel's monarchic beginnings is gradually emerging. Certainly the most enigmatic and unpredictable character is Yahweh himself. The gulf between the omniscient and omnipotent LORD, on one hand, and fallible humans struggling to make their way in the tangle of this world on the other, is central to the "drama of reading" so well described by Meir Sternberg in *The Poetics of Biblical Narrative*. Humans continually strive to put a fence around the words and actions of God in an effort to tame them, but they somehow resist such domestication. Such is a constant theme of biblical literature; God resists human attempts to "pen him in."

The spirit of God, which comes so mightily upon Saul in 10:10, remains elusive to us, just beyond our grasp. Like Saul, Samuel, and their fellow Israelites, we labor to understand the LORD's intentions. As for our grasp of Samuel, the inner and outer man slowly comes into focus. By chapter 10 we already have a clear idea of what motivates him as judge and prophet. And concerning Saul, we now have our first opportunity to get beyond his good looks, his unusual height (9:2), his humility (9:21), and his filial piety. By the end of chapter 10 we feel we have somehow gotten hold of the characters of Saul and Samuel. If divine ultimacy remains mysterious, the path upon which the Deuteronomist takes us is nevertheless filled with a range of valuable insights into the ever-variable human character. The marvel of the author's craft lies in the ability to characterize players in the drama with only the sparsest of explicit evaluation or ideological judgment; that shadowy figment of our imagi-nation, that personified reconstruction of our reading we call "the author," remains a master of indirection.

Perhaps the greatest surprise awaiting the reader in chapter 10 concerns Saul. By means of a brilliant set of interlocking compositional and thematic features, the history of Saul's reign is foreshadowed, his insurmountable problems deftly indicated, and his mysterious rejection already suggested.

First, even before Saul is chosen king by lot in verses 20–24, the narrator already sets him up for failure by clothing him in the discor-dant garb of a prophet. From the beginning of the monarchic history to its very end, no king of Israel except Saul is ever said to prophesy, no king at all ever so much as called a prophet. Given Saul's disastrous royal tenure and his abortive dynastic hopes, the proverb in verse 12, "Is Saul also among the prophets?" (repeated in 19:24), surely expresses a central problem with the reign of Saul, a reign in which there was a tragic mix-up of theocratic roles.[41] God's part in Saul's prophetic activity (v. 10) need not obscure for us the disastrous confusion of monarchic and prophetic offices that coexisted in the person of Saul only to end abruptly and disastrously with him, any more than the divine command to Samuel to make Israel a king should cause us to ignore its essentially idolatrous nature in terms of the story's ideology.

The buildup of Saul as prophet begins with the first words we hear him utter. "Come, let us go back," he says to his servant, "lest my father cease to care about the asses and become anxious about us" (9:5). These words express an understandable filial concern, not particularly unusual for someone in his circumstances. The narrator, however, chooses to highlight these first words of Saul by having Samuel's first sign to him in chapter 10 echo them: "And now your father has ceased to care about the asses and is anxious about you, saying, 'What shall I do about my son?'" (10:2). Certainly this first sign highlights Samuel's prophetic ability to see into the hearts of Saul and his father, or at least miraculously to know almost the very words that Saul and his father had said about the matter. At the same time, the impact on the reader of this prophetic repetition by Samuel of Saul's earlier words works in the other direction. Once Samuel repeats Saul's words, the reader cannot avoid the knowledge that Saul in fact foretold his father's concern— unknowingly, to be sure, and ostensibly through filial empathy, but foretold it nonetheless—even before Samuel mentions it to him. More- over, in the story itself, not only does Saul express his father's state of mind before Samuel does, he also is made unwittingly to foretell the sign itself. Thus, when the reader comes upon the first of Samuel's signs in 10:2, he is reminded that Saul was there before him, as he was there even before Samuel himself. Given that Samuel's information about the finding of the asses is truly wondrous, the rest of this first sign follows as the normal expression of any father in a similar situation, so that Samuel's reference to the father's feelings is no more marvelous than Saul's was. In terms, however, of communication between author and reader, this foreshadowing function of Saul's first reported words in the History, this "prophesying of Samuel's prophecy," is the reader's first hint of the prophetic aura that will surround Saul in chapter 10.

Other compositional means of preparing Saul for the illicit garb of a prophet have already been mentioned: wordplay concerning the word *nābî'* itself as well as concerning the theme of a prophetic "declaring (*higgîd*) about kingship," a theme initiated by God's command to Samuel to solemnly declare to the people the *mišpaṭ hammelek*, the rights and duties of the king (8:9).

Consider first how the wordplay of 9:7 to which we alluded above is continued in chapter 10. If Saul's words to his servant can mean both "What can we bring to the man?" and "What is a prophet to man?" this key statement of Saul's also forms a kind of prophetic *inclusio* with the very end of chapter 10. In verse 27, after Saul is chosen king, "[some worthless fellows] despised him and brought him no present (*lo' hēbî'û lô minḥāh*)." The narrator's words here allow the reader to direct Saul's question toward Saul himself and to answer it: the worthless fellows must have said to themselves something like, "*lo' nābî'*," that is, "We will not bring (a present to him)." Which is also to say, "He is not a prophet," in response to the people's proverbial question, "Is Saul also among the prophets?" (10:11; 19:24). Then recall the paronomastic comparison of Samuel and Saul brought about in verses 14–16 through the use of *higgîd*, "to declare," by both Saul's uncle and the narrator with reference to both Samuel and Saul. This term clearly carries prophetic associa- tions.[42]

The question of Saul's prophetic activities, therefore, is not only dramatized within chapter 10, it is also woven into the very fabric of the story by compositional means such as paronomasia and thematic *inclusio*.

Second, the centrality of Saul's problematic status from the very beginning is best seen in the continuous questioning that accompanies him throughout these opening chapters, but with special intensity in chapter 10.[43] This chapter, which starts with Saul's anointing and proceeds to an account of the people's public acclamation of him as king, begins and ends with a question about him:

> Has not ($h^a l\hat{o}$) the LORD anointed you to be prince
> over his inheritance? (V. 1)
> How can this man save us? (V. 27)

Although, as we have seen above, the opening question functions as an answer, the question form is used nonetheless as if to prepare the reader for Saul's being inundated by questions to and about him throughout the chapter. His character zone is filled with doubt and uncertainty. Surrounded by a dubious aura, Saul is the epitome of a questionable choice. Consider how all the characters in the chapter are reported by the narrator as having questions sometimes for, but more often concerning Saul; so it is with Samuel (vv. 1, 24), Saul's father (v. 2), the people (vv. 11, 22), an anonymous man (v. 12), a proverb (v. 12), Saul's uncle (vv. 14, 15), and, finally, the chapter's worthless fellows (v. 27). Consider also that, although Saul does make statements in chapters 9 and 10 (9:5, 7, 10; 10:10, 14, 16), our introduction to him in chapter 9 is as one who himself continually asks questions:

> Look, if we go what shall we bring to the man? . . . What have we? (9:7)
> Is the seer here? (9:11)
> Declare to me please, where is the house of the seer? (9:18)
> Am I not a Benjaminite from the least of the tribes
> of Israel?
> And is not my family the humblest of all the families
> of the tribe of Benjamin?
> Why then have you spoken to me as you have? (9:21)

Saul, therefore, is a seeker of answers as well as asses, a traveling question mark.

Third, besides this weary dubiety that surrounds him, a somber shadow of sin and guilt is cast upon Saul's kingship from the very beginning by means of chapter 10's depiction of the manner in which he is chosen king (vv. 17–24).[44]

There are only three biblical passages in which someone is taken by lot (*nilkad*) before the LORD: Joshua 7, wherein inquiry of the LORD effects the discovery of Achan who had kept for himself some of the devoted things of Jericho; here in 1 Samuel 10; and 1 Samuel 14 where Jonathan is discovered by lot to be the one who against Saul's command had eaten some food and was thereby responsible for the LORD's silence. That is to say, apart from 1 Samuel 10, the ritual whereby Israel drew near (*liqrôb*) or was drawn near to God to inquire (*liš'ôl*) of him by lot is described only in situations where an unknown person needs to be singled out (*nilkad*) because of some kind of covenantal transgression (Josh. 7:15), shameful thing (ibid.), or sin (1 Sam. 14:38; Josh. 7:20).

The public choice by lot of Saul for king follows this pattern of "seizing the culprit." In the prophetic judgment oracle that precedes, Samuel accuses Israel: "You have this day rejected your God . . . and you have said, 'No! but set a king over us'" (10:19). The manner in which Saul is publicly chosen or taken by lot, therefore, is intended, above all else, to emphasize the guilt and sin inherent in the royal office for which he is taken. Saul, as Israel's first king, is singled out as a personification of kingship's sinfulness.

Finally, in contrast to the self-interested and obstructive features introduced into Samuel's character in chapter 9, Saul strikes the reader as docile, humble, and diffident. He directly obeys his father's command to look for his lost asses (9:3); he does everything Samuel asks him to do in chapters 9 and 10; he is humble about his origins (9:21); as if to emphasize the distance between the forceful prophet and the timid man underneath it all, he is characterized by Samuel as about to be turned into another man (v. 6) and by the narrator as being given another heart (v. 9) through the agency of God; when chosen by lot, he—whether shrewdly or timidly we cannot tell—hides himself among the baggage (v. 22); nor, finally, does he divulge to his uncle the matter of the kingship (v. 16). All in all, Saul appears to be exactly the kind of man whom Samuel would have every hope of molding into a compliant king who would least limit the prophetic and judicial powers Samuel has been accustomed to exercise in the past and now sees threatened. Moreover, if a docile king is just what the prophet Samuel orders, a docile prophet-king is doubly what Samuel, himself the head of the prophets (19:20), would want.

This picture of a hesitant and potentially pliable Saul leads us into a consideration of the character zone of Samuel through chapter 10 and helps to explain why Samuel, after delaying the move to monarchy in chapter 9, will come to be Saul's defender and promoter even in the face of God's clear rejection of him. If the people's request for a king had displeased Samuel (8:6), God's coming rejection of Saul will make Samuel angry (15:10), so much so that he will "turn back after Saul" in response to Saul's pleading (15:31). The motivation for this prophetic about-face has its roots in the characterization of Samuel in the chapters immediately following chapter 8.

Sternberg aptly summarizes the narrator's characterization of Samuel in these chapters: "On the threshold of the monarchy, the outgoing prophet-judge hardly appears in an attractive light."[45] Nowhere is this unfavorable depiction of Samuel better seen than in chapter 10. Take, for example, the reported speech within it. On one hand, the emphasis throughout is on the prophetic words of Samuel. Whereas the other characters utter only brief sentences (in vv. 11b, 12b, 12d [(a proverb)],

14b, 15b, 16b, 22b, 24d, and 27b), Samuel's speech is given prominence in both its content and length (vv. 1–8, 18–19, 24b). The boundaries of Samuel's speech range from the prediction of future events to the reporting of God's prior speech. In both cases, the information conveyed is represented as inaccessible within normal human experience, that is, it is *privileged prophetic speech.*

On the other hand, Samuel's series of signs to Saul in verses 1–8 amounts to something like prophetic overkill. Through the use of thirteen predictive verbs (twelve in the waw-converted perfect and one in the imperfect) Samuel appears almost to be showing off his prophetic powers. The contrast in chapter 9 between the simply predictive statements of Saul, his servant, and the maidservants on one hand, and the truly prophetic words of Samuel on the other, finds an impressive climax here at the beginning of chapter 10 where there can be no doubt about how fundamentally different prophetic speech is from simply predictive speech. Nevertheless, Samuel exhibits his prophetic clairvoyance like a strong man publicly flexing his muscles in an excessive or unseemly fashion. The plethora of predictions is certainly not meant to convince the reader, who shares the narrator's knowledge of Samuel's role and is aware of the people's belief in him as prophet, a belief established long before in the narrative ("And all Israel from Dan to Beer-sheba knew that Samuel was established as a prophet of the LORD," 3:20). So this prophetic show must be for Saul's benefit.

Samuel's threefold prediction leads up to Saul's joining the prophetic band he will meet on his journey, the only sign singled out for specific narrative fulfillment in 10:10. One can argue, therefore, that Samuel is here portrayed as intent upon providing Saul with motivation for joining the prophetic band by showing him how impressive a prophet's powers can be. In addition, since Saul, as we have seen, is presented in these chapters as someone who is as timid as he is tall, his initial experience of prophetic power offers the reader some insight into why he, Saul, initially so hesitant about God's royal plans for him, would gradually accede to Samuel's and the people's insistence that he become their king.

Samuel's conduct in chapter 10, however, does more than convince Saul; it also provides the reader with a character portrait of Israel's last judge and first monarchic prophet, a portrayal that is as critical of his teaching about the *mišpaṭ hannābî*, the rights and duties of the prophet, as chapter 8 was of his teaching about the rights and duties of the king. How Samuel conducts himself here will give an ironic dimension to his self-righteous words at the end of chapter 12: "Moreover, as for me, far be it from me that I should sin against the LORD by ceasing to pray for you; and I will instruct you in the good and right path" (12:23). How precisely do Samuel's words and actions in chapter 10 declare and embody this pedagogic obligation of a prophet? The answer to this question will help to explain why Samuel's protestations of innocence at the beginning and end of chapter 12 belie a defensive self-awareness of his failures as God's prophet.

Interpretations of chapter 10 have understandably focused upon Saul—his personal encounter with prophecy and his eventual acclamation as king by the people. Samuel, on the other hand, although a multidimensional character with important ideological functions in the Deuteronomist's story, is too often seen as a flat, mechanistic trigger who simply propels Saul into the royal office chosen for him by the LORD. Things are not so simple.

Consider, for example, Samuel's formal shift from prediction to command in 10:7–8. His command to Saul to join the prophetic band and to do "whatever your hand finds to do" (v. 7) is, as we pointed out above, in profound tension with his word that Saul later wait seven days at Gilgal until he come to show him what to do (v. 8). These two verses epitomize the entire section of chapters 8–12, foreshadow the tragedy of Saul's kingship, and implicate Samuel in the Deuteronomist's explanation for Saul's downfall. King and prophet may not be united in the same person, yet this is precisely the path upon which Samuel's prophetic words send Saul as they declare and embody the *mišpaṭ hannābî'* in chapter 10.

Personal control appears to be what Samuel is after; Saul as both king and prophet offers a double warrant for royal dependence on Samuel, who himself leads the prophets. As verses 9 and 10 show, God cooperates for a time with this disastrous path, just as he will cooperate for centuries with the mix-up of divine and human leadership that constitutes kingship itself. If the people are not absolved of their sin by Yahweh's reluctant and magnanimous fulfillment of their request for a king, neither can Samuel be exempt from the Deuteronomist's censorious depiction of him as a prophet who fails his commission by leading his people down a false path.

The words of Moses come to mind as commentary on Samuel's conduct at this crucial point in Israel's history: "If a prophet arises among you or a dreamer of dreams, and gives you a sign or a wonder, and the sign or wonder which he tells you comes to pass, and if he says, 'Let us go after other gods,' which you have not known, 'and let us serve them,' you shall not listen to the words of that prophet . . . for the LORD your God is testing you, to know whether you love the LORD your God with all your heart and with all your soul" (Deut. 13:1–3). Kingship in Israel was tantamount to idolatry, as God himself asserts in 1 Samuel 8:8. If we understand that God's allowance of this institution is predicated on its providential powers being limited by the office of prophecy, then the wholesale neutralization of this divine constraint effected by Samuel's encouragement of Saul to be both king and prophet can be seen as tantamount to leading the people once more into the very idolatry God intended to avoid (or at least diminish). The events described in 1 Samuel 10 constitute a striking application of the situation envisioned in Deuteronomy 13: a prophet, Samuel, gives signs and wonders that come to pass; his words lead the people into the idolatry of a prophet-king; the people, in turn, question the situation ("Is Saul also among the prophets? 10:12). Yet ultimately they fail God's test by responding positively to Samuel's blandishments: "'Do you see him whom the LORD has chosen? There is none like him among all the people.' And all the people shouted, 'Long live the king!'" (10:24). The so-called tragedy of Saul is a tragedy also for Israel, as it is for Samuel himself. The LORD chose Saul for kingship; the people are misled into accepting him for prophecy as well. At this point in the story everyone—with the possible exception of Saul—has failed God's test.

One final facet of the story is little emphasized in the literature but significant for our understanding of the rights and duties of the prophet. In anticipation of a fuller discussion when we reach chapter 13, we need to bear in mind that the very last events Samuel predicts to Saul in this chapter will not come to pass. What may be read as a series of commands in verse 8 (Go down to Gilgal and wait until I come to you . . .) is actually a continuation of the predictive waw-converted perfects in this section. Whereas Samuel's command in verse 7 is in the imperative, "Do whatever your hand finds to do," in verse 8 Samuel tells Saul, "You *will go down* before me . . . and you *will wait* seven days until I come and I *will show* you what you are to do." Interpreters rarely spell out the ideological implications of Samuel's failed prediction. Not only does Samuel foolishly push Saul into joining a prophetic band, he also is shown as setting up a situation in which neither his word comes true nor his king acts obediently.

The ideological importance of this (failed) prediction of Samuel in verse 8 is that it foreshadows Samuel's failures as prophet as much as Saul's failure as king. What Samuel is shown predicting here is a king obedient to the divine obligations imposed upon him by God's prophet. Not only will Saul fail to be obedient in the crucial incident at Gilgal; much of the responsibility for his failure must be laid at the feet of Samuel who had encouraged Saul's prophetic independence ("Do whatever your hand finds to do, for God will be with you" 10:7]) at the same time as he has paradoxically commanded strict royal dependence upon prophetic direction. In other words, Samuel is shown placing Saul in a double bind.

This failure of Samuel to appear at the appointed time, as he said he would, brings to mind Deuteronomy 18:22: "When a prophet speaks in the name of the LORD, if the word does not come to pass or come true, that is a word which the LORD has not spoken; the prophet has spoken it presumptuously, you need not be afraid of him." Saul, therefore, can be seen in 10:7–8 as being set up for disaster in a double sense. Not only does Samuel encourage his prophetic taking of things into his own hands; Moses' words about unfulfilled prophecies will further justify this independent action of his at Gilgal. For now, it is enough to realize that the "failed appointment" involves Samuel's failure as well as Saul's.

Chapter 10 ends with the narrator's contrast between "men of valor" who follow Saul and whose hearts God has touched (v. 26) and "worthless fellows" who express serious doubts about Saul (v. 27). The narrator's departure from largely nonjudgmental statements since chapter 8 began is significant. God, who will accomplish his purposes despite the personal plans and inclinations of Samuel and Saul, had promised, "[Saul] shall save my people from the hands of the Philistines" (9:16). As the reader is expected to know, therefore, those who express doubt about Saul ("How can this man save us?") express doubt about God himself: they are indeed "renegades," in Eslinger's apt translation.

On Taking Renewal Seriously (11:1–15)

If any chapter in 1 Samuel gives even the most conservative reader cause for textual emendation of the Masoretic Text (MT), it is chapter 11. For one thing, 4QSam[a] now confirms the Greek text apparently used by Josephus, which contained additional information about Nahash's raids upon the transjordanian tribes.[46] More importantly, however, our abiding desire for the story to make sense, in itself and in its literary context, is severely tested by this chapter's apparent inconsistencies, non sequiturs, and other problematic features—all responsible for the veritable jungle of interpretations that has grown up around the chapter.[47] Nowhere is the need for emendation or the warrant for literary history more apparent than in the story of the siege of Jabesh-Gilead.

Consider the question of narrative flow. Like the transition from Samuel the universally known judge of chapter 8 to Samuel the obscure local seer of chapter 9, the transition from chapters 10 to 11 apparently represents a retrograde movement from a newly acclaimed king to a charismatic judge-savior well known from the book of Judges. The concluding verses, witness to a desire to integrate into the present account a story drawn from a supposed "original Saul cycle," are generally considered to contain clumsy editorial additions. The resulting strain on the fabric of the story is almost too much for the text to bear. The hybrid account that we now have in chapter 11 confusingly pulls us backward in time toward the charismatic leaders of the book of Judges even as it proceeds forward with the story of Saul's kingship. This judicial escapade of Saul's, the commentators tell us, originally had nothing to do with questions of monarchy.

Consider also the obvious need for textual emendation to help the redactor's confused story make sense. No sooner does Saul lead Israel to victory over the Ammonites than the people demand to put to death those who had promoted his kingship! It is perfectly clear, we are told, that one must add either a question mark (*ha-*) or a negative (*lo'*) to the damning statement, in the Masoretic Text, of those men whom the people want to execute:

MT:	Who is it that said, "Saul shall be king over us"? Bring the men, that we may put them to death. (V. 12)
RSV:	Who is it that said, "*Shall* Saul be king over us?" Bring the men, that we may put them to death. (V. 12)
OTHER:	Who was it who said, "Saul shall *not* be king over us!"? Give us the men and we shall put them to death!" (V. 12)

This demand raises a further complication: it is made of Samuel, but then the text confusingly has Saul respond in verse 13.

Consider also the nature of the opening request of the men of Jabesh-Gilead to Nahash for a treaty: the townspeople are willing to act contrary to the tribal confederation by allying themselves to a belligerent outsider without a fight, yet God takes pains to save them anyway. Moreover, Nahash's agreeing to their further request for time to muster sufficient opposition to him lacks credibility. Why would an attacking army agree to such a request?

Consider finally, and perhaps most importantly, the people's apparently superfluous action, in verse 15, of "renewing the kingship (*ḥdš*)," which Samuel himself suggests in verse 14. The people have just acclaimed Saul king in 10:24, but here, in the very next chapter, a renewal of kingship is proposed and carried out. Is this renewal an indication of narrative movement from kingship de jure to kingship de facto—as noted by Wellhausen, who is quoted with approval by McCarter[48]—as well as of historical layering of the text itself?

Granting all these textual and hermeneutic difficulties concerning chapter 11, and recognizing textual variations lying behind or alongside the MT—variation exemplified by ancient witnesses like 4QSam[a]—I nevertheless want to suggest a reading that proceeds from an unemended text and assumes a much closer fit between chapter 11 and its literary context than ordinarily proposed. What does the story say if we remove the heavy hand of ancient redactors and modern emendors and replace it with suggestions of high literary art?

The best place to begin is where the story ends. The siege of
Jabesh-Gilead culminates in an Israelite victory and "renewal of the
kingdom" (vv. 14–15). The word used here (*ḥdš* in the *piel*) means "to
restore or repair" and elsewhere always refers to the renewal or
restoration of something actually destroyed, damaged, or lost.[49] It turns
out, therefore, that both the command of Samuel and the response of
Israel toward renewal of kingship in verses 14–15 are as troublesome to
understand as the people's desire, in verse 12 of the MT, to kill those
who had proclaimed or promoted Saul's kingship.[50] How can the
chapter, as it stands, make any sense at all if one takes this concluding
renewal of the kingship literally, that is, as an action presupposing a
prior dissolution of or serious attack upon kingship since the events
recounted in chapter 10?

The suggestion that the kingship had become dormant since the
narrator had Samuel send everyone home in 10:25 makes some sense
but hardly goes far enough. In this view, a quiescent kingship is simply
revitalized and the need for its renewal only implied. Actually, there is
abundant indication within the chapter of Israel's ignoring and even
opposing its monarchic situation—be it quiescent or active—so that
Samuel's move at the end toward renewal of the monarchy becomes
something of a literal necessity if Israel is to regain its commitment to the
monarchy.

Long-recognized insights of scholars concerning chapter 11 offer us
the beginnings of a solution, provided we put their perceptions to better
use by assuming an artful narrative rather than a clumsy redaction.

Kyle McCarter, citing the classic work of Albrecht Alt, succinctly
characterizes the events of 11:1–11: "It is widely recognized that Saul's
deliverance of Jabesh-Gilead belongs to a type of story, best known from
the Book of Judges, in which an enemy threat is averted by an Israelite
hero whom Yahweh has raised up from among his countrymen. These
were the tales of the so-called 'major judges' (Judg. 3:7–16:31), each of
whom rescued some part of Israel from a foreign threat."[51] Once he has
recognized the thoroughgoing judicial picture presented in chapter 11,
McCarter, like most biblical scholars bent upon historical reconstruction,
uses this insight for purposes of literary and political history rather than
for serious narrative interpretation. It is precisely because these originally judicial stories of Saul are supposed to ill-fit their present monarchic context that McCarter, Alt, and all the rest can construct the various
literary histories they suggest.

What if, on the other hand, we were to suppose that the judicial
picture presented in chapter 11, whatever its actual prehistory, is exactly
what the narrator is emphasizing at this point in the complex story of
Israel's move to kingship? This suggestion of an artful and coherent
story would then lead us with some justification to accept a literal
renewal of the kingship and to reject any emendation of the pivotal

statement in verse 12. The complex characterizations of Israel and especially Samuel are greatly enhanced, indeed enabled, by this chapter's picture of Saul, the judicial rather than monarchic deliverer of Israel.[52]

There is not a hint in chapter 11 before verse 12 that Israel, or any tribe or individual thereof, is conscious of having a king within its midst. The threat from Nahash leads the men of Jabesh-Gilead to send messengers throughout Israel in search of a "deliverer."[53] They find Saul of Gibeah who, like Samson before him, experiences the onrush of God's spirit and an ensuing fierce anger that prepare him for a stinging victory over Israel's enemies (see Judg. 14:6, 19; 15:4). Alt's description of chapter 11 is accurate:

> Saul's charismatic leadership, the military service of the tribes, the overwhelming success; up to this point one would think oneself simply confronted with a story from the Book of Judges, except perhaps that the circle of people who were borne along by the enthusiasm of the leader is wider here than elsewhere. But in the final terse sentences comes the unexpected twist: the victorious tribes bring Saul to their sanctuary and by their act of homage make him what no charismatic leader ever was before: the king of Israel (1 Sam. XI.1–11, 15).[54]

Alt also cites with approval Martin Noth's recognition of the remarkable procedural similarity between the dismembering call to arms of Saul in this chapter and that of the Levite in the story of the Benjaminite outrage from the book of Judges.[55] Unlike Buber, however, neither Alt nor Noth tried to integrate this judicial perception into the larger story line. As for the views of most scholars persuaded by Alt's depiction of a judicial context for the Jabesh-Gilead story in 1 Samuel 11, a typical move is to use this insight to reconstruct a two-staged historical progression toward the monarchy: first a "charismatic type" represented by Saul's kingship, then a permanent dynastic type represented by David's.[56]

The story's progression (perhaps *retrogression* more accurately fits these scholars' view) from Saul, the king acclaimed by the people in chapter 10, to Saul, the "charismatic judge" chosen by God in chapter 11, is not too bothersome to excavative scholarship because such a transition simply signals a tolerance for narrative incoherence that belongs to their ancient redactor's psychological or esthetic profile. The two chapters' variant viewpoints need not be reconciled because they are basically irreconcilable, however illuminating they are for purposes of literary history. Nevertheless, we need only assume an artful and coherent construction in the story's development for many of the jagged details of chapter 11 to fall into place.

To begin with, the judicial echoes in 1 Samuel 11 of Judges 19–21 are far more extensive than Noth's simple recognition of a tribal call to arms

represented by the drastic dismembering of the Levite's concubine in
Judges 19 and of Saul's yoke of oxen in 1 Samuel 11.[57] Literary allusions
and narrative reworking of key details make the ideological and esthetic
connections between the two passages deliberate and extensive.

The pairing of the towns of Jabesh-Gilead and Gibeah in both
passages is obvious and scarcely accidental. On one hand, Jabesh-Gilead
had notoriously refused to join Israel's call against a notorious Gibeah in
Judges 21; on the other hand, a divinely led call to arms to rally Israel in
aid of a besieged Jabesh-Gilead in 1 Samuel 11 issues forth from Gibeah.
There is an aura of urban reciprocity begun in the book of Judges that
will continue far beyond 1 Samuel 11.

Notice that the Benjaminite town of Gibeah, its covenantal treachery,
and its tribe's fate form the main subject matter of Judges 19–21. These
chapters of Judges, as if to emphasize the premonarchic background of
the first pairing of Gibeah and Jabesh-Gilead, are bracketed in the
following way:

JUDG. 19:1:	In those days, when there was no king in Israel, a certain Levite . . .
JUDG. 21:24–25:	And the people of Israel departed from there at that time, every man to his tribe and family . . . In those days there was no king in Israel.

By contrast, the monarchic background of the second pairing of these
two towns, in 1 Samuel 11, is bracketed as follows:

1 SAM. 10:24–25:	And all the people shouted, "Long live the King" . . . Then Samuel told the people the rights and duties of the kingship . . . Then Samuel sent all the people away, each one to his home.
1 SAM. 11:15:	So all the people went to Gilgal and there made Saul king before the LORD at Gilgal.

It is as if the chaotic situation described at the end of the book of
Judges—when there was no human deliverer, whether judge or king, to
set Israel on the right path—deliberately looks forward to a sequel here
in 1 Samuel 11 involving these same two towns. This time, however, a
newly acclaimed king from Gibeah turns out to act, in Jabesh-Gilead's

behalf and at God's behest, precisely like the judge so obviously missing from the last chapters of the book of Judges.

Notice also that the account of the siege of Jabesh-Gilead sends forth some paronomastic rays whose source is in the name of the tribe to which Gibeah belongs, Benjamin (*bin-yāmîn:* "right son"): Nahash threatens to gouge out every right eye (*ʿēn-yāmîn*) of the inhabitants of Jabesh-Gilead, who later respond, "You may do to us what is pleasing (*ṭôb*) to your eyes" (v. 10). If this response plays with Nahash's threat ("You may try to pluck out our right eyes, an action pleasing to *your* eyes"), it more importantly echoes the judge versus king background against which both accounts occur: "In those days there was no king in Israel: every man did what was right (*yāšār*) in his own eyes" (Judg. 21:25).

Notice finally that the outrageous act of the base fellows of Gibeah in Judges 19 causes the tribes of Israel to say:

> "Now, therefore, *give up the men* [the base fellows of
> Gibeah] *that we may put them to death*." (Judg.
> 20:13)

The story in 1 Samuel 11 has the people say (to Samuel) the very same words:

> *"Give up the men, that we may put them to death."*

Nowhere else in the entire Bible do we find these exact words.

Taking these examples of literary allusion, paronomasia, and echoing of reported speech as additional confirmation of the unquestionable judicial emphasis of 1 Samuel 11 so long recognized by scholars, what narrative conclusions can we draw?

Everything in verses 1–11, be it the statements of the narrator or the statements and actions of its characters, contributes toward a conscious and deliberate ignoring of the monarchic status of Saul in favor of depicting him as someone who, like the judges of old, leads Israel to victory under God's inspiration. May we not, therefore, plausibly suggest that this lesson about proper leadership, intended for the story's characters and readers alike, is to be understood as so well learned by the people after their deliverer's victory that they were inclined to recognize the political and theological advantages of retracting their demand for a king, thus reversing the direction they had chosen in chapter 8?

Along this line, may not the entire movement of 1 Samuel 11, in its immediate literary context and intimate dialogue with the book of Judges, render plausible the community's desire to punish those within their midst like the elders who had gathered together at Ramah to request a king from Samuel (8:4–5) or the people who had acclaimed

Saul king in chapter 10? Could not God's deliverance of Jabesh-Gilead through Saul, who acts not like the kings of other nations but like Israel's judges of old, have impressed itself so forcefully upon Israel that it is portrayed as recognizing the practical advantages of extirpating the monarchy from its midst and punishing those in the community most responsible for promoting it? Such considerations allow the Masoretic Text ("Who is it that said, 'Saul shall be king over us!'? Bring the men that we may put them to death" 11:12) to make some sense. "Let Saul be our judge," the people now say, "but no longer our king. We want to retreat from our sinful state by punishing those most responsible for having put us there."

By integrating, therefore, the thoroughgoing judicial nature of the Israelite victory in verses 1–11, a feature emphasized by both narrator and characters alike, with the call in verse 12 to punish those who had wanted a monarchic Israel, the stage is set for the revealing responses of Saul and Samuel to this national call for repentance.

The Art of Prophetic Manipulation

The narrator now uses this story of God's offer to Israel to repent as a vehicle for deftly portraying a complicated range of character, both human and divine. What is remarkable about this account, as generally about this entire section of 1 Samuel, is its ability to characterize without the narrator making explicit evaluative statements concerning the words or actions of the main characters. The verbal economy with which the Deuteronomist achieves authorial purposes is exceptional, however diverse the methods used.

Think about the effect wrought upon our perception of the story's characters by the perfidious pairing of Jabesh-Gilead and Gibeah in Judges 19–21. That the men of Jabesh-Gilead had earlier refused to honor their tribal obligations at Mizpah makes their present treachery in offering convenantal peace to Ammon without a fight (v. 1) simply characteristic. The character zone of Jabesh is already filled with tribal betrayal, so that the treacherous dimensions of its opening gambit with Nahash are easily understood without so much as a raised eyebrow on the part of the narrator. Nahash's arrogant response then forces those who once had failed to honor their own tribal obligations to call upon fellow tribes to honor theirs. The presumption and easy self-deception of the men of Jabesh-Gilead are palpable. If we add to this negative picture of an Israelite town the positive portrayal of a God who delivers it from its dire straits despite its perfidy, we are confronted once again with a mysteriously magnanimous and merciful LORD who, contrary to the abundant words concerning his harsh justice that are found throughout the History, is so often shown as partial to a sinning Israel.

For his part, and in spite of the powerful success brought about by the onrush of God's spirit about him, Saul remains continually dogged by the negative associations of the town of his origin. Once it is paired with Jabesh-Gilead in the gruesome incidents recounted in the book of Judges, Gibeah becomes a hallmark of sin, tribal treachery, and divine disfavor.[58] God's purposes govern all; it is therefore no accident that Israel's first abortive king should hail from Gibeah. That geographic detail about Saul tragically comments upon all the events of his life— even here in what one commentator has chosen to call "Saul's finest hour."[59] His first military victory is colored throughout by a narrative pairing of his own town with the town he successfully rescues. As the story proceeds, it will continue to intertwine Saul of Gibeah with the men of Jabesh-Gilead, even to his death and beyond. For now, in his hour of glory, the failure of Saul's coming reign is also already foreshadowed by the town God chooses for the man of Gibeah to deliver. And all this without so much as a judgmental word from the narrator or any authoritative character speaking for the narrator.

These points being understood, however, the narrator still reserves the most cutting characterization for Samuel himself. After all, if the story in chapter 11 is, as we are suggesting, about Israel's missed opportunity to reverse a monarchic path leading ultimately to exile, then the final rejoicing of Saul and the people (v. 15) is ironic in a tragic sense; and with the tragedy goes a sense of sympathy on the part of the reader toward them because of their missed opportunity. We somehow feel that if only Saul and the men of Israel understood, as we already do, that they were being manipulated by Samuel's personal desires for power and prophetic control and by God's impelling desire to underline the dangerous responsibilities of free will, perhaps things might have turned out differently. By contrast, the words and actions of Samuel in this chapter, as in those that precede and follow, characterize him with a power that no explicit judgments by the narrator could ever accomplish.

Samuel's appetite for control over the man whom God had designated (the *nāgîd*) led him, we have suggested, to encourage Saul's prophetic activities with an expansive but ambiguous argument about freedom of action ("for God will be with you," 10:7). Saul, as a "liberated" prophet-king, paradoxically would be doubly under Samuel's direction: as king he would be limited by Samuel the prophet, as prophet by Samuel the head of the prophets. Saul, by chapter 11, has so been taken in by Samuel's stratagems that even as military leader he issues a call to arms to Israel markedly fixing his own leadership with Samuel's: "Whoever does not come out after Saul and after Samuel[60] so shall it be done to his oxen!" (10:7). Just as the larger narrative permanently pairs the towns of Jabesh-Gilead and Gibeah, and thereby fixes an evaluative comment upon their notorious union, so also does it bind the fates of Samuel and Saul to such an extent that henceforth their careers will be intimately connected. Perhaps in recompense for forging a detrimental union more determinate than God had intended, Samuel will continue to be plagued with the problem of Saul even after Samuel's death, as chapter 28's account of the calling up of Samuel's spirit by Saul will make clear.

Both Saul and Samuel, therefore, are here bound together in the short-circuiting of the people's plan to put an end to monarchy—Saul, however, less actively than Samuel. When the people command Samuel to bring forward the promoters of the monarchy (v. 12), it is Saul who begins the process of deflecting their desires by forbidding any execution on the day upon which "the LORD has wrought deliverance in Israel" (v. 13). His argument is especially effective; not only does it avoid punishment for those who had promoted kingship, it also gives credit where credit is due. The people had stubbornly insisted on having a king like the other nations so that he could "go out before us and fight our battles" (8:20), but Saul now reminds them that it was the LORD who delivered Israel, not himself whether judge or king.

At this point in the narrative Samuel intervenes by issuing a call that recognizes the people's statement in verse 12 as the disavowal of kingship it actually is. With prophetic authority he commands the people to follow him to Gilgal, there to reestablish the royal course they had just rejected. Whatever their motivation, be it obedience to God's prophet or simply a superficial repentance (there is a narrative gap here), the people follow Samuel, their prophet, with Saul's obvious cooperation. Once more they make Saul king (v. 15). Given Samuel's disastrous manipulation of them following their statements in verses 12–13, the irony of the great joy with which the chapter ends is not lost upon the reader. For Saul, his unwillingness to kill those who deserved to die will come back to haunt him in chapter 15, when he is again unwilling to put someone to death. Which chapter's account of the king's refusal to execute is more fundamental to his failures as leader of Israel is not difficult for the reader to decide; the first refusal foreshadows and forms the basis for the second.

Samuel will consolidate his control over the people and Saul in chapter 12, yet his memory there of the events of chapter 11 will turn out to be deficient in a self-serving way. By then old and gray, he will recall that the people, not himself, had insisted on a king during the events surrounding the siege of Jabesh-Gilead. The narrator, confident that the reader will pick up the discrepancy, thereby highlights Samuel's conveniently faulty memory.[61] Samuel's speech in chapter 12, as we shall see, is markedly defensive; this self-righteous tone of a prophet who protests too much is another of the narrator's subtle but effective means of highlighting Samuel's self-interested actions with respect to Saul and the kingship. Details such as this constitute the author's abiding picture of Samuel throughout these chapters. Chapter 11, like the preceding and following chapters, provides us with a particularly uncomplimentary portrait of Israel's last judge and first kingmaker; it actually implicates

Samuel in the people's royal sin more devastatingly than anywhere else in the story.

The Powerful Voice of the Author (12:1–25)

The narrator hardly speaks in chapter 12; apart from simply introducing the reported speech of Samuel and the people in verses 4, 5, 6, 19, and 20 and describing how Samuel's requested thunder and rain affected the people in verse 18, the narrator's voice is silent. At the same time, the Deuteronomist manages to fill this climactic chapter with numerous authorial accents that turn it into a highly evaluative portrait of Samuel and the people. This central feature of chapter 12, wherein the superficial composition of reporting and reported speech contains scarcely any direct word of the narrator yet refracts the profoundly ideological voice of the author everywhere within it, provides us with examples of what Bakhtin calls double-accented, double-styled *hybrid constructions*. Such a construction is

> an utterance that belongs, by its grammatical (syntactic) and compositional markers, to a single speaker, but that actually contains mixed within it two utterances, two speech manners, two styles, two "languages," two semantic and axiological belief systems . . . There is no formal—compositional and syntactic—boundary between these utterances, styles, languages, belief systems; the division of voices and languages takes place within the limits of a single syntactic whole, often within the limits of a single sentence. It frequently happens that even one and the same word will belong simultaneously to two languages, two belief-systems that intersect in a hybrid construction—and consequently the word has two contradictory meanings, two accents.[62]

It may be helpful to describe precisely how the Deuteronomist makes an ideological position present in a passage where the explicit voice of our omniscient guide, the narrator, is scarcely heard. Such an analysis might be useful for evaluating the plausibility of assuming a haphazard or heavy-handedly crude redaction lying behind the composition of the Deuteronomic History as we now have it.

The structure of the chapter is easily described. After a Samuel-centered dialogue between prophet and people in verses 1–5, a people-centered dialogue in verses 6–25 follows, consisting of Samuel's prophetic judgment speech (vv. 6–17), a comment by the narrator (v. 18), the people's response to Samuel (v. 19), and Samuel's concluding speech (vv. 20–25).

The double interchange between Samuel and the people in verses 1–5 sets the tone for the entire chapter: Samuel immediately insists upon establishing the innocence of his past actions as leader of a people whose stubborn sinfulness will form the basis for his words in the rest of the chapter. This contrast between Samuel's beginning insistence upon the utter propriety with which he has conducted his affairs throughout his long career as prophet and judge and his subsequent hammering away at the continued wickedness of the people in demanding a king is significant. It allows us to view Samuel in the uncomplimentary light of putting as much distance as possible between himself and the impious institution of kingship at the same time as we see him continuing to do whatever is necessary to sabotage the very rejection of kingship toward which his words to the people appear to incline.

If the markedly self-defensive posture of Samuel in verses 1–5 allows us to put his following words in proper authorial context, the people's immediate confirmation of his innocence establishes the docile and manipulated accents that will dominate their character zone for the rest of the chapter. The willingness with which the people followed Samuel's direction to renew the kingship in chapter 11 continues on into chapter 12; the people's speech fairly parrots Samuel's, so that it will not be difficult for us to accept their further words and actions in the chapter as proceeding from a community who have become puppets of the prophet. Notice how the narrator has the people respond almost hypnotically to Samuel's protestations of innocence in matters that are all irrelevant to this section's emphasis on the rights and duties of the prophet insofar as they are meant to restrict and guide the rights and duties of the king:

SAMUEL	THE PEOPLE
3: Whom have I defrauded? Whom have I oppressed? Whose ox . . . or whose ass have I taken? 5a: The LORD is witness against you.	4: You have not defrauded us or oppressed us or taken anything from any man's hand. 5b: (He is) witness!

This interchange between Samuel and the people not only establishes the sinless/sinful and the manipulating/manipulated contrasts that will characterize the speech of Samuel and the author for the rest of the chapter, it also rests under the darkening shadow of what we have already observed in the preceding chapters.

On one hand, nothing so far encountered would lead us to doubt either the self-righteous feelings of Samuel concerning questions of fraud, oppression, and bribery or the people's sincerity in confirming his uprightness in these matters. Lurking in the background here is the narrator's earlier contrast between the young and spotless Samuel and the wicked sons of Eli in chapters 2 and 3. Now that Samuel is old and gray, the picture appears not to have changed. On the other hand, the portrait of Samuel painted since chapter 8 has not been a flattering one; it is not accidental, therefore, that the reader senses an attempt by Samuel to concentrate on the strong points of his past behavior while ignoring precisely those areas of his prophetic leadership so soundly criticized by the authorial accents within chapters 8–11. In fact, Samuel will soon be shown downplaying his own crucial role in resurrecting the kingship despite the LORD's behind-the-scenes attempt—God's omnipotence never quite overwhelming human free will—to reverse Israel's monarchic direction through Saul's judgelike deliverance of Jabesh-Gilead in chapter 11.

Another aspect of Samuel's insistence on innocence is a final voicing of his initial displeasure at the people's rankling request for a king to rule in place of him (chap. 8). Samuel now wants the people finally to admit that, in contrast to their dissatisfaction with Eli's sons (2:23) and despite his own sons' bribe taking and perversion of justice (8:3), the people really had little cause to urge a replacement of his rule with that of Saul, the king "asked for (šā'ûl)." Samuel reminds them that he had reluctantly obeyed their voice and made a king over them (12:1); by conveniently glossing over the divine command that he do so, he is able in this way to reemphasize the people's guilt. Samuel's words about himself, however, portray a prophet of highest probity, a leader of magnanimous character.

Nevertheless, the literary context in which the author places these words of Samuel causes them to reverberate with self-serving and highly manipulative accents. Samuel still controls the people's responses, as he controlled them in chapter 11. In both cases, a desire for personal power at the expense of communal welfare seems to underlie his actions and self-justifications. Samuel diverted the people away from repentance in chapter 11; he now diverts their attention away from his central failures by speciously concentrating on areas of responsibility unrelated to his actual failures in leadership.

In the previous chapter the Deuteronomist had just shown him robbing Israel of its repentance, which is still within his hand, yet Samuel's easy promise to return whatever he had taken (12:3) will be contradicted by his continued short-circuiting of the people's repentance as the chapter develops.

These conflicting accents, which we hear in the opening words of Samuel and the people, are examples of a kind of *speech interference* between character and author that disposes us to be sensitive to the many hybrid constructions within the chapter. In verses 1–5 it appears that only Samuel and the people speak. Yet the words expressing the prophet's protestations of innocence and the people's facile compliance with them are subjected to a highly critical evaluation: what has preceded chapter 12 undermines the self-styled innocence of the prophet even as it criticizes the extreme docility of the people.[63]

Because of the double-voiced nature of Samuel's speech in verses 1–5, his words convey to the reader more than Samuel intends to convey to the people. For example, Samuel's two statements, "Behold the king walks before you . . . and behold my sons are with you" (v. 2), apparently referring to two separate phenomena, now take on a parallel relationship that renews the ideological weight of chapters 1–6's allegorical juxtaposition of the having of sons and the request for kings, as well as chapter 11's exposure of Samuel's personal complicity in the rebirth of kingship itself. "Behold the king and my sons testify to my innocence," says Samuel; "Behold the king, that is, 'Samuel's son,' testifies to Samuel's guilt," says the author.

When, also, Samuel says to the people, "This very day, the LORD is witness against you, and his anointed is witness against you" (v. 5), we hear the author speaking these words *of* and *to* Samuel himself. The I-convict-you nature of Samuel's prophetic speech to the people is taken over by the I-convict-you accents of the author to Samuel as well as to the people. That the king continued to walk before the people even to Samuel's old age, that Saul, the LORD's anointed, was still around as king rather than judge, was indeed living witness against Samuel himself. After early overcoming an initial dislike for the idea of a rival to his leadership, Samuel had quickly appropriated to himself responsibility for Saul, "the one asked for," and now he continues to do so. King Saul and all the future kings of Israel have become, in Samuel's words and through his actions, "my sons," witnesses against their father as well as against the people.

Considerations such as these help us hear the authorial voice that is everywhere present in Samuel's and the people's words in verses 6–17, 19–25, as well as the narrator's in verse 18. Both Samuel's and the narrator's words focus upon wordplay involving *rā'āh* ("to see"), *yārē'* ("to be afraid" and "to fear," that is, "to obey [the LORD]") and *rā'a'* in the *hifîl* ("to do evil").[64] This extensive paronomasia in the chapter binds the various speeches together within a consistent semantic field that helps us correlate the ideological positions of narrator and character even as it refracts authorial intentions: the people's "seeing" ought naturally to lead them toward "being afraid" and "fearing the LORD (that is, obeying him)" and away from "doing evil."

When we examine Samuel's speech in verses 6–17, its phraseological composition helps to establish the ideological perspectives according to which the author characterizes him.[65] First, Samuel effectively dissociates himself from personal culpability in kingship's evil by consistently associating the king with the people rather than with himself.[66] Samuel's pointing to "your king" rather than "our king" is further reinforced by the narrator's emphasis upon Samuel's convenient distortion of what has just been recounted in the previous chapter. There, it was Samuel who brought up the matter of renewing the kingdom, with the people then following him in spite of their earlier movement toward repentance (11:12–15); here Samuel's retelling reverses the roles of prophet and people in that renewal: "And when you saw that Nahash the king of the

Ammonites came against you, you said to me, 'No, but a king shall reign over us,' when the LORD your God was your king" (12:12). We see, therefore, that the distance that Samuel places between himself and kingship is patently erroneous from the standpoint of reality as established by the story so far.

Second, the perspective whereby Samuel places the guilty weight of promoting kingship solely on the people's shoulders is reinforced in Samuel's prophetic judgment speech through its depiction of him as too easily accepting kingship as an accomplished and continuing fact, as an institution henceforth to be bound up with the people by some kind of necessity: "If you and your king will follow the LORD, it will be well . . . but if . . . not . . . then the hand of the LORD will be against you and your fathers[!]" (vv. 14–15).[67] This terrible union of people and king is to continue to the very end of Samuel's speech and the author's history: "But if you still do wickedly, you shall be swept away, both you and your king" (v. 25).[68]

Where in God's words to Samuel, or anywhere else in the story so far, does God restrict or forbid Israel from repenting of their decision to ask for a king? Where does God forbid Samuel to move Israel toward repentance over kingship in an attempt to return matters to their preroyal state? Even the LORD will soon repent of having chosen Saul king (15:11); may not the people now repent of having chosen kingship itself?

Third, Samuel's earlier display of prophetic power over future events (10:2–8) is now characteristically followed by a meteorological power play the *sight* of which ("see this great thing," v. 16), he intends, will cause the people's *seeing* how wicked their request for a king is ("you shall see that your wickedness is great," v. 17). *Seeing* this great thing ought to lead first to fear of the LORD and Samuel in the sense of being terrified of them, and then to fear of the LORD and Samuel in the sense of following and obeying them. *Everything in Samuel's speech up to this point seems geared toward effecting the people's repentance.*

The narrator's notice in verse 18 that the people do become afraid of the LORD and Samuel prepares quite naturally for the people's fearful response in verse 19: "Pray for your servants to the LORD your God, that we may not die; for we have added to all our sins this evil, to ask for ourselves a king." Notice how the people, like Samuel earlier, are putting some distance between themselves and Samuel: they speak of "your God" rather than "our God." More importantly, however, the people's words are a cry for repentance similar to their words in chapter 11. There the people desired to kill those who had led the move toward making Saul king, that is, the "elders" of 8:4, whereas here the people, that is, the "all Israel" of 12:1, express fear of the death awaiting them as those who are guilty of acquiescing both to their elders' request for a king and then to the move to renew the kingship recounted in chapter

11. In accepting Samuel's skewed version of who suggested to whom the need for a king in connection with the threat from Nahash (only one chapter removed from the reader of chapter 12, but apparently many years removed from the characters involved in the dialogue of chapter 12) the people therefore request forgiveness from the very person who led them into renewing their sin in the first place, Samuel himself.

At this crucial point Samuel is shown once again short-circuiting the very repentance to which his words and display of power in verses 6–18 would normally lead. Sight giving rise to fright should lead to a fear of the LORD that involves a turning aside (*šûb*) from one's acknowledged sins. But once the people have seen and are afraid, Samuel's words in verses 20–25, now most obviously double accented through the ironically condemning voice of the author, succeed in diverting the people away from a truly effective repentance: "And Samuel said to the people, '*Fear not . . .*'" (v. 20). Authorial accents invest these words with a highly contradictory implication and reveal more about Samuel's motivations than the people apparently realize: Samuel's "Do not be afraid, but serve the LORD" now fuses with the author's unmasking of his, Samuel's, intentions: "Do *not* fear [the LORD by rejecting your king]." The best way to see how incriminating is Samuel's role in fostering this lack of any real follow-through to the people's words of repentance is to compare this account with Samuel's earlier prophetic and judicial intervention in behalf of the people in chapter 7.

The similarities and differences between chapters 7 and 12 have long been recognized by scholars operating from either a source-oriented or a discourse-oriented perspective.[69] What has not been generally recognized by interpreters, however, is a key point of contrast: whereas the earlier scene in chapter 7 led to Israel's repentance ("So Israel put away the Baals and the Ashtaroth and they served the LORD *only*," 7:4), here in chapter 12 Samuel does not demand what he then demanded, namely, that Israel "put away the foreign gods . . . from among you" (7:1). That is to say, Samuel never requires that the people put away "this evil, to ask for a king" (v. 19). Rather, in verses 20–25, as earlier in verses 6–18, he accommodates kingship within a proposed scheme of obedience, that is, of fearing the LORD. Indeed, if it had been the LORD himself who compared the kingship with serving other gods (8:8) yet allowed it to begin nonetheless, now it is Samuel who, in his instruction to Israel "in the good and right way" (v. 21), is shown as accommodating the service of the LORD (v. 20) to the continuing service of these "other gods." Samuel never contemplates or suggests the cessation of an institution that he had gone out of his way to promote, even revivify, while all the while publicly condemning it. The events of chapter 11 portray the LORD as having offered Israel a way out of its royal dilemma. Here, as there, the people allow Samuel to short-circuit their repentance.

The narrative connections between chapters 7 and 12 within the compositional plans of the Deuteronomist need to be emphasized here. On one hand, chapter 7 represents the Deuteronomist's idealized judicial blueprint for the regaining of a land lost in the exile largely through the very institution whose checkered history is set to begin in the very next chapter. On the other hand, chapter 12 can be seen as the final nail hammered into the royal coffin that is about to begin its solemn procession toward ultimate exile. Samuel's and the people's failure to turn aside from kingship in chapter 12 ultimately prepares for Israel's exile—and thus makes necessary the Deuteronomist's historiographic plan for ending it.

What is remarkable about chapter 12 in the light of chapter 7 is what the author does *not* have his narrator and characters say or do. Neither before nor after the people have fearfully acknowledged their sin in requesting a king (v. 19) does Samuel require them to put aside their king and return "to serving the LORD *only*" (7:4). Nothing in the narrative would seem to forbid it. In like manner, once Samuel has persisted in promoting the fact of kingship (all the while blaming the people for it), nothing besides their increasing docility before Samuel appears to stand in the way of their adamantly refusing to follow his lead, just as they so forcefully refused it in chapter 8. There they insisted, "No, but we will have a king over us!" (8:19). Why do they not now reject Samuel's royal accommodation with an equally resounding "No! but we will *no longer* have a king over us"? Their fear, brought about by Samuel's display of power over nature, may mitigate the guilt of their docility, but it does not succeed in removing it altogether.

The command of Moses in Deuteronomy 13 casts a condemnatory shadow over Samuel's accommodating words and helps to explain the people's responsibilities as well as God's motivation throughout chapters 11 and 12 of 1 Samuel: "If a prophet . . . gives you a sign or wonder, and the sign or wonder which he tells you comes to pass, and if he says, 'Let us go after other gods,' which you have not known, *'and let us serve them,'* you shall not listen to the words of that prophet . . . for the LORD your God is testing you, to know whether you *love the LORD your God with all your heart* and with all your soul" (Deut. 13:1–3). Moses' words put Samuel's instruction to "fear not . . . but serve the LORD with all your heart" (v. 20) in proper perspective. Samuel's efforts to sustain and promote the king—that "other god" within Israel's midst—give a double accent to his words: "fear not" hovers dangerously close to "fear not the LORD" so that his instruction "in the good and right path" has become a contradiction in terms.

Thus does the Deuteronomist use verses 20–25 as a comment on and a final evaluation of the prophetic performance of Samuel throughout the crucial events inaugurated by the people's fateful decision in chapter 8; these words of Samuel also constitute the author's postdictive "proph-

ecy" of the ultimate fate of the people of Israel in the light of their
earliest lost opportunities for repentance.

The double-voiced, double-accented statement in verse 23, therefore,
represents Samuel's description of his intercessory and strategic responsibilities as prophet, at the same time that it contains the author's
evaluation of the prophet's performance. Samuel's pious protestations
of innocence at the beginning (vv. 1–5) and end (v. 23) of the chapter
bespeak a claim to Israel of professional uprightness as God's prophet.
In addition, verse 23 ("Far be it from me that I should sin against the
LORD by ceasing to intercede for you; and I will instruct you in the good
and right path") focuses upon Samuel's iniquitous conduct at almost
every stage of monarchy's birth: his personal affront (rather than
indignation in God's behalf) at the people's request for a king; his
partial, and therefore self-serving, description of the rights and duties of
the king; his ready involving of Saul in prophesying; his refusal to accept
the people's repentance at Jabesh-Gilead; his convenient blaming of
Israel alone for kingship's continuance; his easy assumption that "you
and your king" are indissolubly united; and his cultivation of a highly
manipulable king and people. All this testifies to Samuel's failures as the
LORD's prophet. Samuel's hypocritical piety and self-serving conduct
are unmasked by the author's past and present descriptions of his many
impieties. Authorial irony reveals the duplicitous role of Samuel in
continually fostering kingship at the beginning of its disastrous history.

Samuel's final words in this chapter also contain the author's foreshadowing of the fate of Saul at the end of this book and the fate of
Israel at the end of the history: "You shall be swept away, both you and
your king" (v. 25). Given this national fate as a foregone conclusion,
chapter 12 looks back to chapter 7 as the author's proposed solution to
the exile. There Samuel and the people enact a model of national
repentance: the kings of Israel are put away and, under Samuel's judicial
leadership, the people "serve the LORD *only*" (7:4). Samuel, as the
idealized judge of chapter 7, anticipates and supplies what the more
historiographically portrayed Samuel of chapter 12 succeeds in removing: true and effective repentance on the part of the people.

The Mystery of Divine Manipulation

In spite of the powerful characterizing elements in chapters 8–12 and
the uncomplimentary picture of Samuel that they produce, the Deuteronomist nevertheless invests the narrative with a human/divine counterpoint that constantly places the merely human characterizations in
proper perspective. *Yahweh the maker of plot makes Samuel the manipulator of
people pale by comparison.* However Samuel, Saul, or the people choose to
act, the narrator never lets us forget that it is God who is directing traffic.
The LORD commands Samuel to make a king (8:7, 9, 22); the LORD

chooses Saul (9:17); the LORD moves Saul to prophesy (10:10); the LORD publicly chooses Saul by lot (10:21); the LORD gives Saul victory over Jabesh-Gilead (11:6); and the LORD cooperates with Samuel's fear-instilling display of thunder and rain (12:18). It is difficult to avoid seeing the LORD as the one who ultimately sets up Saul for proximate rejection just as he will Israel for ultimate exile. The paradox of kingship, epitomized in Saul's abortive reign, is of an institution that came about through both obedience and disobedience to the LORD's command. The tragedy of King Saul, as of royal Israel in general, ultimately rests in the mysterious coexistence of divine omnipotence and human freedom.

It is in this light that the Deuteronomist's proposed solution to the exile in chapter 7 (the end as a corrective to the deficient picture in chapter 12, the beginning) is finally to be understood; even assuming Israel's ultimate repentance and rejection of kingship, return to the land is not something that is insured. The Deuteronomist, the prophet to come after Moses, whose voice Israel must heed,[70] offers no ultimate certainties. No one better expresses the limitations of the promises to an exiled Israel that the Deuteronomic voice makes through its history than the servant of Saul, who defined the limits of what Israel can expect from any of its seers or prophets: "Perhaps [this man of God] can tell us about the journey on which we have set out" (9:6).

This hesitant "perhaps" turns out to be doubly significant: it both foreshadows the human freedom whereby Samuel will ignore his prophetic responsibilities in instructing the people in "the good and right way" as well as recognizes the LORD's freedom to carry out his own mysterious ways. Thus the Deuteronomist offers no absolute certainties concerning the path that leads away from exile toward a regaining of the land; otherwise the author would be denying to the LORD the very freedom of action that merely human characters are shown to possess.[71] Any greater claim would also exceed the powers of the prophet who, like his counterpart, the biblical narrator, is only the shaper of plot. Whatever one may say about the genius of the Deuteronomist's human characterizations, the LORD will remain, for author and reader alike, ever mysterious.

Four

SAUL AMONG THE BAGGAGE
(13:1–15:35)

So they inquired again of the LORD . . . and the LORD said, "Behold [Saul] has hidden himself among the baggage." (1 Samuel 10)

Cheer up, the worst is yet to come. (Philander Chase Johnson, *Shooting Stars*)

Some scholars marvel at, and puzzle over, the origin of the theological revolution apparent in Israel's monotheistic beliefs within a thoroughly polytheistic environment. Yet there is another revolution, an epistemological revolution, to use Sternberg's apt phrase, represented by the emergence upon the world scene of a kind of narrative that is unprecedented in its artistic and ideological scope. The "sudden" appearance in Israel of such narrative art is as marvelously mysterious and uncanny as the monotheism that infuses the emergent's every page.[1] Rather than immediately giving this novelty a name—like "epic," "fiction," "historiography," or the like—I will conclude this chapter with a description of some basic generic features illustrated by the text.

Broken Appointments (13:1–15)

In spite of some problematic details that defy clear-cut solution—the obviously corrupt opening verse in which numbers relating to Saul's age when he began to rule and to the length of his reign are missing,[2] the town of Jonathan's initial hostile act (Gibeah or Geba),[3] and the precise object of his attack, a Philistine "garrison" or "prefect,"[4]—the main lines of the story are clear. The account of a military confrontation between Israel and Philistia at Michmash Pass (13:15–14:23) is preceded by an ideological confrontation between Samuel and Saul at Gilgal.[5] Samuel had said that Saul was to precede him at Gilgal and to wait there seven days until the prophet came to sacrifice and show him what to do (10:8).[6] But after waiting seven days at Gilgal, Saul himself sacrifices. When Samuel finally appears, it is to make a fateful announcement that is the first direct statement in the story concerning Saul's kingship: it will not endure (v. 13). The rest of the book is a detailed account of Saul's troubled reign until his death in chapter 31.

There is a serious yet wordplayful tone to the narrator's voice as it begins to describe how the reins of Saul's rule start to unravel. Terror of the Philistines encamped in Michmash is so great that those Israelites not succeeding in hiding themselves in caves, holes, rocks, tombs, or cisterns cross the Jordan into Gad and Gilead: Hebrews "cross over" (*ʿibrîm ʿābᵉrû*, v. 7) but in the wrong direction! As many passages in the history indicate, but never so clearly as Joshua 3:1–5:1, "crossing the Jordan" carries with it heavy ritualistic and ideological baggage relating to God's gift of the land to Israel.[7] The contrast between those fleeing "Hebrews" and the few Israelites who tremble after Saul into Gilgal (v. 7) is noteworthy.

But the narrator's central wordplay in this section involves "keeping the commandment of the LORD" (*šāmar miṣwat YHWH*) in Samuel's announcement to Saul:

> You have acted foolishly; *would (lû') that you had kept the commandment of the LORD*. For then (*kî ʿattāh*) the LORD would have established your kingship over Israel forever. But now your kingship shall not be established. (Vv. 13–14)[8]

It is noteworthy that YHWH so far in the story has not been quoted making a promise of an everlasting kingship to Saul's house; the assertion of an everlasting kingship based upon Saul's obedience is made by Samuel alone. As for limitations on royalty, as we saw earlier, the monarchic false start embodied in Saul's kingship—it will not stand—was one of the matters foreshadowed by Elkanah's foreboding words concerning the weaning delay in presenting the "royal" infant Samuel to the LORD: "Do what seems best to you [O Hannah-Israel], only may the LORD establish his word" (1:23).

The immediate emphasis, however, in Samuel's words is on a broken appointment.[9] The logical progression of the paronomasia centers on the semantic range of *ṣiwwāh*, which extends from "to command someone or something" to "appoint someone or something." Samuel's accusation is that, since Saul did not observe the prophet's *appointment* (that is, waiting the appointed time of seven days), this failure is equivalent to not observing God's *commandment* and will result, there-fore, in God not continuing to observe his *appointment* of Saul as *nāgîd* over Israel. The intended logic of the wordplay is clear from the very choice of the word signifying Saul's failed observance, *miṣwāh* (com-mandment/appointment), rather than any of the other equally frequent or likely words Samuel could have been quoted speaking here, such as *mišpaṭ, ḥoq, ʿēdût*, and so forth.[10]

It is clear, therefore, that this initial confrontation between Samuel and Saul prepares the way for much that follows in the book concerning God's rejection of Saul in favor of David.[11] This is nowhere more clearly seen than in the precise words the narrator puts into Samuel's mouth concerning the coming transfer of power: "The LORD has sought out a man of his own choosing [in McCarter's translation]; *and the LORD has appointed him to be prince over his people*" (v. 14). To be sure, Samuel's ignorance about the successor's identity, a characteristic blindness apparent in the groping manner in which he will finally single out David in chapter 16, is as profound at this point as that of characters and readers alike. Nevertheless, it is a playfully omniscient narrator who puts such words of rebuke on the unknowing Samuel's lips in anticipation of the later rebuke of a naked David to Saul's own daughter: "'It was before the LORD, who chose me above your father, and above all his house, *to appoint me as prince over Israel, the people of the LORD.*' . . . But Michal, the daughter of Saul, had no child to the day of her death" (2 Sam. 6:21, 23).

Nothing is more obvious than our story's highlighting of Saul as a royal culprit. Much that we have encountered so far has prepared us for the present scene. After the story of the lustfully impatient men of Gibeah in Judges 19–20 who violently abuse a Levite's concubine, should we expect anything less from this man of Gibeah who impatiently takes matters into his own hands and offers up a sacrifice presumably belonging to a priestly Samuel? Then the Levite's outrageous act of dismembering his concubine—whether she was dead or alive, the reader could not tell—was later followed by Saul's own dismembering of his yoke of oxen in defense of his town's old allies from Jabesh-Gilead (chap. 11). As we have also seen, an aura of dubiety surrounds Saul from the beginning. The questions that have continually surrounded him or issued from his mouth up to now have set us up for the doubtful situation in which he finds himself—what to do now that Samuel has not come at the appointed time and the Philistines are pressing in upon him. Add to all this the loaded implications of Israel's only king ever to prophesy among the prophets or to be publicly chosen by lot like the guilty Achan before him and his "wayward" son, Jonathan, after him, and the first shoe of God's rejection of Saul does not drop unexpectedly.

All of which is true but only half the story.

The problem for many commentators with this chapter in Saul's career has not been its subject matter but its redundant character with respect to the "other" account of divine rejection in chapter 15. These two accounts of Saul's rejection are often taken as signs of redactional prodigality, so that scholars often fail to recognize the complex relationships of these passages to the larger story line. What emerges from any serious effort to contextualize these accounts, in search of and based upon evidence of artful composition, are deftly shaded characterizations serving sophisticated ideological perspectives and producing unsettling theological questions.

For example, the care with which the narrator paints the picture of a laudable and credible Saul, to be believed by character and reader alike, complicates and balances the obvious emphasis of the passage on the coming rejection of the king in favor of another.[12] A clear indication of the story's careful establishing of the veracity of Saul's defense of his actions to Samuel is the narrator's earlier description of the facts exactly as Saul will then recount them, except in reverse order:

NARRATOR	SAUL TO SAMUEL
And the Philistines mustered in Michmash. (V. 5)	"When I saw that . . . the people were scattering from me
But Samuel did not come to Gilgal and the people were scattering from [Saul]. (V. 8b)	and that you did not come at the appointed time and that the Philistines had mustered at Mishmash. (V. 11)

This double establishment of the antecedants of Saul's decision to sacrifice puts his action in a favorable light from the narrator's perspective. Unlike the situation in chapter 15, where disobedience to *God's* command will be precisely the issue, here the overwhelming military superiority of the Philistines, the terrified scattering of most Israelites in spite of Saul's call to arms, and the failure of Samuel to keep his word all conspire to magnify Saul rather than diminish him; with thirty thousand chariots, six thousand horsemen, and uncounted troops like sand on the shore, the Philistines instill such fear in Israel that an already minimal force of three thousand Israelites dwindles down to only six hundred men (v. 15). Nevertheless, while the majority of his people are in hiding or fleeing to Transjordan, a courageous Saul remains in Gilgal with a trembling few. In narrative contrast to his people's terror, Saul "pulled himself together" or "got control of himself" (*wa'et'appaq*, v. 12) and entreated the favor of the LORD by offering sacrifice in Samuel's absence. It is not difficult to see Samuel's subsequent accusation of the king as a trumped-up charge to keep Saul on the defensive and under his prophetic control. That Saul has no response for Samuel in verse 14 is indicative of the prophet's domination of him.

The issue here is the narrator's focusing as much upon Samuel's failures as prophet as upon Saul's failures as king. No matter, then, that Samuel's words foreshadow God's in chapter 15 and David's in 2 Samuel 6; the story all along has been leading in this direction. Saul's ultimate rejection by God is already well established, if only by means of the aura of doubt and suspicion with which a prophetic narrator has so far surrounded him. It is rather the narrator's abiding characterization of Samuel as a prophet whose continual lack of insight in the midst of his repeatedly self-serving actions that has largely eluded commentators, ancient and modern alike.

The sight/insight metaphors in chapter 3 introduced us to a budding prophet whose repeated failure to recognize the LORD's word was an apt beginning to Samuel's career as the narrator would describe it. The LORD has to point out to Samuel in a step-by-step fashion who his designate is (9:16–17), and even so late as the events of chapter 16 God will have to chide Samuel for (still) looking upon "outward appearance" (16:7) in his search for Saul's successor. Coupled with the prophetic blindness with which the narrator hampers Samuel is the prophet's continual obduracy in carrying out the LORD's will. When commanded by God three times to give the people a king, Samuel sent them home (9:22). When the people had recognized their treachery in asking for a king and finally wanted to repent by executing those in their midst most responsible for this sin, Samuel persuaded them rather to renew the kingdom at Gilgal (11:14). We see Samuel acting in the self-serving belief that a subservient king is better for him than a judicial peer. All along the way Samuel has taken every opportunity to gain the upper hand over the rival whom God had forced upon him; he managed double control over Saul by persuading the timid man to experience the heady power of prophecy (10:6). Samuel's own displays of prophetic power were meant to instill awe of himself as well as of God in both Saul (chap. 10) and the people (12:18). All the while he was publicly proclaiming the people's sin in requesting a king, he was secretly conspiring to maintain kingship in such a way that it would be as much as possible under his control. Having played upon the people's guilt in chapter 12, he now focuses upon instilling guilt in Saul in chapter 13. If there must be kingship—the LORD had commanded it—then Samuel will appropriate it for his own purposes. Once having bent Saul to his own will, Samuel will endeavor to keep him there.[13]

The prior words of Moses himself put the Deuteronomist's two-edged account of a failed appointment in perspective: "When a prophet speaks in the name of the LORD, if the word does not come to pass or come true (*lo' yābô'*), that is a word which the LORD has not spoken; the prophet has spoken it presumptuously, you need not be afraid of him" (Deut. 18:22). Samuel's delay in coming at the appointed time ("And Samuel *did not come* (*w^elo' bā'*)," 13:8; " 'You *did not come* according to the stipulated time,' " 13:11) and Saul's not waiting for him as Samuel had predicted (" 'You shall wait *until I come* to you,' " 10:8) mean that Samuel's prophetic word *did not come to pass* (*lo' bā'*) in this instance.

Verses 1–15 of chapter 13 are thus about Samuel's present failure as prophet as well as Saul's future failures as king. The "missed appointment," after all, is as much Samuel's as Saul's. This basic fact allows us to see how once again the author can turn the condemnatory words of Samuel against the prophet himself, so that some of Samuel's and the narrator's words turn out to be *hybrid constructions* in which the author puts Samuel's prophetic career in an unflattering light.

In contrast to the manner discussed above, in which the narrator's previous words establish the veracity of Saul's explanation in verses 11–12 (double-voiced words reinforcing each other), there are other double-voiced constructions here where speech interference is the result: the author's accents conflict with Samuel's.

When Samuel, for example, makes Saul's broken appointment equivalent to not observing God's commandment ("You have not kept the *commandment/appointment* of the LORD," v. 13) and thus punishable by God's not allowing Saul's royal appointment to stand ("The LORD *has appointed* [another] to be prince over his people," v. 14), the logical sequence works just as well against Samuel himself. Since it was Samuel who in fact missed the prophetic appointment that he foretold in chapter 10, these words of his come across as directed by an ironic author against the prophet himself, even as the prophet directs them against the king. Since the narrator has taken care to illustrate in manifold ways how Samuel had abused his prophetic office for the sake of personal control over king and people, *and thereby made Saul's kingship his own*, this kingship of his, that is, the one unduly appropriated by Samuel, will not stand; the LORD will seek out another, of his own prior choosing rather than Samuel's subsequent one. That is to say, if God chose Saul against Samuel's will, he will soon reject Saul against Samuel's will. In chapter 16 God will characterize Samuel as looking on outward appearances, whereas he, God, "looks on the heart" (16:7); here in chapter 13 someone is foretold as the man according to God's heart (13:14), in contrast to Saul, the author implies, who is according to *Samuel's* heart.

As if to accent Samuel's utter domination of Saul, Samuel's words, "Your kingdom *shall not stand* . . ." (v. 14), are followed not by any response or objection on Saul's part, but by the narrator's words about Samuel, "And Samuel *stood* . . ." (v. 15). Then, to reinforce the guilt by association that will dog both their lives to the end, the narrator continues, "And [Samuel] went up from Gilgal to Gibeah of Benjamin" (v. 15): the character zone of the self-serving prophet is once again joined to that of the failed king. Having Saul completely under his thumb, Samuel travels to the city of sin that from the beginning has stood for Saul's tragic reign.[14] Why else does the narrator have Samuel go up to Gibeah?

The Journey from Gilgal to Gilgal (13:15–14:52)

The literary crafting of the story about the battle of Michmash Pass (13:15–14:23) is extraordinary. The way in which this account is contextualized can provide a number of beginning illustrations of a new narrative genre being born, as it were, before our eyes.[15] Almost any section of the History offers us similar material, as our readings of previous sections have tried to show. Nevertheless, because these aspects of Israelite narrative have a profound literary-historical impact on matters of genre and ideology, it may be useful at the end of this chapter for the reader to compare the literary-historical implications of our reading with those of other readings based upon traditional redactional models, be they "authorial" like Noth's or editorial like most others. What emerges from almost all these source-oriented readings is the picture of a genre that involves nothing more than a crude amalgam of traditions sewn together in a basically external fashion by summarizing and connective speeches. In spite of claims by some source-oriented scholars concerning the Deuteronomist's historiographic genius,[16] the literary product *they* describe hardly deserves the encomia they lavish upon it. Scholars rarely recognize what is innovative and important about the novel narrative of the Deuteronomic History as a whole, about that space where genre, ideology, and art intersect to reinforce one another.

The high degree of stylized language throughout the accounts of the battle of Michmash Pass (13:15–14:23), Saul's laying of an oath upon the people (14:24–35), and the seizing of Jonathan by lot (14:36–46) are clear indicators that numerous esthetic features found throughout the chapter work together to integrate it internally and contextualize it externally.[17]

The Battle of Michmash Pass (13:15–14:23)

Scholars have commented on the historiographic aura of factuality that surrounds the story of Michmash Pass,[18] but few have recognized the highly esthetic manner in which all this "factual detail" is structured. The result of such structuring is an account in which a number of authorial positions are ritually thematized even as the discourse itself is artistically stylized.[19] After the narrator's technological and strategic exposition in 13:15–22, the battle account itself begins and ends using key words that provide a helpful introduction to the story's main ideological concerns: in geographic terms, the battle takes place at Michmash "Pass" (*maʿᵃbar*, 13:23), only to "pass over" (*ʿābᵉrāh*) into Beth-aven (14:23). Between these two verses, some form of the root *ʿābar*, "to cross over," is found on the lips of the narrator, Jonathan, and the Philistines:

"Come let us *pass over* on yonder side (*mēᵉ̆ēber*)." (14:1)
Between *the passes* where Jonathan sought *to pass over*. (V. 4)
"Come let us *pass over*." (V. 6)
"Behold, we will *pass over*." (V. 8)
And the Philistines said, "Look, *Hebrews* (*ᶜibrîm*)." (V. 11)
As for the *Hebrews* who had been with the Philistines. . . . (v. 21)

The highly stylized language here in chapters 13 and 14 is reminiscent of Joshua 3:1–5:1, which served similar ideological perspectives: the essence of a "Hebrew" is one who "crosses over." Only here the ritual whereby Jonathan and his companion are enabled to cross over to the Philistine side of the pass—thereby to initiate the Hebrews' victory—connects up through a number of interlocking devices with the ritual later in the chapter whereby Saul seizes Jonathan by lot in the face of Yahweh's refusal to answer.[20] All this will go to show how the chapter's frequent display of "factuality" conceals much narrative artificiality: artifice using "fact" to represent a particular view of the world, artistry and "history" working together to serve ideology.

The most obvious connection between the battle account in verses 1–23 and the lot account in verses 36–46 is the repetition of the first account's key word in the second. Whereas the history's two previous reports of seizing a culprit by lot (Josh. 7 [Achan] and 1 Sam. 10 [Saul]) describe a similar ritual, only here in 1 Samuel 14 is there a selection whereby one group, all Israel, is put "on one side (*lᵉᶜēber*)" and another group, Jonathan and Saul, is put "on the other side" (v. 40). Clearly, the taking of sides is a central ritualistic and stylistic feature uniting the two stories that begin and end chapter 14. In the first story Jonathan and his companion are on one side, the uncircumcised Philistines on the other; in the second story, first the leaders of the people (v. 38) are on one side and Saul and Jonathan on the other, then when the people "escape" (v. 41) the issue turns on Saul and Jonathan being on opposite sides, with Jonathan eventually being taken (v. 42).

Second, both accounts revolve around contrasting rituals of divine inquiry. Jonathan employs his ritual in hopes of concluding, "We will *go up*; for the LORD has given [the Philistines] into our hand" (v. 10); Saul inquires of God, "Shall I *go down* after the Philistines? Wilt thou give them into the hand of Israel?" (v. 37). In Jonathan's case, his diffident "perhaps" (v. 6) results in God giving the required sign (v. 10), but in Saul's the certainty hoped for by inquiring of God is frustrated by God's refusal to answer (v. 37), which then explains Saul's move to find an answer by lot. Saul's rituals are sacral affairs seeking certainty from God either by official priestly inquiry or by a priestly casting of the Urim and Thummim. On the other hand, Jonathan's ritual is a less confident, more secularized affair, which recognizes and embraces uncertainty from the start; Jonathan's "sign to us" from God is not to be coerced but only hoped for. Saul forces an answer by lot when none is initially given through sacred inquiry; Jonathan's procedure is less dogmatic: he prefaces it with a "perhaps," will not act without a sign, and understands from the start that it may not be given (" 'If they say to us, "Wait until we come to you," ' then we will stand still in our place, and we will not go up to them,' " v. 9).

The circumstances surrounding each ritual reinforce the secular/sacral contrast between them. Jonathan is accompanied by a lad, his armor bearer (*nosē', kēlayw,* v. 1), whereas Saul's constant companion is Ahijah, who bears the ephod containing the sacred lots (*nosē' 'ēpôd,* v. 3).[21] Jonathan's initiative is actively military and issues in success; Saul's is motivated by sacred ritual, which explains his lack of military initiative against the Philistines in this chapter. Saul wants to go down against the Philistines to despoil them but is inhibited by God's failure to respond; all his lot casting accomplishes is his ceasing to pursue his enemy (v. 46). Moreover, when Saul's troops do participate in this chapter's routs of the Philistines, they do so only after Saul has interrupted the priestly casting of lots: "And Saul said to the priest, 'Withdraw your hand' " (v. 19). Clearly, successful military action against the Philistines "on that day"[22] results from Jonathan's desacralized ritual resulting in a "sign" rather than Saul's "sacred" procedures resulting, as we shall see, in a travesty of one.

The different voices that respond or not to Jonathan's and Saul's proposed courses of action also reinforce the ideological emphasis of this chapter on Jonathan's initiative in contrast to Saul's passivity.[23] The narrator has both the Philistines (v. 12) and Israelites (v. 28) "answer" Jonathan but then tells us that "[God] did not answer [Saul] that day" (v. 37) and that "there was not a man among all the people that answered [Saul]" (v. 39). Of course, many dialogues take place between Jonathan and his companions on one hand and between Saul and his on the other in this chapter, but even in these cases the ideological balance is tipped in Jonathan's favor. As if to foreshadow God's coming lesson to Samuel—"for the LORD sees not as man sees; man looks on outward appearance but the LORD looks on the heart" (16:7)—the narrator has Jonathan's armor bearer speak with clearly divine accents in approval of Jonathan's proposed course of action, whereas Saul's interlocutors, divine and human, either do not respond or, when they do, approve in merely human fashion:

JONATHAN'S ARMOR BEARER: "Do all that is *in your heart;*
                            turn, behold I am with you
                            according to your heart." (V. 7)

SAUL'S PEOPLE: "Do whatever is good *in your
                            eyes.*" (V. 36)
                            "Do what is good *to your eyes.*"
                            (V. 40)

The people respond to Saul's proposals as humans typically do, by appearance only; Jonathan's armor bearer sounds very much like the LORD, who looks upon the heart.

Such textual features help us see how the opening battle account begins with a "demythologized" ritual of divine inquiry, one whose stylized details clearly contrast with their stylized counterparts in the sacral lottery account later in the chapter. One process of divine inquiry, Jonathan's, is placed in a positive light; another process, Saul's, is full of shadows. What precisely the Deuteronomist is for or against, as symbolized by these opening and closing rituals, needs now to be specified in greater detail: the story of Saul's oath upon the people forms the connecting link between the stories of Michmash pass and the lottery and provides background for both.

Saul's Oath upon the People (14:24–35)

Everything about the oath story serves to discredit Saul's growing obsession with ritualistic insurance against possible defeat. If his son had once before taken the initiative against the Philistines (13:3), at least there Saul responded with his own initiative. Yet even then Saul's concerns were centered on ritual once Samuel's delay had provoked further disarray among Saul's small band of followers. But here in chapter 14 a pall of passivity has settled upon Saul's band of six hundred men. Present with Saul is the ark of God—surprisingly enough with Ahijah, the Elide priest, in place of Samuel. Only when Saul manages to interrupt the priestly ritual of casting lots (v. 19) do his troops participate in the rout of the Philistines begun by Jonathan. Once the battle passes on to Beth-aven (v. 23), the narrator reveals that Saul had forbidden Israel food that day "until evening and I am avenged on my enemies" (v. 24). This oath fills Saul's character zone with that excessive concern over ensuring the success of one's efforts already dealt with in detail by the Deuteronomist in the negative depictions of judges like Gideon and Jephthah; it reminds us as well of Samson's abiding concerns about personal vengeance upon his enemies.[24] Saul's oath also brings to mind the vow Hannah made in chapter 1, its *do ut des* perspective contrasting with the more magnanimous characterization of Elkanah. All in all, this combination of sacral factors surrounding Saul—emphasis on the presence of the ark and an ephod-bearing priest, the psychological and religious need for an oath to insure victory and vengeance, formal divine inquiry to predict it, and finally the lottery as a backup for a failed inquiry—now puts a negative cast upon Saul's impatient sacrificial act in chapter 13 and deepens the significance of God's rejection of him in chapter 15. We begin to see that something in Saul's character is inclining him toward usages of Yahwistic ritual that border on sorcery and divination.

The narrator's account of Saul's oath forbidding the people to eat until evening makes all this eminently clear—except for the tendency of commentators to misread it. For example, scholars usually understand Jonathan's statement in verse 30 as claiming that the slaughter of the Philistines had not in fact been as great as it might have been. Yet how this interpretation makes sense, given the definite statements of the narrator at the beginning and end of the oath account that the salvation and slaughter had indeed been significant (vv. 23, 31), is itself beyond understanding were it not for the redactional models of most commentators that allow such readings.

What if the narrative *does* portray agreement between the narrator and Jonathan concerning the great slaughter wrought by the LORD upon the Philistines? A coherent picture then emerges, provided one deals accurately with two significant features of the story: the contrary-to-fact meaning of Jonathan's reference to the people's eating of the spoil (v. 30) and the timing of the narrator's account of the people's swooping upon (?) and eating of the spoil (v. 32).

The sequence of events leading up to Jonathan's statement in verses 29–30 is straightforward: first the battle of Michmash Pass and its expansion into Beth-aven up through verse 23, then the narrator's introduction of Saul's oath in verse 24, and then the incidents in the forest when Jonathan unknowingly eats a small bit of honey while the people remain fasting. The situation seems clear: the slaughter of Philistines has been great and no one eats until Jonathan does in verse 27. Then Jonathan, informed of his father's oath, criticizes it in verse 29 and states, "Furthermore (*'ap kî*), if the people really had eaten (*lû' 'ākol 'ākal*) from the plunder of their enemies which they found [implied: but they didn't eat] then indeed (*kî 'attāh*) the slaughter among the Philistines would not have been great (*lo' rab'tāh*) [implied: but it was great]" (v. 30). Both the narrator's own words before and after (vv. 23, 31), as well as the syntax of Jonathan's statement itself, support the contrary-to-fact sense of Jonathan's words. Consider Samuel's previous words to Saul, in which we find a similar contrary-to-fact construction: "If you had kept (*lû šāmartā*) the commandment of the LORD your God [implied: but you did not] . . . , then indeed (*kî 'attāh*) the LORD would have established your kingdom forever [implied: but he has not!]" (13:13). In each statement, both the context and the syntax support the sense of what might have been.

Once Jonathan has his say in verses 29–30, the narrator resumes describing the battle; fighting extends even to Aijalon (v. 31) some fifteen miles from Bethel. But now the people's fasting proves too much for them. Whereas they were faint in verse 28, they now are "very faint" in verse 31 and succumb to their hunger: "The people flew upon (?) the spoil . . . and ate [them] with the blood" (v. 32). When precisely do the people begin to eat? Commentators usually place the people's "break-fast" at night, despite the narrative's mention of night only following the eating in verse 32 and the rolling of the great stone in preparation for the ritual slaughter that takes place "that night" in verse 34. After all this, Saul then proposes to despoil the Philistines "by night until the morning light" (v. 36).

The narrative's chronological contrasts are clear in their ideological implications: Israel's victory at Michmash Pass takes place by day against the backdrop of Jonathan's deritualized inquiry (vv. 8–12) and the interruption of Saul's sacral one (v. 19); their defeat of the Philistines even to Aijalon takes place "that day" (v. 31), during which they break their fast and Saul's oath. But victory attends them nonetheless, so that Jonathan's small infraction and the people's great one (itself magnified even further by their blood sin) serve to highlight the uncanny "prediction" of Jonathan earlier, in a statement that puts human concerns about oaths and ritual slaughter in the proper perspective of the LORD's ultimate freedom of action: "Perhaps the LORD will work for us; for nothing can hinder the LORD from saving in matters great or small" (14:6). Whether the slaughter (of Philistines or their animals) be of many or few, ritually pure or no, whether the eating be great (like that of the people with their spoil) or small (like that of Jonathan with his honey), Jonathan's "perhaps" puts all human ritual certainties, as well as God's ultimate freedom to act or not, in proper perspective. Even the statement of this section's "hero" in verse 30, "Then indeed the slaughter among the Philistines would not have been great," by so limiting God's freedom, is filled with the interfering voice of the Deuteronomist. Oath or not, God will not be penned in by human beliefs: the victory remains great even in the midst of the people's serious breaking of Saul's oath.

On the other hand, Saul's ritualistic actions in this chapter take place mostly at night, be they the proper ritual slaughter of Philistine spoil (v. 34), Saul's proposal to despoil the Philistines "by night until dawn" (v. 36), or, perhaps, even the abortive divine inquiry and subsequent lottery.[25] It is according to this day/night contrast that the ideological functions of the seizing of Jonathan can be properly illuminated.

The Seizing of Jonathan (14:36–46)

Saul's unsuccessful inquiry of God and the subsequent seizing of Jonathan by lot recall that earlier inquiry of God that itself followed the seizing of Saul by lot (10:20–24). At that time, in contrast to now, God did answer the people of Israel by offering them and the reader an image of Saul that may very well turn out to be the hallmark of his abortive reign: "Behold, he has hidden himself among the baggage" (10:22). Enigmatic at the time, to say the very least, the picture was nonetheless striking and memorable, especially when juxtaposed with the narrator's immediate description of Saul's majestic height in 10:23 and Samuel's accolade about his singularity: "There is none like him among all the people!" (10:24). Who is this man of contradiction, timid yet tall, filled at times with divine (chap. 11) and human (chap. 13) initiative, yet sometimes strangely passive and hesitant (chap. 14)? The account of the seizing of Jonathan provides us not only with a unifying vision of all that precedes it, but sets the stage for the rejection of Saul in chapter 15.

Fear made the Israelites hide themselves "in caves and in holes and in rocks and in tombs and in cisterns" (13:6); fear of failure and defeat makes Saul also hide himself among the baggage of rite, inquiry, and oath, the implements or appliances of sacred ritual. Saul's ritual dismemberment of his yoke of oxen in chapter 11, his characteristically impatient sacrifice of the burnt offerings in chapter 13, his calling for the ark of God and the priest of Shiloh with the sacred lots, and, finally, the formal divine inquiries that surround his character zone and even play upon his very name (*šā'ûl šā'al*)—under all this baggage does the narrator show us Saul progressively, almost obsessively, hiding himself.[26]

Saul's son, on the other hand, provides a counterpoint to his father's acts of ritual concealment: Jonathan begins his attack at Michmash Pass by revealing himself: "The Philistines said, 'Look, Hebrews are coming out of the holes where they have hid themselves'" (14:11). Characteristic of Jonathan and his companion, therefore, is their revealing of themselves (*wayyiggālu*, v. 11) by leaving the rocks; typical of Saul, however, is his command to have the people roll (*gollû*) a sacrificial rock toward him (v. 33). Jonathan reveals himself in order to fight by day; Saul hides among the implements of ritual in order to fight by night (v. 36). Jonathan's companion looks to what is in the heart (v. 7); Saul's entourage only to what is apparent to the eyes (vv. 36, 40). People, both Israelite and Philistine, "answer" Jonathan (vv. 12, 28); neither God nor human "answers" Saul (vv. 37, 39).

It is in light of these contrasting characterizations and of the people's breaking of their fast and Saul's oath in verse 32 that the seizing of Jonathan in verses 36–46 is to be understood. Not only do God and human not answer Saul, Saul's ritualistic casting of lots twice seizes the wrong side: if the "sin" (v. 38) concerns who broke the fast, then the people should have been taken rather than the other side, the "many or much" rather than the "few or little." Moreover, if the choice has to be between Saul and Jonathan, then everything in the story up to now has conspired against Saul.

It seems, therefore, that Saul's use of the sacred lots results in the least guilty of all sides having been taken (Jonathan) and the more guilty among them having escaped (Saul and the people). Nevertheless, Saul now characteristically utters another oath (that Jonathan surely die) and only the people's intervention saves Jonathan's life (vv. 44–45).[27]

This theme of the king's disposition to punish or not runs through the stories of Saul like a dark thread and will touch upon God's definitive rejection of Saul in chapter 15. What is already clear is that Saul more than once allows those who are portrayed as deserving of death to escape punishment. During the people's attempt in chapter 11 to repent of kingship by wanting to kill those most responsible for promoting it, Saul intervened, and with Samuel's help the kingdom was renewed (11:13–14). Here in chapter 14, it is Saul again who by vowing to execute his own son instead of the people cursed by his oath averts punishment from those he knows to be most guilty.

But the narrative also provides an added twist: if Saul intervened to save the king's people in chapter 11, the people now intervene to save the king's son in chapter 14. In both cases deliverance of Israel is proposed as the mitigating factor. Whether characters attribute that deliverance directly to God, as Saul states (11:13) or to humans, as the people state (14:45), the Deuteronomist's abiding message is that there is no simple formula for salvation or disaster. Jonathan's words in 14:6 best express the author's ideological perspective: from God's side, nothing—few or many, big or small—can hinder salvation if the LORD so choose; from the human side, the operative word remains *perhaps*. For a Hebrew, to cross the line, as Saul is shown doing, is to enter the Philistine territory of sorcery and divination.

In the midst of all these problems surrounding Saul, the narrator is careful to describe Saul's military consolidation of his kingship in 14:47–52.[28]

Surely the Bitterness of Death Has Passed (15:1–35)

The ability of the Deuteronomist to capture the essence of the story in a single image is extraordinary. The long and complicated account of kingship in Israel began with an intricate parable that spanned the first seven chapters of 1 Samuel. Everything in this introduction found its focus in the diamond-hard description of the royal Eli, grown old and heavy, falling backward off his throne to die of a broken neck. Thus did the Deuteronomist epitomize the introductory parable of Israel's disastrous romance with kingship. In a similar manner and with the same hard-edged strokes, the author now captures the heart of the story of Saul in the figure of the captured Agag who (cheerfully?) comes before Samuel with hopeful feelings of deliverence. "Surely the bitterness of death has passed," Agag says to himself an instant before he is hacked to pieces by Samuel.[29] Agag's pregnant statement colors what Saul, Samuel, and Israel do and say here, just as the abiding grief of Samuel over Saul's rejection by God casts a somber shadow upon the entire chapter.[30]

The Ambiguity of Repentance

The word *repentance* wonderfully captures the central concerns of this chapter. In its power to express either a contrite change of heart or a definite change of mind, *repentance* provides the reader with a focal point that integrates the perspectives of narrator and characters alike. What happens when God repents, when humans repent? And what is the exact relationship between divine and human repentance? This second account of God's rejection of Saul as king is a profound meditation on the human foolishness that believes humans can restrict divine freedom even in the context of human freedom. That is to say, much of the discourse of the narrator and characters in chapter 15 combines to shatter Agag's (and the reader's) feelings of certainty.

Take first the fundamental question of whether God can repent (*NHM* in the *nifal*). The reader knows for sure that God can and does repent, because the omniscient narrator begins the account of the confrontation between king and prophet with a direct reporting of God's words to this effect (v. 11) and ends it with the narrator's statement about God having changed his mind over Saul's kingship (v. 35). Between verses 11 and 35 Samuel's assertion that God, not being human, does *not* repent (v. 29, twice) is thus subjected to the critical evaluation of the narrator and shown to be off the mark.[31]

Matters are really more complicated than this: when one thinks further about how *repent* (*niham*) is used both inside and outside the History, its inherent ambiguity puts the reader in a precarious position. As Jeremiah 18:8–10 illustrates most pointedly, God's change of heart toward Israel may be from the imposition of good to that of evil, or vice versa. God's repentance, therefore, may mean either God's punishment or compassion, justice or mercy, depending upon the context. For example, God's "repentance" in Judges 2:18 signifies compassionate mercy toward Israel in the face of its enemy's onslaughts, whereas here in 15:1, 35 it stands for the opposite of God's merciful compassion toward Saul in the face of his repeated failures.

As for God, so for humanity. Israel's "repentance" toward Benjamin (Judg. 21:6, 15) brings to that tribe a merciful solution to a previous punishment; Israel's move with respect to Benjamin is from treating that tribe badly to treating it well. Conversely, Exodus 13:17 talks about the people "not repenting" of having left Egypt, that is, about their not changing their mind from viewing the exodus as good to seeing it as bad.

It is the antecedant situation, therefore, that helps to explain whether anyone's change of mind or heart is merciful or not, or strictly just or not, or anything else or not, vis-à-vis another person; conversely it is the context that determines whether one's *not* changing his or her mind translates, for example, into effective punishment or compassionate mercy with respect to someone else. When God (v. 11) and the narrator (v. 35) speak about God's repenting over Saul's kingship, they speak of a divine change of heart that moves judicially from Saul's weal to his woe; when Samuel, on the other hand, speaks about God as one who does not repent (v. 29), he professes a belief in a God who will not change his mind toward a merciful forgiving of Saul, that is, who will not change his mind about punishing Saul.

By focusing this account of Saul's rejection upon the central idea of repentance, the Deuteronomist invests the story with a maximum of clarity in asking profound ideological questions and a minimum of didacticism in answering them. Not only must we ask in what direction the divine change of heart may travel—from benevolence to malevolence or vice versa—we are bound also to inquire about the circumstances that will dispose the LORD to move in one direction or the other. This leads to a consideration of the play and place of human repentance with respect to its divine counterpart, and here again the story in chapter 15 employs an abundance of resources to deal with this question in a profound, if unsettling, manner.

Human repentance comes about through a recognition and proclamation of sinfulness. Thus we hear Saul's "I have sinned" (vv. 24, 30) and Israel's "we have sinned" (for example, 7:6; 12:10; 1 Kings 8:47). But what is the Deuteronomist's position concerning the connection between divine and human changes of heart? Is the human change of heart away from moral evil a necessary precondition or disposing element for God's repentance away from punishment toward merciful beneficence? Here, once again, the author of the History avoids simplistic formulations; throughout the entire book of Judges, but most succinctly in Judges 2, we find that God's merciful "change of heart" (2:18) away from punishing Israel for their idolatry is preceded by no mention of a corresponding repentance on Israel's part. Here in chapter 15, however, the opposite is the case: everything in the text leads toward a repentant Saul at odds with an unmerciful God, just as the book of Judges had contrarily depicted a predominantly merciful God at odds with a continually unrepentant Israel. Nor does the Deuteronomist avoid a third combination concerning divine and human repentance. In 2 Samuel 24 David repents of his sin of numbering the people: "I have sinned greatly in what I have done" (v. 10); God, for his part and after killing seventy thousand, finally comes upon Jerusalem and repents of the evil, saying, "it is enough" (v. 16). In short, there is no necessary correlation within the History between the experiencing (in contrast to the promising) of divine repentance as mercy and the human move toward repentance as precondition (or predisposing factor) for such mercy. Even though the telling of many authoritative characters in the

History, God included, appears to assert such a connection, the narrator's omniscient and constant showing of what happens in the course of Israel's history contradicts such assertions time and time again.

The relationship between divine and human repentance becomes even more complicated when we ask, in what precisely does Saul's sin consist in chapter 15? What is Saul repenting of? Clearly, Saul sinned by "sparing or having compassion on (*ḥml*)," those upon whom God forbade him to have compassion (vv. 3, 9, 15). Saul spared the sinful Agag and the choicest of his animals, but after he repents, God does not have compassion on or spare the sinful Saul. This connection between the people of Israel's obligation not to spare the guilty (*lo' ḥāmal, lo' ḥûs*) and their experiencing a merciful or compassionate LORD (*rāḥām*) finds its exemplary statement in Deuteronomy 13:17: "None of the devoted things shall cleave to your hand: that the LORD may turn from the fierceness of his anger, and show you mercy, and have compassion on you, and multiply you, as he swore to your fathers."

From first to last, therefore, the story in chapter 15 is about Saul's sin in sparing the guilty Agag and God's subsequent refusal to spare the guilty Saul. Nevertheless, the story is about much more. Between the limits of an (un)repentant God on one side and repentant Saul and Samuel on the other lies a world of difference.

The Errors of Contagious Repentance

Were we heuristically to imagine God's punishment like a kind of infectious disease he spreads among the sinful, we could then describe the ideological concerns of this chapter as revolving around whether human repentance acts like an antibiotic that tends to clear up such infection or an inoculation that forestalls future infection or, finally, a procedure that may in fact involve only the injection of a sterilized but inert substance. Human repentance so pervades this chapter that any apprehension of its powers as a cure-all for the ravages of divine wrath turns out to be the greater disease about which the Deuteronomist writes. The story in chapter 15, as elsewhere in the History, is about the salvaging of God's freedom in the light of human freedom.

The clearest penitent in the chapter is, of course, Saul himself. Not only does he finally repent of the sin of sparing those devoted to the LORD; his triple recognition that he had sinned (vv. 24, 25, 30) includes also a turning away from his attempted concealment of this sin from Samuel. At first he admits no guilt (v. 13). Then, prodded by Samuel, he admits to his part in sparing Agag's life but still dissociates himself from the people's sin in sparing the choicest animals (vv. 20–21). Finally, faced with Samuel's unequivocal condemnation in verses 22–23, he acknowledges his full complicity in the entire affair: his repeated "I have sinned" (vv. 24, 30) and "my sin" (v. 35) include a recognition of his sinful sparing of both Agag and the animals (as the narrator had described it in v. 9) and his subsequent repudiations of wrongdoing in verses 13 and 20. Saul is doubly repentant: of his sin and of his attempt to conceal that sin from Samuel.

So far we can hardly fault Saul for finally owning up to his faults. Nor can we condemn him for asking Samuel for divine forgiveness and mercy: "Now therefore, I pray, pardon my sin and return with me, that I may worship the LORD" (v. 25). The question Saul raises here is whether sincere repentance has some kind of compelling force to effect the LORD's turning from punishment to mercy. The dialogue between Samuel and Saul in verses 24–30 revolves around whether the LORD will repent of his repentance. That is to say, given that the LORD has changed his mind about Saul and has decided to move from weal to woe, a fact understood by both Samuel and Saul, will God in turn move from contemplated woe to effective weal with respect to Saul? Just as the prior dialogue between them (vv. 12–23) had Samuel successfully disposing Saul to move from concealing to recognizing his sin, so in the dialogue that ensues (vv. 24–30), Saul successfully disposes Samuel to work toward effecting God's repentance of divine repentance. In this case however, Saul's success in converting Samuel to his own point of view spells failure for both in converting God to theirs.

It is helpful to see precisely how the Deuteronomist centers this dialogue of Samuel and Saul upon their disagreement over whether human repentance from sin can or will effect God's repentance from punishment. The key word here is *šûb*, which is used in this chapter, as often elsewhere, to indicate either human repentance or the sin that precedes it. It is, therefore, an apt word to indicate the uncertain extremes of human moral destiny.

First God expresses Saul's sin as "he has turned back (*šāb*) from (following) me" (v. 11). Once Samuel has convinced Saul of this sin, Saul then asks Samuel to forgive him and "turn back with me" (v. 25). The penitent overtones of this request convey something like "accept my repentance" and easily follow upon Saul's request to Samuel to pardon his sin. The tendency of commentators to understand *šûb* here as only a local affair (but where are Samuel and Saul supposed to be returning *from?*) has caused many to ignore the penitential meaning of Saul's request. The absence of any clear indication of where Samuel and Saul are supposed to be, before their "turning back" in verse 31, inclines one to conclude that the geographic sense of *šûb*, if present at all, is only a vehicle for its primary meaning here of "to repent."

Notice how the Deuteronomist described the idealized account of Israel's "exilic" repentance in chapter 7: in response to Samuel's admonition, "If you are returning (*šābîm*) to the LORD with all your heart . . . " (v. 3), the people gather at Mizpah and confess, "We have sinned against the LORD" (v. 6). Similarly, when Solomon offers his prayer of dedication, he refers to Israel's future exilic situation as follows, "Yet if they repent (*wᵉšābû*) and make supplication to thee . . . saying, 'We have sinned . . . '" (1 Kings 8:47). In addition, the occurrence of *šûb* by itself and without the usual explicit complement indicating either from what (*min*) or to what (*lᵉ* and *'el*) is used within the History—as also outside it—to indicate either acts of sin (for example, Josh. 23:12; Judg. 2:17; 8:33) or acts of repentance from sin (for example, 1 Kings 8:48).

Once we understand that Saul's request to Samuel in verse 25 is to cooperate with his, Saul's, repentance in order to dispose God to repent yet once more and thus reinstate Saul's kingship, we begin to understand the verbal tug of war this request prompts. Samuel at first refuses to "return/repent" with Saul for, he believes, the cause is lost: the kingdom has already been given to one better than Saul (v. 28). Moreover, Samuel argues, "The Glory of Israel will not lie or repent; for he is not a man that he should repent" (v. 29).[32] Then, once again, Saul confesses his sin and invites Samuel to join him in making penitential supplication to the LORD for forgiveness and a merciful reinstatement of his kingship (v. 30). Thus twice importuned, Samuel finally accedes to Saul's pleading, and both "return/repent" so that Saul may prostrate himself before the LORD (v. 31).

What Saul has finally convinced Samuel of is the advisability here of hoping that sincere human repentance will bring about merciful divine repentance. Samuel's initial anger over God's repentance effecting a rejection of Saul has been transformed in this dialogue to hope for a further repentance of God that would effect a reinstatement of Saul as king.

True repentance, however, demands that Saul's failure to kill Agag be rectified. Whereas in chapter 12 Samuel had, for his own purposes, short-circuited the people's repentance over their sin of asking for themselves a king, that is to say, he did not demand that they put away the "guilty" king from among them, here it is in Samuel's best interest personally to dispatch the guilty king (Agag) from among the people, and thus complete Saul's repentance: so Samuel "hewed Agag in pieces before the LORD in Gilgal" (v. 33).

It is in the context of this shared hope that God would repent of the evil he had decreed for Saul that we see the full meaning of the encounter between Samuel and Agag. The irony that fills the words of the narrator quoting Agag ("And Agag came to him cheerfully [?]. Agag said, 'Surely the bitterness of death has passed,'" v. 32) is directed at Samuel and Saul as well as at Agag. Agag stands and falls for Samuel and Saul as surely as Eli sat and fell for all Israel's kings in chapter 4. Agag hopes until the very instant before he dies; Samuel hopefully grieves over Saul, that is to say, is not able to let go of him or accept his rejection by God, until the LORD in chapter 16 destroys all hope by sending him out to find and anoint David. As for Saul, like Agag, he hopes against hope, until the very obsession with divination that lost him the kingship in the first place forces him at last to face the truth of his rejection in the person of the woman of Endor (chap. 28).

This miniature account of Agag's final moments is shaped by the Deuteronomist's ironic message concerning misguided human views about God's mercy and compassion. Agag's execution allows the Deuteronomist to foreshadow the sorry fate of Saul and Samuel as the rest of the book will chronicle it. Agag's death signifies a lack of progeny. Samuel's words, "So shall your mother be childless among women" (v. 33), return us to the guiding metaphor of chapters 1–7 and represent the end of royal "progeny" for both Saul and Samuel: Saul's dynasty is finished before it begins; nor will David ever be swayed by Samuel as completely as Saul was.

Agag's "surely (*'ākēn*)," therefore, ties in not only with Saul's repentance but even with the very sin for which Saul is condemned. It is no accident that Saul's rebellion and stubborness are likened by Samuel to "the sin of divination" (v. 23). All along, we have seen the Deuteronomist emphasizing Saul's overdependence upon the certainties of ritual and the rituals of certainty. The "teraphim" (v. 23) will deceive Saul later (19:13, 15); and toward the end of Saul's life, after Samuel's death, divination will once more bring them together (chap. 28). Here, as throughout the book of Judges, the Deuteronomist denigrates humanity's unwarranted striving for certainty. As a dramatic symbol of Saul's miscalculating belief that human repentance will effect God's, Agag's "surely" has its counterpoint in the authorial accents we discovered earlier in the words of Saul's servant about the then unnamed prophet of chapter 9 ("*Perhaps* he can tell us about the journey on which we have set out," 9:6) and the "perhaps" of Saul's son in 14:6. For humans to expect more than a "perhaps" or to contrive to ensure more than God's freedom allows is a kind of divination that seeks to limit the freedom of God. The reader is not to demand more of the narrator than Samuel and Saul ought to demand of God: the Deuteronomist, as a prophet like Moses—but unlike Saul—is no sorcerer.

The Neglected Sins of Samuel

"The people" of chapter 15 are the neglected sinners of the story. Because the author's focus is on God, Samuel, and Saul, the people are hardly present for the narrator: they steal the booty like Saul does, but punishment for their sin never becomes an issue here. If the narrator of chapter 15 ignores the people's sins, most commentators have neglected Samuel's. From the beginning, the portrait of Samuel painted by the Deuteronomist has not been a flattering one. Consider now how the negatively charged character zone of Samuel continues on into chapter 15.

One esthetic indicator that Samuel remains negatively associated with the failed king is the continual placing of "the night" as an element within the prophet's character zone, just as it was within the king's in chapter 14. There, Jonathan's military successes by day were contrasted with Saul's ritual excesses by night (14:34, 36); here in chapter 15, "Samuel was angry and he cried to the LORD *all night*" (v. 11) concerning Saul's rejection. Then Samuel confronts Saul with the words "Stop! I will tell you what the LORD said to me *this night*" (v. 16). The darkness of God's displeasure envelops both Saul and Samuel, binding them together. We recall that the first revelation of God to Samuel takes place at night (chap. 3), nor should we be surprised that our last revelation of Samuel will take place "by night" through the medium of Endor, at Saul's command (28:8, 20, 25).

Samuel's angry crying to the LORD when told of Saul's rejection (15:11) also continues the obstructive characterization of Samuel we have been taking care to emphasize. God is shown working not only through Samuel but often around him. An essential part of the drama of the prophet's career lies in the suspense built up by the narrator over Samuel's repeated delaying tactics: the reader keeps wondering how God will achieve his purposes, given the human freedom he allows his prophet. One of the effects of the story is to see how divine omnipotence manipulates human weakness without destroying human freedom. Even when we see Samuel reluctantly confronting Saul with the unpalatable fact of God's rejection of the king (vv. 12–23), we are immediately given an inside view of Samuel's skewed motivation in conveying God's message to Saul: if Samuel knows for a fact that God can repent in the interests of justice, nevertheless the prophet is made to profess a belief that God therefore will *not* repent in the direction of mercy: "For [the Glory of Israel] is not a man, that he should repent" (v. 29). The irony of the second part of the dialogue between Samuel and Saul (vv. 24–31) is that Saul rightfully convinces the prophet that Samuel's belief is erroneous, just before the climax of the story indicates that a merciful God is not constrained to be so in every case. The destiny of Saul—like that of Josiah and Israel after him—shows how human repentance, however good and necessary, does not limit God's freedom to act, however mysteriously, in ways that do not correspond to human understandings of mercy.

Samuel, both before and after his change of heart on this point, is shown to be—like his mother before him—the author's spokesperson for the errors of authoritarian dogmatism. To believe that God *will* accomplish humanity's idea of mercy is, in this instance at least, as mistaken a position as to believe that God *must* punish according to human views of strict justice.[33] A dramatic irony of chapter 15 consists of

Saul convincing Samuel to go from an error of principle to an error of fact; as it turns out, God can be merciful, but in this case will not be so. It is thus doubly ironic that the prophet of God misjudges the future—once again. An authorial voice of critical traditionalism uses Saul to convict Samuel of the mistaken belief that God does not forgive, just as it convicts both Saul and Samuel of mistakenly believing that God will repent if only humans do so. The narrator uses these events at Gilgal to drive home the ideological position that even if humans repent, there is no assurance that God will; if God need not punish, neither does he need to show mercy.

We are thus led to see how the Deuteronomist in chapter 15 has succeeded in dramatizing the ambiguities of repentance, of changing one's mind or heart, not only with respect to God and Saul but even with respect to Samuel. If God repents and yet does not repent, if Saul repents yet may not remain king, so also Samuel repents yet remains under the author's evaluative cloud. Beneath the imploring words of Saul to Samuel, "Repent with me" (vv. 25, 30); of Samuel to Saul, "I will not repent with you" (v. 26); and of the narrator to the reader, "And so Samuel repented after Saul" (v. 31), we hear the interfering voice of the Deuteronomist as it continues its largely negative characterization of the prophet Samuel.

It is the prophet's duty to preach repentance and a bonus to his audience when he practices what he preaches; it is Samuel's lot to do both in chapter 15 and still fail. When Saul asks Samuel to "pardon (*sā' nā'*) my sin" (v. 25), the reader hears authorial accents about Samuel's role in Saul's sins: "Bear (*sā' nā'*) my sin," the Deuteronomist has Saul ask Samuel. Samuel and Saul are again inextricably bound together for failure in the story.[34] Between the two, the reader's sympathies probably lie more with Saul, who appears—so far at least—more sinned against than sinning, more manipulated than manipulating, with Samuel just the opposite. Nevertheless, over both tragic figures stretches the mysterious hand of God.

Genre and Literary History: An Illustration

It remains now to situate the above reflections within that larger literary-historical context alluded to at the beginning of the chapter.[35] My purpose is not to construct an absolute temporal scheme within which to place the kind of narrative we see in chapters 13–15 (as representative of the Deuteronomic History as a whole) but rather to suggest the emergence, whenever that emergence is supposed to have taken place, of something novel in ancient Near Eastern literature, perhaps in world literature.

Instead of trying to name this new kind of literature—is it "fictionalized history" or "historicized fiction," "historiography pure and simple" or "epic, not myth"?—we might contrast its generic characteristics with those literary expressions "of a specific societal Gestalt" usually placed under the useful umbrella term *epic*.[36] At this level of abstraction all kinds of more concrete *gattungen* incorporated into a particular narrative work (including *epic* in the narrow sense) lose their individual identities in the service of an overriding esthetic and ideological conception.[37]

This somewhat negative procedure of describing in part what the Deuteronomic narrative is not—it is not like, for example, all those works we traditionally term epic in the narrow sense—is necessary, it seems to me, given this book's claim that the Deuteronomist's work is fundamentally novel, that is, without sufficiently obvious literary progenitors.[38]

Simply using chapters 13–15 as a case in point—and every page of the History provides equal opportunity for such reflections—we see a new kind of writing that is thoroughly imbued with what Bakhtin called "the internally persuasive word" as opposed to the purely "authoritative word." We see, moreover, a narrative style that is not distanced like traditional epic, a style in which a sense of contemporaneity infuses its every page about the past. These two general features, the internally persuasive word and the profoundly contemporaneous words about the past—both so well developed by the time we view them here for the first time in ancient Near Eastern literature that we are forced to call their appearance sudden—account in large part for the mysterious conjunction of contradictory adjectives that best describe the Deuteronomist's work: innovative yet traditional, fresh yet mature, modern yet ancient. For those who cannot or no longer choose to meditate upon the religious mystery of monotheism's "sudden" emergence upon the ancient Near Eastern scene, the more prosaic mystery of a new kind of narrative within the world of ancient texts may prove excitement enough for many a scholarly career, perhaps for many a lifetime.

Everywhere we look in the ancient Near East for texts that command authority—call them epic, myth, or what you will—such texts seem to come from on high and demand acceptance. Bakhtin best describes this kind of discourse:

> The authoritative word demands that we acknowledge it, that we make it our own; it binds us internally; we encounter it with its authority already fused to it. The authoritative word is located in a distanced zone, organically connected with a past that is felt to be hierarchically higher. It is, so to speak, the word of the fathers. Its authority was already *acknowledged* in the past. It is a *prior* discourse. It is therefore not a question of choosing it from among other possible discourses that are its equal. It is given (it sounds) in lofty spheres, not those of familiar contact. Its language is a special (as it were, hieratic) language. It can be profaned.[39]

When we look at the Deuteronomic History in general, and 1 Samuel 13–15 in particular, the authoritative nature of the narrator and some of the characters is beyond question. Deuteronomic narrative's truth claim comes across as supremely authoritative. In this respect the History's generic similarities to many myths and epics from the ancient Near East are both numerous and obvious.

And yet, to borrow an apt formulation from Sternberg but for my own purposes and without implying our agreement in the matter under discussion, the History's obvious claim to authority may be the truth, but it is certainly not the whole truth. For within its supremely authoritative pages we find an ever-present fusion of "authoritative word" with what Bakhtin calls "the internally persuasive word."[40] Texts that succeed in uniting both authorial consciousnesses within them are rare: I am suggesting that the type of first-millennium narrative represented here by the History probably did it first and perhaps does it as well as any since. It is this profoundly successful integration of the authoritative word with the internally persuasive word that constitutes the first significant feature of that remarkable generic innovation represented by the Deuteronomic History.

The truth is that the biblical narrator demands acceptance on the part of readers; the whole truth, however, is that the narrator's internally persuasive discourse also invites interpretation from them. This fused feature of the text helps to explain the marvelous prodigality with which the narrator strews esthetic, ideological, and historiographic riches throughout the story, even while compelling readers to accept it.

Take the narrator's characteristic avoidance of direct and explicit evaluation of character or event from chapter 8 onward. Even when it is elsewhere less reticent concerning explicit evaluation, the narrator's overall style is to point rather than say, reflect rather than project; the narrator is a master of indirection and thus continually requires direct interpretation.

Consider, for example, the genius with which the narrator meshes the highly stylized nature of the discourse in chapter 14 with the highly ritualized aspects of the characters' actions: stylization reinforces ritualization. We have here a good example of how the internally persuasive word invites interpretation. From the first appearance of Jonathan in 13:2 to the temporary cessation of hostilities with the Philistines in 14:46, nothing is more obvious than that the son is made continually to upstage the father. But for what purpose? (And with what finesse!) How does esthetic largesse correlate with ideological impact? For those who care to take the time and expend the effort, this text justifies the time and effort: the building of the story around a meditation on what it means to be a Hebrew (*ʿibrî*), the contrastive exposition of sacral and "secular" ritual (for example, the casting of lots; formal divine inquiry; the seeking of signs; the taking, keeping, and breaking of oaths; the situational appropriateness of sacrifice; the pure and impure slaughter of booty, both human and animal), the effects of deliberate and indeliberate sin, the initially striking image of Saul among the baggage now being filled out with narrative colors having an ideological texture, the Hebrews' hiding among the stones and Saul's having one rolled into his presence with both actions in contrast to Jonathan climbing out from under the rocks, the armor bearer's insight into the heart versus Israel's sight of the eyes—all this is in a story somehow interposed, commentators tell us, between two rejection scenes (chaps. 13 and 15) in editorial innocence or insensitivity.

All along the way, the story invites one to think about why God favors Jonathan even as he disfavors Saul. One ultimately wrestles with how to gain insight from a narrator who seems to claim authoritatively that it is humanity's fate, even nature, to remain ignorant in the face of God's omniscience, yet ever compelled to strive for knowledge and understanding.

Second, chapters 13–15 are an apt illustration of the abiding contemporaneity that infuses almost all the Deuteronomist's pages about the past. In spite of possessing the convention of omniscient reliability, the narrator's style is not distanced after the manner of traditional epics, which look to the national past as a foundational epoch and view the present and future as its weak shadows at best. Rather, nothing in the History seems to be for itself; it is for the present and the future.[41]

Notice, for example, how the narrator fills the tale with temporal indicators that set up the "that day (of narrative time)/this day (of narrator's time)" contrast, which is at the heart of the narrative act itself. The narrator's "day of battle" (13:22), and the repetition of "that day" in 14:18, 23, 24, 31, and 37 both correspond to the characters' "today" or "this day" (14:33, 38, and 45). At the same time, all of these "days" contrast with the "this day" of the narrator's present so plaintively heard, yet all the while remaining unsaid: "For the ark of God existed at that time—and also the sons of Israel!" (v. 18). What separates the Deuteronomist's use of the past from other ancient Near Eastern texts is the insistence on making the reader's "now" present, as it were, in the past. Moses' words best represent the History's model for a historical, ideological, and esthetic lack of distance: "Nor is it with you only that I make this sworn covenant but with him who is *not* here with us *this day* as well as with him who stands here with us *this day* before the LORD our God" (Deut. 29:14–15). When, therefore, the narrator points out that both the ark and the sons of Israel were there in the land "on that day," the situation in which narrator and audience find themselves infuses every word: the ark is no more and Israel is in exile. Like the book of Deuteronomy itself, the that day/this day contrast is essential to everything emphasized in the History as a whole.

This profound contemporaneity allows the Deuteronomic voice to shape its story of the past toward maximal benefit for its present. Just as the Deuteronomist's past account of the fall of the house of Eli and the rise of Samuel (chaps. 1–7) is shaped in every way for the benefit of the present account of the rise (and fall) of kingship (1 Sam. 8–2 Kings 25), so also the past of the entire History itself is shaped for the benefit of the Deuteronomist's present and future audiences to an extent that seems to set it apart from other authoritative but distanced literature of the ancient Near East. Hammurabi might propagandistically dictate the reading of the *Enuma Elish* so as to promote obeisance to Marduk's king among his contemporary audience; so also the Bible has been and will continue to be used in authoritative ways for contemporary audiences. But in addition, the novelty of, indeed the literary revolution inherent in, the Deuteronomic text is its mastery of ways to explain and persuade as well as command, provoke thought as well as require obedience.

The Deuteronomic narrative style, for all its authoritative manner, still involves a profound contemporaneity and sublime relativity that revels in the mystery and ambiguity of life. No matter that the reader gives the narrator of chapters 13–15 and the God within them their basic due of communicative omniscience and reliability; the story that begins with Jonathan's initiative and ends with Saul's rejection never fails to highlight life's rich complexities. To make people marvel, to provoke humanity toward an ever-present quest for the truth, even as we are disposed to recognize our relative ignorance—this is the fundamental perspective of this new kind of narrative. This "novelty" whereby everything in the past is for the present, whereby, for example, the full potential of this man, Saul, and the fate of the nation that promoted him is known from the beginning as a foregone conclusion, involves a paradox: the story is already known, but it is the fashioning of the plot that makes all the difference for the reader's present and future. This is of the essence of critical traditionalism.

Five

THE APPEARANCE OF DAVID
(16:1–19:24)

Who can foretell for what high cause
This darling of the Gods was born. (Andrew Marvell, *The Picture of Little T.C.*)

Though music oft hath such a charm
To make bad good, and good provoke to harm. (William Shakespeare, *Measure for Measure*)

Mad world! Mad kings! Mad composition! (William Shakespeare, *King John*)

Chapter 16: Providing for David

Chapter 16 is about the choosing of David first by God (vv. 1–13)[1] and then by Saul (vv. 14–24). As such, the introduction of David into the story marks the beginning of that conjunction of rivals that will remain the central concern of the rest of the book.[2] It is immediately obvious that Saul is shown unknowingly choosing as his musician and armor bearer the very person whom God has just anointed as his royal replacement.[3] God's lesson to Samuel in the first half of the chapter—humans see only appearances but God the heart of the matter—sounds a note that will resound throughout the coming history. Double stitched into the entire chapter are two key words, *rā'āh*, "to see," and *bā'*, "to come." Somehow these two *leitworts* provide a guide to the reader as the chapter plays between appearance and reality.[4]

Appearance and Reality: Old Business (16:1–13)

The opening story of Samuel's anointing of David finishes off old business by providing the reader with the final strokes of the author's harsh characterization of Samuel that was foreshadowed in chapter 3. Samuel will reappear briefly in the company of David and standing as head over the prophets (chap. 19) and will play a final role after death in chapter 28. Nevertheless, the opening scene of the present chapter constitutes the second element of a kind of authorial *inclusio* bracketing the prophetic career of Samuel. Verses 1–13 finish off Samuel even as they continue to play out the finish of Saul. Before turning to an examination of the entire chapter as it affects the story of Saul and David, it will be profitable to spend some time describing how narrative details within these opening verses complete a picture of Samuel begun in chapter 3 and pursued with vigor thereafter.

As discussed above in chapter 1, 1 Samuel 3 was full of language about the diminution of sight and light—no frequent vision, eyesight growing dim, not being able to see, a lamp not yet extinguished—metaphoric language about a conspicuous lack of insight exhibited largely, but not exclusively, by Samuel. Thrice called by the LORD, Samuel was not yet able to recognize his voice and needed to be directed by a blind old priest, who was himself the very object of the LORD's punishing words. Certainly the opening scene of Samuel's career marked an inauspicious beginning; references to the diminution of sight and seeing combined with a Samuel whose hearing was not yet attuned to divine accents. This account of sensory deprivation provided a picture of a young man remarkably lacking in prophetic power. Yet all this could have easily been attributed to the neophyte's youth and lack of experience, and, anyway, the chapter ended with a reference to the LORD not having allowed any of Samuel's words to fall to the ground, so that "all Israel knew that he was established as a prophet of the LORD" (3:19–20).

Once the narrator removes the idealized garb with which Samuel has been clothed up through chapter 7, the portrait of Samuel from chapter 8 onward is remarkably and consistently unflattering—so much so, in fact, that the author is now able to complete the sorry story of Samuel's career in a particularly explicit manner in chapter 16. Having forgiven the neophyte for his first faltering prophetic steps, the reader has come to recognize that Samuel's frequent stumbling is characteristic of the man himself rather than his youth. The hesitant lad of chapter 3 and the stumbling old man of chapter 16 form a prophetic *inclusio* that confirms the powerfully negative characterization of Samuel forming the stuff of the intervening chapters. Read superficially, as it is usually done, the career of Samuel is of a loyal, if human, advocate of God; the heart of the matter, as the Deuteronomist describes it, is that Samuel remains, to the end, insensitive to the interests of God.

Chapter 16, like chapter 3, is filled with references to sight and seeing: the root, *rā'āh*, "to see," appears ten times (vv. 1, 6, 7 [four times], 12, 17, and 18 [twice]); *nbṭ*, "to look upon," occurs in verse 7; and eyes are referred to in verses 7, 12, and 21. But what is significant about both parts of the *inclusio* these chapters form is that the account of God's rejection of one in favor of another—Samuel in place of Eli and David in place of Saul—serves also to evaluate the prophet chosen by God to convey his words of rejection or selection: " 'For the LORD looks on the heart' " (v. 7) refers not just to God's present selection of a king but also to the author's final evaluation of a prophet.

Whether the reader is supposed to take the Deuteronomist's inclusive evaluation of Samuel as comment upon the very nature of human prophecy or more narrowly as condemnation of Samuel for not living up to his prophetic potential is a question probably not susceptible of definitive answer. Certainly, Samuel stands condemned for many of the manipulative, self-serving turns in his career, as our reading of the text has been intent upon underlining. Nevertheless, to what extent Samuel's continual failure to see is to be understood as every prophet's necessary situation or simply this prophet's culpable one is not so clear.[5]

Leaving aside this larger question, it is nevertheless obvious that Samuel continues to be depicted in an unflattering light here in chapter 16. For example, the distance between divine and prophetic foresight, that is to say, the difference between God's effective commands or predictions and his prophet's ineffectual ones is clear from the very words God utters to Samuel in verses 2–3: "You shall take . . . and say . . . and invite . . . *and I will show you what you are to do.*" These commands/predictions recall Samuel's previous words to Saul: "You shall go down . . . and wait until I come to you *and I will show you what you are to do*" (10:8). The contrast is striking: Samuel made a prediction in chapter 10 but did not carry through in chapter 13; his God speaks here in chapter 16 and is shown immediately fulfilling what he promised.[6] In terms of the recipient of these commands/predictions, Samuel scores even more poorly than Saul: at least the king was shown reacting to the crisis of Samuel's broken appointment with some initiative and ingenuity, whereas here the prophet still needs to be led by the hand, as was the case in his youth (chap. 3) and midcareer (for example, 9:15–17). No slouch at determining the best course of action in terms of self-interest, Samuel still needs God to lead him step by step through the movements of divine providence. Appearances may dictate one thing, but the LORD demands another.[7]

Notice also how the narrator characterizes Samuel at the beginning of chapter 16: the LORD is reported as inquiring about the prophet's state of mind using an imperfective verb form: "How long will you grieve over (*mit'abbēl*) Saul?" (v. 1). In terms of its emotive register, this question recalls Elkanah's original question to Samuel's own mother in chapter 1: "And why is your heart sad (*yēra' l'bābēk*), am I not worth more to you than ten sons?" (v. 8). God can be heard confronting Samuel with the same kind of aggrieved implication: "Why do you continue to mourn? Am I not worth more to you than ten Sauls?" We have already seen in sufficient detail why Samuel grieves: God had rejected someone whom Samuel had so successfully molded to his own power-driven specifications. Now that God was forcing him to go and choose another, his will must be done—but not before Samuel is further blackened by the Deuteronomist's pen.

The manner in which the narrator fills the character zone of Samuel with emotional overtones having a number of negative implications is not limited to these details in verse 1. For if the reader has just experienced Samuel hacking to pieces a mistaken Agag, whose last thought in life was a poignant "*surely* the bitterness of death is past" (15:32),[8] the Deuteronomist now portrays Samuel as a mistaken prophet who somehow believes that God likes to replace tall kings with tall successors: "*Surely*," Samuel says to himself in the presence of a tall Eliab, "the LORD's anointed is before him" (v. 6), just before God cuts Samuel down to size with the words, "Do not look on his appearance or on the height of his stature *for I have rejected him*" (v. 7). Tall Eliab, therefore, stands for tall Saul both in the mind of a mistaken Samuel, who cannot completely let go of Saul, as well as in the discourse of a correcting LORD, who speaks more harshly of Eliab than Samuel does of Eliab's brothers.[9] We find here in God's words a *hybrid construction*, in which two accents sound—one God's and another the author's. Even as we hear the LORD contrasting Eliab's physical stature with the reality of divine rejection, we also hear the author contrasting Samuel's prophetic reputation with the reality of divine evaluation.

Samuel now leaves for Ramah (v. 13), there to die and be buried (25:1).

Appearance and Reality: New Business (16:1–24)

An intriguing feature within the two stories of the choosing of David— God's choice of him to be king (vv. 1–13) and Saul's to be his musician and armor bearer (vv. 14–24)—is that God's emphasis upon his own manner of choosing as opposed to the human (perception of inner reality versus that of mere appearance) is in apparent conflict with the Deuteronomist's emphasis upon mere externals concerning David. We learn that the spirit of the LORD came mightily upon David (v. 13) and that a young man in Saul's court was sure that "the LORD is with [David]" (v. 18), yet David himself curiously says nothing throughout his momentous introduction into God's and Saul's service. And the only actions he is said to perform are the tending of sheep and the playing of the lyre (vv. 11, 23).

Our first contact with David shows him to be largely passive, mostly an object of contemplation, someone strikingly pleasing to the eye and ear. He is young and ruddy, the narrator tells us, with beautiful eyes and handsome to look at (v. 12); he is a skillful musician, a man of valor and of war, prudent in speech and of good presence, Saul's young servant relates (v. 18). We stand here before the Deuteronomist's David much as we would before Michelangelo's statue and are struck by the figure's grace and beauty. In both cases we know that there must be more to David than mere appearance: the play between sight and insight surely motivates chisel and pen. Nevertheless, we first come upon this David of the History as someone standing, as it were, motionless before Samuel and Saul—both of them losers caught gazing upon the quintessential winner. We are invited by the Deuteronomist to reflect upon how utterly becoming, yet basically irrelevant, is David's uncommon ability to please the eye and ear.

So there is more here than meets the eye. Notice that the chapter is filled with instances of what Alter calls "dialogue-bound narration," that is, narrator's words "verbally mirroring elements of dialogue which precede them or which they introduce."[10] A general trait of biblical narrative, as Alter points out, dialogue-bound narration nevertheless occurs within and around chapter 16 more often than one might expect; the narrator's voice seems to go out of its way to corroborate the truth of the characters' discourse. That God's words fit reality scarcely needs any narrative confirmation, yet we are directed by both the narrator and God towards Samuel's inner grieving: "But Samuel grieved over Saul (15:35). . . . The LORD said to Samuel, 'How long will you grieve over Saul . . . ?'" (16:1). More to the point, the special ability of God and the narrator to "look on the heart" (v. 7) is generalized in this chapter to become a privilege of the unlikeliest of its characters. Thus Saul's servants also know about the matter that the narrator has just shared with the reader: "Now an evil spirit from the LORD kept tormenting [Saul]. And Saul's servants said to him, 'Behold now, an evil spirit from God is tormenting you'" (vv. 14–15).[11] Not only do they know what is bothering Saul, his servants even have the correct remedy for the problem: "'when the evil spirit from God is upon you, he will play [the lyre], and you will be well.'. . . And whenever the evil spirit from God was upon Saul, David . . . played [the lyre] . . . so Saul was well" (vv. 16, 23). If the inner life of Samuel or Saul is open to their fellow characters' eyes, so also is this chapter's main focus of appearances: David is himself known by the most minor of characters as intimately as God and the narrator describe him: "And the spirit of the LORD came mightily upon David from that day forward . . . One of the young men answered, '. . . and the LORD is with [David]'" (vv. 13, 18).

It is not difficult to suggest an obvious function for this generalized picture of characters' privileged information about Samuel, Saul, and David: how better to put into sharp relief the ignorance of the one human character in the story who ought to know such things but does not, the prophet Samuel? Samuel's penchant for appearances, already criticized by God in verse 7, is further underlined by the narrator's juxtaposition of the prophet's ignorance about David on one hand, and a mere youth's insight about him on the other.[12]

If these matters of sight and seeing help to underline the distance between a privileged insight, shared by many in the chapter, and Samuel's chronic shortsightedness, they also indicate how Saul is once again paired with his prophetic partner as an object of the narrator's discursive attacks, even as Saul, bereft finally of Samuel, will bear the brunt of the author's critical evaluations throughout the rest of the book. For by the very structuring of the chapter, the Deuteronomist contrasts God's choice of David with Saul's: the difference between the two, as between God and Samuel, concentrates upon the various ways they see.

That both God's sight and Saul's are contrastively paired in the two halves of the chapter is seen first by each character's use of *rā'āh* in its relatively rare meaning of "to look for and choose," that is, "to provide for oneself" (as in the word *providence*). God sends Samuel to Jesse for, he says, "I have provided for myself (*rā'îtî lî*) a king from among his sons" (v. 1). Similarly, Saul tells his servants, "Provide for me (*r*ᵉ*'û nā' lî*) a man who can play well" (v. 17).[13] Thus God's choice of David is described in visual terms and then deliberately followed by Saul's visual choice of him.

Whereas, therefore, verses 1–13 internally contrast Samuel's looking upon appearances with God's looking upon the heart, the larger contrast of the chapter is between God's providence and Saul's. In this way once more, we encounter Samuel and Saul united by the Deuteronomist's unflattering depiction of them. If indeed humanity tends to judge by appearances, rarely managing to get to the heart of the matter, ought not God's king, as well as his prophet, do a better job than others in counteracting this human tendency? Here again it is not altogether clear whether Saul's shortsightedness is to be attributed to his personal makeup or simply to human nature itself. What is clear, however, is that Saul is shown bringing into his own household the very man who will replace him as king. It is Saul as well who is the object of God's words, "Man looks on the outward appearance" (v. 7), for the reader already knows that God, unlike Saul, looks upon the heart (v. 7) and that David is the man after God's own heart (13:14). The heart of the matter is that even if the presence of David intermittently frees Saul from the evil spirit that will more and more come upon him, David, the new vessel of God's spirit (v. 13) must finally overwhelm him.

Perspectives

It remains now to look more closely at some narrative means whereby the author conveys the main ideological positions in the chapter. This involves a discussion of the play of shifting perspectives—temporal, psychological, and spatial—that are apparent in both the narrator's words and those of the characters.

Take, first, the precision with which issues of divine rejection and selection are developed. Over the course of time, God's decisions are incorporated into the story only gradually, in stages, as it were, so that one sees main ideological distinctions translated into, and transmitted through, sequential terms. The figure of Eliab presents us with a useful example of the Deuteronomist's practice. God's words to Samuel about Eliab, "I *have rejected* him" (v. 7), form a kind of sequential bridge between God's rejection of Saul and his selection of David in both a narrative and ideological sense. Whereas Samuel says of all Jesse's sons between Eliab and David, "The LORD has *not chosen* them" (v. 10, compare also vv. 8 and 9), Eliab's status is more pronounced in God's words, "I have rejected him." Never having enjoyed the kingship and never going to, Eliab is an exemplar of divine rejection, albeit a weaker one than Saul is. On one hand, the series Saul-Eliab-the six middle sons of Jesse articulates the negative range of divine providence extending from full rejection to the absence of selection; David's introduction, on the other hand, introduces us to the positive mysteries of divine selection. The crux of the narrator's story again consists of the unbridgeable gap between human and divine providence—human sight versus God's insight. God's rejection of Saul is ultimately impenetrable; God's weaker rejection of tall Eliab is also. We thus move toward God's selection of David, a move itself full of mystery.

The temporal sequencing of basic ideological categories is also seen in the shifting of God's spirit with reference to Saul and David. If it is clear that God's spirit comes mightily upon David "from that day forward" (v. 13), and that it departs (once for all?) from Sa...l (v. 14), the introduction of an *evil* spirit from God, intermittently coming upon Saul and leaving him through David's musical performances, foreshadows the developing struggle between the two protagonists that will constitute a large part of the book's remaining stories. If appearances shimmer and shift, so also does the heart of the matter, which, after all, gradually bodies forth in time, a something not quite amenable to absolute, once-for-all statements, however much the History is full of them.

Notice, second, how "the heart of the matter (*lallēbab*)" (v. 7) works itself out in the chapter with respect to the characters' apparently unusual ability to penetrate the minds and hearts of their fellows—a characteristic normally reserved for God and the narrator. This privileged ability to take on and express what Uspensky calls "the internal psychological point of view"[14] is especially relevant here in chapter 16 where the very distinction itself is thematized around the explicit statement of God in verse 7. The chapter's unusual amount of dialogue-bound narration mentioned above serves another important ideological function: it shows that the heart of the matter is multilayered and relative, so that human looking upon the heart, however accurate or insightful it is, can turn out to be, from God's deeper point of view, mere appearance.

When, therefore, the authority of the narrator confirms the judgments of Saul's servants about what ails him and about its remedy (vv. 14, 23), and when the young man's judgment about God being with David has already been corroborated by the narrator (v. 13), these examples of dialogue-bound narration not only put Samuel's short-sightedness in proper perspective, they also underline the complexity hidden in God's simple distinction between appearance and reality. All this privileged information from the mouth of the narrator or the characters—whether about the spirit of God leaving Saul and entering David or about the evil spirit of God entering and leaving Saul intermittently—actually divulges little about the heart of the matter: what makes David God's favorite?

Third, and perhaps most important, the intricate manner in which the narrator weaves into the story the second of this chapter's key words, *bā'*, "to come," that is to say, the way in which the narrator shifts *spatial* perspectives, has important ideological implications for the chapter's basic distinction between human sight and divine insight.

The precise way in which *bā'*, "to come," is used in verses 1–5 provides a clear example of this term's ideological implications for our story. These opening verses are about Samuel's trip from Ramah to Bethlehem at the LORD's command. From the point of view of God and his prophet, it is a going whose real purpose is to anoint a king. So God commands, "Fill your horn with oil and *go* . . . for I have provided for myself a king" (v. 1). But Samuel, fearing Saul's displeasure, answers, "How can I *go* . . . ?" (v. 2). We thus possess information about the trip's true purpose, the anointing of Saul's successor; we look upon the heart of the trip. But then God responds to Samuel's fears by inventing a subterfuge, thus creating the apparent reason for the trip: "And the LORD said, 'Say "I have *come to sacrifice*"'" (v. 2). The narrative distance here between "coming" and "going" represents the ideological distance between appearance and reality.

The narrator then describes what happens when Samuel arrives in Bethlehem: "He *came* to Bethlehem . . . The elders *came* to meet him . . . and said, 'May *your coming* be peaceable.' And he said, 'I *have come* . . . to sacrifice . . . Come* with me *to the sacrifice*'" (vv. 4–5). No matter that God speaks to Samuel or vice versa, that Samuel speaks to the elders of Bethlehem or vice versa, or finally that the narrator speaks to the reader. In all these cases the spatial shifter indicating movement from Ramah to Bethlehem is *a going* (*hālak*) when its true purpose is being referred to, and *a coming* (*bā'*) when its sacrificial subterfuge is in focus. From God's spatial perspective (Ramah), Samuel *goes to anoint*; from the point of view of those at his destination (Bethlehem), Samuel *comes to sacrifice*.

Of course the sacrifice is never reported as taking place in the story because the anointing of David is the heart of the matter, whereas the sacrifice is only outward appearance, something that apparently achieves no greater reality in the story than God's and Samuel's verbal expressions about it as the "purpose of the trip." The use of *bā'*, "to come," in this chapter can thus be seen to carry with it an important ideological connotation: it comes with mere appearances the way "to go" goes with core reality.[15]

The actual anointing scene is then described (vv. 6–13). First, various verbs of motion are associated with instances of human judgment:

MOTION	SUBSEQUENT JUDGMENT
When they *came* . . .	[Samuel] said [about Eliab], "Surely the LORD's anointed is before him." (V. 6)
[Jesse] *made* Abinadab *pass* before Samuel.	And [Samuel] said, "Neither has the LORD chosen this one" (V. 8)
So Jesse *made* Shammah *pass*. . . .	And [Samuel] said, "Neither has the LORD chosen this one" (V. 9)
So Jesse *made* seven of his sons *pass* before Samuel.	And Samuel said, . . . "Neither has the LORD chosen these. (V. 10)

Once again, "to come" is associated with mere appearance, whereas another verb, "to make pass, to present," is associated with the heart of the matter.

Then comes the central movement in the scene: it is associated with the reality of divine judgment:

And [Jesse] sent and *made* [David] *come* (*waybî'ēhû*).	And God said, "This is the one" (V. 12)

The various terms by which locomotion is expressed by narrator and characters alike in verses 1–13, and related to questions of divine and human judgment involving appearance and reality, indicate, therefore, that the *leitwort bā'* (in the *qal*) is consistently associated there with mere appearance, whereas other verbs of motion—like *hālak, he^{ce}bîr*, and even *hēbî'*—are joined with statements about "what really is." This correlation between expressions involving spatial shifts and judgments involving shifts between appearance and reality in the story of God's choice of David for king can help us sort out the ideological implications of similar spatial shifters in the story of Saul's choice of David to be his musician and armor bearer.

In the second half of the chapter, Saul, as we have seen, commands his servant to provide him (*rā'āh lî*) a musician, just as God provided for himself (*rā'āh lî*) a king in the first half. Saul says to Jesse, "Send David to me" (v. 19), just as Samuel said to Jesse, "Send and take him" (v. 11). But whereas the narrator describes David's spatial shift from tending sheep to standing before Samuel by using the verb *hēbî', "to make someone come, to bring someone" ("[Jesse] sent and made [David] come," v. 12), David's movement from Bethelehem to Gibeah in the second half of the chapter is described differently: "And David *came* to Saul and stood before him" (v. 21). The result of this locomotion was that Saul loved David and made him his armor-bearer, requesting Jesse to allow David to enter his service, "for he has found favor in my eyes" (v. 22).

The foregoing analysis suggests that it is no accident that Saul wants David "to be brought (*wah*^{a}*bî'ôtem*)" (v. 17) to him, but that David in fact "comes" (v. 21). As with the ideological implications of *bā'* earlier in the chapter, so also here: "to come" means to be seen according to appearances, as people see, rather than according to the inner truth, as God sees. The shifting spatial perspectives indicated by the narrator's precise choice of words help to indicate the ideological perspective of the author. It may appear to Saul and his retinue that David is the answer to their problem; up to a point he is. Nevertheless, the heart of the matter, as the reader already knows, is that Saul is really helping to bring about his own downfall. God's "having David brought" to Samuel marks its true purpose: to make a king; David's "coming to comfort Saul" merely masks its true purpose: to unmake one.[16]

Through all the various narrative means we have so far discussed—the interweaving of *rā'āh* and *bā'*, the frequent use of dialogue-bound narration corroborating the fundamental insights of human characters, the presentation of David as a pure object of contemplation pleasing to human eye and ear and chosen of God, the use of double-voiced language like "God is with him" (apparently nonthreatening to Saul's ears within the story, but signaling to the reader how much a threat David is to Saul's throne) or *la*^{ca}*mod lipnê* (with its progressively more active meanings)—through all these means the narrator of chapter 16 indicates basic ideological positions on matters of interest and importance and provides the reader with an elevated position concerning appearance and reality vis-à-vis the weaker vision of the story's human characters.[17]

Nevertheless, however much the narrator reveals by these means, the "heart of the matter" remains concealed; David's good looks and impressive appearance—like his coming successes—go only so far in providing insight into the mysteries of divine providence. The narrative distance extending from David's "being made to come" before Samuel (v. 12) to Saul's wanting "to have David brought before him" (v. 17) and finally to David's actual "coming to stand before Saul" (v. 21) expresses the full range of human experience: from the constraints of divine providence to the desires of the human heart to the false comforts of outward appearance. "For the LORD sees not as man sees."

Chapter 17: Recognition as a Central Problem

The account of David's remarkable defeat of Goliath offers a serious challenge to anyone intent upon illustrating the narrative coherence of the present text.[18] That David is said to bring the head of Goliath to

Jerusalem (v. 54) but is himself then brought before Saul "with the head of the Philistine in his hand" (v. 57) is only a minor distraction: one might see the narrator indicating first the head's ultimate place of rest and only then its first stop at the beginning of its journey toward that ultimate destination. Much more disruptive to the reader's sense of equilibrium is the dual conversation about David's identity in verses 55–58. These short interchanges between Saul and Abner and between Saul and David provide an amazing climax to an already amazing story: after having met David and loving him greatly (16:21) and after himself clothing his beloved armor bearer (16:21) with armor in the midst of a conversation about the advisability of David fighting Goliath (17:31–39), how can Saul possibly ask, "Whose son is this youth?" (v. 55)? It is true that Jesse's name never came up in their earlier conversation in which David, only once and without naming him, referred to his father (v. 34). Nevertheless, Saul's servant originally introduced the subject of David to Saul by calling him "a son of Jesse" (16:18), and Saul is subsequently described by the narrator as sending messengers to Jesse, saying "Send me David, your son" (16:19). It is indeed a puzzling matter to have Saul puzzle over David's identity after such dealings with him.[19]

The way commentators typically deal with this narrative puzzle is neither puzzling nor unpredictable. For example, Saul's quest for David's identity is often thought to be part of a second account of David's fight with Goliath, an account "interpolated somewhat heavy-handedly into some manuscripts of the completed story . . . "[20] This literary-historical solution is less speculative than most of its kind, since it is supported by the Codex Vaticanus (LXX[B]), "the most direct witness of the Old Greek in 1 Samuel," which completely lacks those portions of chapter 17 described by scholars as part of a "second account."[21]

Nevertheless, whatever may be the literary history hinted at by the various manuscript traditions, and however justified commentators are in trying to visualize how the MT got into its present muddle, it is precisely the assumption itself—that the MT represents here a narrative muddle—that needs to be reexamined in its own right.[22]

Let us assume that Saul's questions about David—even after the youth enters his presence in verse 57—are to be taken seriously. Under this assumption, Saul's questioning might be understood in various ways. On one hand, it might be seen as indicative of something like a beginning loss of memory on Saul's part or even the gradual onset of madness, a condition that would then reinforce the previous chapter's account of Saul's intermittent bouts with God's evil spirit. On the other hand, Saul's question to Abner in verse 55 and to David in verse 58 might have some other narrative meaning besides Saul's inability, for whatever reason, to recognize a person already well known to him.

Chapter 17: Repetition as a Central Characteristic

One way to get at a predominant effect of reading chapter 17 is to concentrate on its many forms of repetition. Repetition within a text is, of course, an important feature by which biblical commentators postulate two or more sources lying behind a particular sentence, verse, pericope, chapter, section, book, or combination of books. Indeed, repetition in biblical studies has long been the mother of source-oriented learning. Chapter 17 seems to provide the reader with a treasure trove of such repetitive forms and structures; it is abundantly redundant at many levels of the text.

For example, the story line itself is built around the repetitive words and actions of its characters. Goliath comes forward to taunt the Israelites "day and night for forty days" (v. 16). He repeats his words of defiance, reported in verses 8–10, at least once (v. 23), and one should probably understand him to have uttered this taunt very many of the eighty times he stepped forward to take his stand. Also, "day and night for forty days" is symbolically redundant, since it results in Goliath stepping forward twice that number, forty, which itself symbolizes completeness. Like Goliath, Israelites in the story also repeat what they have just said. The news reported in verse 25 as spreading throughout the Israelite ranks is first repeated to David in verse 27. But then the words of verse 25 are again repeated to him in verse 30. Of course, people tell David the same thing twice because he asks them the same question twice, once in verse 26 before his conversation with Eliab and then again in verse 30 after it. Did David not understand the answer the first time? But since "they answered him again as before" (v. 30), there is nothing new, is there, in what David hears the second time around? So what *is* the purpose of the second interchange? The words that David spoke twice are then repeated to Saul (v. 31), who immediately sends for him. Then, within the short story he tells Saul, David manages to smite (*hikkāh*) a thieving animal twice (v. 35) and kill him twice (vv. 35, 36). Why such doubling?

The narrator seems also to possess the characters' penchant for repetitive discourse. Within the reporting speech of the chapter, we encounter the piling up of related words and phrases, mostly verbs. The Philistines "gather" and "are gathered" (v. 1). Jesse's three eldest sons "go," then "go after Saul," and then "go into battle" again—all in verse 13—only to "go after Saul" once more in the very next verse. Within Goliath's speech to the Israelites in verses 8–10, the narrator's second "and he said" (v. 10a) is as redundant there as is the case further on, when the narrator's second "and David said" (v. 37a) redundantly occurs within David's speech in verses 31–37.

The narrator also tends to pile different verbs one upon the other, thus creating logjams of action throughout the chapter. Already by the end of verse 2, opposing forces encamped twice, were gathered twice, gathered, and lined up to meet. David breathlessly rises, leaves, takes, goes, and comes, while his father commands and the army shouts and (perhaps) even goes out—and all of this accomplished in only one short verse, verse 20. The narrator's account of the contest between David and Goliath (vv. 48–54) is itself action packed, averaging over five verbs per verse, with eight verbs occurring in verse 48 and nine in verse 51.

One of the most obvious repetitive features within the chapter, a characteristic that pervades both the reporting speech of the narrator and the reported speech of the characters, is the unusual frequency of demonstrative pronouns: there are twenty-five occurrences in fifty-eight verses. The narrator uses demonstratives to point to locations, words, or characters,[23] while characters themselves point mostly to Goliath but also to David, days, and other things.[24] No other chapter of 1 Samuel, apart from chapter 29, contains such a proportion of these pronouns. Why is chapter 17 so demonstrative?

Artful Composition (17:1–24)

This chapter's high degree of stylization—a kind of narrative ritualization—works together with its varied patterns of repetition to provide many signs of artful composition.

Look first at the story's description of the battle scene in verses 1–24. It is striking that these verses are structured in a narrative manner that mirrors the geography of the scene described in verses 1–3. After verses 1–2 put the Philistine and Israelite ranks into position, verse 3 pictures for us the position they are in: "And the Philistines were standing (*ʿomᵉdîm*) on the mountain on the one side (*mizzeh*) and Israel was standing (*ʿomᵉdîm*) on the other side (*mizzeh*) with a valley between them." In addition, the sequence of six perfective verb forms in verses 1–2 and two imperfective participles with a nominal clause in verse 3 introduces an alternation of perfective/imperfective verb forms that will continue through verse 24.

One side of this chapter's opening description of the battle scene extends through verse 11 and is expository in nature, so that the presence of imperfectives within it functions to represent action that is habitual or condensed, that happens over a long period of time and needs to be indicated as briefly as possible. The imperfectives of verse 3, therefore, indicate the respective positions of the opposing armies over the course of a protracted period of time—at least forty days, according to verse 16.

The exposition continues: after Goliath *came out* (v. 4),[25] the narrator visualizes for us in verses 5–7 what Goliath *looks like* throughout the forty days he came forward. In verses 5–7 the narrator describes Goliath mostly without the use of verbs, and never with a perfective verb form:

at his most active, Goliath "is clothed (*lābûš*)" in verse 5, while his shield bearer "goes before him (*hōlēk*)" in verse 7. After Goliath's taunt in verses 8–10, presumably repeated whenever he came forward, the description of the battle scene without David ends with the words, "When Saul and all Israel *heard* . . . they were greatly afraid" (v. 11).

The other side of the narrative battle scene is not expository but part of the chapter's series of events: a description of what happens at the battle scene when David finally arrives (vv. 19–24). Like the first side, it also contains a double alternation of perfective/imperfective verb forms. First the narrator presents us with a synchronic view of what is happening at the time during which the very first actions of David in the narrative event take place: "Now while Saul and they and all the men of Israel were in the valley of Elah fighting (*nilḥāmîm*) with the Philistines, David arose . . . and left . . . and took. . . ." (vv. 19ff.). This piling on of perfective verb forms continues until the narrator switches back to a synchronic viewpoint once more: "Now while [David] was speaking (*mᵉdabbēr*) with them, behold the man . . . , Goliath by name, comes up (*ᶜôleh*) from the ranks of the Philistines" (v. 23a). The narrator then continues the story with perfective verbs until this side of the battle scene (vv. 19–24) ends like the first side (vv. 1–11): "And they feared greatly" (vv. 11, 24). By contrast, however, the Israelites *heard* and were afraid in verse 11, but *saw* and were afraid in verse 24.

These two narrative sides of the battle scene are related to each other as exposition to story proper. In both cases the use of imperfective verb forms plays a crucial role, yet their function in either case is entirely different. Just as the piling on of imperfectives in the book's opening exposition (1:1–8) indicated action of a condensed or habitual nature, while the imperfectives of 1:9ff. brought the reader into the synchronic perspective of the characters within the story,[26] so also here in chapter 17. That aspect of action indicated by "standing" (v. 3), "being clothed" (v. 5), and "going" (v. 7) is continual or habitual action, taking place over a long period of time and serving the expository emphases of verses 1–11. On the other hand, the "fighting" (v. 19), "speaking" (v. 23a), and "coming up" (v. 23a) in the second battle scene are more synchronic in emphasis and correspond to the fact that verses 19–24 are part of the story proper. These last three imperfectives give the reader an action picture of what is going on during David's arrival upon the scene.

Between these two battle scenes—the expository side lacking David (vv. 1–11) and the narrative event having him (vv. 19–24)—lies a narrative "middle ground" which introduces David into the story (vv. 12–18). These verses are the narrative focal point of the contest's antecedants, just as the valley of verse 3 is the geographic locus of the contest itself. What is interesting about this introduction of David into the story is its composite nature: it too, like the battle scenes that bracket it, is both exposition and story proper.

Within the expository section of David's introduction (vv. 12–16), the alternation of perfective and imperfective verb forms, together with a number of nominal clauses that Alter would term "pre-temporal exposition,"[27] completes the expository picture helpful for understanding the story itself, that series of narrative events that begins in verse 17. Verses 12–16 offer us on one hand a vivid visual picture of a motionless David in contrast to his active brothers (vv. 12–14), and a constantly moving David (v. 15) in concert with a habitually active Goliath on the other (v. 16).

The artful manner in which David is placed between his brothers and Goliath by means of the narrator's expository discourse is impressive. Preceded by the perfective actions of his brothers (they "went . . . went . . . went [v. 13] . . . and went" [v. 14]), David, by contrast, is presented as commuting between Bethlehem and Saul's camp through the use of two imperfective verb forms: "David was going back and forth (*hōlēk wāššāb*) from Saul to tend his father's sheep at Bethlehem" (v. 15). These two imperfectives, like those preceding them in the chapter, represent repeated habitual action, condensed in a few words.

The temporal opposition between David and his brothers is even more complex than this: there are actually three contrasts in verses 12–15. We first have a verbless David in verse 12 in contrast to the piling on of three imperfective forms of *hālak* upon his brothers in verse 13. Then in verse 14a a verbless David is again contrasted with his active brothers, who once again are said in verse 14b to have gone after Saul. Finally, the four perfective forms of *hālak*, with David's brothers as their subjects (vv. 13–14), are in temporal contrast to the two imperfectives that indicate David's habitual actions in verse 15.

The juxtaposition of David and Goliath in verses 15–16 is just as precise. Here, however, we see how the same expository function of habitual, repeated action is accomplished by contrasting verb forms. On one hand, David's repetitive actions are described by two imperfective participles; Goliath's repeated actions, on the other hand, are represented through the narrator's use of a perfective verb form, "he approached (*wayyiggaš*)," followed by adverbial phrases indicating repetition: "night and day for forty days." The verbal forms may be different, but their expository function remains the same.

Once this expository introduction of David is accomplished, the narrator immediately begins the story itself in verse 17 by reporting what Jesse said as David prepared to travel to Saul—once again (vv. 17–18). Notice how David's actions are habitual in verse 15 but individual in verses 17–18: we are to understand that this particular time he makes the trip back to Saul, he is to take specific things to his brothers and their commander and to return some kind of token to his father. Thus this middle section of verses 1–24 introduces us to David through expository material (vv. 12–16) and through the start of the narrative event (vv. 17–18).

By means of the constant alternation between perfective and imperfective verb forms in verses 1–24, the narrator is able to construct a complex "visual" picture of the actions—some repeated, others individual—leading up to the battle soon to be recounted. Characters' speech here is minimal and downplayed, in contrast to the series of dialogues within verses 25–47, where it predominates. Instead, the narrator of verses 1–24 offers the reader a number of visual images that freeze the action, whether habitual or not, at key points in the narrated past: the respective armies standing on their mountains (v. 3); Goliath motionless, as it were, before he speaks, giving the narrator time to cast an eye over him for us (vv. 5–7); David commuting between Bethlehem and Saul (v. 15) until he comes this time to the battle scene to play his part in it; the Israelites and Philistines frozen in battle (v. 19); and finally, David caught in the act of speaking just as Goliath comes up for a final taunt (v. 23a).

Such a highly stylized opening of this chapter as I have so far described it inclines toward the recognition of a carefully crafted construction, whatever its literary history may be claimed to be. There is already, in my opinion, enough evidence to suggest that the literary hands that crafted the account as it now stands bear little resemblance to the heavy-handed description of them (heavy-handed in a double sense) fashioned by many commentators.

Artfully Composed Dialogue (17:25–47)

If the chapter's opening section is constructed around a kind of visualized matrix in which perfective and imperfective aspects of past narrated events are juxtaposed, a series of dialogues involving David now concentrates on the hearing of the word in preparation for, and in further contrast to, the doing of the deed: we encounter David's dialogues within the ranks (vv. 25–30), with Saul (vv. 31–39), and with Goliath (vv. 43–47).

As verses 1–24 were mostly narration, so verses 25–47 are mostly dialogue, and here even more than there the degree of stylization is high. But whereas the first section's emphasis on narration allowed a great deal of double vision—we see "what happened" in its frozen or ongoing form as well as in its completed form—this section's emphasis on dialogue allows a change of perspective based mostly on hearing what was said, so that much of its formal stylization necessarily centers around the *repetition of reported speech*, with or without variation in form and meaning.

The most generalized aspect of this repetition of reported speech is, of course, the presentation itself of a series of dialogues centered around David: first he converses within the ranks, then with Saul, and finally with Goliath. This sequencing of dialogues allows us to hear David from a number of different perspectives. Unless we appreciate how formal stylization of speech[28] is the hallmark of these dialogues, we may miss out on an important function of such repetitive speech and will view as simply redundant a recurring feature that is intimately connected with the ideological dimensions of the story.

David's dialogues within the ranks (vv. 25–30) indicate just how formalized such repetition can be, for the narrator sets out on a repetitive journey of questions and answers that remarkably mirrors the formal pattern of verses 1–24.

Using the spatial pattern in verse 3 of this side/middle/that side, verses 25–30 now do mostly with dialogue what verses 1–24 did mostly with narrative. After the expository statement of an anonymous Israelite (v. 25) sets up the following conversations within the ranks, we encounter a triple series of question-and-answer constructions that emphasize repetition without variation.

On one side, David's question to his fellows in verse 26, "What will happen to the man who kills this Philistine?" represents the first words spoken by David in the Bible. The people's answer is immediately repetitious in a number of ways: not only do they answer "in the same way as before" (thus v. 27a echoes v. 25), not only do they repeat part of David's question, "Such will happen to the man who kills him" (thus v. 27b echoes v. 26), the people also are shown repeating their words just as Goliath did in the previous section, "Goliath spoke the same words as before" (thus v. 27 echoes v. 23). This first instance of a question-answer construction is one side of David's dialogues within the ranks; the other side of the dialogue occurs at its end and exactly mirrors the first side: "And [David] . . . spoke in the same way; and the people answered him again as before" (v. 30).

Between these two sides of the dialogue occurs the middle ground of David's conversation with Eliab, and it too is constructed along a question-answer pattern, but one even more complex than those surrounding it. First Eliab asks David two questions (v. 28), and then David answers him with two questions (v. 29). But the stylization goes deeper: just as Eliab's discourse itself contains the answer to one of his questions ("Why have you come down? . . . You have come down to see the battle," v. 28), so also David's response equivalently contains the answer to one of his own questions ("Is it not [$h^a l \hat{o}$] a word?" means, "Is it not a word? Yes, it is.").

We see, therefore, that these dialogues within the ranks are repetitious on a number of different levels: the discursive structure of verses 25–30 mirrors the narrative structure of verses 1–24, just as both mirror the spatial structure of the battle scene as set out in verse 3; the people and David are both reported as repeating their exact words, just as Goliath is reported repeating his exact words in the preceding narrative; within the dialogue itself, the people are said to repeat exactly in verse 27 what someone said in verse 25, then are said to repeat this again in verse 30b in response to David's repetition, in verse 30a, of the question he already asked in verse 26; and finally, just as Eliab answers his own question during his questioning of David, so David answers his own question in his response to Eliab. It is difficult to imagine a more stylized presentation of dialogue than that which the narrator gives us in verses 25–30.

The narrator again uses repetition of reported word to move the reader into the next dialogue, that between David and Saul: "When the words which David spoke were heard, they repeated them (*wayyaggidû*) before Saul and he sent for him" (v. 31). This next dialogue is in many ways the most *telling* of all the dialogues in verses 25–47; not the least reason for this is that it contains a report of David telling a story to Saul. Meant to convince the king of David's worthiness to fight Goliath, this story-within-a-story is remarkable for its predominant use of imperfectives that make present for Saul events taken from David's past. In other words, David is shown here narrating to Saul in much the same manner as the narrator does to the reader in the chapter's opening verses (vv. 1–24): David gives Saul a visual picture of his defeat of the lion and the bear. Here are David's words:

Perfectives	Imperfectives
STORY (Vv. 34–35)	
When your servant was (*hāyāh*) a shepherd among the flock of his father,	the lion and the bear would come (*ûbā'*) and take (*wᵉnāsa'*) a lamb from the flock. And I would go out (*wᵉyāṣā'tî*) after him and I would smite him (*wᵉhikkitîw*) and snatch [it] (*wᵉhiṣṣaltî*) from his mouth.
But [if or when] he rose up (*wayyāqom*) against me	I (would [?]) seize (*wᵉheḥᵉzaqtî*) [him] by his beard and smite (*wᵉhikkitîw*) and kill him (*wahᵃmîttîw*).
POINT OF STORY (V. 36a)	
And David said:	
Your servant killed (*hikkāh*) both the lion and the bear	Now this uncircumcised Philistine is (*wᵉhāyāh*) like one of them,
for he has defied (*ḥērēp*) the ranks of the living God.	

David tells his story by alternating perfective and imperfective verb forms. In fact, his mode of storytelling, which employs mostly imperfectives alternating with a few perfectives, is the mirror image of the narrator's in the previous section (vv. 1–24), which used mostly perfectives alternating with a few imperfectives. Nevertheless, the combination of exposition and narrative event, together with the precise alternation of perfectives and imperfectives, motivates David's story just as it did the narrator's in the first section. This is a notable example of structural repetition in the chapter.

Notice how the string of imperfectives in verses 34–35[29] makes the entire story of the lion and the bear exposition, as it were, for the point David wants to make to Saul in 36a through the use of another imperfective: Goliath *is* like one of them (the lion and the bear). Who might tall Goliath stand for in the point of the narrator's story? And whose son is the servant of such an individual?

Besides David's story-within-a-story, consider also how the entire dialogue between David and Saul is stylized through the varied repetition of "to go (*hālak*)." Here repetition serves stylization as narrator and characters proceed through various modes of David's *going* to fight Goliath: (1) *Desire:* "I will go," David says (v. 32); (2) *Inability:* "You are not able to go," Saul responds (v. 33); (3) *Command:* "Go . . . ," Saul says (v. 37); (4) *Desire:* "He wanted to go," the narrator says of David (v. 39a); and (5) *Inability:* "I am not able to go . . . ," David finally says (v. 39b). Through all these repetitions of "to go," we see that this dialogue, like the preceding one, has two sides flanking a middle ground: "to go" combining both desire and inability is on either side, with its occurrence as command holding the middle ground.

The formalization of dialogue through David's story-within-a-story and the narrator's strategic deployment of *hālak* emphasize the shifting perspectives of repetitious speech that varies both form and meaning, whereas the earlier dialogue within the ranks represented repetition of speech without variation in form or meaning.

The third dialogue involves the two combatants themselves, David and Goliath (vv. 43–47). It does not appear to be as stylized as the two preceding it. Goliath opens with a question (v. 43) and then issues a command, "Go to me . . . "[30] David's response, in which he repeats his description of the Israelite ranks as they relate to Goliath's defiance (vv. 45–47) is significant from the point of view of our discussion of repetition. David asked his fellows in verse 26, "Who is this uncircumcised Philistine that he should defy *the ranks of the living God?*" Similarly in verse 36 he talked to Saul about Goliath: ". . . since he has defied *the ranks of the living God.*" Here in verse 45 David also talks of "the *God of the ranks of Israel* whom you have defied." These repetitions about the ranks are at variance with Goliath's description of them in verse 10 as well as an Israelite's in verse 25, both of whom refer simply to "the ranks of Israel." No one in this chapter emphasizes the interests of God more than David does, and nowhere more so than here in the third dialogue of this section.

David also repeats himself when pointing out that the defeat of Goliath has a double meaning—that all the earth *may know* that there is a God in Israel, and that Israel *may know* that their God does not save with sword and spear (vv. 47–48). David's twofold meaning to the contest recalls Joshua's twofold meaning to the setting up of stones in another highly ritualized account, that of the crossing of the Jordan (Josh. 4:7, 24).[31] In both passages, there is one meaning for the peoples of the earth and another for Israelites. Here in 1 Samuel, the meaning of the contest for Israelites ("this assembly") involves the relative uselessness of sword and spear, and, further, the meaning for Israelites is itself double; the sword and spear to which David refers are not only Goliath's, which David will render useless with his sling, but also Saul's armor and sword, which David has already put aside (v. 39).

Combat (17:48–54)

If the first section of this chapter is mostly narrative and the second mostly dialogue concerning the antecedents of the coming contest, verses 48–54 describe the contest itself and constitute pure narration. That is to say, there is nothing in this section but description, with no admixture of obvious interpretation on the part of the narrator. Its piling on of verb upon verb (all perfective forms with only a single nominal clause, in v. 50) fits its emphasis upon the act of narration itself. The density of the verbs in this section—thirty-six of them in only seven verses—appears to be the main means of stylizing the account of the contest itself by having the narrative imitate the active, rapid movement of the military events described therein: the narrator narrates as quickly as David runs in verses 48 and 51, or as the ranks flee and pursue in verses 51 and 52.

With the completion of this third section of the chapter and with the defeat of the Philistines, the story itself is over. But does the narrator's story have a point as David's did earlier in the chapter? David identified "this uncircumcised Philistine" with the bear and the lion of his story; what is David like for Saul, and Saul for the reader? The double dialogue that concludes the chapter—that between Saul and Abner and between David and Saul—is very much the point of the narrator's story and will provide a focus for the discussion to follow: who is this king who would ask such a question as "Who is this youth?"?

Repetition and Recognition (17:55–58)

The narrator certainly succeeds in getting the reader's attention at the end of the chapter: Saul's question to Abner in verse 55 falls upon one's ears like a thunderclap. An amazing turn of events it assuredly is, but just as amazing is the easy dismissal of these verses as crudely incoherent within the story as it stands. Why would some guiding intelligence take care in verse 15 to make David's situation there consistent with the events of the preceding chapter, but then allow to stand, or worse still incorporate, a conclusion that is inconsistent not only with chapter 16 but also with Saul's and David's meeting in the middle of chapter 17? How could the entire chapter show so many signs of formal stylization and structural repetition, in narration as well as dialogue, only to collapse into a jumble of incoherence at the end?

That Saul's question about David is expressed not just once but three times in these four verses should at least alert the reader that Saul's questioning is being emphasized here with a vengeance. It simply will not do to dismiss these verses with a redactional shrug; such an attitude robs the story of its esthetic brilliance and ideological complexity, even as it severely weakens the drama of reading. Having thus lost confidence in the chain of events at such a critical turn in the story—the beginning of David's military activity—we are doomed henceforth to suspect the narrator whenever the story places our comprehension between a rock and a hard place. Suspense, curiosity, surprise, doubt, and even mystery lose their full power to engage us if we so easily attribute our struggle to comprehend to that self-excusing catch-all termed *the redactor*. Perhaps by doing so, we simply remove from our shoulders the responsibility of reading.

How might one suggest that the reader is supposed to struggle with Saul's behavior here, that his and our questions are an appropriate culmination of the story of David's defeat of Goliath and Israel's defeat of the Philistines? Once again, repetition is the mother even of discourse-oriented learning.

Verses 55–58 continue this chapter's emphasis on repetition: in not recognizing David, Saul is made to ask the same question twice, first of Abner (v. 55) and then of David himself (v. 58). After Abner swears that he does not know, David ultimately responds, "I am the son of your servant, Jesse the Bethlehemite" (v. 58). What is structurally interesting about this double interchange of question/answer is that both interchanges bracket a middle ground that contains Saul's question yet a third time, as imbedded in a command to Abner: "And the king said, 'Inquire whose son the youth is'" (v. 56). In verses 55–58 we find once more a narrative structure that mirrors the battle scene described in verse 3.[32]

Notice also how verses 55–58 continue the pattern of pointing so unusually predominant in the preceding verses. As remarked above, no other chapter of the book, apart from chapter 29, contains so many demonstrative pronouns. Once we see Saul looking out upon David advancing on Goliath, and hear him ask twice, "Who is *this youth* . . . Who is *this stripling*?" we are reminded of the tones of derision so often accompanying the use of demonstratives earlier in the chapter. We may even suggest that this act of pointing with derision is a principal reason why there are so many demonstratives in the chapter. A chief means whereby the Israelites refer to Goliath in a disparaging manner is to call him *"this* man" (v. 25), *"this* Philistine" (vv. 26, 32, 33, 37), *"this* uncircumcised Philistine" (vv. 26, 36). When Eliab asks David, "Why *this* going down of yours? . . . I know your presumption and the evil of your heart . . . " (v. 28), he begins his question with a disparaging demonstrative. When David rejects the helmet and armor with which Saul has clothed him, he speaks of them with demonstrative derogation, "I cannot go with *these*" (v. 39). And even when he corrects Israel for its overreliance on sword and spear (an attitude accounting for its fear of Goliath's power and confidence in Saul's), he refers to Israel as *"this* assembly" (v. 47).

By the time readers get to Saul's double reference to *"this* youth . . . *this* stripling," we may wonder whether Saul is asking Abner such a question as much out of derision as amazement. Does Saul's reaction at *seeing* David ($w^e kir\hat{o}'t$, v. 55) mirror Goliath's at seeing him:"And when the Philistine *saw* David . . . he disdained him" (v. 42)? That Saul continues to point to things through demonstrative language complements the narrator's continuing to structure the dialogue along the lines previously described in the chapter.

Notice finally that David, when speaking to Saul, refers to his own father as *"your servant* Jesse." Such language is not as innocent as it sounds. Not only does it correspond to David's previous reference to himself as "[*Saul's*] *servant*" (vv. 32, 34, 36), it establishes connections with Goliath's opening challenge, "Are you not *servants of Saul*? . . . Then we will be your *servants* . . . Then you shall be our *servants*" (vv. 8–9), and with the talk within the Israelite ranks, "Whoever kills [Goliath] . . . the king will make his father's house *free in Israel*" (v. 25)[33]

The foregoing features of verses 55–58 help us to hear some accents present in Saul's opening exchange with Abner. The derisive tones present in Saul's double use of the demonstrative pronoun connect up with David's last words to Saul in verse 39: "I cannot go *with these things* [you have given me]." David was as doubtful about his chances with armor as Saul apparently is about David without it. The situation is thus set up wherein the reader is not certain, at the point of Saul's questioning Abner, whether the king had understood David in verse 39 to mean that he could not go up *at all* to fight Goliath. When David put off the armor, did he seem to Saul to put off the contest also? Perhaps Saul was not aware—in contrast to the reader—that David still intended to approach the Philistine but without any armor (as v. 40 narrates him doing). Perhaps, also, there is a matter of distance. Are David's features recognizable where Saul stands as he watches the youth go forth?

By the end of Saul's first question, it is still possible for the reader to assume that Saul's failure to recognize David is somehow explicable according to the story's previous details.

When Abner also fails to recognize David, or, more precisely, when he swears that he does not recognize him, the derogatory tones of Saul's question, followed by an answer of Abner that is no answer at all ("As your soul lives, O King, I cannot tell") recall details of the account of Israel's defeat of the Philistines in chapter 14. There, Israel defeated the Philistines primarily through the initiative and leadership of Jonathan, with Saul himself at first unaware of his son's initiative (14:3, 17) and taking a decidedly secondary role in the victory; here, Saul is reported as not participating in any way in the Philistine defeat, which is shown to be inaugurated by David's courageous acts. Thus Jonathan plays a similar role in chapter 14, with reference to Israel's victory and Saul's inaction, as David here in chapter 17. Moreover, in chapter 14 victory over the Philistines is followed by Saul inquiring of God and receiving no answer (14:37), then voicing suspicions about "his son" and again receiving no answer from the people (14:39). So too, Abner has no answer for Saul.

By 17:56, therefore, such factors as we have been discussing might make it possible for readers to accept that Saul might not be aware that David was going forward to battle, just as he was unaware of Jonathan's going in chapter 14.

Then the narrator uses verses 57–58 to force readers to reject any surmise we might have made to explain Saul's first question as *simply* a visual failure to recognize his own armor bearer. For the narrator now brings David into the king's presence (v. 57), and we discover to our amazement that Saul is still asking the same question. With David standing before him, Saul's repetition of the question he asked Abner cannot be explained by any inability to see David or misunderstanding of his intentions.

That this second question is, as is sometimes suggested, an indication of something like an abnormal loss of memory or even the gradual onset of madness would need further confirmation as the story progresses and therefore will not be developed here. Rather, a less drastic tack can be taken, one that does have some basis in the scene's antecedents. What does Saul's question in verse 58 indicate if we take the story's previous details seriously?

Once recognizing the lad standing before him as David, his own armor bearer and musician, Saul asks him a question containing a number of accents that serve the story well. "Whose son are you, O youth?" recalls, with gentle self-irony, Saul's lack of confidence in him earlier ("You cannot go . . . for you are but a youth," v. 33). Looking at the head of the Philistine in David's hand, Saul also uses his question to express genuine amazement that David, after announcing his intentions to him, has been able to "carry it off." His father Jesse is not a giant like Goliath; how then could he have defeated one? Finally, Saul's question carries with it a threat of coercion, for Saul thereby asks David formally to renounce Jesse's paternity in favor of his own. After all, after David came before Saul to serve him (16:21), the youth began dividing his time between his father's flock and Saul's court (17:15). Now that David has proven his military usefulness to Saul by leading the Israelites in victory over Goliath and the Philistines, the king recognizes how necessary it is that David give his full allegiance to him by renouncing Jesse's paternal hold over him. Saul's question to David, therefore, is a compelling directive for the youth to call him father, just as he later would call David son (24:16). At the same time, it recalls Samuel's warning about the future actions of the king requested by the people: "He will take *your sons* . . . and he will appoint for himself 'commanders of thousands'" (8:11–12; see especially 18:13).

For his part, the narrator uses Saul's questions to continue variations on the theme of repetition. If the narrator has already emphasized repetition of dialogue without variation in form or meaning (Goliath is supposed to have said the same thing exactly in v. 23 as in vv. 8–10; David asks the same question in v. 30a as in v. 26 with his words being repeated before the king in v. 31; and the people's words in v. 25 are reported as being repeated exactly as before in v. 27 and again in v. 30), if, moreover, the narrator has emphasized repetition with variation in form and meaning (*hālak* in vv. 32–39), here with Saul's question to David in verse 58 the narrator introduces another form of speech repetition, one that with little variation in form appears to convey simple repetition of meaning but actually conveys great variation of meaning. "Whose son are you, O youth?" may sound very much like "Whose son is the youth, O Abner?" but the intent, effect, and circumstances are entirely different. That shifting of perspectives through repetition, which has motivated the narrator's story so far, now gives this final and formal twist to the story's climax.

As for David, his straightforward answer carries with it a refusal to respond as Saul would have wished, and the chapter ends on a note of defiance that will necessitate Saul's immediate and coercive reaction: "So Saul took [David] that day, and would not let him return to his father's house" (8:2). Saul's desire to have David serve him alone carries with it a threat of violence that is not lost upon David or the reader. Once again the threatening questions at the end of chapter 14 connect up with this one at the end of chapter 17: in both cases the only straight answer Saul gets is from the son to whom he asks a question (14:43; 17:58). We begin to understand that David, like Jonathan before him, is putting himself in danger by answering Saul: "As the LORD lives . . . though it be Jonathan, my son, he shall surely die . . . Here I am, I will die . . . You shall surely die, Jonathan" (14:39, 43, 44). "Whose son are you, young man? . . . I am the son of your servant, Jesse the Bethlehemite" (17:58).[34]

As if to confirm our suspicions that David is now under threat by Saul like Jonathan in chapter 14, the narrator immediately follows this interchange between David and Saul with Jonathan's reaction to it: "When [David] had finished speaking to Saul, the soul of Jonathan was knit to the soul of David, and Jonathan loved him as his own soul" (18:1). Jonathan, who has had his own run-ins with Saul, is pleased with David's simple yet defiant response. As the people saved his life in chapter 14, so will he save David's in the story to come. So we are given notice in 18:1 that the souls of David and Jonathan are to be as united in the story as those of Samuel and Saul.

A Shift in Perspective

In chapter 18 we find a ragged shifting between exposition and narrative event combined with temporal discontinuities between the events themselves.[35] After verses 1–4 relate what happened immediately following the conversation in 17:57–58 between David and Saul, verse 5 shifts to a narrative summary of David's successes as head of Saul's army. Then verses 6–11 analeptically carry us back to David's return after defeating Goliath and Saul's reaction to the women's rejoicing about this, before moving us forward to the king's troubled attempt to kill David the next day. Verses 12–16 then shift to more summary about David's military successes and everyone's subsequent acceptance of him— everyone, that is, except Saul. This section is characterized by five imperfective verb forms condensing the action described therein: David was successful (*maskîl*, vv. 14, 15); all Israel and Judah was loving (*'ōhēb*) him as he would go and come (*yōṣē' wābā'*) before them (v. 16). Verses 17–27 then recount the negotiations leading up to David's marriage to Michal in verse 27, and the chapter ends with more summarizing statements in verses 28–30 about Saul's abiding hatred (*'ōyēb*) of David in response to his success and esteemed reputation.

Repute and Reputation (18:1–30)

Chapter 18 is unlike anything we have encountered so far in the story of Israel's romance with kingship. Coming immediately after a double dialogue in which the words of Saul, Abner, and David were so laconic that the reader was forced to supply almost all the background, motivation, meaning, and significance necessary to understand them (17:55–58), and in contrast to the narrator's consistent pattern of minimal evaluative comment since chapter 8, the predominantly internal psychological perspective of chapter 18 could not be more striking.

The narrator's constant display of omniscience, revealing to the reader the significant thoughts, emotions, and motivations of the characters, involves an important change of direction. Why such narrative revelations and why now? We need first to consider the nature of these revelations before suggesting answers.

The narrator lays bare Saul's mental and emotional life with as much a display of narrative omniscience as Samuel's display of prophetic omniscience for Saul's benefit in chapter 10. We are allowed to penetrate the king's thoughts in verse 8b, which contains privileged information about his emotional state in 8a. Later, as Saul lifts his spear against David in verse 11, we find out exactly what was in his mind at the time. Immediately after the narrator reports what Saul told David in his marriage offer of verse 17a, we are told in 17b exactly what Saul intended by such an offer.[36] When the matter of Michal is raised, the narrator prefaces Saul's words to David (v. 21b) with the narrator's own question to the reader about Saul's intentions (v. 21a).

If we were not enlightened about what was going on in Saul's mind and heart when he questioned Abner and David at the end of chapter 17, we are told everything about it in chapter 18: Saul got very angry and displeased in verse 8a at the women's song; he did not hurl his upraised spear at David because he was afraid of him in verse 12; he stood in awe of him in verse 15; and it pleased Saul that Michal loved David in verse 20. Not content to reveal Saul's reactions to particular circumstances in the story, the narrator also uses imperfective verb forms and other means to indicate Saul's abiding thoughts and feelings: "Saul was eyeing (ʿōwēn) David from that day forward" (v. 9), and "Saul continued to fear David and was hostile (ʾōyēb) to David continually" (v. 29). While few of the inner reactions of Saul toward David are withheld from us, neither are we left with any doubt about most everyone else's reactions to David: Jonathan's soul was knit to David's, and he loved him as his own soul (vv. 1, 3),[37] David's success in battle pleased the people, even Saul's servants (v. 5); all Israel and Judah loved David (v. 16), as did Michal, Saul's daughter (v. 20). The chapter ends with a statement summarizing all these insider views: "So David's name was highly esteemed" (v. 30). The combined effect of such narrative revelations is to impress upon the reader that as everyone else loved David, to that extent did Saul hate him.

The narrator also uses an intrinsic perspective to expose Saul's deviousness. Saul's words to David in verse 17a seem to be the reward foreshadowed by the words of the Israelite soldiers in 17:25, but the narrator takes care to reveal in 17b that such benevolent words mask malevolent intentions. Not content simply to contrast Saul's evil thoughts with his well-sounding words, the narrator must also indicate the opposition between Saul's words and the present circumstances: Saul offers to David a daughter already given to another. Thus Saul's words are shown to conflict both with inner and outer reality. Similarly, the king's second marriage offer to David is couched in words that indicate Saul's pleasure over, and the people's love for, David (v. 22), but the reader has just been told of the king's evil purpose in v. 21; and, finally, Saul's words about the significance of the one hundred Philistine foreskins as an act of vengeance upon his enemies are immediately followed by the narrator's explanation that Saul intended the request to finish off David rather than diminish any Philistines (v. 25).

It seems, therefore, that all of a sudden in the story everything is laid out for the reader in black-and-white fashion. Why did Saul fear David? Because the LORD was with him (v. 12). Why did David have such esteemed success? Because the LORD was with him (v. 14). Why did Saul continue to fear David? Because the LORD was with him (v. 28). And what something looks like "in the eyes of" everyone in the chapter—all the people, Saul's servants, Saul himself, and even David—is continually revealed to the reader (vv. 5 [twice], 8, 20, 23, 26).

The narrator's sudden fondness for transparent characters, however, should not obscure for us the opaque characterization of David.[38] Jonathan gives everything to David—his robe, his armor, his sword, bow, and girdle, his covenant, his love, and even his very soul (vv. 1–4)—whereas David is not reported as giving anything in return. Nor does the narrator give us very much intrinsically belonging to David. In contrast to others in the chapter, David's inner life and motivation are almost completely hidden. If we are told that David was pleased with Saul's designation of a marriage gift (v. 26)—our only notice of David's feelings in the chapter apart from his responses of self-abasement in verses 18 and 23, which are clearly matters of form[39]—we are still required to puzzle out why David is so pleased. Was it because, being poor, he was attracted by the opportunity both to purchase a marriage gift with soft rather than hard currency and to give twice as much as required, thus impressing the king by again overwhelming the Philistines? Whatever the reason for his pleasure here, we learn nothing else in the chapter about what is going on within David's soul. We know why Jonathan makes a covenant with David, but not how or why or even if David reciprocates at this point. And why would David so foolishly turn his back on a raving Saul, not once but twice in verse 11? Chapter 18 tells us a lot about Saul's inner life, but almost nothing about his rival's.

God's Spirit and Saul's Prophesying

Why such baring of souls here? One central fact is relevant: this chapter begins the story of the personal rivalry between Saul and David that will fill the rest of the pages of this book. It seems important to the narrator, therefore, that we understand from the start the role that God and Saul each play in such a competition. But even so, if the narrator's revelations succeed in clarifying the motivations of Saul, they still leave unanswered many questions concerning God's mysterious designs. Nowhere is this curious conjunction of human failing and divine mystery so intensely addressed than in the matter of Saul's prophesying. For on the very day following David's triumphant return from killing Goliath, "an evil spirit from God rushed upon Saul and he prophesied within his house" (v. 10). During this divine seizure, Saul sought to kill David.

This striking scene—the divinely frenzied Saul with his spear raised to pin to the wall the one who twice turns his back on him (v. 11)—looks backward and forward to clarify as well as obscure the story of the two royal rivals. In line with the other features of this chapter that reveal, the scene closes an important ideological gap that has plagued the reader up to now—that concerning the disastrous commingling in Saul's person of king and prophet.

Our reading of chapters 8–12 sought to clarify the Deuteronomist's position on the relationship between the *mišpaṭ hammelek*, the rights and duties of the king, and the *mišpaṭ hannābī'*, the rights and duties of the prophet: Saul's abortive reign as well as Samuel's flawed career are to be understood as intimately connected with the tragic admixture of royal and prophetic activity first prophesied and encouraged by Samuel, and then enthusiastically embraced by Saul in chapter 10. Samuel's words to Saul there, "You will meet a band of prophets . . . Then the spirit of the LORD will come mightily upon you and you shall prophesy with them *and be turned into another man*" (10:5–6), now come back to haunt both Saul and Samuel on one hand, and to enlighten the reader on the other. As Saul now stands with upraised spear behind an unsuspecting David, the admonition of Samuel on how Saul is to act when prophesying serves further to clarify for us the situation according to Saul's troubled mind: "Now when these signs meet you, do whatever your hand finds to do, *for God is with you*" (10:7). Thus Saul now seeks to kill David with the abandon that comes with the rush of God's spirit.

The precise words of the narrator, however, serve as a formal condemnation of Saul's and Samuel's behavior back in chapter 10, even as they continue to condemn the pair in chapter 18. For the narrator here characterizes the spirit of God that rushes upon Saul causing him to prophesy *as an evil spirit*: "And on the morrow an evil spirit from God rushed upon Saul and he prophesied within his house" (18:10). "Do whatever your hand finds to do," Samuel had counseled. So Saul now says to himself, "I will pin David to the wall" (18:11). Samuel's encouragement to Saul then, ". . . for God is with you" (10:7), is now subjected to the narrator's correction: "because the LORD was with [David] but had departed from Saul" (18:12). We look back on that earlier scene and realize what Samuel had failed then to point out to Saul to the harm of both: the spirit of God that causes the king to prophesy is invariably evil, and the king upon whom it rushes does not have God with him, whatever Samuel asserts. We see Samuel and Saul paired once more under the shadow of the narrator's condemning words.[40]

This image of Saul with the upraised spear, upon whom David turns his unsuspecting back not once but twice yet still escapes, also foreshadows and contextualizes the double opportunity of David to kill a defenseless Saul in chapters 24 and 26. Here Saul refrains from action out of a profound fear of David; there David will refrain out of respect for the LORD's anointed (24:10; 26:23).

The Dangers of Didacticism

Such revelations as the narrator has chosen to lavish upon the reader in chapter 18—Saul's inner life and evil intentions, the emotional swings of the people toward David and of Saul away from him—come dangerously close to propagandistic or didactic writing in David's behalf, were it not for the deeper mysteries such revelations continue to engender. No matter that Saul's perfidy is here described in unambiguous terms, or that the people's love for David is unqualified. Brooding over the entire scene is the dichotomous spirit of God and the opaque characterization of David. However clearly Saul may be condemned by the narrator's words, we cannot avoid repeating that Saul is still as much sinned against as sinning, that he is still being driven by the mysterious actions of God, as he was once manipulated by the self-serving schemes of Samuel. Samuel may have foretold and encouraged Saul's disastrous prophesying, but it is God's (evil) spirit that brings it about. And the reader continues to wonder if the evil spirit of God that intermittently descends upon Saul is not just as much cause as effect of Saul's evil actions.

As for David, his inner life and motivations remain hidden from the reader, so that the emphasis of this chapter on the LORD being with him (vv. 12, 14, 28) maintains as much mystery as it dispels. David's question to Saul, "Who am I that I should become the king's son-in-law?" (v. 18), not only reverberates with Saul's previous question to him, "Whose son are you, young man?" (17:58), it also reflects the question that the reader keeps asking about David: who is this youth that he should become the LORD's king?

Because Saul's rejection—like his and David's election—is so mysterious, the story remains ideologically gripping even as it comes perilously close, here and there, to pitfalls of didactic writing. We continue to pity Saul because the narrator reveals the king's thoughts only *after* God's evil spirit has taken him over a number of times (16:23; 18:10). (These thoughts of Saul's are to be distinguished from his verbal defenses after, say, being accused by Samuel in chaps. 13 or 15.) We continue to be charmed by David even as his contemporaries were, yet all along we hope not to be misled, as Goliath and Saul were, by mere appearance. David may be a charmer, but we still wonder whether his uncommon good looks might just as easily go the epithetic way of Saul's height or Goliath's awesome presence: "For man looks on appearances, but the LORD looks on the heart" (16:7). And so far, despite repeated assurances that the LORD was with David, and despite our certitude that David is indeed that "man after God's heart" about whom Samuel prophesied in 13:14, the Deuteronomist, the LORD's mouthpiece, still keeps carefully hidden from us the heart of David.

Stylized Repetition (19:1–24)

A brief description of the discourse within chapter 19 will indicate how stylized repetition of all kinds succeeds in structuring the text.[41] The chapter focuses upon Saul's attempts to "put David to death"[42] and David's success in escaping him.[43] There are four parts to the chapter: (1) after Saul announces his murderous intentions, Jonathan gets Saul to make peace with David (vv. 1–7); (2) but God's spirit incites Saul to attack David (vv. 8–10); (3) Michal saves David from Saul's further attempts to kill him (vv. 11–17); (4) God's spirit finally causes Saul and his messengers to prophesy rather than kill (vv. 18–24).

Each of these four sections contains imperfective verb forms that give a synchronic view to the action: Jonathan tells David that Saul is seeking to kill him ($m^e baqq\bar{e}\check{s}$ $lah^a m\hat{i}t$, v. 2), and Michal warns David that unless he escapes ($m^e mall\bar{e}t$) at night, he will be put to death ($m\hat{u}m\bar{a}t$) on the morrow (v. 11). Similarly, the narrator shows us Saul sitting ($y\bar{o}\check{s}\bar{e}b$) with his spear in his hand and David playing on his lyre ($m^e nagg\bar{e}n$, v. 9), while later Saul's messengers see the prophet prophesying ($nibb^e\hat{i}m$) and Samuel presiding ($^c\bar{o}m\bar{e}d$ $niṣṣāb$) over them at Ramah (v. 20).

Saul's son saves David's life in the first section and Saul's daughter does the same in the third section; God's evil spirit, which is associated with Saul's prophesying (18:10), incites him to attempt killing David in the second section, but the same spirit of prophecy keeps Saul and his servants too busy to kill David in the fourth section.

Many repetitive features also appear within and between the four sections of this chapter. The narrator makes Jonathan's warning to David to "be on your guard in the morning, for my father is seeking to kill you" (v. 2) strangely prophetic in another context: "Saul sent messengers to guard David and to kill him in the morning" (v. 11). If David strikes the Philistines and they flee (v. 8), Saul subsequently seeks to strike David and *he* flees (v. 10). In line with this deliberate comparison between Israel's fight with the Philistines and Saul's with David, the war continues to rage (or again rages) in verse 8, just as Saul continues to send (or again sends) messengers to kill David in verse 21. If Saul sends messengers three times to David's house (vv. 11, 14, 15), he also sends them three times to Ramah (vv. 20, 21). Whereas Michal covers David's bed with his clothes (v. 13), Saul strips off *his* clothes and lies naked all day and night (v. 24)—a graphic picture of how the narrator hides David and bares Saul throughout the last two chapters. The narrator quotes Saul vowing, "[David] shall not be put to death" (v. 6) and then contrasts this with Michal's warning to David, "If you do not escape tonight, you shall be put to death tomorrow" (v. 11). In verses 20–21, the narrator refers to the messengers three times as "they also (*gam hēmmāh*)"; in verses 22–24 Saul is referred to four times as "he also (*gam hû'*)."

This chapter also contains details that set up repetitive echoes backward and forward in the History. When Michal saves David's life by letting him down through the window of her home (v. 12), we quite naturally recall another heroine, Rahab, who let Joshua's spies down through the window of her home, thus saving their lives (Josh. 2:15). In similar fashion, Saul's query to the daughter who used *teraphim* to trick him ("Why have you deceived me thus?" v. 17) allows the reader to recall this incident later on in the story when another woman well acquainted with *teraphim*, the woman of Endor, turns Saul's accusing question against him: "Why have you deceived me?" (1 Sam. 28:12).[44] It seems as if Samuel's condemnation of Saul in chapter 15, "for stubbornness is as iniquity and idolatry (*ťrāpîm*)," comes back to taunt him in chapter 19 and haunt him in chapter 28.

Prophetic Murder and Escape

This chapter's main preoccupations—Saul's attempts to kill David and David's escapes from such attempts—illustrate the ideological dimensions of prophecy within the progression of the larger story line. Between Saul's attempts and David's escapes lies the topic of Saul's implication in prophecy. It may be helpful, therefore, to review the various modes of Saul's murderous attempts and David's successful escapes.

Through chapter 19, Saul is shown trying to kill David either personally or through the agency of others. He personally attacks David only when the spirit of God is upon him. Thus in 18:10–11 he gets so far as to lift his spear when David turns his back on him twice, but he is held back by fear of David. Then in 19:9–10 he tries once more to pin David to the wall, but David, forewarned earlier by Jonathan of Saul's murderous inclinations, escapes. Again in 19:23–24, Saul seeks to take David, but the king's frenzied prophesying while lying naked before Samuel all day and night allows David once more to escape (20:1).

Saul also tries to kill David through the agency of others. He first does this secretly by encouraging David to "be valiant for me and fight the LORD's battles" while intending the Philistines to fight his own battle with David and kill him (18:17). He also demands a wedding gift of one hundred Philistine foreskins, again hoping that the Philistines will execute David for him (v. 25).[45] The narrator then steps up Saul's campaign against David in chapter 19 by reporting Saul's open command to Jonathan and all his servants to kill David (v. 1). After the narrator has Saul utter a prophecy that ironically predicts the course of events in the rest of the book ("As the LORD lives, [David] shall not be put to death," 19:6), Saul sends messengers three times to David's house to kill him (19:11–17) and then sends messengers three more times to Samuel's place at Naioth to take him for the same purpose (19:18–24).

For his part, David is shown escaping Saul's attacks in a variety of ways: through Saul's fear of him in 18:12; by his own military valor in 18:27 when he kills those Philistines whom Saul had intended to be his executioners; with Jonathan's loving help in 19:1–7 when Jonathan succeeds in changing Saul's mind; by fleeing and escaping in 19:10 when David changes his location; with Michal's loving help in 19:13 when David is absent under his clothes; and finally with God's help in 19:24 when Saul is present without his clothes.

Woven into this account of Saul's murderous attempts and David's successful escapes is the thematic thread of Saul's evil prophesying. From the very beginning of Saul's reign to the end of his life, Saul is attached to prophetic activity. When God's spirit comes upon him in chapter 10 Saul prophesies, thus—as we have suggested—defiling God's anointed. In chapter 18 when God's spirit again comes upon him—a spirit now explicitly designated as "evil" by the narrator in verse 10—Saul again prophesies and tries to kill David, God's anointed. Then in 19:8–10 God's evil spirit again comes upon him—that same evil spirit that caused Saul to prophesy in chapter 18—and he again tries to kill God's anointed. Finally in 19;23 God's spirit once more comes upon Saul, who prophesies all day and night, thus allowing God's anointed to escape.

Saul, David, and Prophecy

By continuing to emphasize the theme of Saul's prophesying, chapter 19 helps us realize how significant is the precise distribution of references to prophets and the act of prophecy in the books of Samuel. "To prophesy" is often said to occur during the reign of Saul, that is, in 1 Samuel, *but no one is said to prophesy during the reign of David, that is, in 2 Samuel.* The prophet par excellence of Saul's reign is, of course, Samuel, whom the narrator nevertheless tends to avoid calling a prophet after chapter 8 (Samuel is designated a prophet only once thereafter, in an aside before the anointing of Saul, 9:9). As for David, he is associated with two prophets, Gad and Nathan.

When we inquire how the two royal rivals are said to conduct themselves vis-à-vis prophets and prophecy, the contrast in the books of Samuel is striking: Saul has an active, David a passive relationship to prophecy.

Take first the matter of initiative. It is Saul who invariably seeks out the prophet by actively inquiring of God in times of need: thus he looks for and finds "a prophet" in 1 Samuel 9, and thus he is said actively to inquire of God through prophets in 1 Samuel 28:6, 15. On the other hand, wherever a "prophet" is said to speak to David, David has rarely taken the initiative in such cases. Thus David passively waits in his stronghold until "I know what God will do for me" (1 Sam. 22:3), that is, until "the prophet Gad" (v. 5) tells him what to do. Thus it is God who seeks David out—and not vice versa—through "the prophet Gad" in 2 Samuel 24:11 and "the prophet Nathan" in 2 Samuel 12:25.

The one instance where David is described as approaching a "prophet" for help is illuminating; his act of initiative in this case is rewarded with incorrect advice. Thus "The king said to *Nathan, the prophet,* 'See now, I dwell in a house of cedar, but the ark of God dwells in a tent." And Nathan said to the king, 'Go, do all that is in your heart; for the LORD is with you' " (2 Sam. 7:2–3). Nathan's misleading answer, soon to be corrected by God's initiative in the following verses, is dramatically similar to Samuel's disastrous directive to Saul at the beginning of *his* career, "Do whatever your hand finds to do, for God is with you" (1 Sam 10;6). It is no accident that in both cases the king's initiative with respect to prophecy leads him astray.

The rule, therefore, in the books of Samuel is this: whereas it is God who seeks out David through the "prophet," it is rather Saul who seeks out God through the "prophet." Could it be that, for the Deuteronomist, God appropriately takes the initiative with prophets, but humans should not?

In line with this prophetic rule in the books of Samuel is the absence of any reference to prophets, prophecy, or prophesying whenever David *does* take the initiative in inquiring of the LORD. Thus in chapter 23 David uses the priestly ephod to inquire of and receive an answer from the LORD (vv. 10–12). Similarly in chapter 30, David has Abiathar, the priest, bring the ephod: "And David inquired of the LORD," who then answered him (vv. 7–8).

The contrast between David and Saul is clear: Saul is intimately associated with prophecy, David not; and when Saul inquires of the LORD (*šā'ûl šā'al*), he often receives no answer (as in chaps. 14 and 28), but when David does so, he usually receives one (as in chaps. 23 and 30).

Second, as we have been suggesting all along, Saul's involvement with prophecy is disastrous for his reign because his association with this divine activity goes much deeper than mere consultation: he is encouraged by Samuel and even inspired by God to join the prophets through active participation. Just as the narrator characterizes as "evil" the spirit of God that causes Saul to prophesy (confirming our view of Samuel's prophecy and Saul's prophesying in chap. 10 as evil), so also the murderous conduct of Saul in chapter 19 characterizes as evil his and his servants' prophesying at the chapter's end. "Is Saul also among the prophets?" (19:21) asks a question about one of Saul's most abominable practices.

David, on the other hand, is never personally implicated with any act designated by the narrator as prophecy, nor does the root appear even in circumstances where we might consider its presence a possibility, as when David feigns madness in 21;12–15 or during his naked leaping and dancing before the ark of God in 2 Samuel 6. In fact, David often seems to be in *dangerous* circumstances when prophesying comes his way: Saul's frenzied prophesying almost does David in in chapters 18 and 19, even as it appears to save his life at the end of chapter 19.

The occurrence of *higgîd,* "to declare," as a key word in chapter 19 connects up with the narrator's consistent implication of Saul and distancing of David with respect to prophecy and prophetic speech. As discussed above in relation to chapters 9 and 10, the verb *higgîd* is central to prophetic rhetoric, especially when there is a question of the LORD's designate: the prophet "declares" about and to the LORD's *nāgîd.* Although it is not exclusively a prophetic term, *higgîd* is especially appropriate where prophetic matters are at issue, and this is precisely the case in chapter 19, where we find *higgîd* used more often than in any other chapter of 1 Samuel,[46] and where the etiology of the saying about Saul's prophetic role motivates the entire conclusion of the chapter (vv. 18–24).

In sections one (vv. 1–7) and three (vv. 11–17), both Jonathan and Michal speak of David using prophetic rhetoric that is in stark contrast to all the prophetic activity in verses 18–24. First Jonathan, speaking in tones that are clearly prophetlike, is said to "declare" (vv. 2, 3, 7) to David information that saves his life: Jonathan introduces a "now therefore (*wᵉᶜattāh*)" and follows it with a series of waw-converted perfects that counsel and foretell how David will indeed escape from Saul's clutches: "You will stay . . . and hide . . . and I will stand . . . and find out . . . and report to you" (vv. 2–3). Jonathan carried through with his plan "and reported to David all these words" (v. 7). Then Michal follows her brother's prophetic rhetoric with prophetlike speech of her own: "But Michal declared to [David], 'If you do not escape tonight, tomorrow you will be killed'" (v. 11). Yet Jonathan's directions and Michal's predictions have nothing of the prophetic spirit about them, in spite of all the prophetic rhetoric with which they are expressed: son and daughter simply speak and act in reaction to Saul's murderous words (v. 1) and in accord with their own love for David. On the other hand, important information about where David is hiding and about the fate of Saul's first delegation of messengers is declared (*hûggad*) to Saul (vv.

19, 21), and while there is nothing prophetic about these conveyances of information to Saul, they are surrounded by the onrush of God's prophetic spirit upon Saul and his servants. As we pointed out above, just as chapters 9 and 10 contrasted the "prophetic" rhetoric of normal predictive speech with that of a real prophet (that is, the predictive speech of everyone else in the chapters, in contrast to that of Samuel), so also here in chapter 19 a contrast is set up between David's escapes through Jonathan's and Michal's apparently prophetic speech, and his escape through Saul's actual prophetic activity. David escapes *from* prophecy in verses 1–17 but escapes *through* prophecy in verses 18–24. Nor should we forget that David is shown escaping in verses 8–10 from the same spirit of God that sought to kill him during Saul's prophesying in 18:10–11. David's escapes from Saul are an escape from prophecy itself, from the evils that result from its illicit commingling with kingship.

It would seem, therefore, that the narrator uses the characterization of Saul to write against all divinatory uses of prophecy and the characterization of David to exemplify correct royal attitudes toward prophecy. The graphic picture of a prophesying Saul lying naked before Samuel, the one who all along had encouraged such activity, while David is fleeing from Naioth in Ramah (19;24–20:1), summarizes the narrator's ideological perspective. Saul is the one who all too often wants to force God to speak to him, even as God himself forces prophecy upon him. For Saul, the divine becomes divinatory. On the other hand, David is remarkably shielded by the narrator from too intimate a connection with prophets or prophetic activity.

Six

THE KING'S FUGITIVE
(20:1–23:28)

They do but flatter with their lips, and dissemble in their double heart. (King David, Psalm 12)

And after all, what is a lie? 'Tis but the truth in masquerade. (Lord Byron, *Don Juan*)

Coherence and Characterization (20:1–21:1)

Poor Jonathan: his naive defense of Saul in response to David's realistic fear for his life at the beginning of chapter 20 makes little sense in terms of the story's antecedents. Having once been directed by Saul to kill David, why would Jonathan counter David's concerns with arguments in behalf of Saul?

Poor Saul: in 17:55–58, the king, like an ancient sufferer from Alzheimer's disease, failed to recognize David, his own musician and armor bearer, as the one whom he himself had sent out against Goliath.[1] Now in chapter 20, Saul is again made to appear oblivious of past events—a forgetful monarch who is emblematic of an oblivious redactor. In verse 26 Saul raises a royal eyebrow in apparent wonder over David's absence from the king's table—an absence not particularly puzzling, we would think, given Saul's earlier directions to his son and servants to kill David (19:1), his castigation of Michal for helping David escape the murderous clutches of his servants, and his many attempts to take and kill David at Ramah. To portray Saul's surprise as something genuine rather than feigned, the narrator describes Saul's "puzzlement" first as unspoken thought (v. 26), and only then as spoken word (v. 27).[2]

Poor David: even he seems to speak with inconsistent speech in this chapter. After explaining to Jonathan that Saul has probably hidden royal intentions out of consideration for Jonathan's feelings (v. 3), David then goes on to suggest to his friend that an accommodating king ought to be believed: "If [Saul] says, 'Good!', it will be well with your servant . . . " (v. 7). Already exposed many times to the king's treachery, why should David now believe in Saul's honesty? Can the present carrier of such naivete become the brilliant strategist of future stories?

A typical way to accommodate these features of chapter 20 is to emphasize its independence as a tradition incompatible with the events described in chapter 19. David's coming and going within Saul's court in chapter 20, Jonathan's denial of his father's murderous inclinations, and Saul's wonder at David's absence from the royal table—all this incoherence is thought to have literary-historical roots. Many scholars assume that ancient redactional processes are responsible for these breaks in the story of Saul's break with David,[3] and we are sagely counseled not to expect the kind of narrative continuity or coherent characterization that is consistent with modern sensibilities.

Whatever the literary history of this section, it does seem possible to make a case for credible characterization within it. Indeed, if we were to read the story *as if* its continuing characterizations of Saul, David, and Jonathan made sense, we might even come to believe that the story in chapter 20 contains a profound meditation on the dual theme of covenant and communication. The account describes in detail a bilateral covenant between Jonathan and David that, like Ehud's sword in Judges 3, is two-edged in thrust, and it brackets the covenant with plans by David and Jonathan that portray human communication itself as two-edged—and this in a double sense.

Look first at the Jonathan of chapter 20: one continues to see in him traits that are characteristic of preceding chapters. Unlike David and Saul, who are not above deception when the situation warrants it, Jonathan is straightforward in speech and act. When confronted with David's fears, Jonathan's first reaction is to express belief that Saul would never go back on his oath not to put David to death (19:6). Were his father ever to recant, Jonathan is convinced, he would immediately inform his son about it. But then, when David continues to press the issue ("But truly . . . I am but a step away from death!" v. 3), Jonathan's reaction is immediate and unqualified: "Whatever you say, I will do for you" (v. 4). Jonathan is not one to hedge his bets. It is true that Jonathan is devious in his answer to Saul's question about David's whereabouts (vv. 28–29), but here he is carrying out David's plan rather than his own. If Jonathan *does* deceive, therefore, such duplicity does not befit his character as easily as it would Saul's—or David's, for that matter. Jonathan misleads, but only out of an uncompromising loyalty to David; he accommodates himself to David's duplicity, rather than initiating any himself.

All this is very much in character with the Jonathan we have observed since chapter 14, someone who speaks and acts with uncommon directness, and to whom subterfuge is alien. When confronted with his unwitting act against his father's oath, Jonathan is not afraid to criticize Saul's "troubling of the land" (14:29). When questioned by his father, Jonathan immediately responds, "I tasted a bit of honey. . . . Here I am, I will die" (14:43). From the first moment he sees David, "he loved him as his own soul" (18:1), nor does he so far deviate from that love. Thus, when David suggests that Saul may be deceiving him, Jonathan finds it difficult to believe that father is not like son in straightforward words and deeds.

Jonathan's protestation to David, "If I knew that it was determined by my father that evil should come upon you, would I not tell you?" (v. 9), depicts Jonathan's uncomplicated directness—yet emphasizes his lack of knowledge as well. This aspect of Jonathan's character—the ignorance that stems from an uncomplicated view of people and events—is the source of much of the authorial irony that permeates the story.[4] For one thing, the covenant between the simple heir who will never take the throne, and the complex, sometimes devious, character who will, is followed by another pact, suggested this time by Jonathan: the ritual of the arrows is occasioned not really by David's but by Jonathan's ignorance of danger roundabout.[5] In the coded message of the arrows, the only matter that David did not already know is that now, finally, Jonathan is no longer ignorant of affairs.

The characterization of David himself takes on an intriguing complexity once one assumes that a progressive (albeit indirect) illumination of his character rather than an artless process of redaction motivates the story. It makes little sense for David now to believe that any favorable utterance of Saul about him is credible. When, therefore, David suggests to Jonathan that any word of approval by the king over David's absence would mean that "it will be well with your servant" (v. 7), it is difficult to take David seriously, either from the perspective of the text's antecedents (where Saul has sought to kill David many times) or from the internal characteristics of chapter 20 itself (where David, believing himself a step away from being murdered by Saul, would then trust the king's word). David cannot be serious here—unless, of course, his entire strategy in having Jonathan lie about his absence is to provoke Saul to an angry outburst that would remove Jonathan's misconceptions, not his own.

Saul's outburst is predictable to David and credible to the reader precisely because chapter 20 has been carefully foreshadowed by 18:1–3, which already set up the terms of the present story by commingling the covenant of David and Jonathan (18:1, 3) with Saul's prohibition of David to return to his father's house (18:2).[6] This last element is the detonator embedded in the message that David suggests Jonathan tell Saul. Given such a preparation for the present story, David and the reader may now suspect that any explanation of David's absence from the king's table involving a return to his father's house for "a yearly sacrifice for the whole family" would be especially provocative to Saul. Everyone should know this, except, it seems, Jonathan, who naively follows David's plan, only to become the object of his father's verbal ire (v. 30) and deadly spear (v. 33). Saul's very choice of words in speaking disparagingly of David three times in verses 27–31 as "the son of Jesse" makes the connection between the covenant and the prohibition of Saul in both 18:1–3 and chapter 20 even more direct, so that Saul's anger becomes entirely predictable, David's subterfuge deviously effective, and Jonathan's naive ignorance remarkably characteristic. So unyielding is Jonathan's perception of things that it takes Saul's hurling of his spear at him to make him finally realize that his father is determined to put David to death (v. 33). And it is a mark of his love for David, and his forgetfulness of self, that Jonathan's ensuing anger at his father is not over the attack on his—Jonathan's—life, but over the king's treatment of David (v. 34).

As for Saul, once one assumes that his questioning of Jonathan has nothing at all to do with being surprised about David's absence and everything to do with learning about Jonathan's participation in it, his reaction to Jonathan's specific response is of a piece with previous events. Believing that Jonathan has allowed David to return home in direct disobedience to his prohibition, Saul immediately assumes that his son is as devious as he, and that Jonathan's support of David has been motivated by conspiracy: Jonathan, he believes, "has chosen the son of Jesse" (v. 30) to further his own chances of one day ascending the throne. So Saul criticizes Jonathan's behavior according to his own mistaken idea of its motivation: "For as long as the son of Jesse lives upon the earth, neither you nor your kingdom shall be established" (v. 31). How foolish, Saul is saying, to believe that a living son of Jesse could ever benefit this foolish son of Saul. When even this tack fails to convince Jonathan, Saul loses all patience and hurls his spear at his naive and shortsighted son.

Through all the crucial incidents in this chapter, a key aspect of the narrator's characterization of its central figures is a continual avoidance of anything to do with David's inner motivation or true purposes. Why does the narrator seem averse to invading the inner psychological life of Saul's chief rival? Whereas the narrator's voice often reveals to the reader Saul's true purposes, as well as his inner thoughts and feelings,[7] and often speaks of others' inner thoughts and feelings, especially their love and esteem for David,[8] it gives us almost nothing in the entire five chapters since David's appearance (chaps. 16–20) that can be described as an inner psychological view of David.[9] This dimension of the narrator's characterization of David is crucial for an appreciation of the History's overall ideological position on the man who will dominate the story until his death in 1 Kings 2—and beyond it.

Bilateral Covenant in Two-Edged Speech

Apart from announcing David's flight from Ramah to visit Jonathan (v. 1a), their going into the field (v. 11c), and the sworn love between them

(v. 17), the narrator does nothing in verses 1–23 except report the words of David and Jonathan. A bilateral covenant that stipulates Jonathan's obligation to inform David about what goes on within the royal household and David's pledge to preserve Jonathan's household forever constitutes the central matter of this dialogue. Nevertheless, each partner makes a proposal to the other in connection with David's absence from court: first David suggests that Jonathan use the subterfuge of a familial visit to explain the matter to Saul, and then Jonathan devises a ritual with arrows to disclose to a hidden David Saul's reaction to such an explanation. 20:24–21:1 then narrates the carrying out of these plans and concludes with Jonathan's reiteration of the oath of mutual protection that he and David swore earlier in the chapter. David leaves and Jonathan returns to Gibeah.

What is striking about the reported words of David and Jonathan in verses 1–23 is the preponderance of definitive, forceful, strident, and emotionally charged language that permeates these verses. The finite verb is strengthened or emphasized by a preceding infinitive absolute of the same stem no fewer than seven times in verses 1–21;[10] both David and Jonathan frequently invoke the LORD's name in solemn oath, self-imprecation or blessing;[11] the partners repeatedly protest, implore, and react in the strongest of terms;[12] and they frequently punctuate their statements with the deictic *hinnēh*, "behold."[13]

Certainly all of this emphatic or heightened language is appropriate to the danger of the situation and the protagonists' covenantal response. Their words underlie the emotionally charged manner in which they enter into this solemn covenant of mutual protection. Nothing is clearer than that the threat of Saul breathing down the neck of David, and the desire of Jonathan that David never breathe down his, fill their dialogue with a vehement urgency that is meant to tackle both problems at once—and forever. Thus, Jonathan is twice made to invoke the matter of the covenant in order to underline its centrality within the story (vv. 23, 42). The covenant represents a united front of David and Jonathan in the face of Saul's murderous intentions.

Verses 1–23, then, is about the language of mutual fidelity. But how faithful are these men who swear their oaths in behalf of one another? On one hand, Jonathan's love for David—in both its covenantal and personal dimensions—is unquestioned: from the beginning of their association, the narrator has assured us of Jonathan's true and abiding feelings for David (18:1; 19:1; 20:17). On the other hand, because of the narrator's practice so far of keeping the inner life of David opaque, we have only this character's words and actions to go by; author will keep reader in suspense until David's future actions establish or negate the same kind of fidelity we know to be part of Jonathan's persona.

It may not be accidental that the account of the covenant first mentioned in verse 8 is preceded by David's suggestion on how to deal with his absence at the king's table. Briefly put, David directs Jonathan to lie, that is, to use duplicitous language. Here we have the first indication in the story that David can dissemble when it is in his own interest to do so. The question remains open, then, whether David is dissembling as he swears the oath that Jonathan makes him swear (v. 17).

Besides the dangerous duplicity of language, another threat to the covenant appears in this chapter, one established by the passage's preoccupation with the double-voiced nature of language. And here it is no accident that Jonathan's suggestion is to inform David through a ritual in which Jonathan's words are programmed to mean two truthful things at the same time. One's language is always duplicitous when what one says is knowingly false, but it is only double voiced when what one says is superabundantly true. While it remains an open question whether David, who counsels dissembling, might vitiate the covenant by his own dissembling, it is unquestionably true that Jonathan, who proposes speech as straight as an arrow, also twice utters a covenantal formulation that is more true than even he may comprehend. The manner in which the Deuteronomist builds the story around a possibly devious David and a certainly unswerving Jonathan is a measure of its esthetic and ideological brilliance.

Intimations of Love and Language

The author uses a number of verbal and structural means to organize the story in chapter 20. In addition to playing with *šālaḥ*, "to send," throughout the chapter,[14] and repeatedly using the number three,[15] the narrator structures the first half of the chapter (vv. 1–23) dealing with a triple pact of love and language around eleven "if-then" statements, parceled out first to David's dissembling plan to explain his absence (vv. 5–7), then to the covenant of mutual love (vv. 8–17), and finally to Jonathan's plan to communicate to a hidden David through double-voiced language (vv. 18–23).[16] The integration of these three pacts or plans between David and Jonathan—pacts to lie, to love one another, and to utter what is doubly true—produces a number of authorial messages that go to the heart of the Deuteronomist's story.

We have already touched upon two aspects of the text that provide intimations of the author's point of view. First, the object of David's dissembling plan and Jonathan's straight-as-an-arrow plan is to enable Jonathan, not David, to discover that Saul still harbors murderous intentions, and then to convey this discovery to David. (A knowlegeable Jonathan is the fugitive's lifeline and pipeline to Saul's court, as 23:16—18 illustrates.) As between David and Jonathan, then, the first irony built into the story is that, whereas Jonathan appears to believe that he is communicating lifesaving information to David, the reader understands that it is really David who schemes to convey information to

Jonathan. Although in either case it is David's life that needs saving, and although Jonathan indeed is instrumental in saving that life through the communication of crucial information, still Jonathan, not David, is the primary recipient of such information in the chapter. If we read the story superficially—and redactional assumptions may incline one in this direction—then the message of the arrows tells David that Saul is really after him; read rather more seriously, the message is simply that Jonathan finally knows. Second, the account of the covenant between David and Jonathan needs to be understood, perhaps even qualified, by the two aspects of language symbolized, on one hand, by David's devious plan preceding the account, and on the other by Jonathan's double-voiced stratagem following it. Because the narrator continues to give us an utterly transparent Jonathan and a largely opaque David, the reader must suspensefully search out all the words and actions of David for possible signs of fidelity or infidelity toward Jonathan, who, as everyone knows, is loyalty personified.

But there is more. In the ritual of the arrows, whereby Jonathan's words mean one thing to his lad and quite another to David, the narrator explicitly sets up an epistemological contrast between the three characters: "But the lad knew nothing, only David and Jonathan knew the matter" (v. 39). And the matter is complex. Take the words of Jonathan to David in verse 23, repeated and applied across generations in verse 42: this formula, " the LORD is between you and me forever," is already multivoiced insofar as it expresses the almost contradictory nature of the protagonsits' relationship in the story.[17] On one hand, "between" expresses the union of love and fidelity enacted in the covenant and the hoped-for perpetuity of that union. Much will depend here on the faithfulness of the characters themselves, and it will be the ensuing story that clarifies the matter for us: dissembling and deviousness remain a continual threat. On the other hand, nothing is clearer in the ongoing story about the throne of Israel than that the LORD stands *for* David and *against* Jonathan.[18] No matter how many oaths they make or how deep their love is for each other, the LORD has already determined evil for Saul's house: he remains "between" David and Jonathan, who are thereby placed in an either-or situation.

But if Jonathan's arrow ritual is about the conveyance of double-voiced language, language that can be superabundantly true, then perhaps it is but a small step to suggest further that this triangulation of characters, with the hierarchy of knowledge they collectively possess (David and Jonathan knowing the matter, but the lad knowing nothing, v. 39), represents double-voiced communication not only between character and character, but also between author and reader:[19] Jonathan here is an apt figure for the author speaking to a reader who, like David, is "hidden" (vv. 5, 19). In addition to Jonathan being the embodiment of straight talk and the opposite of all that is devious and duplicitous, he is portrayed here also as the initiator of language that means more than it says, the inventor of a pact like that between author and audience, whereby what is said or heard, written or read, needs to be transmuted onto a higher level or toward a deeper understanding. In chapter 20, Jonathan rather than David speaks in double-voiced language that is superabundantly true both to character and reader alike. Perhaps we are meant to hear the Deuteronomist speaking to us in the multivoiced words of Jonathan, who speaks erroneously *to* David, but who also speaks unknowingly and omnisciently *about* him to the History's audience: "You [David] shall not die. Behold, my father does nothing either great or small without disclosing it to me; and why should my father hide this from me?" (v. 2).

The ritual of the arrows, then, may suggest that self-conscious dimension to the History that we have often mentioned in reference to its two opposing "voices": an overriding voice of "critical traditionalism" in constant opposition to a voice of "authoritarian dogmatism." If it is accurate to say that the History comprises a multifaceted mystery in the events and characters that fill its pages, then there may be an evaluative dimension to the contrast set up between David and Jonathan on one hand and the lad on the other: "Only David and Jonathan," who know the double-voiced nature of the words Jonathan spoke, "knew the matter"; "the lad," who knows only one meaning to Jonathan's words, "knew nothing." Superabundance and plurality rather than narrow uniformity of meaning characterize the truth claim of the Deuteronomist, and we will continue to read about the complexities of knowledge and about the complications arising from its absence in the history that follows. Such hermeneutic musings are appropriate to the episodes here in chapter 20, where words using the root *YD^c*, "to know," occur more often (twelve times) than in any other chapter of the book.

David and Ahimelech at Nob (21:2–11)

Given our characterization of David as duplicitous in having Jonathan explain his absence from the king's table, it would appear at first sight as if the fabricated story he tells the unsuspecting Ahimelech is characteristic: Saul has not charged David with a secret matter, nor do we believe that there will follow any young men who need the bread that David requests. The dialogue is at times obscure to our modern ears, and its syntax often awkward,[20] yet there is something of narrative interest here, especially concerning David's alibi, the bread he requests of Ahimelech, and the sword he takes from him.

It would be small consolation to Ahimelech, standing accused of conspiracy in the next chapter, to learn that David's deceptive story appears remarkably true from the wider perspective of the Deuteronomist's audience. Nevertheless, David's speech to Ahimelech is as much double voiced as deceptive, as much like Jonathan's speech to his lad in the field as like David's earlier lie about his absence from Saul's table. What David is about these days remains hidden from almost everyone around him in the story. The narrator's earlier description of the situation provides a succinct description of the difference between David's contemporaries and the Deuteronomist's: "But the lad knew nothing, only David and Jonathan knew the matter" (20:39). And the matter, simply put, is that David is "the one sent" by the LORD to be king over Israel. The previous chapter's central wordplay was around *šālaḥ* ("to send," "send for," "send to, or "send away"), and most of the time David was the subject or object of these missional actions (20:5, 12, 13, 22, 29, 31). David is "the one sent," and this central description of what he is secretly about at this point in the story is epitomized by the encoded words of Jonathan, and his decoding of them to David: "But if I say to the youth, 'Look, the arrows are beyond you,' then go; *for the LORD has sent you away*" (20:22). The journey upon which David has now embarked, all alone, is one in which he is a real but secret king, fleeing from Israel's fugitive king. The LORD told Samuel, "[Israel] has rejected *me* from being king over them" (8:7) and later tells him, "I have rejected [*Saul*] from being king over Israel . . . and have provided a king for myself among [Jesse's] sons" (16:1). David is the king whom the divine king has secretly sent to rule over Israel, so that against this background David's words, while deceptive to anyone not in on the secret, are still profoundly double voiced: they are false in their obvious meaning, but true to a few people in the story and to all of the Deuteronomist's audience outside it. "The king [not Saul, but the LORD] has charged me (*ṣiwwanî*) with a matter and said to me, 'Let no man know anything of the matter about which *I am sending you* (*šoleḥᵃkā*) and with which I have appointed you (*ṣiwwîtkā*)'" (v. 2). These words reverberate with those that Samuel earlier spoke to the very man about whom Ahimelech thinks David is speaking: "The LORD has sought out a man after his own heart, and has appointed him (*wayṣawwēhû*) to be prince over his people" (13:14).

In addition to David's opening speech—which we are characterizing as deceptively simple rather than simply deceptive—the matters of the questionable bread and of the exceptional sword of Goliath also illustrate how intricately composed is the larger storyline.

Consider the matter of the bread: a main function it has in the story is to indicate that David receives what is not clearly or indisputably to be eaten. The bread, being holy, is questionable food. Yet Ahimelech "gave him the holy bread" (v. 6). The ritual matter at Nob recalls the earlier matter of Jonathan's eating of honey in chapter 14 in unwitting violation of Saul's prohibition during the battle of Michmash Pass.[21]

This detail about ritually questionable food illustrates nicely how details from the events of chapters 13–14 echo throughout this story in order to present David as *Saul's replacement*: David's fugitive exploits in the face of Saul's opposition mirror Saul's past exploits in the face of Philistine opposition.[22] Like Saul of old, David is clearly outnumbered by his enemy. Saul numbered only six hundred men (13:15) and was opposed by the Philistines' thirty thousand chariots, six thousand horsemen, and innumerable troops (13:5); David will have only four hundred men by 22:2 and six hundred men by 23:13 and is opposed by Saul, who is said to have mounted three thousand men against him by 24:2. Like Saul earlier, whom the people followed trembling (13:7), David is met by Ahimelech, who comes out trembling to greet him (21:1). Why would Ahimelech, having done nothing, be so afraid to meet with David, when later he exhibits no fear whatsoever at the beginning of his meeting with the king himself? These details appear haphazard from a mimetic point of view but are pregnant with meaning from the reader's wider perspective: outnumbered by his enemy, David's character zone, like Saul's earlier, is filled with fear and trembling.

Then there is the matter of the sword. After offering him questionable food, Ahimelech provides David with military sustenance as well. And here once again, comparison with chapters 13–14 is suggestive. There, Jonathan not only eats questionable food in unwitting opposition to Saul's oath, he also provides Saul with the type of military assistance that carries the day for the king. In chapter 14, Jonathan's military initiative, in contrast to Saul's passivity, follows hard upon the LORD's rejection of the king in 13:8–15; in much the same manner, Ahimelech's handing over of the sword of Goliath to David is a priestly reiteration of the handing over of kingship from Saul to David. Wrapped in a cloth, the sword lies hidden behind the ephod—like David's hidden status. Ahimelech says, "If you will take it, then take it, for there is none besides it (*'ên 'aheret zûlātāh*) here." And David answers, "There is none like it (*'ên kāmôhā*). Give it to me" (v. 10).

It is an easy matter to recognize the central significance of Ahimelech's handing over of the sword of Goliath to David. This sword, by itself a narrative instrument recalling that earlier victory whereby David had demonstrated not only his God-given right to lead Israel but Saul's losing of such power as well, is now surrounded by royal references that underline its narrative significance in a new context. No sooner does David receive the sword (v. 10), than he travels to Gath, where the servants of Achish are made to exclaim, "Is this not David, the king of the land?" and to repeat the acclamation of the Israelite women, "Saul has slain his thousands, and David his ten thousands" (v. 12).

Just as pointedly, however, the transference of the sword to David is wrapped up in a brief dialogue that indicates the symbolism of the act itself. The statements "there is no other besides it" and "there is none like it" reverberate with echoes that indicate how the giving of the sword symbolizes the divine transfer of royal power from Saul to David, and, even further, the mystery of such a divine change of heart. These two idioms are so infrequent—in the History as well as outside it—and so focused in their few referents, that the thrust of their meaning here should not go unnoticed. Hearing David's description of the sword, we should recall the words that Samuel used when he introduced to Israel the man whom the LORD had chosen to be their king: "Do you see whom the LORD has chosen? There is none like him (*'ên kāmôhû*) among all the people" (10:24). The sword, as David now describes it, clangs with royal associations of *the unique one* chosen by the LORD to be king, Saul himself. There is but one man chosen by the LORD—but David is now that man. The priestly transfer to David of the sword that is wrapped in a (royal?) garment and hidden behind the ephod speaks of the holy and mysterious transfer of royal power from Saul to David. This "one and only" aspect of God's chosen one is something filled with mystery: how can David, by taking the sword like which and beside which there is no other, replace the man like whom there is no other? Such a mystery depends upon one even more fundamental, that of the one and only LORD. David and Ahimelech clothe the sword with words that, albeit once used of Saul, still refer almost exclusively to the LORD everywhere else: the object of God's unique choice stands for the unique LORD himself. Once David is installed as king in Jerusalem and the matter of his "everlasting" kingship revealed in the vision of Nathan, it is no accident that David prays to the LORD in words that recall the very sword of Goliath, even as they tie together the unique choice of David with the unique LORD:

> For thou knowest thy servant, O LORD God. Because of thy promise and according to thy own heart, thou hast wrought all this greatness, to make thy servant know it. Therefore (*ʿal kēn*), thou art great, O LORD God, for there is none like thee (*'ên kāmôkā*) and there is no God besides thee (*wᵉ'ên 'elohîm zûlātekā*). (2 Sam. 7:21–22)

This prayer of David gathers up many of the themes that tie together the present story: humans with their limited intelligence striving to understand the mysterious events now being recounted.[23]

Despite all these larger realities suggested by the double-voiced language of David and Ahimelech, the reader still realizes in how deceptive a manner the fugitive has dealt with the priest. Unlike Jonathan's words in the last chapter, which accurately meant one thing to his lad and something else to David, David's words deceptively mean one thing to Ahimelech and truly mean another to everyone to whom the great God has made it known—privileged characters and readers alike. Like Jonathan's lad and most Israelites in the story, Ahimelech knows nothing of the matter; unlike them, however, Ahimelech will pay with his life for ignorance of David's deception. At the same time, in terms of the Deuteronomist's audience, presumably in exile with their national house demolished, the ignorance and fate of Ahimelech are precursors of their own. The Deuteronomist seems to be telling readers, as David speaks to Ahimelech about "the king's mission," that it is the LORD, rather than Saul, David, or any of their royal successors, who is king over Israel: "[Israel] has rejected me from being king over them" (8:7). Ultimately, this is "the secret matter" that Israel would forget over the course of its monarchic history, and for which it would pay so high a price.

Foreshadowing Interruptions (21:12–22:5)

In his insightful discussion of narration and dialogue in biblical narrative, Robert Alter discusses the interruption of David and Ahimelech's dialogue by the narrator's reference, in 21:8, to the presence at Nob of Doeg, one of Saul's servants: "Doeg's denunciation will trigger a general massacre of the priests of Nob, with the Edomite acting as executioner as well as informer, so his appearance in our passage . . . is also an apt piece of foreshadowing."[24] This example, whereby the account of David's visit at Nob in 21:2–11 contains within it an ominous intimation of the account of Saul's slaughter of the priests of Nob shortly to follow in 22:6–23, actually represents an oscillating mode of narration that powers a number of the stories here toward the end of 1 Samuel. If David's visit to Nob is interrupted in order to prepare for and foreshadow Saul's slaughter of its priests, in similar fashion the entire Nob story in chapters 21–22 is itself interrupted by narrative material that in large part foreshadows the ebb and flow of the larger storyline beyond that slaughter.

In 21:11–15 (the brief account of David's briefest of visits to Achish, king of Gath) and in 22:1–5 (the account of David moving his family to Moab but himself and his band of malcontents to the land of Judah, at the LORD's command), the narrator chiastically foreshadows the two-staged nature of David's flight from Saul: David will lead Saul a merry chase first within Judah itself (22:6–26:25) and then outside it with Achish (27:1ff.). Before finishing the story of Nob, the narrator interrupts the "normal course of events" to provide us with an intimation of what is to happen beyond Nob.[25] At the same time, such details as David feigning madness before Achish to save his own life underline the dissembling and deception that continue to fill the character zone of David, even at this early stage in his career.

Saul's Massacre of the Priests and Inhabitants of Nob (22:6–23)

When Saul accuses his servants of conspiracy in verses 7–8, he uses language about the appointment of commanders and of the bestowal of field and vineyards that is reminiscent of Samuel's limited discussion of the *mišpaṭ hammelek*, the rights and duties of the king, in chapter 8. Perhaps Saul here believes that David has already offered such enticements to the king's disloyal servants; or else the king is berating his servants for foolishly shielding a man who as pretender is unable, and as Judahite successor would be unwilling, to do for Benjaminites what he, Saul, has already done for his kin. Another feature that beclouds the story is Doeg's accusation that Ahimelech had inquired of the LORD for David (v. 10), a priestly action never mentioned by the narrator in 21:2–11, yet corroborated by Ahimelech when responding to the king: "Is today the first time I inquired of God for him?" (22:15).[26]

What is especially clear about the account of the destruction at Nob and the massacre of its priests at Gibeah is the narrator's continuing to pattern the story after the events of chapter 14. There, it was Jonathan who was the object of Saul's murderous intent; here it is Ahimelech. We find a local hint that Ahimelech is playing here a kind of Jonathan role in the particular conjunction of death and ignorance that permeates their speech in chapters 20 and 22. In 20:2 Jonathan responded to David's worries, "You shall not die. Behold, my father does nothing either great or small without disclosing it to me." These words are almost a mirror image of Ahimelech's response to Saul, followed by Saul's reply, " 'Your servant knows nothing about this matter great or small.' And the king said, 'You shall surely die.' " In Jonathan's formulation, knowledge of things great and small goes with life; in Ahimelech's case, ignorance of matters great or small will lead to death. Alerted by such language to their similar roles with respect to Saul—who has just tried to kill Jonathan again in 20:33—we can see a number of connections between the son in chapter 14 and the priest in chapters 21–22. Intimations begin with the matter of ritually questionable food, as we have suggested above. Jonathan's eating of honey in violation of the king's oath is followed by Ahimelech's giving of ritually questionable bread to David in assistance to the king's enemy. Both unwitting offenses against the king induce the same response from Saul:

> "You shall surely die (*môt tāmût*), Jonathan." (14:44)

> "You shall surely die (*môt tāmût*), Ahimelech." (22:16)

In Jonathan's case, Saul's death sentence is short-circuited by the people:[27] "So the people ransomed Jonathan, that he did not die" (14:45); in Ahimelech's case, Saul's servants are also opposed to the king's pronouncement but are able only temporarily to short-circuit Saul's command: "But the servants of the king were unwilling to put forth their hand to fall upon the priests of the LORD" (22:17). So it fell upon a foreigner, Doeg the Edomite, to kill Ahimelech and his house.

The two episodes in chapters 21–22 concerning the priests of Nob set up, first, a portrait of David in 21:2–11 as "the new Saul," the one chosen by God and aided by Ahimelech as Jonathan aided Saul in chapters 13–14, and, second, the depiction of Saul in 22:6–23 as the same old Saul, who still wants to execute the most unlikely of his subjects, whether beloved son or faithful priest.[28]

In Quest of Answers (23:1–28)

Kyle McCarter perceptively notes that, from chapter 23 on, there is a sharp contrast between David, who continually receives divine guidance "at every turn," and Saul, to whom "Yahweh will refuse to communicate his will in any accepted manner."[29] Indeed, the entire section comprising chapters 20–23 constitutes a meditation on the various effects of knowledge or the lack of it upon character and reader alike. One way to comprehend the confusing zigzag of Saul on the hunt and David on the lam is to see chapter 23 against the background of chapters 20–22 and to discuss how the various characters are presented in terms of their knowledge or ignorance. That such an approach is appropriate to the material is easily illustrated by simply plotting the distribution of words using the root *yādaᶜ*, "to know," throughout the entire book of 1 Samuel: this simple exercise reveals that chapters 20–23 contain over one-third of all the occurrences of this root in the entire book.[30]

Chapter 23 illustrates the epistemological disadvantage under which Saul operates in his quest of David. The contrast between David's knowledge and Saul's makes it crystal clear that David has the upper hand throughout.

The most obvious contrast, as McCarter has emphasized, is that David has continual access to divine information, whereas Saul is forced to rely solely on human informants as he pursues David. Leaving his family in the safekeeping of the king of Moab, David characteristically says, "Pray let my father and mother come out (?) with you, till I know what God will do for me" (22:3). Saul, on the other hand, speaks about conspiracy to those who do not disclose matters to him (22:8, 13) and about mercy to those who do (23:21), but in both cases it is human information about which he is concerned. In chapter 23, David inquires of the LORD four times (vv. 2, 4, 11, 12) and four times receives an answer. By contrast, ever since his disastrous attempts to inquire of the LORD in chapter 14 Saul no longer inquires of God and apparently relies only on human sources of information for guidance in his various enterprises. The LORD, of course, spoke to Saul through his prophet when he rejected him in chapter 15, yet the priestly ephod no longer remains an option for the king. Thus Saul's preponderant military resources are counterbalanced by David's divine sources, not the least of which are prophetic foreknowledge of his ultimate victory over Saul and priestly foreknowledge (through divine inquiry) of many steps along the way.

Second, chapter 23 ends on a note that illustrates how this contrast in intelligence is not simply between David's divine and Saul's human knowledge, but also between David's human knowledge and Saul's. In an episode that gives rise to the place-name, "Rock of Escape," David is hastening away from Saul on one side of the mountain, and Saul is closing in upon him on the other, when the king receives word about a band of raiding Philistines and has to abandon the chase. Here we see that even Saul's reception of information by human means works by divine providence on behalf of David.

When we look more closely at the four instances of God's communication of privileged information to David in chapter 23, there appears to be a significant difference between the first two occurrences and the last two. In verses 1–5, God responds to David's inquiries with answers that involve more than a yes/no response: "The LORD said to David, 'Go and attack the Philistines and save Keilah'" (v. 2); "And the LORD answered him, 'Arise, go down to Keilah, for I will give the Philistines into your hand'" (v. 4). On the other hand, God's next two responses are one-word affairs: "He will come down (*yērēd*)" (v. 11) and "they will surrender [you] (*yasgîrû*)" (v. 12). What distinguishes these responses is their varying degree of articulateness and the intervening arrival of Abiathar "with an ephod in his hand" (v. 6), a strategically placed piece of information that sets off the two following inquiries as priestly affairs, in contrast to the two that precede. A literary-historical explanation of verse 6 might see it as indicative either of an original separation of verses 1–5 from verses 7–13, or of verses 7–13 as a subsequent expansion of what comes before.[31] An alternate attitude might attribute more narrative significance to the arrival of the priestly ephod than simply the late arrival of necessary expository information. Perhaps the narrator's attention to detail and precision of speech highlight the varying kinds of divine communication to which David had recourse during this critical period.

On one hand, the presence of the priestly ephod, with its suggestion of sacred lots, fits the yes/no background of Yahweh's two responses in verses 11 and 12. On the other hand, before the notice of Abiathar's arrival, David's inquiry of the LORD produces divine statements that formally resemble the prophetic word of God to David in 22:5. ("Do not remain in the stronghold; depart and go into the land of Judah.") If we therefore suggest that the first set of inquiries in chapter 23 is prophet-like, and the second set priestly, the question naturally arises why there is no mention of prophet or prophecy in verses 1–5, which speaks of divine inquiry rather anonymously. One answer would recall the discussion, in our last chapter, of the Deuteronomist's attitude in hardly ever having David initiate or seek out prophetic activity, while Saul is often intimately associated with prophetic activity, to his harm. When David *does* approach a prophet on his own initiative, as in 2 Samuel 7:1–3—a rare occurrence—he receives a wrong answer, which God must subsequently correct.

It seems possible, therefore, that three kinds of divine inquiry are open to David as he seeks to avoid Saul. The most passive situation, from David's side, is an explicitly prophetic one, in which David must wait until the LORD sees fit to come to him through prophecy: "[David] said to the king of Moab, 'Pray let my father and mother stay with you till I know what God will do for me . . . Then the prophet Gad said to David, '. . . depart and go into the land of Judah'" (22:3–5). The Deuteronomic view of prophecy emphasizes God's initiative in communicating with humanity, rather than human initiative in seeking such communication. A second mode of inquiry is represented in 23:1–5: here David takes the initiative, so that prophets or prophecy are not explicitly mentioned, and the mode of inquiry is left vague. God's answer may be *like* a prophet's response in its more fully articulated form, yet David's initiative in seeking out a divine course of action precludes the narrator from referring to God's answer as prophetic. Nor does the priestly ephod have any role in this second kind of divine word: what is highlighted here is an unmediated or, at any rate, unspecified communication of God to David. Finally, the arrival of Abiathar with ephod in hand signals a third mode of divine inquiry. Here, as described with precision in verses 7–13, the LORD's discourse fits the priestly situation in the oracular yes/no response presumably given David.[32]

If David's divine channels of communication are well emphasized in chapter 23, this is not to minimize the constant recourse to human intelligence that plots the course of events within it. Both sets of divine inquiry are themselves prompted by David's human network of intelligence gathering: "They told David" in verse 1, and "David knew" in verse 9. At the same time, the narrator emphasizes Saul's scrupulous (because sole) recourse to human intelligence: "Saul said, 'Go, establish once more, know and see . . . See and know and return to me *with sure information*'" (vv. 22–23). Having already been disappointed that David was no longer trapped in Keilah, Saul now seeks to make sure his prey is present for the taking. In fact, this chapter's emphasis on the constant vibrating of lines of communication is seen first in the unusually large number of references to the giving or receiving of intelligence, then in the less usual manner in which the messages themselves are sometimes reported, and finally in the frequent use of imperfective verb forms.

Besides the person-to-person communications between Saul and the Ziphites in verses 19 and following, and between the messenger and Saul in verse 27, the chapter refers at least six more times to David's (vv. 1, 9, 25) and Saul's (vv. 7, 13, 25) intelligence on crucial matters. The narrator also departs from the preferred practice of directly reported speech by using indirect report (signaled by *kî*, "that") at least twice: verses 7, 13 (see also 22:6, 21).[33] Finally, the frequent use of imperfective verb forms within the directly quoted messages crossing back and forth within the camps of David and Saul may evoke the urgent necessity of finding out what is now the case. The news, if not new, is useless: thus Saul, in learning that David, who was at Keilah, no longer is there, had to give up the expedition (v. 13). We get a sense of the "presentness" of these messages through the imperfective verb forms that abound within them: David is told of the Philistines' "fighting and robbing" (v. 1); the Israelites talk of their own "fearing" and of the LORD's "giving" (vv. 3–4); David talks to Abiathar of Saul's "seeking to come" (v. 10); Jonathan talks of his father's "knowing" (v. 6); and the Ziphites speak of David's "hiding himself" (v. 19). At the same time, the narrator emphasizes the synchronistic nature of the events being described by noting David's knowledge that Saul "was devising evil against him" (v. 9) and by writing, near the end of the chapter, about David "making haste to get away from Saul" and Saul "closing in around David" (v. 26). Just as the large number of emotion-laden and oath-filled expressions in chapter 20 underlined David's and Jonathan's urgent need for mutual protection and for the trustworthiness necessary for such protection, so here in chapter 23 the urgency and necessity of useful information is conveyed by the frequent use of imperfective verb forms.

It is against this background of a pressing need for *human* intelligence that is frequent, well analyzed, and up to date, that the reader feels the full impact of David's constant access to *divine* communication.

The Narrator's Message: Knowledge and Destiny in 20:1–23:28

The problem with messages is that you can take them or mistake them, a fact complicated even further if the message is derived from a narrative that is filled with indirection. But when even the content of the message seems to be about the intricate twists and turns of knowledge itself—and its communication or absence—then any discussion of such messages runs the risk of being excessively sinuous or convoluted. Still, it seems worthwhile to summarize the manner in which double-voiced speech in chapters 20–23 revolves around an epistemological spine to form something like a double helix.

Chapter 20 deals with matters of knowledge more directly than any other chapter in the book. Filled with knowing expressions ("Your father certainly knows," "let not Jonathan know this," "then know," "if I really knew," "do I not know?" "so Jonathan knew," "the lad knew nothing," "only David and Jonathan knew the matter"), the episode of the covenant between David and Jonathan is peppered with expressions of oath and imprecation through which those who converse seek to establish the truth of their assertions and the trustworthiness of their promises. David's plan for duplicitous speech precedes this covenant account, and Jonathan's stratagem for double-voiced communication follows it. Their proposals revolve around this covenantal core in two directions at once: whereas, on the surface, Jonathan is to find out information for David's sake and then to communicate it to his friend in the field, the basic thread of the story twists around its core in the opposite direction, that of getting Jonathan to know what David already knows. Only when Saul casts his spear at him in verse 33 does Jonathan finally realize what David tried to convince him of back at verse 1, and it is this late realization that is at the heart of Jonathan's message to David when he shoots his arrows. David's plan also goes in two directions at once: it is about the conveyance of false knowledge to Saul and of true knowledge to Jonathan. Finally, the covenant itself, as epitomized twice by Jonathan's concluding formulations in verses 23 and 42, twists in opposite directions at the same time. The LORD is indeed "between" David and Jonathan: even as the covenant of their love unites them, the providence of the LORD divides them.

Consider the remarkable juxtaposition of the words of Jonathan, who naively believes that "my father does nothing either great or small without disclosing it to me" (20:2), to those of David, who, self-consciously or not, proclaims to Ahimelech that "the king has charged me with a matter, and said to me, 'Let no man know anything of the matter about which I send you, and with which I have charged you'" (21:3). In terms of the story itself, the paradox is established whereby Jonathan's sincere conviction is utterly false and misguided, whereas David's deceptive statement is remarkably accurate: few Israelites are yet aware of David's true position as the one charged by the LORD to be king over them. In similar fashion, the reader of the History finds superabundant significance in the priestly transference of royal power symbolized by the giving of the sword of Goliath, sheathed in words recalling the divine choice of Saul: next to the LORD, besides whom and like whom there is no other, stands David, who by receiving the sword beside which and like which there is no other, takes the place of the one like whom there is no other. Then, near the end of chapter 23, the reader of the History listens to Saul's response to the Ziphites, who offer to surrender David to him: "May you be blessed by the LORD; for you have had compassion on me (*ḥml*)" (v. 21). We recall with sadness that Agag was himself the one upon whom Saul disastrously had compassion (15:3, 9). Thus Saul's statement in 23:21 reverberates with the earlier episode, so that both Agag's fate and Saul's rejection are conjoined and reenacted in Saul's words: spoken gratefully to the Ziphites, they sound ominously upon our ears.

Finally, and perhaps most importantly, however misguided Jonathan sometimes is in terms of the story, and however more astute David appears to be, it is Jonathan who as instigator of double-voiced rather than duplicitous speech turns out to be the more appropriate figure for refracting the hidden voice of the Deuteronomist.

Seven

PROVIDENTIAL DELAYS
(24:1–26:25)

"Then must the Jew be merciful."
"On what compulsion must I? tell me that." (William Shakespeare, *The Merchant of Venice*)

Nothing excites a biblicist's historical impulses more than a series of parallel episodes strung out along the storyline like a string of pearls. If "these chapters (24, 25, 26) show David being saved from himself, or rather from the consequences of deeds potentially disastrous to his own interests," and if in all three chapters "David refrains from violence against an enemy,"[1] then, indeed, such repetition inclines many interpreters to fond thoughts of redaction. It is to be expected, then, that Klaus Koch in a classic form-critical work gives prominence to 1 Samuel 24 and 26 by placing them second (after Gen. 12, 20, 26) in his series of analyses of duplicated stories.[2] Certainly like that earlier triple variation on the theme of the ancestor of Israel in danger, not just chapters 24 and 26 but all three episodes in chapters 24, 25, and 26 can be viewed as redaction-related variations on David's success in avoiding any action that would later jeopardize the integrity of his rule.[3] But what if I foolishly refuse to hand over the fruits of my interpretative labors to anonymous redactors who, as Nabal would say, "come from I do not know where"? And what if the story of David's sparing of Nabal's life, flanked by the twin stories of David sparing Saul's life comprise a narrative unit that, like Abigail herself, has discretion and good judgment, quite apart from any literary-historical considerations one might entertain?

Inner Continuities (24:1–26:25)

In addition to the thematic threads that bind together the stories in these three chapters—threads that commentators usually distinguish only as a preliminary step to unraveling from them genetic strands of tradition— a number of formal features help these chapters build a bridge between what precedes and follows. The importance of these features lies in their power to unify even the many details that distinguish the episodes from one other, thus providing guidance from within the text itself for uncovering some of the ideological concerns that motivate the stories.

Take the distribution of the verb *biqqēš,* "to seek," or "to search for." From 19:2, where we read for the first time that "Saul, my father, seeks to kill [David]," to 27:4, where Saul "sought for [David] no more," this action of seeking or striving has Saul almost exclusively as its subject,[4] and David is almost always the object of Saul's seeking. Even when David is not the object, as in chapter 23 (where Saul is seeking to destroy Keilah), this seeking is still "on [David's] account" (23:10). Further, it is David dead that best expresses Saul's pursuit of him.

Throughout chapters 19–28, this constant depiction of Saul as the seeker and David as the one whose life is sought casts light upon the episode involving Nabal to make of him an obvious replacement or stand-in for Saul so that David's mercy toward him in chapter 25 is as toward Saul in chapters 24 and 26.[5] When Abigail refers to "those who pursue you and *seek your life*" (25:29), these words ill befit her husband; in terms of the larger story in chapters 19–28 they refer almost exclusively to Saul. It is Abigail also who makes explicit the connection between "seekers after David" and Nabal: "Now then let your enemies and those who *seek to do evil to my Lord* be as Nabal" (25:26). Saul is the foolish one, and the foolish one is Saul.

Another formal element that ties together these chapters is their frequent use of *wᵉᶜattāh,* "now, therefore," the rhetorical device that moves from antecedents to consequences, cause to effect, background to main topic of concern. Like the preponderance of *yādaᶜ* in chapters 20–23, over one-third of the occurrences of *wᵉᶜattāh* in 1 Samuel are found in chapters 24–26.[6] Whether the speaker be Saul, David, Abigail, her young man, Abishai, or David, almost everyone in these chapters is especially intent on force of argument or persuasion, often with homiletic overtones. We ought, therefore (*wᵉᶜattāh!*), to consider how many matters in chapters 24–26 are especially worth emphasis or argument, and *wᵉᶜattāh* is a helpful, formal signpost in this regard. A related sign of the highly rhetorical flavor of the episodes in chapters 24–26 is the frequent use and balanced distribution of *hinnēh,* "look now". Like *wᵉᶜattāh, hinnēh* often functions as a focusing agent for a speaker who is intent upon making a point, and these chapters are filled with this deictic form.[7]

A final indication that the characters are caught up in something like a frenzy of rhetoric in these chapters is the frequent use of questions, many of them of a purely rhetorical nature. That is, the questions are forceful declarations masquerading as requests for information; most of these questions occur in chapter 26.[8] A good example of just how rhetorical these questions can be is the one Saul asks David in 24:17: "Is this your voice, my son David?" Spoken after he had looked behind him to see who was there, and especially after the speaker before him had gone on for seven full verses, during which he referred to Saul as "my father" (24:12) and spoke in terms that easily revealed his identity, Saul's utterance is actually a declaration of recognition put into question form for rhetorical effect.[9] The rhetorical aspect of Saul's question is even clearer in 26:17, where the narrator makes it explicit: "Saul recognized David's voice, and said, 'Is this your voice, my son David?' "

The highly rhetoricized speech of characters in chapters 24–26 is but one indication of the utterly contrived nature of the stories themselves,[10] whose details appear to convict even the narrator of rhetorical overkill. Look at the skirt of Saul's robe, which David holds before Saul as they speak (24:12). As visible proof of David's good intentions toward Saul, it is difficult to surpass—until the reader, like Saul and Abner, looks again to see Saul's spear and jar of water being flaunted by David in 26:16 and by the narrator in the story itself. The reader of ancient or modern times can scarcely imagine a more powerful means of conveying David's fidelity toward "the LORD's anointed." Who of us, maligned by an unjust, perhaps even irrational, superior, has not dreamed of the perfect response that would stop our accusers in their tracks and put them on their knees begging for our forgiveness and goodwill? But how many of us are so fastidious and insecure that we would require the scene to be played out twice, even three times, before we considered our goal of self-justification fully achieved and our detractors sufficiently groveling before us? It seems as if the conjunction of episodes in chapters 24–26, whether it be by redactional or authorial means (with all the coded implications I have been assigning to these adjectives throughout this book), condemns the text to that lack of tact we assign to the worst kind of didactic writing. Like Nabal, such excess is rough and unmanageable, obvious in its foolish designs. This is in large part the evaluative implication we are left with when commentators, as they often do, write about these chapters as part of an original apology for David.[11]

The highly stylized, that is, artificial nature of the LORD's active protection of David in these chapters parallels the excessive claim to divine intelligence David has enjoyed in the preceding chapters. Nothing illustrates the self-confidence he has in the LORD's protection more than David's placing himself in the most vulnerable position imaginable, at the feet of his murderous pursuer even before he has a chance to indicate to Saul how vulnerable the king was earlier within the cave. Knowing that Saul will recognize him as he bows down with his face to the earth, David is shown acting out, with great abandon, his role as the LORD's chosen one. David and the reader know here what the narrator and God have taken great care to convince them of in preceding chapters, and what Saul is made to confess at the end of chapter 24: "Now therefore (*wᵉᶜattāh*) I know that you shall surely be king, and that the kingdom of Israel shall be established in your name" (24:21). The difference between Saul, on one hand, and David and the reader, on the other, is that the latter already know these things before Saul is shown the hem of his own garment. In the parallel account, when David is again most vulnerable, when he and Abishai are alone within Saul's camp surrounded by Saul's three thousand chosen men, the narrator abandons an implicit appeal to God's protection of David for an explicit statement about it: "So David took the spear and the jar of water from Saul's head; and they went away. No man saw it, or knew it, nor did any awake; for they were all asleep, because a deep sleep from the LORD had fallen upon them" (26:12).

The didactic bluntness of the narrator's apparent message to the reader about God's protection of David is also seen in the account of Nabal in chapter 25. Here, as in a morality play where a character's name may exemplify his or her inner character, David is protected from killing that Saul figure, Nabal the foolish one, through the providential persuasion of Abigail. This beautiful woman, full of discretion and understanding, is, like that other non-Israelite before her, Rahab, privy to knowledge providentially known only to (some) Israelites and the reader:

> *Rahab:* "I know that the LORD has given you the land . . ."
> (Josh. 2.9)
>
> *Abigail:* "For the LORD will certainly make my lord a
> sure house" (25:28)

In chapters 24 and 26, where David's impulses are most laudable, the LORD protects him when he is most vulnerable; in chapter 25, when he is once more vulnerable—but this time because his impulses are most damning—the LORD again protects him.

Nevertheless, where the text runs the greatest risk of falling apart through a series of three overly didactic lessons that seem to exemplify cheap propaganda rather than great literature, the care with which these episodes are strung out along the larger storyline rescues them from superficial charges and demonstrates instead their artistic and ideological integrity. The deeper meaning of these three stories resides in their literary context, just as Saul's three questions to Abner and David do in an earlier chapter (17:55–58). Where the physical and ideological integrity of the text has been most vulnerable to commentator's attacks, there the literary skill and ideological brilliance of the Deuteronomist come to the rescue. It may be worthwhile to discuss how each episode in chapters 24, 25, and 26 resonates with episodes that precede it, and how the stakes in each confrontation surpass the purely personal by engaging complicated ideological issues.

Narrative Connections

A signal that past events provide background for the confrontation between David and Saul in chapter 24 sounds when Saul recognizes David in words that seem to belie recognition: "Is this your voice, my son David?" (24:17). Here is a rhetorical question very much like Samuel's opening question in an earlier confrontation between the king and his prophet in chapter 15: "What is *this voice* of sheep in my ears and *this voice* of oxen which I am hearing?" (15:14). In the course of this conversation in chapter 15, Saul revealed to Samuel what the narrator had already told the reader: "Saul spared (*wayyaḥmol*) King Agag" (15:9). Accused of sparing the king, Saul three times acknowledged his sin (*ḥāṭā'tî* and *ḥattā'tî*, vv. 24, 25, 30), yet the LORD did not repent of his repenting that he had made Saul king over Israel (v. 35). During this emotional meeting between Samuel and Saul, Saul seized and tore off (*qāraʿ*) the skirt of Samuel's garment, an action seized upon by Samuel: "The LORD has torn the kingdom of Israel from you this day, and has given it to a neighbor of yours, one better than you" (v. 28). The king of Israel spares a king condemned by the LORD, thereby incurring the wrath of the LORD. Saul's initial defense of his actions, that his decision to spare Agag's life was not disobedience to the LORD's voice, and that it was the people who had spared the best of the spoil (15:20–21), turns on a decisive gamble that Saul loses; his penalty is loss of a kingdom.

Chapter 24 illustrates how David, when confronted with a similar situation—whether to kill a king already rejected by God, a king, moreover, who has many times sought to kill him—similarly decides not to kill the king, but in this case the decision is portrayed as a correct one. Everything in chapter 24 seems to justify David, even as everything in chapter 15 seemed to condemn Saul. Consider the incident in the cave: the darkness there symbolizes uncertainty concerning how David's certain future will intermesh with Saul's uncertain end. David's men incite him to violence by telling him that the LORD has delivered Saul into his hand and that he may do whatever he wants. But what exactly is to be done with Saul? This question is precisely what makes the story so suspenseful from chapter 13 on: once David is chosen and Saul rejected, *how will David obtain the kingdom already given him by God?* David's decision, so much like Saul's, is not to kill the king, and its rightness is symbolized by an action that is much like the action in chapter 15 that symbolized Saul's error: as Saul *tore off* the skirt of Samuel's robe (*kᵉnap mᵉʿîlô*), David now *cuts off* the skirt of Saul's robe (*kᵉnap hammᵉʿîl*).[12] The first action and its effect are ragged, the second sharp and incisive. The loose ends unraveled in the first account now appear in a more clearcut fashion: David's cutting off the skirt of Saul's robe is mentioned three times in chapter 24 (vv. 5, 6, 12) and symbolizes even more cleanly the transfer of royal power from Saul to David.

When, therefore, he twice confronts Saul with the words "the LORD be judge between you and me" (vv. 13, 16), David's double allegation is not simply personal (whereas Saul had continually sought to kill David, David has now refrained from killing Saul) but also deeply ideological: when God incited Saul to kill a king and his people, Saul refused (chap. 15); when men in the LORD's name now incite David to kill Saul, David refuses (chap. 24). Both make a decision in their own kind of darkness, but Saul's decision not to kill was humanly inspired ("I have sinned because I feared the people and obeyed their voice." 15:24), whereas David's is apparently divinely inspired.[13]

Nevertheless, the dialogue between David and Saul in chapter 24 also betrays the self-interested motivation of both of them. On one hand, nothing is emphasized more in this chapter than that David refused to kill Saul because he was "the LORD's anointed" (vv. 7, 11; see also 26:9, 11, 16, 23): the reader cannot help realizing that the speaker of these words is *also* the LORD's anointed.[14] And so it turns out that David perhaps is shown not wanting to do anything himself that could also provide a precedant for his own murder later. On the other hand, Saul's words in verses 20–21, in which he prays that a man's sparing of his enemy should be rewarded by God (v. 20), and therefore ($w^{ec}att\bar{a}h$) that David's reward will be certain kingship (v. 21), also issue in a second consequence: "Now, therefore ($w^{ec}att\bar{a}h$), please swear to spare me and my seed" (v. 22). The reader remembers that after all Saul's loss of kingdom was provoked by the same situation he invokes in 24:20: "If a man finds his enemy, will he let him go away safe . . . ?" Saul's argument is that David ought to spare Saul's house and name, as Saul once tried to spare Agag.

Chapter 20 also puts this first confrontation of Saul and David in perspective. David's cutting off ($k\bar{a}rat$) the skirt of Saul's garment (vv. 5, 6, 12) and his oath not to cut off ($k\bar{a}rat$) Saul's descendants after him (v. 22) recall the covenant that David and Jonathan "cut" in chapter 20. When God "cuts off" everyone of David's enemies, David is not to "cut off" his loyalty from Jonathan's house (v. 15): "So Jonathan cut [a covenant] with the house of David" (v. 16). In chapter 20 Jonathan formalized this relationship by twice uttering the double-voiced statement: "(Behold) the LORD *is* between you and me . . . forever" (vv. 23, 42); likewise David in chapter 24 twice utters a similar statement that is also double voiced in its own way: "The LORD *judge* between me and you" (vv. 13, 16). As Jonathan and David were both united and divided by the covenant there, so David and Saul are both united and divided by their mercy here: Saul had spared Agag unwisely, but David has spared Saul providentially.

When we turn to chapter 25, Nabal is obviously related to the Saul of chapters 24 and 26 insofar as he is a similar object of mercy: David chooses not to kill the man who has returned evil for good.[15] However, a number of other details within the story reinforce the role of Nabal as a Saul figure and help to explain why chapter 25 is placed between the two stories involving Saul. First, as pointed out above, Abigail herself prays that all David's enemies, "those who seek (*biqqēš*) to do evil to my LORD be as Nabal" (25:26). In terms of the larger story in chapters 19–28, the only seeker of David is Saul: Saul is as Nabal, and Nabal as Saul. Second, David curiously refers to himself as Nabal's son: "Pray give whatever you have at hand . . . to your son, David" (25:8). As Saul stands for David's father under the law, so Nabal stands for Saul within the story.

Even more intriguing than these minor points of contact is the particular response that Nabal makes to David's request for food. Prefacing his statement with a double question ("Who is David? Who is the son of Jesse?" 25:10) that recalls the triple question of Saul ("Whose son is this youth?") and David's response ("I am the son of Jesse," 17:55–58), Nabal goes on to speak very much as Saul would have liked Ahimelech to speak when David similarly requested food from the priest: "There are many servants nowadays who are breaking away from their masters" (25:10). This is exactly the case from Saul's perspective: David has broken away from his master, Saul. In both chapters 21–22 and chapter 25, David requests food from someone whose life is subsequently put in jeopardy by the request: Saul kills Ahimelech and his entire house for giving the food, while David wants to kill Nabal and his house for refusing it. The difference between the two is that the LORD is said to have restrained David from murdering his enemy (25:26, 33). Here in chapter 25, the contrast between David and Saul, therefore, is not simply between one man who seeks to murder the other and the other who does not; it is between Saul, who in fact slaughtered an entire house, and David, who also wants to slaughter an entire household but is restrained from doing so by the LORD. Once again, as in chapter 24, the contrast is between past decisions of Saul that are condemned and present actions of David that are shielded from condemnation.

After chapter 24 had made clear that David would not personally lift a hand against Saul nor would allow anyone else to do so, the story of Nabal further reveals Saul's fate by having Nabal's fate prefigure it: each must die to enable, or at least benefit, David's rule. The connection between Nabal's death and David's rise is wonderfully captured in a detail of the story that illustrates its allusive quality. When Abigail invokes the image of God slinging out the life of David's enemies as from the hollow of a sling (25:29), an allusion to David's miraculous defeat of Goliath in chapter 17 is hard to avoid. When we read there that David "put his hand in his bag and took out a stone and slung it" (17:49), and then read here that Abigail's news caused Nabal to become as a stone

(25:37), the allusive circle is complete: David's enemy has been slung out like a stone from his sling, an allusion to David's victory over Saul as much as over Goliath.[16]

By the time we arrive at the second account of how David spared the life of Saul, chapter 26, the central matter that has motivated the entire section, indeed the entire second half of the book, now becomes explicit. What is to be done with Saul now that God has rejected him? Assuming that David will not kill Saul, how then will he die? Nabal's manner of death gave one possibility: "The LORD struck (*wayyiggop*) Nabal and he died" (25:38). David now spells out the triple possibility that results from his double refusal to murder Saul: "And David said, 'As the LORD lives, the LORD will smite him [*yiggopennû*, that is, Saul will suffer the same fate as Nabal] or his day shall come to die [that is, Saul will die a "natural" death] or he will go down into battle and perish [that is, Saul's actual fate as chap. 31 will describe it, but with an additional narrative twist]' " (26:10). The importance of this third episode about the fate of David's enemies in general, and of Saul in particular, lies not only in the increased explicitness with which the subject matter is treated, but also in its continuing dialogue with past events. Chapter 26 continues to rehearse the past even as it foreshadows the future.

The variant that best illustrates the Deuteronomist's use of previous accounts to cast light on present happenings is the jar of water and spear of Saul that are emblematic of David's decision not to kill Saul: "So David took the spear and the jar of water from Saul's head and they went away" (26:12). Just as the story of Abigail contrasted David's treatment of Saul with Saul's treatment of the priests of Nob, so also does the account here in chapter 26 reaffirm such a connection. Whereas David's taking of bread and the sword of Goliath caused Saul to murder the priests of Nob, here his taking of water and the spear of Saul embodies a refusal to murder. And if repetition is the mother of learning, then there is added significance in David's self-interested motivation for not murdering Saul: David's triple appeal to the evil of putting forth one's hand against "the LORD's anointed" (24:7 (twice), 11) is now repeated four more times: 26:9, 11, 16, 23. One may miss this section's more arcane allusions, but it is not easy to avoid its constant repetitions. At the same time as David is constantly shielded from blame, his motivation, like Saul's, is shown to be repeatedly self-serving.

Toward the end, the chapter contains a response of Saul to David's mercy that is even more explicitly repentant than that in chapter 24: there he could only acknowledge that David was more righteous than he (24:18); here he fully acknowledges, "I have sinned," and further promises no more to harm David (26:21). A notice in 27:4 indicates that Saul kept his side of the bargain: "And when it was told Saul that David had fled to Gath, he sought for him no more" (27:4).

By the end of chapter 26, the matter of Saul's death has been ominously raised three times, but what neither character nor reader yet knows is its manner. Will God strike him as he did Nabal? Will he die of natural causes? Or will he fall in battle? Whatever turns out to be the case, one puzzling aspect of the story will remain: why is it taking so long to dispose of Saul? We already suspect that there is something of a providential delay in this deferred denouement. But what does the providential delay itself signify?

The Scope of Providential Delay

There is an expansive vision in 1 Samuel, apparent throughout the book, that absolves it from damaging charges of didacticism. Even here in chapters 24—26, where a predeterminate view of David's rise and Saul's fall is most explicit, the theme of a mysterious and providential delay in the affairs of God and humanity complicates the story in ways that repeat what has already occurred and foreshadow what is to come. Indicative of this recurring pattern of delay found throughout the entire History is the painful process through which Saul is slowly removed from the scene. Well over half the book of 1 Samuel finds Saul sitting among the ashes of his kingship, and the reader who looks upon him during this period is tempted to repeat the words of Job's wife: "Curse God and die" (Job 2:9). But the tragedy of Saul's reign, like that of Job's life, strikes a responsive chord in one's heart that will never go away; nor will the triumph of David's reign, like Job's reinstatement in God's good graces, ever dissolve it. For Saul's reign is simply a preview of David's, and of every king of Israel and Judah after him. In fact, Saul's reign appears to be the Deuteronomist's prefiguring image of kingship itself as described throughout the History. We might try to put this matter in perspective before Saul's end arrives.

At the beginning of 1 Samuel, Hannah delayed the presentation of Samuel before the LORD until her child was weaned, a delay that provoked Elkanah's puzzling reply: "Wait until you have weaned him; only may the LORD establish his word" (1:23). As we suggested in the first chapter, Elkanah's statement introduced a central puzzle of the book: once having chosen Saul, why did the LORD reject him, and in rejecting him, how can the LORD's word be said to have been established? The false start of Saul's reign is a major puzzle within the book of 1 Samuel—and its central image. But now that the end of Saul's reign draws near, we begin to see that false start and providential delay are simply two ways of expressing the inexpressible mystery of God's dealings with Israel, and that the abortive reign of Saul is but a prefiguring of that abortion of God's rule which is kingship itself. Once Israel rejects God by demanding a king (8:7), it will take the rest of the History to describe the slow and painful process of God rejecting Israel.

Having already been alerted to this theme of false start and providential delay through the weaning of Samuel, we find the note repeated in many ways throughout the History. In its most generalized form it expresses and explains the puzzling admixture of strident threat and long-suffering partiality that describes the LORD's dealings with Israel from the beginning of the History to its end. No period better exemplifies this disparity between the telling and showing of God's justice than the period of the judges[17]—that is, until one realizes that even this period is but a reflection of every period in Israel's history from the giving of the ten words to the destruction of the temple. In this sense, given that Saul's reign prefigures the false start and providential delay that is David's reign, the apologetic thrust by which the quality of David's mercy toward Saul is strained in chapters 24–26 loses much of its didactic appearance.

Even now, when the triumphs of David's house lie mostly before the son of Jesse, the destruction of the nation—in the mind of the Deuteronomist exemplified by the introduction of kingship itself—already lies behind the reader of the History. What triumphalism can the "sure house" of David signify, whether prophesied by the man of God in 2:35, assured by Abigail in 25:28, or promised again by Nathan in 2 Samuel 7, once the exile has come upon Israel? If this disaster was providentially delayed by Davidic rule, this delay involves a false start already prefigured by Saul's rule before it. And once the temple itself lay destroyed, was not this destruction foreshadowed in the providential delay and false start described in 2 Samuel 7, where Nathan first approved David's plan to build a house, and then God determined that Solomon, not David, would build it? And is not the temple itself, in its solidity and age, testimony to a puzzling delay of divine retribution? The building of such a monument by an already rejected institution is itself a reflection of false start as providential delay. In truth, the History in many places seems like a complex hologram: at any point in the text one may come upon a generalized image of the entire History.

Perhaps it can be said that the very writing of the History is the best expression and final proof of the mysterious value and significance of this generalized principle of providential delay and false start. Perhaps the History endures as a literary monument because it *documents* the value of painful delays and keeps a continually disobedient Israel upon the stage long enough for a magnificent history to be written.

It seems, therefore, that God's repenting of having made Saul king, caused by Saul having spared a king from one of the nations, drags on for seventeen chapters because this delay is simply a repetition of a larger pattern affecting Israel itself. When Samuel hacks Agag to death, we almost hear the prophet saying to Saul, "Like Agag, whom the LORD makes to perish before you, so shall you perish, because you would not obey the voice of the LORD your God." But then, these words are really only an echo of those spoken by the greatest prophet of them all, Moses, who at the beginning of the History foretold its end: "Like the nations that the LORD makes to perish before you, so shall you perish, because you would not obey the LORD your God" (Deut. 8:20). Between Moses's issuing of this threat and God's fulfillment of it lies the borders of the History itself. However mysterious the delay in divine execution, the writing of the History demonstrates how providential it was for all of us who read it and see the vibration beneath.

Biblical Israel, like the Israelite monarchy that encompasses its later stages, and perhaps even like biblical humanity, which precedes both,[18] represents an experiment or experience that somehow succeeds in its very failure. It may be that this is what the providence of the Deuteronomic History—and in it—is all about.

Eight

SAUL AND HIS SONS: THE
END (27:1–31:13)

Losers must have leave to speak. (Colley Cibber, *The Rival Fools*)

In my beginning is my end. (T. S. Eliot, "East Coker")

David's Strategy and the Narrator's Plan (27:1–12)

David's escape to the land of the Philistines serves a narrative purpose wider than ensuring his physical safety.[1] In line with the previous chapters' emphasis on freeing David from any implication in the coming death of Saul, David's escape neatly reminds the reader that David is still breathing down Saul's neck. At the very moment when Saul "sought for [David] no more" (27:4), the narrator moves David into Achish's camp so that the ensuing conflict between the Philistines and Israel introduced in 28:1 will initially put David in a situation where he might confront Saul once more, not in an obscure cave or during a royal nap but in open battle. Will this possibility ever take place? Chapter 29 seems to end suspense by having the lords of the Philistines help David escape from future charges of bloodguilt, as Abigail helped him do so in chapter 25.

Having been given the city of Ziklag (27:6), David continues the duplicitous relationship with Achish that he began by feigning madness before the Philistine king in chapter 21. Attacking the inhabitants of the land, David leaves "neither man nor woman alive" (27:9). If he had resolved to kill only the males in Nabal's household, he now succeeds in killing all the inhabitants of the land whom he attacks, male and female alike, lest anyone report his treacherous behaviour to Achish (27:11). Chapter 27 ends with the narrator revealing the inner thoughts of Achish (as the inner thoughts of David were divulged at the beginning) in demonstration of David's successful treachery: "And Achish trusted David, thinking, 'He had made himself utterly abhorred by his people, Israel . . . therefore he shall be my servant always' " (27:12). When the Philistine later proclaims to David, "I know that you are as blameless in my sight as an angel of God" (29:9), Achish will be made to look as much the fool as Nabal was in chapter 25. At the same time, the reader's recognition of Achish's foolishness carries a corresponding realization of David's growing duplicity.[2] One continues to wonder whether David's dealings with various Israelites might not conceal similarly self-serving motives. However successfully David is shown escaping the clutches of Saul, he cannot escape the scrutiny of the reader. The story of David's rise to power is contrived as much against him as for him.

The manner in which the narrator shifts perspectives in chapters 27–31 is worth mentioning. Once the triptych of providential delays in chapters 24–26 is completed, an oscillating pattern of narration first noted in chapter 21 moves the story along toward Saul's death in chapter 31. This weaving back and forth between the "flow of the story" and various "interruptions" is more calculated than commentators recognize. David's move to Philistine country in chapter 27 (already foreshadowed in 21:10–15) is followed by Saul's seeking for answers in chapter 28. But then chapters 29–30 concern David's return to Philistine country and his distancing from anything to do with Saul's death. Similarly, chapter 28's prophecy of Saul's death finds its conclusion only later in chapter 31. Thus chapter 28 "interrupts" the natural flow of the story moving from chapter 27 to 29–30, just as chapters 29–30 "interrupt" the natural progression by which events flow from chapter 28 to chapter 31. Chapters 27–31 may very well indicate a narrative sensibility in which modern concepts like "narrative flow" and "narrative interruption" easily merge through the shifting perspectives of the narrator.[3]

Rise of Samuel, Fall of Saul, and Shroud of Kingship (28:1–25)

Ever since Samuel and Saul first crossed paths in chapter 9 the story has combined their character zones and fused their fates so completely that one has only to come upon their final confrontation in chapter 28 to feel how fitting a conclusion it is to their association. Threads that bound them together throughout the story are interwoven into the account of their meeting at Endor to provide an ancient instance of Henry James's modern dictum: "What is character but the determination of incident? What is incident but the illustration of character?"

One thread that has bound together Israel's last judge and first king from the start is Samuel's inducement of Saul to commingle the roles of prophet and king, thus provoking disastrous consequences for both of them. The strangely restrained references to Samuel's death in 25:1 and 28:3 appear to be faint praise indeed for a man who has played such a crucial role in guiding Israel on the royal path it now travels. Perhaps this doubled reticence carries its own negative evaluation of Samuel's career, and perhaps nothing condemns Samuel more than his progressive prophetization of Saul in an attempt to increase his own waning power over Israel. A second thread we have been emphasizing is Saul's gradual descent into sorcery and divination, a movement first recognized in the ritual baggage among which Saul fruitlessly hid in chapter 14. His oath of fasting, his frustrated efforts to inquire of the LORD, his casting of lots to seize the culprit, and his preference for doing things "at night" were all indications of Saul's divinizing of acceptable Israelite rituals in an excessive effort to ensure the success of his enterprises— like Gideon before him. This characterization prepared the reader for Samuel's accusations of divination and idolatry in 15:23. With Saul's gradual leanings toward divinatory practices comes a corresponding refusal of the LORD to answer him in any way. The LORD was profuse in answering David by Urim (23:6–12), by prophets (22:5), and, perhaps, even by dreams (23:1–5),[4] but when Saul inquired of the LORD, "the LORD did not answer him" in any of these ways (28:6).[5]

Many elements in the account of chapter 28, therefore, find their narrative antecedents in the story's progressive prophetization of Saul, his growing divinatory obsession, and God's continuing silence: Samuel receives a kind of narrative recompense for prophetizing Saul by having to appear before him in a disruptive divinatory apparition: Saul's inclination toward sorcery and divination ends up in a mediumistic prophecy of his death;[6] and God ends his silent treatment of Saul by communicating news that turns out to be terminal.[7]

What does Samuel look like as he is called up? When Saul asks the woman of Endor about his outline (*ta'ar*), she responds, "An old man is coming up; and he is wrapped in a robe (*me'îl*)." And immediately, "Saul knew it was Samuel" (v. 14). In this shadowy outline the reader sees an outline of the entire book of 1 Samuel: Samuel's birth and death encompass the book and express its central topic, the birth and death of kingship in Israel. Nothing clothes Samuel and Saul alike in kingship better than the robes they wear throughout the book.

From the earliest days of his youth to his resurrection in chapter 28, Samuel wears a robe representing the royalty that was wrapped around Israel during the course of the story. When Samuel first started ministering to the LORD at Shiloh, his mother Hannah began a practice of making a small robe (*me'îl qāṭon*), which she would take him each year when she went up to Shiloh (2:19). That young, berobed Samuel is now an old man and dead, and the robe has become a shroud. During his career, Samuel's robe was torn by Saul (15:27), an action Samuel interprets as the tearing away of the kingdom from Saul. Jonathan's robe played a similar role when he stripped it off to hand over to David (18:4), again signifying the transfer of royal power, the kingdom, from Saul's house to David's. Then David himself cut off the end of Saul's robe in 24:5, presenting Saul and the reader with a cleaner, more clearcut image of the seizing of kingship. When Saul had seized Samuel's robe, the kingdom was torn from Saul's grasp; when David cut Saul's robe, it was delivered up into his hands. This robe of royalty appears one final time in 1 Samuel, now wrapped around a dead person. In line with the conjoined character zones of Samuel and Saul throughout the story, Samuel is clothed in a dead man's robe as he foretells the imminent death of Saul and his sons. The robe as shroud enfolds Saul's death as well as Samuel's.

But the episode at Endor signifies much more than the demise of one king and the rise of another. The woman resurrects Samuel for Saul so that the narrator may resurrect a royal corpse for the Israelite reader. Chapter 28, with its fulfillment in chapter 31, is part of an inclusive reprise of the royal parable on the rise of Samuel and the death of Eli at the beginning of the book. The account of the death of Saul and his sons is also about the death of Israel and its kings.

Consider the circumstances surrounding chapters 1–7 on one hand and chapters 27–31 on the other. In both cases, war with the Philistines provides the occasion for a prophecy in which the death of an Israelite leader's sons is foretold.[8] The death of Saul and his sons prophesied by Samuel in chapter 28 is an uncanny reenactment of the parable that introduced the history of kingship in Israel. One may even suggest that Saul's reign itself acts like a kind of shadow parable by which the reader is meant to look forward to David's day and beyond—even to the exile—and see there the same false start and providential delay that embodied Saul's rule. As the rise of Samuel was a parable on the fall of kingship at the beginning of the book, so the resurrection of Samuel functions in a similar way at its end. God's vision to Samuel happened at night (chap. 3); so does Samuel's vision to Saul (28:8, 25).

Not only do Eli's and Saul's sons die at the beginning and end of the book[9] (the first pair are symbolic kings and the second trio potential ones), but Israel also falls into "the hands of the Philistines" (see 7:3, 14, and 28:19). As suggested above in chapter 2, the double defeat of Israel in 1 Samuel 4, together with the capture of the LORD's ark and its sojourn in Philistine country, carried exilic overtones that complemented the downfall of kingship seen in the collapse of Eli's house. In much the same way here at the end of 1 Samuel, the prophesied defeat of Israel and the collapse of Saul's house are accompanied by an enforced sojourn of the LORD's anointed, David, in Philistine country. There are both ideological significance and narrative symmetry in the Philistine interludes of chapters 5–6 on one hand and chapters 27, 29–30 on the other. Is it accidental that both *ark* of the LORD and *anointed* of the LORD remain in Philistine country a sufficient number of months to cause serious harm within it: "The ark of the LORD was in the country of the Philistines seven months" (6:1); "And the number of days that David dwelt in the country of the Philistines was a year and four months" (27:7)? During these sojourns, when the LORD's ark and the LORD's anointed were lost to Israel, their presence in Philistine country caused havoc—the plagues within the Philistine pentapolis on one hand, and David's raids upon the inhabitants of the land on the other.

If there is a kind of gross anatomical similarity between the beginning of our story and its end, there are also a number of details that chronicle the differences between the Samuel-Eli encounters as parabolic beginning to the royal story and the Samuel-Saul encounter as its shadowy end. We were foretold the death of Eli's sons through the narrator's revelation in 2:25, the word of a man of God in 2:27–36, and Samuel's vision in chapter 3. This was a time when "the word of the LORD was rare . . . there was no frequent vision" (3:1), and when "Samuel did *not yet* know the LORD and the word of the LORD had *not yet* been revealed to him" (3:7). But since then, the idolatrous reign of kingship intervened in the person of Saul, whose divinatory tendencies are emphasized in chapters 14–15, and now, finally, in chapter 28. The "not yet" of the LORD's word to Samuel has become the "no longer" of the LORD's word to Saul: "And when Saul inquired of the LORD, the LORD did not answer him, either by dreams, or by Urim or by prophets" (28:6). Saul complains, "God has turned away from me and answers me *no more*, either by prophets or by dreams" (28:15).

In these plaintive words, it is not especially difficult to hear the voice of Israel in exile, looking across the divide that separates its life from its past and reflecting upon a centuries-old dalliance with kingship. In the beginning, a young Samuel and old Eli had encountered the pristine word of the LORD ("It is the LORD," Eli tells Samuel, 3:18). But then kingship wrought its first idolatrous effects upon Israel, and an old Samuel and his new master, Saul, are now implicated in a prophetic word clothed in divination: the woman of Endor expresses the idolatry of kingship when she sees an old man clothed in a royal robe and "rising up from the earth like a god" (28:13).[10]

The narrator's choice of a prophetic medium—or a mediumistic prophet—by whom Saul learns of his impending death is a final link between the fate of Saul and the ultimate exile of Israel. When Moses forbade Israel to allow mediums and wizards in its midst, he pointed to such abominations as causes for God's dispossession of the people whom Israel was to force out of the land (18:10–11). If this teaching is understood in the context of Moses' prophetic threat in 8:20, "Like the nations that the LORD makes to perish before you, so shall you perish because you would not obey the voice of the LORD your God," it becomes clear that Saul's initial putting away of mediums and wizards (28:3, 9) and his subsequent consultation of a medium in chapter 28 map out the fate of Israel in a particularly appropriate way. When the end of *Israel* draws near, the narrator once again will point to the abominable practices of one king, Manasseh (2 Kings 21:6), and the reforms of another king, Josiah (2 Kings 23:24), both dealing with mediums and wizards in their own way and to no avail. Israel's disastrous end, like

Saul's, is bound up with royal sorcery and idolatry. The reader may now realize that when Hannah says of Samuel, "He is Saul (*šā'ûl*) to the LORD" (1:28), she is referring not just to her son's lifelong counterpart and narrative double, Saul—and to every king who came after them— but even more poignantly to the nation who gave birth to them all.

Whether the woman of Endor's final preparation of a feast for Saul and his servants (28:24–25) and her concern "that you may have strength when you go on your way" (v. 22) have any ideological significance for the final fate of Israel in the History is not particularly clear—except that the last image we have of the last Judahite king is of the exiled Jehoiachin dining every day of his life at the table of the king of Babylon (2 Kings 25:30).

The Spoils of David (29:1–30:31)

The inclusive function of the account of the campaign between Israel and Philistia at the end of 1 Samuel is signaled by the Philistines gathering at the very place where they gathered at the beginning of the book, Aphek (4:1 and 29:1). The beginning story of the defeat of the Israelites by the Philistines and the capture of the ark is now replayed with specific details pointing back to this earlier account and its significance in the story. There, the capture of "the ark of the covenant of the LORD of hosts who is enthroned on the cherubim" (4:4), with the royal overtones attached to this designation and with all the other royal features comprising the parable of kingship in chapters 1–7, underscored the connection between the establishment of kingship in Israel and the captivity of Israel in Babylon. As mentioned above, the "royal" ark remained in Philistine country seven months (6:1), as the anointed of the LORD remained there sixteen months (27:7). Both presences are destructive within their land of sojourn—a series of plagues within the Philistine pentapolis, and a series of deadly raids by David against the inhabitants of the land in chapters 27 and 30. The Philistines are powerless to prevent either ark or anointed of the LORD from becoming "an adversary to us" (29:4). Moreover, as the narrator took care to emphasize the ignorance of the Philistines displayed in their misrepresentation of Yahwism (for example, 4:8), so also chapter 29 emphasizes Achish's profound ignorance of the adversary within his midst: "I know," Achish responds to David, "that you are blameless in my sight as an angel of God" (29:9).

So while the surface of the story deals with David's escape from culpability in the coming death of Saul and his three sons, the larger issues continue to be those concerning exile: the small band of Israelites exiled in Ziklag is subjected to a further captivity as the Amalekites overcome Ziklag and carry off everyone within it "both small and great" (30:2).[11] But David's rescue of everything captured by the Amalekites quickly follows: "David recovered all that the Amalekites had taken. . . . Nothing was missing whether small or great, sons or daughters, spoil or anything that had been taken: David brought back all . . . and the people said, 'This is David's spoil' " (30:18–20). Like Hannah's bitterness of soul and weeping at not having a son (1:10), David and the people's weeping (30:4) and the people's bitterness of soul "each for his sons and daughters" (30:6) are now turned to joy with the recovery of those who had been made captive. Still, it is not lost upon the reader that David and his small band of Israelites remain in exile in Ziklag.

The strange interlude recounted in chapters 29–30 is a reflection upon the spoils of David (*šᵉlal dāvid*, 30:20) as the portion of *all Israel* (*yaḥdaw yaḥᵃloqû*, 30:24): Israel's share in the spoils of David's kingship ultimately turn out to be exilic in nature. In spite of Josiah's reform, when the words of the book of the covenant were read in the hearing of "all the people both small and great" (2 Kings 23:2), the History will record one final exile as part of David's spoil: "Then all the people both small and great . . . arose and went to Egypt" (2 Kings 25:26). The related issues of culpability and fate—afflicting individual and nation alike—circle around the interlude at Ziklag like vultures over a corpse. That corpse is both the beheaded body of Saul and the exiled body of Israel, and both belong to "the spoils of David." What ties together Ziklag and Babylon?

Notice how the words of David sound like a clarion call within the chapter. When wicked and base fellows within David's band of four hundred men who had defeated the Amalekites refuse to share the spoil with the two hundred men who had been too exhausted to follow David, he made a statute and ordinance, in effect "from that day forward even to this day" (v. 25): "For as his share is who goes down into battle, so shall his share be who stays by the baggage; they shall share alike" (v. 24). Apparently directed solely at the specific issue at hand—who is to enjoy the booty captured from the Amalekites?—the statement integrates the entire account in a number of interesting ways: the story revolves around more than one instance of characters who have been "left behind."

The first instance is the Egyptian lad, servant to an Amalekite who "left me behind because I fell sick three days ago" (30:13). The lad leads David to the Amalekite camp and is thus responsible for their defeat at David's hands.[12] David shares the spoil of this victory by (presumably) preserving the life of the lad left behind. Then, of course, come the two hundred men of David's band, left behind because they were too exhausted to cross the brook Besor (v. 10); they also share in the spoil of the four hundred who went down in battle. Next come the elders of Judah, to whom David sends presents from the spoil of the enemies of the LORD (30:26). Not having participated in the battle itself, they receive a share nonetheless.

All of these characters in the story help the reader to understand the larger issue involved in these concluding events. For besides the Egyptian, the exhausted two hundred, and the elders of Judah, one other character does not participate in a battle yet shares in its spoil: if the battle is between the Philistines and Saul's army, the one left behind by the Philistines is David himself. Far from exculpating David from any part in the death of Saul and the defeat of the Israelites, the stories in chapters 29–31 do not shrink from placing responsibility for the death of Saul and the defeat of Israel upon the shoulders of David himself: apparently willing to go down (29:4) or up (29:9) in battle against Saul and his own people,[13] David is constrained to return to Ziklag, and he is left behind as the climax approaches. Nevertheless, the Deuteronomist uses David's own law and statute to put the story in perspective. Having been left behind by the lords of the Philistines, David more than anyone else shares in the spoils resulting from Saul's death. In fact, both benefit and blame are laid at David's feet by his own words: "For as his share is who goes down into battle, so shall his share be who stays by the baggage; they shall share alike" (30:24). Most immediately, David bears the responsibility for Saul's death as surely as Saul would have for David's, had David died at the hands of the Philistines in chapter 18. More profoundly, however, the evils of kingship remain the spoils of David as well as of Saul, so that blame belongs to him who remains behind to rule (David), as well as to him who goes down into battle to die (Saul). The king who hid himself among the baggage when called upon to rule (20:22) is replaced by one who stays by the baggage (30:24) as he waits for a chance to rule.

At ideological issue also in all this is the culpability of Israel itself in the exilic fate that finally befell it, foreshadowed by the beginning parable of chapters 1–7 and the shadow parable of chapters 27–31. The details of Saul's end are a conclusive comment on Israel's: to have demanded a king to rule over it was an act of political and communal suicide.

The End Is the Beginning (31:1–13)

When the people "refused to listen to the voice of Samuel and said, 'No, we will have a king over us . . . *that our king may go out before us to fight our battles*' " (8:20), their political fate was sealed as surely as Saul's personal fate is here in chapter 31. As all Saul's men died "on the same day together" (*yaḥdaw*, v. 6), and as those who go down into battle and those who stay by the baggage both share alike (*yaḥdaw yaḥ*ᵃ*loqû*, 30:24), so the fate of Israel and its king is the same: "You shall be swept away, both you and your king" (12:25). The details of Saul's death provide us with the Deuteronomist's final comment in the book on the fatal union of Israel and its kings.[14]

The most obvious connection between the details of Saul's death and the evils of kingship is the similarity between the reactions of a wounded

Saul and those of a wounded Abimelech in Judges 9. As David Jobling has effectively demonstrated,[15] the account of Abimelech's abortive attempt to become king over Israel offers the reader a powerfully proleptive view of the Deuteronomist's coming history of kingship in Israel. Wounded in battle, both Abimelech and Saul ask their armor bearers to kill them lest they bear the ignominy of being killed by one who is uncircumcised (in Abimelech's case by a woman, in Saul's by the Philistines). The differing responses of their armor bearers is significant: Abimelech's young man thrusts him through (Judg. 9:54), but Saul's is unwilling to kill his master, forcing the king to commit suicide and disposing the armor bearer to do likewise (31:4–5).

If, as I suggest, the rise of Samuel and the fall of Saul form a kind of parabolic *inclusio* about the role of kingship in the exilic fate of Israel, then the particular manner in which Saul dies may form the Deuteronomist's epitaph over the corpse of Israel buried in Babylon: kingship, despite all its glories, constituted for Israel communal suicide. Moreover, at the level of the History's characterizations, the unwillingness of Saul's lad to do him in, as well as Saul's final abhorrent act of self-destruction, may tell us something about the lesson offered an exilic Israel. Perhaps Saul's final sin is more tragic than his earlier sins: as he impatiently took matters into his own hands in chapters 13 and 15, and impatiently tried to force God's hand in chapter 14, Saul one last impatient time refuses to let the LORD's providence run its course and takes matters into his own hands by ending his life.[16] However, whereas Abimelech's lad obeyed his master, Saul's is unwilling, and this may be the course that the Deuteronomist charts for an exilic Israel. Despite its fear of being made sport of by its Chaldean masters (as Saul feared the Philistines making sport of him, 31:4), Israel may not have lost everything in the exile: it may very well hope for a new exodus. In a final splendid irony, the words of the Philistine priests and diviners to their plagued compatriots in the book's opening parable whisper in Israel's ears at the end of the book and provide sound advice to a nation in exile: "Why should you harden your hearts as the Egyptians and Pharaoh hardened their hearts? When he had made sport of them, did he not let the people go, and they departed?" (6:6). As the ark was returned leaderless to the land of Israel (chap. 6), so might Israel one day return kingless to its own land. After all, this is very much what is to take place under Ezra and Nehemiah.

NOTES

Introduction

1. The cautionary remarks of Eslinger, *Kingship of God in Crisis* (Sheffield: Almond Press, 1985), pp. 467–68, on the relationship of text criticism and interpretation perceptively indicate some of the problems involved in this matter.
2. P. D. Miller and J. J. M. Roberts, *The Hand of the Lord: A Reassessment of the "Ark Narrative" of 1 Samuel* (Baltimore: Johns Hopkins Univ. Press, 1977).
3. Ibid., pp. 71–73.
4. See for example, J. T. Willis, "An Anti-Elide Narrative Tradition from a Prophetic Circle at the Ramah Sanctuary," *Journal of Biblical Literature* 90 (1971), pp. 288–308.
5. See also J. T. Willis, "Samuel Versus Eli," *Theologische Zeitschrift* 35 (1979), pp. 201–12. This article documents the double standard that Miller and Roberts use in identifying their original ark narrative and effectively demonstrates how they arbitrarily distinguish original from redactional passages.
6. Miller and Roberts, *Hand of the Lord*, p. 23.
7. Ibid., pp. 19, 21.
8. As I will indicate below in chapter 1.
9. M. Sternberg, *The Poetics of Biblical Narrative* (Bloomington: Indiana Univ. Press, 1985), chap. 1. For other excellent introductions to discourse-oriented study of biblical narrative, see Robert Alter, *The Art of Biblical Narrative* (New York: Basic, 1983) and Adele Berlin, *Poetics and Interpretation of Biblical Narrative* (Sheffield: Almond Press, 1983). As some scholars have foreseen, the new movement toward discourse-oriented study of biblical narrative is especially welcome to more conservative biblical scholars, who subscribe, for example, to a dispensational hermeneutics in which human composition is guided by the inspiration of the Holy Spirit. Thus, from a denominational perspective, whereas the more liberally based scholar (most often a historical critic) largely ignores or at most confusedly mentions the growing body of discourse-oriented studies, a conservative writer like John A. Martin, who often mentions the guidance of the Holy Spirit on biblical writers, freely quotes with approval academic colleagues—but denominational or theological opponents—like Fokkelman or Alter, toward whose more holistic approaches to biblical narrative he is quite naturally congenial. From Martin's perspective, the more persuasively the artistry of biblical narrative is shown to be, the more obviously does modern scholarship operate *ad majorem Dei gloriam*. See J. A. Martin, "Studies in 1 and 2 Samuel: Parts 1 to 4," *Bibliotheca Sacra* 14 (1984), pp. 21–42; 131–45; 209–22; and 303–14. This fundamentalist welcoming of holistic approaches to biblical material was foreseen by James Barr in a review of Childs's *Introduction to the Old Testament as Scripture*, in *Journal for the Study of the Old Testament* 16 (1980), pp. 12–23.
10. Miller and Roberts, pp. 1, 17.
11. Martin Noth, *The Deuteronomistic History* (Sheffield: Almond Press, 1981), p. ix. This

volume, referred to as ET in subsequent notes, is a translation of the first part of Martin Noth, *Überlieferungsgeschichtliche Studien*, (2d ed. (Tübingen: Niemeyer, 1957). I will be quoting from Noth's 3d edition of 1967.

In contrast to Nicholson, John Van Seters characterizes the matter quite differently: "Returning to Noth's thesis of a single Dtr history, we find that the reactions to it vary from qualified approval to rather strong rejection." John Van Seters, *In Search of History* (New Haven and London: Yale University Press, 1983), p. 232.

12. With respect to 1 Samuel, very little of the book, according to Noth, was composed by Dtr: these passages include 2:25b, 34–35; 7:2–8:22 (but Dtr adapted earlier sources in 7:11b–12a, 16–17; 8:2); 10:17–27a (but Dtr utilized earlier local sources in 10:21b–27a); 12:1–25; 13:1. Dtr primarily used earlier traditions in composing the text of 1 Samuel, largely leaving these traditions unchanged. Such sources included stories about Samuel (1:1–4:12), Saul (9:1–10:16; 10:27b–11:15; 13; 14), and David (4:1b–7:1; 16:14–2 Sam. 5:25). After Dtr composed his work, subsequent editorial additions are represented by passages such as 4:18b; 15:1–16:13. In the rarest of cases, as concerning 10:8, Noth admits to being undecided whether a pericope "was inserted before or after Dtr" (Noth, p. 63 [ET: p. 125]). Noth therefore sees only about one-tenth of 1 Samuel as coming from Dtr's hand; the rest is simply either already written traditions that Dtr has selected, compiled, and arranged (Noth, p. 90 [ET: p. 77]), and that his own words interpret, or else subsequent additions to his history.

For an assessment of Noth's tradition-historical methodology as exemplified in his work on Pentateuchal traditions, see my *Biblical Structuralism* (Chico: Scholars Press, 1977), pp. 174–201.

13. Noth, p. 3. (ET: pp. 2–3).

14. Ibid., pp. 12, 96. (ET: p. 11, 84).

15. Ibid., pp. 98, 99. (ET: p. 86, 87).

16. Ibid., pp. 73, 89, 100. (ET: pp. 63, 76, 88).

17. Ibid., p. 54. (ET: p. 47).

18. This inexplicable distance between the work as described and the work as evaluated is typically found in source-oriented treatments of the History, as the following discussion will continue to illustrate.

19. Frank Cross, *Canaanite Myth and Hebrew Epic* (Cambridge, MA: Harvard Univ. Press, 1973), p. 287.

20. Ibid., p. 288. So far as I can tell concerning 1 Samuel, Cross sees the hand of this second Deuteronomist (Dtr²) only in 12:25 (p. 287). Cross distinguishes two ancient sources used by his primary Deuteronomist (Dtr¹), both of them of northern provenance but the first older than the second: (A): 9:1–10:16; 11:1–15; 13; 14; and (B): 7:3–17; 8:1–22a; 10:18–25a; 12; 15.

21. Ibid., p. 289.

22. According to Cross, *Canaanite Myth*, almost everything in Deuteronomy–2 Kings except Deut. 4:27–31; 28:36ff., 63–68; 29:27; Josh. 23:11–13, 15ff.; 1 Sam. 12:25; 1 Kings 2:4; 6:11–13; 8:25b, 46–53; 9:4–9; 2 Kings 17:19; 20:17ff.; 23:26–25:30; and perhaps Deut. 30:11–20; 1 Kings 3:14.

23. Ibid., pp. 284, 288, 250.

24. Noth, *Deuteronomistic History* p. 54. (ET: p. 47)

25. Ibid., p. 96. (ET: p. 84).

26. Cross, *Cannanite Myth*, p. 288. Cross's theory of a dual redaction of the History has found strong support in subsequent studies by other scholars. For example, see Richard D. Nelson, *The Double Redaction of the Deuteronomistic History* (Sheffield: Almond Press, 1981) and R. E. Friedman, *The Exile and Biblical Narrative* (Chico, CA: Scholars Press, 1981). The story of more than two redactions is recounted in G. E. Gerbrandt, *Kingship According to the Deuteronomistic History* (Atlanta: Scholars Press, 1986), who inclines toward Cross's two-staged adaptation of Noth's position. However, Gerbrandt believes that Dtr² probably had an ideology closer to Dtr¹ (and contributed more additions to it) than Cross's theory allows (Gerbrandt, *Kingship*, pp. 17–18). In addition, Gerbrandt thinks it unlikely in principle that the History would ever have seriously questioned such a long-established institution as kingship. Although I seriously disagree with Gerbrandt's reading of 1 Sam. 8–12, I nevertheless welcome his approach to interpretation, which follows the lead of scholars like A. D. H. Mayes (see below) by reading these chapters much more holistically than others are

accustomed to do. Brian Peckham's recent *The Composition of the Deuteronomistic History* (Atlanta: Scholars Press, 1985) also supports a two-staged theory in the composition of the History, yet it differs in many respects from other descriptions of the specific process involved. A. D. H. Mayes's *The Story of Israel Between Settlement and Exile* (London: SCM Press 1983) is, as its subtitle states, a redactional study of the History. In addition to its general strengths in synthesis and assessment of previous research, together with original views of its own, Mayes's work clearly and specifically supports the major conclusions of Cross's theory.

27. Cross, *Canaanite Myth*, p. 289.
28. In contrast to all this reconstructive effort, my approach to the History, in the present reading of 1 Samuel, as in *Moses and the Deuteronomist* (New York: Seabury, 1980), simply tries to give a more satisfactory account of how the real text, whatever its pre-texts, may be not only creative but also ideologically, historiographically, and esthetically valuable to ancient and modern readers alike.
29. Van Seters, *In Search of History*, pp. 307, 359.
30. Ibid., pp. 3, 15, 16, 39, 51, 362.
31. Van Seters's literary-historical discussion of 1 and 2 Samuel (pp. 249–91 and 346–53) is extremely detailed and not always clear, especially when referring to "redactional," "secondary," or "later" additions (to the History or to the History's already written sources?). Which of these additions are pre- and which post-Dtr is sometimes obvious from his discussions, sometimes not. My understanding of his historical reconstruction of the process of composition of 1 and 2 Samuel is therefore tentative: (1) *pre-Dtr passages* include 9:1–10:16 (mostly, but see below); 11:1–13, 15; 13:2–4a, 5–7a, 16–23; (2) *Dtr passages* include chaps. 1–8; 10:17–27; 11:12–14; 12; 13:4b, 7b–15; and the Story of David's Rise, 16:14—2 Sam. 7 (8?); and (3) *post-Dtr passages* include 15:1—16:13 and, most importantly, the Court History, 2 Sam. 9—20, 1 Kings 1—2. (I am not sure which of the following "redactional additions" are pre- and which post-Dtr: 9:9, 15–17, 27a,b; 10:1, 7–8, 14–16; 13:4b, 7b–15a.)
32. Van Seters, *In Search of History*, pp. 290, 359.
33. This phrase is used with obvious approval by Van Seters, *In Search of History*, p. 39.
34. For example, ibid., p. 49.
35. Ibid., pp. 17–18.
36. For example, Henry Immerwahr, whom Van Seters praises for his analyses of Herodotus's paratactic style, never analyzes Herodotus the way Van Seters analyzes the History. In fact, Immerwahr very clearly opposes the type of genetic analysis exemplified in Van Seters's discussion of the History. Immerwahr writes,

> "Genetic theories operate upon the assumption that traces of such earlier conceptions survive in the final version, and that we can recognize them unequivocally for what they are. This is true, however, only when the final stage is very incompletely finished, and a number of remnants of earlier concepts are evident which conflict with the final stage and have neither been eliminated nor adjusted. The genetic approach is by necessity largely negative in its judgment of the final versions, since it cannot succeed without finding imperfections, and thus is apt to lead us away from a sympathetic understanding of the text. Furthermore, a knowledge of style and structure is a prerequisite rather than a consequence of the study of origins, since all too often the inconsistencies on which such a study is based turn out to be stylistic peculiarities." (Henry R. Immerwahr, *Form and Thought in Herodotus* [Cleveland: Western Reserve University Press 1966], p. 8.)

These words turn out to be a trenchant critique of most genetic theories on the composition of the Deuteronomistic History in general and of Van Seters's entire analysis of the History in particular (chaps. 8–10 of *In Search of History*).

37. J. P. Fokkelman, *Narrative Art and Poetry in the Books of Samuel*, vol. 1, *King David (2 Sam 9–20 and 1 Kg 1–2)* (Amsterdam: Van Gorcum, 1981).
38. Charles Conroy, *Absalom, Absalom! Narrative and Language in 2 Sam 13–20* (Rome: Pontifical Biblical Institute, 1978).
39. One might also refer to numerous studies of R. Alter, A. Berlin, H. Frei, R. Polzin, J. Rosenberg, M. Sternberg, and many others, all appearing well before the publication of *In Search of History* and all emphasizing, in theory or in practice, "the integrity of the text" and "narrative style and techniques," matters that Van Seters discusses in theory but fails to incorporate in his analyses of the History. To equate discourse-oriented treatments of biblical narrative with "structuralism," as Van Seters apparently does, is

to indicate a lack of awareness on these matters. The part is mistaken for the whole, and then the whole is condemned on account of the part.

40. Van Seters, *In Search of History,* pp. 38, 40, and *passim.*

41. Those who still defend specific genetic theories like the documentary hypothesis or the double edition of the History often fail to realize that the explanatory need and force of such literary-historical reconstructions have been severely challenged by contemporary discussions of narrative poetic matters such as repetition, point of view, voice structure, plot, etc. The very motives for producing specific genetic theories—motives such as internal contradictions, stylistic variations, repetitive features, and so forth—now appear much less compelling than previously. Few modern geneticists within biblical studies appear willing to meet these challenges to their theories, so that one searches in vain for a literary-historical defense of old views on the narrative function of repetition or contradiction. The strangely defensive and irresponsibly dismissive tone and content of John S. Coolidge's recent review of Meir Sternberg's *Poetics of Biblical Narrative* in *Catholic Biblical Quarterly* 49 (1987), pp. 324–25, is a rather extreme response to such challenges. The uninformed nature of *In Search of History* on literary-critical matters that it itself terms crucial to its own thesis is simply indicative of a discipline lamentably out of touch with contemporary concerns within the humanities—concerns that need to become central to biblical scholarship.

One of the few scholars I know of who has taken up the challenge to genetic theories within biblical studies is Jeffrey Tigay, who has recently edited an important new book, *Empirical Models for Biblical Criticism* (Philadelphia: Univ. of Pennsylvania Press, 1985). Tigay is concerned to show how criticisms of many genetic theories of composition as unrealistic can now be countered by external analogues such as cuneiform evidence for, say, the literary history of the Gilgamesh Epic. Tigay believes that such analogues "can only serve to show what is plausible or realistic by showing what has happened elsewhere" (p. 17). In choosing among external analogues from various times and places for such literary techniques of composition, Tigay insists, "If we are indeed dealing with wide-spread common-sense techniques . . . ancient Near Eastern and post-biblical Jewish analogues . . . will nonetheless retain a preeminent position among extra-biblical models used by biblical scholars" (p. 18). Tigay concludes in chap. 1 ("The Evolution of the Pentateuchal Narratives in the Light of the Evolution of the Gilgamesh Epic") that "it seems nonetheless clear that the stages and processes through which this epic *demonstrably* passed are similar to some of those through which the Pentateuchal narratives are *presumed* to have passed" (p. 27).

To his credit, Tigay has shown, for the first time and in a convincing manner through many ancient examples, that the types of genetic theories of composition that biblical scholars have produced in modern times have a literary-historical justification that is realistically motivated. Nevertheless, since there are few internal empirical models and insufficient empirical evidence to help us decide in most cases which of the various genetic theories is to be preferred over its competitors, the present situation in biblical studies, in which most competing genetic theories of composition remain by and large unfalsifiable and equally speculative, will remain unchanged by Tigay's demonstrations.

The use of external analogues to show how literary-historical research in biblical studies is, generally speaking, realistically motivated is mostly irrelevant, first, to the specific interpretation of specific texts, and, second, to one's ability to choose one specific genetic theory over its rival. If, for example, a particular reading of a text plausibly challenges the very basis for applying a specific genetic theory to that text in the first place—by arguing, say, against supposed incoherences or tensions in the text—then any such genetic theories, however realistically based through external analogues, may be irrelevant to this specific text. In such a case, the application of this or that genetic theory may be unnecessary, even though we all recognize that the text probably had a complicated process of composition behind its present form. Moreover, even when hypotheses of the text's historical composition are found to be necessary (as when no amount of interpretational effort appears to remove the narrative "noise" heard in the text), the use of external analogues still leaves the scholar unable, most of the time, to choose between one or the other specific theory except in the most trivial cases, as for example in deciding why 1 Sam. 13:1 is incoherent.

To be more specific, even if we agree with Tigay that the literary history of the Gilgamesh Epic renders plausible those biblical theories that assume a "separate tale → combination of tales profile" (pp. 29–35), there still is no way to choose among the countless specific theories that share this general conception, nor can one be sure that in this or that ancient text the general rule applied. Tigay, in my opinion, has accomplished less than he may have intended. As is apparent from p. 43 n. 91 and *pace* his strong defense elsewhere of "general conceptions" (for example, p. 30 n.34 on Jastrow), specific theories about specific texts is essentially the heart of the matter: even specialists in the Gilgamesh Epic disagree about essentials in its evolution. Tigay's comparative application to biblical studies ("A comparison of [at least four different stages in the evolution of the Gilgamesh Epic] with each other reveals a pattern of decreasing degrees of adaptation of earlier sources and versions," p. 35) strives to set up an empirical basis for distinguishing editorial from authorial influences in a text. But without specific documentary evidence of various stages of the biblical text— which Tigay in fact has for the Gilgamesh Epic—biblical theories that claim to distinguish such influences remain entirely speculative. Henry Immerwahr's remarks on genetic theories in classical studies, quoted above in n. 36, remain apposite to Tigay's claims.

Tigay himself inadvertently offers a kind of proof that such essential questions as editorial versus authorial influences on a text—questions central to almost all genetic theories—must remain speculative until actual ancient versions are found that testify to earlier literary historical stages of the biblical text. As Tigay's references to Jastrow acknowledge (for example, pp. 30, 51), only the discovery of ancient witnesses has enabled us to distinguish which of Jastrow's specific literary historical suggestions about specific texts bears any resemblance at all to empirical reality. Tigay's approving quotation of Eissfeldt's statement, "The important point is . . . not this or that individual dissection of the material but the total outlook" (p. 51), belies the weakness of this view. In literary matters of both the genetic and poetic variety, specific interpretations of specific texts are everything.

Tigay's book, therefore, is both important and trivial. It is a convincing argument against all those who hold that genetic study of biblical texts is ill founded. It argues correctly that such genetic theories are "realistic in general conception." At the same time, however valuable this accomplishment may be, one feels that it is finally trivial since scholars who deny the Bible's long and complicated genesis are really not taken seriously today within scholarly circles. It is revealing that Tigay and the contributors to his volume rarely deal substantively with scholars like Alter, Berlin, Fokkelman, Polzin, Rosenberg, or Sternberg, who while acknowledging the plausibility, indeed the certainty, of complex processes of composition still expose or undercut uninformed or excessively narrow attitudes of most geneticists toward features of ancient texts like repetition, point of view, reported and reporting speech, and so forth. Tigay unfortunately limits the bulk of his remarks concerning "opponents" to the limited and sometimes outdated views of scholars like Cassuto or Kitchen. Tigay's central argumentation is comparable to a physicist writing a book against creationists: the book purports to show how the many often conflicting theories explaining the genesis of the universe are all "realistic in general conception" because there exist empirical bases for the genesis of the universe.

For another discussion of Tigay's research on the Gilgamesh Epic as it applies to biblical criticism, see Adele Berlin, *Poetics and Interpretation of Biblical Narrative*, pp. 129–34.

42. Van Seters, *In Search of History*, p. 359.
43. It was Samuel Sandmel's opinion that "an oblivion to the text itself seems to me the greatest defect in present-day biblical scholarship." Sandmel, "The Haggada within Scripture," *Journal of Biblical Literature* 80 (1961), p. 108. Twenty years later, Robert Gordis, in a response to James Barr's generally unsympathetic review of his *The Book of Job* (New York: Jewish Theological Seminary of America 1978), raised two important methodological or theoretical points that my reading of 1 Samuel emphasizes throughout. See Gordis "Traumatic Surgery in Biblical Scholarship: A Note on Methodology," *Journal of Jewish Studies* 32 (1981), pp. 195–99. First, in reference to the ease with which scholars delete or transpose portions of the MT for text-critical or literary-critical reasons, Gordis rightly remarks, "But critical scholars have for so long

engaged in these radical procedures that they have ceased to recognize that they are at best provisional and frequently highly questionable, *because the given text is a datum and the emended, deleted or transposed text is a hypothesis*" (p. 198, emphasis Gordis's). Second, Gordis is one of the few scholars—Fishbane is another—who have recognized the importance of hidden or inexplicit reported speech in the study of biblical literature. Although he does not invoke any philosophy of language or broad literary-critical stance that would support his position (as, for example, Bakhtin's), Gordis has written a number of articles over the years (conveniently listed on p. 197 of his reply to Barr) on what he terms "virtual quotation," and he has come to recognize the importance of this aspect of biblical narrative poetics.

44. My emphasis on the final text requires me to write a few words about how I view my own perspective in relation to what is generally called "canonical criticism" as exemplified, say, by Brevard Childs in his *Introduction to the Old Testament as Scripture* (Philadelphia: Fortress Press 1979) or James Sanders in his *Canon and Community* (Philadelphia: Fortress Press 1984). I obviously welcome their greater emphasis on the various final forms of the biblical text. Nevertheless, I have serious reservations about certain supposed similarities we have in approaching the text. First, while Sanders, in my opinion, generally recognizes that "a necessary task *barely begun* [emphasis mine] is that of analyzing the structure of whole biblical books or larger literary units" (Sanders, p. 62), and although Sanders asserts that canonical criticism "includes both a particular perspective and a set of tools and techniques" (p. 21), neither scholar seems very much aware that, on the literary front at least, there must be more to such tools and techniques than simply applying the same old literary-historical questions and answers to the text. Like most of their biblical colleagues, both Childs and Sanders appear oblivious to their responsibility, given their stated interest in the canonical shape of texts, to detail for their audience what philosophy of language or discourse-oriented models they use or would suggest others to use in determining the holistic readings of canonical texts they advocate. Second, whereas both scholars write primarily for a community of believers, I write primarily for a community of scholars; the difference is crucial. I propose the usefulness for biblical interpretation of specific approaches to literature drawn from what Sanders calls—with subsequently disparaging tones—"secular literary criticism" (p. 7).

Chapter 1: Hannah and Her Son: A Parable (1:1–4:1a)

1. R. Alter, *The Art of Biblical Narrative* (New York: Basic Books, 1981) pp. 81–87.
2. See my *Moses and the Deuteronomist* (New York: Seabury Press, 1980). I recognize with everyone else, of course, that the division of the text into books is itself artificial and must have taken place much later than the composition of the History. Nevertheless, by whatever process this division took place, the import of my remarks on "first chapters" in the History is that this process, by and large, has recognized and remained faithful to the structural plan of the History that I assume existed in the original composition. Just as the text's present chapters very often map out the natural breaks in the story, so also with these larger segmentations. It may be that the beginning of 1 Kings will present a problem in this respect, but the beginnings of the books of Joshua, Judges, and now 1 Samuel indicate to me a recognizable pattern of introductory summaries of larger issues of the "book" that follows.
3. Echoing within these words, as throughout this book, is the philosophy of language and literary stylistics of the group of Russian theorists that has come to be known as "The Bakhtin Circle." How this circle came to be and who composed it make up a fascinating story that is only now being told in the West. The central figure of this group was Mikhail Bakhtin, who according to Michael Holquist "is gradually emerging as one of the leading thinkers of the twentieth century." M. Holquist, ed., *The Dialogic Imagination: Four Essays by M. M. Bakhtin* (Austin and London: Univ. of Texas Press, 1981), p. XV. So far as I know, neither Bakhtin nor those associated with him ever applied their literary theories to biblical material. See the recent biography of Bakhtin by Katerina Clark and Michael Holquist, *Mikhail Bakhtin* (Cambridge, MA, and London: Harvard Univ. Press, 1984). In addition to the works of Bakhtin, Voloshinov, and Uspensky (the last-named is not part of the circle but has used Bakhtin's insights) referred to in the Works Cited section of my *Moses and the Deuteronomist*, pp. 219–22, I

have found the following books and articles helpful in understanding and applying the theoretical insights of Bakhtin and his group: M. M. Bakhtin, *Rabelais and His World* (Cambridge, MA: Harvard Univ. Press, 1968); M. Bakhtin, "The Problem of the Text (An Essay in Philosophical Analysis)," *Soviet Studies in Literature* (Winter 1977–78), pp. 3–33; Gary Paul Morson, "The Heresiarch of *Meta,*" *PTL: A Journal for Descriptive Poetics and Theory of Literature* 3 (1978), pp. 407–27; Krystyna Pomorska, "Mixail Baxtin and his Verbal Universe," *PTL* 3 (1978), pp. 379–86; I. R. Titunik, "M. M. Baxtin (the Baxtin School) and Soviet Semiotics," *Dispositio* 3 (1976), pp. 327–38; I. R. Titunik, "Bachtin and Soviet Semiotics," *Russian Literature* 10 (1981), pp. 1–16; and V. V. Ivanov, "The Significance of M. M. Bakhtin's Ideas on Sign, Utterance, and Dialogue for Modern Semiotics," in *Semiotics and Structuralism: Readings from the Soviet Union,* ed. Henryk Baran (White Plains, NY: International Arts and Sciences Press, 1974), pp. 310–67.

4. Boris Uspensky, *A Poetics of Composition* (Berkeley and Los Angeles: Univ. of Calif. Press, 1973), p. 83.

5. The best work I know of on the function of exposition in narrative is Meir Sternberg, *Expositional Modes and Temporal Ordering in Fiction* (Baltimore: Johns Hopkins Press, 1978).

6. This basic distinction between the frequentative or habitual function of the imperfectives before v. 9, and their synchronic function in vv. 9ff. is already clearly seen by S. R. Driver in *Notes on the Hebrew Text and the Topography of the Books of Samuel* (Oxford: Clarendon Press, 1913), pp. 5–14.

7. *Mānāh 'aḥat 'appāyîm* is given a convincing interpretation ("one portion, a *pim* in value") by David Aberbach in a short note in *Vetus Testamentum* 24 (1974), pp. 350–53: "1 Sam 1:5: A New Interpretation". Aberbach concludes that 1 Sam. 1:5 "quite clearly implies that Hannah received a substantial portion of meat from her husband, and a *pim's* worth was indeed a considerable quantity" (p. 353). Such an interpretation, besides involving no textual emendation as previous explanations do, also fits in nicely with the characterization of Elkanah as I shall develop it in this chapter. The reader will notice that I am inordinately attracted to interpretations that avoid disturbing the text, provided that they fit the context.

8. If we were to conclude that the narrator's viewpoint is significantly different from that of the two characters in vv. 5–6, then we would have an instance not only of the reporting of concealed speech but also of *pseudoobjective motivation,* which occurs (to adapt Bakhtin's words) when "the logic motivating the sentence seems to belong to the [narrator], that is, he is formally at one with it; but in actual fact, the motivation lies within the subjective belief-system of his characters, or of general opinion" (M. Bakhtin, *Dialogic Imagination,* p. 305). In either case, whether pseudoobjective or not, parts of vv. 5 and 6, apparently in the narrator's own voice, form also the concealed speech of the characters.

9. Bakhtin, *Dialogic Imagination,* pp. 292, 314.

10. In an interesting article postulating what he calls "the yearly family sacrifice," M. Haran, "Zebaḥ Hayyamîm," *Vetus Testamentum* 19 (1969). pp. 11—22, plausibly connects up Elkanah's practice in 1 Sam. 1 with the accounts of David's absenting himself from Saul's table in 1 Sam. 20 and the people's sacrifice in 1 Sam. 9 (where Samuel first meets Saul). Haran's reconstruction, if correct, would add to the many connections or literary allusions that my reading will make between these opening parabolic chapters of 1 Samuel and the rest of the book. It is clear, however, that Haran's source-oriented approach to 1 Samuel is radically different from my discourse-oriented one, and that, consequently, I am appropriating his interesting proposal for my own purposes (and perhaps, from his perspective, misappropriating it).

11. See Polzin, *Moses and the Deuteronomist,* pp. 181–83.

12. S. R. Driver, *Notes on the Hebrew Text,* p. 15, long ago pointed out the extensive wordplay involving *šā'al* in connection with the name of Samuel in 1 Sam. 1 and 2.

13. So, typically, K. McCarter, *1 Samuel,* vol. 8 of the Anchor Bible (Garden City: Doubleday, 1980), p. 63. A recent article, "A Study of Precise and Partial Derivations in Biblical Etymology," by Yair Zakovitch, *Journal for the Study of the Old Testament* 15 (1980), pp. 31–50, has appropriately questioned the common view that an original birth story of Saul has been transferred here to Samuel's story. Zakovitch examines a

series of double etymologies in the Bible and concludes that they testify to varying sensibilities between ages toward the etymological explanation. However, whether in this case in 1 Samuel—or elsewhere for that matter—one can draw diachronic conclusions from such double derivations is much less clear to me than to Zakovitch. The quotation from Bakhtin with which I introduce this chapter indicates how diachronically stratified is even the most clearly contemporaneous features of life and literature.

14. Once again I remind the reader that when I refer to the "Deuteronomist," I do not intend to refer to any hypothetical historical individual. I am simply personifying that artful intelligence I find behind the History, whatever its process of composition may have been. See my *Moses and the Deuteronomist*, p. 18.

15. G. W. Ahlström, "1 Samuel 1:15," *Biblica* 60 (1979), p. 254, proposes to translate *q'šat rûaḥ* in 1 Sam. 1:15 as "hard, obstinant or stubborn of spirit." Such a suggestion, if correct, would add to the many negative features of this chapter's characterization of Hannah as we are reading it. Needless to say, Hannah's stubbornness of spirit in wanting a son is a fitting preface to Israel's desire for a king, as the History will later characterize it in chap. 8.

16. The Song of Hannah is often compared to Ps. 113, but, as my reading suggests, 2 Sam. 22 (Ps. 18) has many more striking intrinsic and contextual similarities to 1 Sam. 2:1–10. A significant connection between 2:1–10 and 2 Sam. 22 (Ps. 18) was already emphasized by R. A. Carlson (but for his own source-oriented purposes) in *David, the Chosen King* (Stockholm: Almqvist & Wiksell, 1964), pp. 45ff., 227, and 246, and more recently, in a canonical context, by B. Childs, *Introduction to the Old Testament as Scripture* (Philadelphia: Fortress Press, 1979), p. 274.

17. This distinction between David's "horn" and Saul's "vial (*pak*)" of oil is noted by P. Miscall, *1 Samuel: A Literary Reading* (Bloomington: Indiana Univ. Press, 1986), p. 59.

18. See 1 Kings 15:23; 16:5, 27; 22:46; 2 Kings 10:34; 13:8, 12; 14:15, 28; 18:20; 20:20.

19. McCarter, *1 Samuel*, p. 76. The place of the Song of Hannah within 1 Samuel is commented upon by S. R. Driver, *Notes on the Hebrew Text*, pp. 27–28: "And indeed in style and tone the Song throughout bears the marks of a later age than that of Hannah. . . . The presence of the Song here does not prove more than that it was *attributed* to Hannah at the time when the books of Samuel were compiled . . . Its insertion may even belong to a later period still." The tendency in discussing the song is to remove it from its literary context and to treat it as a typical song of thanksgiving: thus, for example, R. W. Klein, "The Song of Hannah," *Concordia Theological Monthly* 41 (1970), pp. 674–84, and most recently *1 Samuel* (Waco: Word Books, 1983), pp. 12–20. For a general introduction to the song, see J. T. Willis, "The Song of Hannah and Psalm 113," *Catholic Biblical Quarterly* 34 (1973), pp. 139–54. Willis compares the Song of Hannah to a number of early poems isolated and discussed over the years by Albright and his students (Exod. 15; Num. 23–24; Deut. 32, 33; Judg. 5; 2 Sam. 22 (= Ps. 18); Hab. 3; Ps. 29; and Ps. 68) and believes "it is quite possible that [the song] is also early or at least that its author imitated . . . ancient poetry" (p. 141). Willis then examines the well-known similarities of the song to Ps. 113 and suggests on analysis that "both songs were ultimately influenced by a common milieu" (p. 154).

For my purposes, what is important about Willis's discussion of all these early poems, especially with respect to their language and thought (pp. 146–48), is that his larger goal (showing how the Song of Hannah is similar to a group of nine or so early poems in biblical literature) apparently distracted him from recognizing, within his own catalogue of verbal and conceptual features, the overwhelming similarity of the Song of Hannah to 2 Sam. 22, in contrast to all the other poems he discusses. If one joins my analysis of the relationships between the song and 2 Sam. 22 to Willis's, it is clear from both studies that these two poems enjoy an intimate interrelationship that is striking. My reading of the History suggests the narrative reasons for such a relationship. The internal similarities beween the Song of Hannah and 2 Sam. 22, as well as their literary contexts, suggest kinds of artful connections that surely are not accidental.

20. This section's important contrast between the lad Samuel and the two sons of Eli is recognized as crucial to the coherence of 1 Sam. 1–3 by R. Péter-Contesse, "La structure de la Sam 1–3," *Bible Translator* 27 (1976), pp. 312–14. See also J. T. Willis, "An Anti-Elide Narrative Tradition from a Prophetic Circle at the Ramah Sanctuary,"

Journal of Biblical Literature 90 (1971), pp. 289–90, and "Cultic Elements in the Story of Samuel's Birth and Dedication," *Studia Theologica* 26 (1972), pp. 38ff.

21. For example, Miller and Roberts's *The Hand of the Lord* (see the Introduction, above), on the supposed redactional nature of the Samuel material in these chapters. For a detailed response of J. T. Willis to Miller and Roberts's contention that 1 Sam. 1–7 does not constitute a coherent literary unity, see his "Samuel Versus Eli," *Theologische Zeitschrift* 35 (1979), pp. 201–12. Willis offers many convincing examples of Miller and Roberts's apparently arbitrary method of calling some interconnections proof of the same source or tradition and others proof of redactional activity. Willis's work on 1 Sam. 1–7 remains the best analysis of the unity of 1 Sam. 1–7 so far published. I find much of Willis's discourse-oriented research thorough and convincing. Willis's arguments for literary coherence and his detailed exposures of the caprices of redactional theories of composition are welcome exceptions to the mass of source-oriented studies of this material. When, however, Willis himself tries to answer source-oriented questions, such as the *Sitz im Leben* of 1 Sam. 1–7, I find his discussions as speculative as those with whom he disagrees. Willis's published work is a good example of how difficult it is for scholars to integrate within their own work what Willis himself describes as "two fundamentally different attitudes toward the biblical text" (p. 207).

22. If one were to change the introductory verb in 2:23 to an imperfective form to fit the pattern of the rest of the chapter preceding the oracle, then Eli's words to his sons would be part of the exposition rather than part of a separate narrative event.

23. One of the unfortunate features of many source-oriented analyses is the typical and premature consideration of repetition, on whatever level of the text, as dysfunctional.

24. In a survey of magical or superstitious practices referred to within certain biblical passages or lying behing them, E. F. de Ward, "Superstition and Judgement: Archaic Methods of Finding a Verdict," *Zeitschrift für die Alttestamentliche Wissenschaft* 89 (1977), pp. 1–19, ends his article by suggesting that *pll* here in v. 25 may denote superstitious methods of trial or ordeal. What is more significant to me in de Ward's survey is the frequency with which he mentions Saul in connection with divinatory practices. My reading of Saul's career in 1 Samuel will underline the place of Saul's divinatory tendencies in contributing to his downfall.

25. For example, vv. 9, 10, 12, 13 (twice).

26. 2:25b. This difficult statement about the relationship between human obduracy and divine purpose is one of a handful of such passages in biblical narrative. M. Tsevat's succinct discussion of these troublesome passages, "The Death of the Sons of Eli," in *The Meaning of the Book of Job and Other Biblical Studies* (New Jersey: KTAV Publishing House, 1980), pp. 149–53, remains a highly suggestive statement about competing voices in the Bible concerning divine and human responsibility and response, God's power and human powerlessness, the Bible's rationalism and its mystery. Nowhere are all these issues so extensively treated and so intensively focused than in the span of the History that deals with Israel's monarchic existence. As stand-ins for Israel's kings in this opening parable, Eli's sons—and the death God has in store for them—are apt conveyances for the easy rationality and the disastrous mystery of kingship in Israel as the History will recount it.

27. Scholars have spent much energy dealing with the unintelligibility of the text in a number of places, for example, in vv. 29, 32; nevertheless, the oracle is clear enough elsewhere for us to make some general statements about its import and relationship to its context.

28. If we assume that the oracle of the LORD refers primarily to Eli's immediate successor, Samuel, and perhaps also to a long-range successor such as Zadok, this means that the oracle is also multivoiced about the succession of *priestly* houses: first, from Eli's Levite house to Samuel's (1 Chron. 6 makes Elkanah and Samuel descendants of Aaron), and, second, from Eli's house to Zadok's. However, there is a sense in which the application of this prophecy to Zadok does not fit in with details within the oracle itself. If in v. 28 "the house of [Eli's] father" means "the house of Aaron," then it is difficult to see how the oracle can be looking forward to Solomon's choice of Zadok in 1 Kings 2:35, since it predicts that not only Eli's seed but "the seed of the house of your father," that is, Aaron, will be cut off (v. 31). But then this same detail would help us conclude that the oracle is referring to a non-Aaronide successor of Eli, that is, a non-Levite. If Samuel's rise is what the oracle is immediately

addressing, then Samuel himself must also be a non-Levite, whatever 1 Chron. 6 says about his descent from Aaron. At any rate, it is revealing that 1 Samuel indicates nothing more about Samuel's background in this regard than that he is the son of an Ephraimite (1:1). Perhaps the most one can say about the priestly accents of this multivoiced oracle is that Samuel turns out to be a surer candidate for Eli's successor than Zadok—or even Abinadab, for that matter. See W. T. Willis, "Samuel Versus Eli," *Theologische Zeitschrift* 35 (1979), pp. 201–12, who also defends Samuel as Eli's successor here.

29. Vv. 2, 11, 18, 20, 21, 26; 3:1.
30. The common recognition that the linen ephod of Samuel is somehow related to that of David in 2 Sam. 6:14 is another feature of the presentation of Samuel having royal, even Davidic, overtones. My assumption and argument throughout the first seven chapters of 1 Samuel is that many of the exegetical cruxes that are recognized so often in the secondary literature have a thematic and narrative dimension that is scarcely ever considered in such discussions. Thus, in a short note on "the linen ephod," *Vetus Testamentum* 24 (1974), pp. 505–7, N. L. Tidwell discusses 1 Sam. 2:18 in connection with 2 Sam. 6:14 in order "to reinstate the more widely held view that the linen ephod of Samuel and David was a priestly vestment" (p. 505), yet it will never occur to this author to inquire why the future judge of 1 Sam. 2 and the present king of 2 Sam. 6 are joined in the narrative by this priestly vestment. It is as if details in the story such as the linen ephod worn by Samuel and David have only historical, rather than historiographic, esthetic, or ideological, dimensions for biblical research.
31. We see in this integration of the personal and the communal, the private and the public, a common trait that runs through much of biblical narrative. Joel Rosenberg's recent *King and Kin: Political Allegory in the Hebrew Bible* (Bloomington: Indiana Univ. Press, 1986) is an important and provocative examination of this theme. In particular, his chapter on "From House to House" (pp. 113–23) examines the polyvalent usage of *house* in biblical narrative, especially in the books of Samuel. His entire book makes a strong general case, along the entire text of Gen.–2 Kings, for the kinds of allegorical connections that I am specifically suggesting between 1 Sam. 1–7 on one hand and the subsequent royal history on the other. Once Rosenberg has established, as I believe he has, how political allegory permeates the entire fabric of biblical narrative, then those allegorical relationships I am suggesting in 1 Samuel no longer need appear as *ad hoc* or artificial attempts to interpret and integrate what has long been considered disparate and artlessly combined material. Such literary interconnections as Rosenberg and I are suggesting for the History, Rosenberg has also shown to exist in biblical narrative outside the History.
32. 2:29, McCarter's translation.
33. This promise to David had been foreshadowed by Abigail's words, "For the LORD will certainly make my lord a sure house (*bayit neʾĕmān*) . . . " (1 Sam. 25:28).
34. The questions about the relationship of *nēr* to *nîr* and about the possibility of *nîr* meaning "dominion" or "royal prerogative" are well known, and specific answers need not detain us here. The statement, "the *nēr* of God had not yet been extinguished," involves at the very least a royal reference based on wordplay (*nēr* here playing on *nîr* as used in 1 Kings 11:36; 15:4; and 2 Kings 8:19 so that "the lamp of God had not yet gone out" sounds like and brings to mind "God's royal dominion had not yet ceased") or—if *nēr* and *nîr* can both mean "lamp"—an even stronger royal reference based on their metaphorical use for royal rule in 1 Kings 11:36; 15:4; 2 Kings 8:19; and consequently here in 1 Sam. 3:3. For a discussion of the *nēr/nîr* question, see Paul Hanson, "The Song of Heshbon and David's Nîr," *Harvard Theological Review* 61 (1968), pp. 297–320, and Richard Nelson, *The Double Redaction of the Deuteronomistic History* (Sheffield: Almond Press, 1981), pp. 108–9.
35. J. Gerald Janzen has written a convincing article detailing how chap. 3 "as a whole is to be read against the background of chapter 1, especially in respect to the latter's language and portrayal of closure and opening of the womb" (p. 91): " 'Samuel Opened the Doors of the House of Yahweh' (1 Samuel 3:15)," *Journal for the Study of the Old Testament* 26 (1983), pp. 89–96. It seems to me that my suggestions about the royal dimensions of these chapters simply add an additional layer to most of the interconnections that Janzen points out concerning chaps. 1 and 3. In fact, once one sees with Janzen's help that chap. 3 continues the "having of sons" theme begun in chap. 1, then, as a surrogate for "the having of kings," "the opening of the doors of the house of

Yahweh" points not only mediately to the royal voice that, as in the Song of Hannah, rejoices in kingship, but finally also to the Deuteronomist's voice, which overlays this joyful theme with accents that give it an exilic, antimonarchic tone: the doors of the house of Yahweh will once again be opened when Samuel, representing also the ideal judge (as in chap. 7) closes the door once for all upon a kingship that, as represented by Eli, had grown old, fat, and blind.

36. Referred to by K. McCarter, *1 Samuel*, p. 98.
37. In a discourse-oriented study, Michael Fishbane, "1 Samuel 3: Historical Narrative and Narrative Poetics," in *Literary Interpretations of Biblical Narratives*, volume 2, ed. K. R. R. Gros Louis and J. S. Ackerman (Nashville: Abingdon Press, 1982), pp. 191–203, has gathered together a number of phonemic, paronomastic, thematic, metaphorical, and structural observations on 1 Sam. 3. The sight/insight interplay that Fishbane describes for chap. 3 was independently developed by J. T. Willis for chaps. 1–4, in "Samuel Versus Eli," *Theologische Zeitschrift* 35 (1979), p. 207. For his part, Fishbane shows in a discourse-oriented way what another scholar in a source-oriented study can only assert without offering much justification: "This author is still tempted to conclude that the chapter is a literary creation" (p. 389). R. Gnuse, "A Reconsideration of the Form-Critical Structure in 1 Samuel 3: An Ancient Near Eastern Dream Theophany," *Biblische Zeitschrift* 29 (1985), pp. 379–90. As with most source-oriented studies, Gnuse's article shows only an incipient understanding of the real text's complicated artistic construction, while at the same time it overwhelms us with its proposed connections to Oppenheim's hypothetical dream-theophany genre in its ancient Near Eastern context. Gnuse modestly does not refer in his article to his own book on the same subject, published the previous year: *The Dream Theophany of Samuel: Its Structure in Relation to Ancient Near Eastern Dreams and Its Theological Significance* (Lanham, MD: University Press of America, 1984).

Chapter 2: Ark in Exile: The Parable Continues (4:1b–7:17)

1. See the bibliographies in Miller and Roberts, *The Hand of the Lord* (Baltimore and London: Johns Hopkins Press, 1977) and A. F. Campbell, *The Ark Narrative (1 Samuel 4–6; 2 Samuel 6): A Form-Critical and Tradition-Historical Study*, (Decatur, GA: Scholars Press, 1975)
2. A welcome exception to this pattern is the work of J. T. Willis, whose two articles, "An Anti-Elide Narrative Tradition from a Prophetic Circle at the Ramah Sanctuary," *Journal of Biblical Literature* 90 (1971), pp. 288–308 and "Samuel Versus Eli," *Theologische Zeitschrift* 35 (1979), pp. 201–12, while concerned additionally with source-oriented questions, are still the best discussions I know of concerning the compositional unity of 1 Sam. 1–7.
3. Only in V. 13, where the man of Benjamin comes upon Eli "sitting upon his 'throne' watching," does the narrator use verb forms of this type. It is clear that Eli is being presented here from the contemporaneous viewpoint of the messenger. At the same time, Eli's central role as a royal figure throughout these chapters makes it especially appropriate to picture him in this abiding way: Eli functions in these opening chapters as a royal figure.
4. We shall soon see how this "obviously erroneous statement" contains more than a grain of truth. For now, Israelite readers mistakenly revel in the dullness of heart of their traditional enemy. The construal of this statement as appropriate from "the mouth of a heathen" is found in S. R. Driver, *Notes on the Hebrew Text and the Topography of the Books of Samuel* (Oxford: Clarendon Press, 1913), p. 47.
5. See above, pp. 39–44.
6. See Sternberg's general discussion of levels of narrative knowledge, *Poetics of Biblical Narrative* (Bloomington: Indiana Univ. Press, 1985), pp. 163–72.
7. Miller and Roberts, in *Hand of the Lord*, remove Samuel from their "Ark Narrative," as we have seen in the Introduction.
8. McCarter, *1 Samuel*, vol. 8 of the Anchor Bible, (Garden City: Doubleday, 1980), p. 113. David Gunn, "Narrative Patterns and Oral Tradition in Judges and Samuel," *Vetus Testamentum* 24 ([1974]), pp. 286–317, discusses the "News of Defeat" pattern of Sam. 4:12–17 and 2 Sam. 1:2–4 and concludes, concerning it and the other patterns he analyzes in this article, that direct literary dependence is out of the question. My reading argues the opposite.

9. S. R. Driver, *Notes on the Hebrew Text*, p. 48, recognizes that "the original sense of the word" as *good* tidings is inappropriate here; he unconvincingly suggests that this sense "has been forgotten." We are arguing that the use of *bissēr* here is intricately connected with its use elsewhere in the history.
10. This same confluence of thematic elements is present when 1 Sam. 4–6 is compared to 2 Sam. 6, as shown below.
11. See my discussion of this in the Introduction in connection with Miller and Roberts's views.
12. John Wilkinson discusses various interpretations of the plague in an interesting medicophilological article, "The Philistine Epidemic of I Samuel 5 and 6," *Expository Times* 88 (1977), pp. 137–41. Wilkinson's conclusion is that "we can be justified in identifying the Philistine epidemic in I Samuel 5 and 6 as one of bubonic plague with a high degree of probability" (p. 140).
13. A characteristic of certain literature as described by M. Bakhtin in *Rabelais and His World* (Cambridge, MA: Harvard Univ. Press, 1968), *passim.*
14. See Miller and Roberts, *The Hand of the Lord,* 9–17 and *passim.*
15. A. T. Campbell, in "Yahweh and the Ark: A Case Study in Narrative," *Journal of Biblical Literature* 98 (1979), pp. 31–43, contends that there is "a consensus on the nature of the text as theological narrative and considerable agreement on the interpretation of its central sections, over against disagreements on the extent of the text, its unity, and the time of its composition" (p. 31). Campbell illustrates "how dependent the theological interpretation is on the delimiting of the extent of the text" (p. 33). Because "there has never been unanimity on the relationship between 1 Samuel 4–6 and either 1 Samuel 1–3 or 2 Samuel 6" (pp. 33–34), Campbell believes that the evidence tends to be selectively assessed, thus putting into question any subsequent theological interpretation. Campbell then evaluates the evidence (section II) in order to show how chaps. 1–3 and 2 Sam. 6 relate to chaps. 4–6. A major conclusion of his (over against Miller and Roberts and Schicklberger) is that 2 Sam. 6 necessarily belongs to the Ark Narrative: "The ultimate substantiation of the claim for unity is the inner logic of the narrative itself. What is begun as Yahweh's action in 1 Sam 4 does not reach equilibrium until Yahweh's action in 2 Sam 6" (p. 41).

   Campbell is perceptive and articulate in his exemplification of the relationship between determining the extent of the text and interpreting its theology. Nevertheless, calling for theological interpretation "at every level" of a text, Campbell ends his discussion with two throwaway lines that indict the enterprise upon which he and the colleagues he quotes in this article have been engaged: "The final text is, of course, the most identifiable level. To treat that fully for the Ark Narrative, in its present context, would be quite another story" (p. 43). That this enterprise is indeed "quite another story," one that none of the concerned scholars have been concerned enough to tell, is, in my opinion, both methodologically and ideologically unfortunate for the present situation in biblical studies.

   Campbell's statements, as his own research illustrates, proceed along the assumption that the best way to understand the final text is first to construct a plausible picture of the history of its pre-texts. He seems unaware that the opposite sequence and, as Sternberg maintains, the absence of any prescribed sequence at all in the two enterprises are alternatives that have at least equal academic respectability. Apparently assuming that "classical literary critical procedures" (p. 43) would exhaust the store of tools and techniques with which to examine the final text, this position inadvertently reveals serious gaps in its comprehension of wider humanistic approaches to the study of ancient literature. It never occurs to Campbell to wonder whether the function of repetition, the play of perspectives, character, and characterization, voice structures, plotting, and other central narratological questions might have an essential bearing on determining "levels of the text," whether poetic (concerning the final text) or genetic (concerning various pre-texts). And if he is aware of such matters, then where is his consideration of any of these important questions or of the scholars who incorporate them in their studies? This is an especially pertinent question to one whose main purpose in his article is to examine the relationship between determining the extent of the text and developing a picture of its narrative theology. (In this regard, it is revealing that, apart from a brief note mentioning Willis, Campbell dismisses through inexplicable silence all the considerations that Willis has raised in a series of articles concerning the unity of 1 Sam. 1–7, considerations that challenge Campbell's, Miller and Roberts's, and Schicklberger's determinations of the extent of the text.)

Second, perhaps Campbell's not having got around to telling this other story (about the final text) has implications that extend beyond questions of methodology into areas of academic ideology. As I suggested in the Introduction, a relevant matter in this regard may be a scholar's view of the final text: does it appear so incoherent, ideologically speaking (because of the complicated process that the scholar believes lies behind its historical composition and because of the supposed crudity of its redactors), that any full-blown account of it as "narrative functioning as a vehicle for theology" (p. 43) would be an unsatisfying and embarrassing exercise?—unsatisfying because the scholar believes the final text makes little sense theologically, and embarrassing because one would thereby advertise to nonspecialists that the textual object of one's specialty, biblical narrative in its final form, is an incoherent mess. And who would want to proclaim to others that one is a master of such imperfect material? So one confines one's research to pre-texts, and never actually gets around to the final story.

16. As Miller and Roberts rightly point out (*Hand of the Lord*, pp. 39, 55, 56), the *glh* of 4:22 and the *kly zhb* of 6:8 also point in this direction. However, they never apply these features to the exile itself, only to their pre-text, as my Introduction indicates. See below, n. 20, for other references to exilic aspects of the ark narrative.

17. Note also in 6:6 how God made sport of (*hit'alēl*) the Egyptians.

18. For a useful discussion of Rost's position, together with a review of the literature, see A. F. Campbell, *Ark Narrative*.

19. The stopover is seven months in 1 Samuel and three months in 2 Samuel.

20. For a source-oriented treatment of some basic questions here, see J. Blenkinsopp, "Kireath-Jearim and the Ark," *Journal of Biblical Literature* 88 (1969), pp. 143–56. Blenkinsopp, as is usual, develops proposals for reconstructing the historical situation, basing himself in part upon assumptions of the literary history of the ark narrative. Thus the present text is assumed to be historiographically unreliable, but certain source-oriented theories help this scholar sort out and propose a plausible historiographic reconstruction. But what does serious doubt about its literary historical assumptions mean for the plausibility of Blenkinsopp's historical reconstructions?

G. W. Ahlström, "The Travels of the Ark: A Religio-Political Composition," *Journal of Near Eastern Studies* 43 (1984), pp. 141–149, sees the ark narrative as "a literary fiction with a tendentious, religio-political thread" (p. 142). Ahlström, in referring to H. Timm (Die Ladeerzahlung [1 Samuel 4–6; 2 Samuel 6]," *Evangelische Theologie* 29 [1966], pp. 520ff.), assumes its author to be exilic, so that "psychologically the ark narrative would have been encouraging for the people of the exile" (p. 143). For Ahlström, "the ark narrative should be seen as a literary composition which has intentionally conflated Shiloh with Kireath-Jearim-Jerusalem up through the story of the imprisonment and travels of the ark" (p. 149).

Ahlström's study as well as Blenkinsopp's are excellent examples of how a source-oriented perspective may proceed both *from* and *toward* extremely fragile discourse-oriented positions concerning the biblical text. In many respects neither history nor literature benefit from this procedure.

21. McCarter, *1 Samuel*, p. 137.

22. See 2 Sam. 6; 1 Kings 6; 8; 19.

23. See *Moses and the Deuteronomist* (New York: Seabury, 1980).

24. For a thorough discussion of the depiction of Samuel in 1 Sam. 1–3 as consonant with the book's subsequent depiction of him as an adult, as well as for a proposed *Sitz im Leben* of the opening chapters in 1 Sam., see J. T. Willis, "Cultic Elements in the Story of Samuel's Birth and Dedication," *Studia Theologica* 26 (1972), pp. 33–61.

25. See above p. 5.

26. This is a matter often emphasized since the appearance of M. Noth's *Überlieferungsgeschichtliche Studien* (Tübingen: Niemeyer, 1943).

27. See Polzin, *Moses and the Deuteronomist*, pp. 155, 161–162.

28. See, for example, K. McCarter, *1 Samuel*, p. 143.

29. Polzin, *Moses and the Deuteronomist*, pp. 176–77.

30. Deut. 6:13; 10:12, 20; 11:13; 13:5; 28:47; Josh. 22:5; 24:14, 18, 19, 21, 22, 24; Judge 2:7; 10:16; 1 Sam. 7:4; 12:14, 20, 24.

31. It is no coincidence that most of these pericopes are found in the sections of the

History that Noth designated as part of Dtr's organizing, structural speeches. A source-oriented explanation for the theological implications of the catchword *sub* in these passages of repentance can be found in H. W. Wolff, "The Kerygma of the Deuteronomistic Historical Work," *The Vitality of Old Testament Traditions* ed. W. Brueggemann and H. W. Wolff, (Atlanta: John Knox Press, 1975), pp. 90– 97.

32. See *Moses and the Deuteronomist*, chap. 4, for a discussion of the language in Judge. 2 and subsequently.

33. It is noteworthy in 1 Kings 8 that vv. 33–34 and 46–50 involve a progressive wordplay on related verbs: *šābāh* (to take captive) → *šûb* (to repent) → *hᵉšîbôt* (to return [Israel to the land]).

34. McCarter, *1 Samuel*, p. 150. Focused here as elsewhere almost exclusively on questions of literary history, McCarter fails to consider how the Samuel and David parallels function in the final form of the history; he thereby ignores a fundamental responsibility of interpretation—a failing typical of modern biblical scholarship, as the introductory chapter above sought to show.

35. See the Introduction, nn. 22 and 26.

Chapter 3: The Monarchy Begins (8:1–12:25)

1. In the midst of an ocean of literary-historical analyses, a number of scholars have perceptively highlighted some of the more significant narrative features in 1 Sam. 8ff., chapters that are especially important for our understanding of the rest of the monarchic history because they deal with beginnings. "The primacy effect" in narrative so clearly discussed by Meir Sternberg, *Expositional Modes and Temporal Ordering in Fiction* (Baltimore and London: Johns Hopkins Univ. Press, 1978), *passim*, is of particular relevance here. What the narrator focuses on, and how the narrator arranges the particular events and reported speech selected for the tale, will prove important guides for what follows chaps. 8–12 in the history.

In recent years there has been a growing tendency to treat chaps. 8–12 in a more unified manner than previous scholarship was accustomed to do. In 1966, M. Tsevat wrote an article in Hebrew which was later translated into English under the title "The Biblical Account of the Foundation of the Monarchy in Israel," in *The Meaning of the Book of Job and Other Essays* (New York: KTAV, 1980), pp. 77–99. In the English version Tsevat asserts that "the story of 1 Samuel 8–12 [cannot be argued] to be composite and imperfectly integrated" (p. 78). Nevertheless, he weakens this assertion considerably in the course of his discussion by resorting to a "list of additions" (p. 78), mostly antimonarchical, to account for those sections of chaps. 8–12 that in his opinion fail to cohere with the larger unit on the question of the monarchy (pp. 83, 97–99).

Dennis McCarthy has written an influential article, "The Inauguration of Monarchy in Israel," *Interpretation* 27 (1973), pp. 401–12, suggesting that the work of the Deuteronomistic school is everywhere present in chaps. 8–12, making them "a coherent account and explanation of the inauguration of kingship in Israel" (p. 404). He believes that "the internal structure of the pericope is too sophisticated to be the product of accidental growth and simple retouches; it shows a controlling conception, the mark of an author, and this conception is integrated into the intricate structure of the Deuteronomistic history as a whole" (p. 408). Despite McCarthy's admirable summary of the artistic integrity of chaps. 8–12, he, like many of the scholars since Noth who are intent on seeing Dtr as an author rather than editor, bases his arguments for such unity upon a plausible literary history of the pericope. He writes principally of matters "regarding antecedents" and exhibits little awareness of the types of poetic tools and techniques that were soon to be called for by wider-ranging scholars like Alter, Berlin, or Sternberg. Commonsense arguments about the "coherence of the text" predominante in his discussion, and there is little analytic sophistication of a poetic (rather than genetic) nature in his procedures. McCarthy appeals to a wider scholarship than many in discussing the growth of literature, oral and otherwise (for example, A. Lord and the Chadwicks), but by and large he believes that one demonstrates coherence—as opposed to just asserting it—by suggesting plausible ways in which presumed pre-texts were reworked by some guiding intelligence. Like most biblical scholars of the time, McCarthy apparently felt that other procedures merited no serious consideration.

A. D. H. Mayes, "The Rise of the Israelite Monarchy," *Zeitschrift für die Alttestamentliche Wissenschaft* 90 (1978), pp. 1–19, goes into "the problem of the origins of the
traditions in 1 Sam (7)8–12" (p. 3). He calls this problem "The Literary Question" (pp.
3–17) and believes that "M. Noth's treatment of [chaps. 7–12], with some modifica-
tions, remains valid" (p. 11). One modification Mayes would insist upon is that "it is too
simple to describe [the Deuteronomists' attitude to the monarchy] as anti-monarchical"
(p. 11). For Mayes also, the best way, perhaps the only way, to understand "the literary
question" is to ask and answer questions of literary history. Why, methodologically
speaking, must this be so? In a subsequent book, *The Story of Israel Between Settlement
and Exile* (London: SCM Press, 1983), Mayes gives an answer: the poetic and genetic
approaches to biblical narrative cannot be integrated and probably cannot even
interact. "These are in fact essentially different approaches, neither exclusive of the
other; if confusion is to be avoided, it is difficult to see how they can interact" (p. 21). It
seems to me that in so characterizing source- and discourse-oriented approaches to
biblical narrative, Mayes has not been able to think through the complicated relationship of a poetics of literature to the questions of literary history that are his main
concern. As Meir Sternberg shows in the opening chapter of *The Poetics of Biblical
Narrative* (Bloomington: Indiana Univ. Press, 1985), genetic approaches always imply
poetic assumptions and vice versa, so that any assertion of such stark separation
between them as Mayes offers is probably misguided, however difficult we all admit it
is to offer more than a few examples of profitable interaction.

David Gunn has a number of interesting and valuable observations on chaps. 8–12
in *The Fate of King Saul* (Sheffield: Almond Press, 1980). His recognition of the
ambiguous depiction of Saul's prophesying in 1 Sam. 10 (p. 63) is certainly on the
mark, as my discussion below will argue. Also, his attention to apparently unimportant
aspects of the text that help us sort out important ideological issues helps to explain his
uncanny ability often to go to the heart of the matter—if not with respect to that
illusory goal of what a text "really means," at least with regard to plausible solutions to
what strikes many of today's readers of the Bible as textual cruxes. Gunn emphasizes
the role of a critic "as one whose most important task is to discriminate between, and
mediate, aesthetic and moral values" (p. 16). This basic attitude of Gunn's, as well as
his courage to go wherever the text leads him—however ambiguous and unpalatable
the result—characterize his work and help to explain why it has a power and influence
that often surpass studies that are apparently more detailed and technical. All this
being said, I believe that Gunn's characterization of Saul lacks some balance in its
neglect of features of the story that support Saul's culpability in matters of religious
importance.

In his voluminous discussions of secondary literature and in the painstaking close
reading he has provided, L. Eslinger, *Kingship of God in Crisis* (Sheffield: Almond Press,
1985), is often helpful on 1 Sam. 1–12. Especially noteworthy are his emphasis on
Samuel's balking at the LORD's command and initial failure to obey it, his linking up
of the explicit parallels between Samuel and Saul (for example, 1:1–2 like 9:1–2; the
use of *ša'al* in the Samuel birth story), and his underlining of the sense of mystery and
uncertainty developed by the narrator. Equally helpful in his recognition of Buber's
original insights about the *leitwort*, *higgîd*, in these chapters and its connection with
nāgîd, the "declared one" of the LORD, and about the servant's words in 9:7 ("What
shall we bring [*nābî*] to the man?") as the narrator's hint concerning the identity of the
anonymous man of God.

At the same time, I differ with Eslinger in his contrastive depiction of the LORD,
who is portrayed as against the monarchy, but unsympathetically so, by a narrator who
is in favor of it in a limited way. Nor do I agree with Eslinger's belief that Samuel at
first fails to obey God's command to make Israel a king "out of a sense of loyalty" to the
covenant (p. 281).

Meir Sternberg's description of Samuel the prophet as the ironic butt of the
narrator in chap. 9, in *the Poetics of Biblical Narrative*, pp. 94–96, is eminently consistent
with the narrator's pejorative depiction of Samuel in chaps. 8–12 as I will characterize
it below. Sternberg, like Buber, Eslinger, Miscall, and others, picks up on the *nābî*
wordplay in 9:7 but gives it a denigrating twist in correspondence with the other
features of the prophetic portrait he finds in chap. 9. As I will suggest in my analysis of
this chapter, the wordplay on *nābî* is even more ideologically central than previously
recognized.

Peter Miscall's recent *1 Samuel: A Literary Reading* (Bloomington: Indiana University Press, 1986) is filled with original insights and suggestions. I remain cautious about Miscall's overall approach but consulting him is almost always profitable. In the present section, his emphasis on the ambiguous questions, *mah nābî* in 9:7 and on the abiding wordplay involving *higgîd* (pp. 53ff.), his perceptive description of the negative aspects of Saul's being chosen by lot in chapt. 10 (pp. 64ff.), and his suggestion about the *qeren/pak* alternation which sets off David's anointing from Saul's (p. 59) are indicative of his contributions.

David Jobling's new study on Deuteronomic political theory is centrally concerned with 1 Sam. 8–12. In chap. 2 of *The Sense of Biblical Narrative: Structural Analysis in the Hebrew Bible II* (Sheffield: Almond Press, 1986), pp. 44–87. ("Deuteronomic Political Theory in Judges and 1 Samuel 1–12"), Jobling proposes to study the part of "The Primary Narrative" (Jobling's borrowing of D. N. Freedman's designation for Genesis –2 Kings) that extends from Judges 2:11 to 1 Sam. 12 and that "broaches the question, 'What form of government is appropriate for Israel?'" (p. 45). Unlike most of his colleagues who deal with this material, Jobling asks, "What . . . is the final form of the Deuteronomic History doing?" (p. 45), and, unlike most of them, he assumes that he has a responsibility toward the final form, just as whoever was responsible for it took responsibility for the complex statement concerning monarchy contained within it. He also points to the interpretational limitations of most redactional theories about the History. After considering the entire section in totality (part 1), Jobling offers a detailed reading of Judg. 6–9, suggesting that this pericope offers a proleptically balancing perspective that "point by point . . . opposes the view of kingship embodied in the Saul of 1 Sam 8–12" (p. 85). Judg. 6–9 is mostly negative where 1 Sam. 8–12 is mostly positive concerning the monarchy. Jotham closes off kingship for Israel as decisively as Samuel leaves it open. Jotham, as "the worthy refusor" of throne, is to the protomonarchical story in Judges what Jonathan is to the monarchical story in 1 Samuel. The Gideon-Abimelek episode in Judges puts into perspective the complex Deuteronomic debate over judgeship-kingship, just as the Saul episode in chaps. 8–12 contextualizes it within 1 Samuel, but with one important difference: the first episode is a proleptic corrective of the second, and both together illustrate how "the deuteronomic treatment of monarchy is a classic example of talking around a contradiction" (p. 46). I know few who in wrestling with the narrative logic of this large block of material offer a more perceptive and persuasive account of it than David Jobling does here. With so many incisive suggestions in his discussion, I can mention only a few of them before offering some suggestions concerning areas where Jobling's reading is questionable or ways in which he might strengthen the general force of his argumentation.

If one agrees that the judicial cyclical system expressed in Judg. 2:11–3:6 is meant to be in effect through 1 Sam. 7, then Jobling's emphasis on gaps in the history (periods when judges do not rule Israel) being programmed into the cycle and then expressed in many of the stories that follow it is most illuminating in its literary and ideological implications. The judicial gap, say, of Judg. 17–21 both illuminates and is illuminated by the subsequent judicial gap in 1 Sam. 4:19–7:2. This insight allows Jobling to illustrate how the judicial system involves problems of political discontinuity that the monarchic system in many ways sought to solve. (For some other apposite remarks on the question of monarchy and [dis]continuity, see S. Talmon, "The Biblical Idea of Statehood," in *The Bible World*, ed. Gary Rendsburg, et al. [New York: KTAV, 1980], pp. 239–48.) At the same time, Jobling shows how crucial one's understanding of 1 Sam. 7 is for establishing, or at least suggesting, a coherent Deuteronomic perspective on the judgeship-kingship debate, especially as this chapter relates to 1 Sam. 8–12 wherein "the text is so arranged as to view the rise of monarchy within the logic which the judge-cycles established and to invite comparison between the two systems of government" (p. 51). One final illustration of Jobling's many insights into the text is the way in which the story's "judge-logic" influences 1 Sam. 8's characterization of the people's request for a king as "*the apostasy which starts a new judge cycle,* and the Ammonite oppression [as] the consequent punishment!" (p. 65).

Because of insights like these, Jobling is able to arrive at a number of important conclusions concerning Judges–1 Samuel that deserve our attention. At the same time, two significant aspects of his discussion invite serious questions: first, his application of

Judg. 6–9, as a proleptic treatment of the theme of monarchy, to the rest of the History, and second, his understanding of 1 Sam. 8–12 as presenting a significantly positive view of kingship in stark contrast to the negative picture of it in Judg. 6–9. A portion of his concluding statement deserves to be quoted since it establishes the significant relationship between the two pericopes:

> 1 Sam 8–12 thus betrays the need for another view which it itself cannot express because of the constraints it is under. I wish to suggest that, within the totality of the Deuteronomic History, Judg. 6–9 provides that other view proleptically. If the whole narrative of the judge-period prepares us generally to read 1 Sam. 8–12, Judg. 6–9 does so much more specifically. The rise of monarchy has happened before! Judg. 6–9 adjusts our reading of 1 Sam. 8–12, as it were, in advance. Being under no constraint to portray kingship positively, it can explore thoroughly its dubious aspects. (p. 85)

It is clear from Jobling's discussion of Judg. 6–9 in how many significant ways this pericope is a proleptic view of that Israelite kingship first set in motion in 1 Sam. 8 by the people's request for a king. However, a serious obstacle to the way Jobling applies this generally convincing account of Judg. 6–9, as proleptic to 1 Sam. 8–12, is his requiring us to accept a foreshadowing incident as meant to counter or significantly correct the subsequent events it foreshadows. What Jobling is suggesting is a significant incoherence between proleptic portrait and its future reality, as depicted by the same editors guiding the larger story line. How much more plausible and elegant it might be to suggest, as I believe the case to be, that Judg. 6–9 is a condemnation of kingship that proleptically anticipates the similarly negative picture of it in 1 Sam. 8–12. Moreover, the positive picture of kingship that Jobling suggests for 1 Sam. 8–12 appears to me to set it off too sharply from chaps. 13–31. On two counts, then, that are central to his reading—a proleptic account that opposes the ideological account of kingship it foreshadows, and an account of the inauguration of kingship in 1 Samuel that opposes the account of its development within the book—Jobling does not entirely succeed in showing how what the Deuteronomists say about monarchy is sufficiently coherent, either literarily or ideologically, to merit our attending to the complexity he insists is central to their position. It appears to me, on the other hand, that many of Jobling's insights and conclusions in this chapter of his book support a greater coherence within the History than Jobling allows, and that if, as he suggests, Judg. 6–9 does foreshadow 1 Sam. 8–12, it does so in a supportive way. 1 Sam. 8–12 is, as my reading below will indicate, ideologically much more consistent with what follows it in the History than Jobling would allow.

I suggest two possible reasons for what I consider are Jobling's misapplications of some of his crucial insights in this valuable study. First, in his discussion outside of Judg. 6–9, and especially in 1 Sam. 8–12, Jobling fails to consider passages in terms of their voice structure. Thus, whereas in Judg. 8–9 he sometimes attends to this feature—as when he points out the ideological relationship of Jotham's voice to that of the narrator to the benefit of his reading (p. 70ff.)—in 1 Sam. 8–12 his failing to do so results in an apparently gratuitous identification of Samuel's words with the ideological perspective of God and the narrator, and in the positive picture of kingship based upon them. It is possible, as I argue in my reading, that Samuel's position vis-à-vis the narrator and God turns out to be significantly negative both before and after chap. 8. Whether this is so, however, depends on a thorough discussion of the various ideological portraits that the narrator paints of the characters, yet Jobling never addresses this question in 1 Sam. 8–12.

Second, Jobling ends up with a greater incoherence in the Deuteronomist's ideology on kingship than is warranted because his normal approach to the study of the text—first paradigmatic, then syntagmatic analysis (p. 15)—is, I suggest, contrary to the order of study suggested by the genre that he is reading: the primary *narrative*. His habit of doing an "isotopic analysis" before a detailed systematic reading of the narrative (his "syntagmatic analysis") is a central cause of his otherwise inexplicable reading of 1 Sam. 8–12 as predominantly positive toward monarchy. Jobling's emphasis on isotopic analysis, while providing us with many valuable insights into the text, probably also explains why he can articulate the contrast between chaps. 8–12 and chap. 13ff. so starkly. (In this regard, his statement that he departs from his normal practice when dealing with "enclosing and enclosed narratives" [p. 15] is doubly confusing: any narrative passage is always at least partially enclosed [that is to say, either surrounded by narrative on one side and by closure on the other, as at the end of a narrative, or, as at the beginning of a story, a passage introducing a subsequent narrative] and most often entirely closed, that is, entirely surrounded by another narrative.)

In all these studies, only Sternberg, writing on biblical narrative in general, comes close to giving us a beginning perspective on the forgotten individual in the chapters under consideration, Samuel himself. His crucial role in the "fate of King Saul" has largely been neglected by commentators; the interpretations of 1 Samuel that result turn out to be flat and unconvincing in their characterization of this central figure in the story.

2. For example, 2:12, 17 (twice), 25, 26; 3:1, 19; 5:5, 6, 11; 6:19; 7:13.

3. Within chaps. 8–12, perhaps only 10:26, for example, is explicitly evaluative.

4. A notable exception to this move toward more complex characterization may be the figure of Jonathan, as David Jobling has persuasively argued in *The Sense of Biblical Narrative I* (Sheffield: Almond Press, 1978; reprint, 1986), pp. 4–26.

5. K. McCarter, *1 Samuel*, vol. 8, p. 161 of the Anchor Bible, argues well for a contrastive relationship between chaps. 7 and 8, even though he has not recognized the larger introductory implications of these opening chapters of 1 Samuel, of which chap. 7 is the idealized conclusion. For his part, David Jobling is perceptive in his emphasis on "the *impasse* at 1 Sam. 7 and its resolution," *The Sense of Biblical Narrative II*, pp. 62ff. My own resolution to the problem of 1 Sam. 7 is an alternative way out of the impasse.

6. In a note in *Vetus Testamentum* 31 (1981), pp. 79–80, Scott L. Harris proposes to read v. 8 of MT as having had an original *mem* that has dropped out, giving us an original *kn hmh 'sym gm-mlk* ("so they are also making a king"). This suggestion makes evident sense in context and is accepted wholeheartedly by Lyle Eslinger, *Kingship of God in Crisis*, pp. 265ff. Nevertheless, it appears to me that the supposed contradiction between vv. 7 and 8, which occasions such a suggestion, "a perennial problem for scholars who have tried to assess Yahweh's words to Samuel concerning kingship" (Harris, p. 79), is really not much of a problem. After all, the people did request of Samuel what Samuel reports to God. God simply interprets (in v. 7) as rejection of God the request of the people which he refers to in v. 8 as "what they are doing to you," that is, to Samuel. That is to say, what they were doing to Samuel was requesting of him a king, which request God, when informed of it, maintains is tantamount to rejection his divine rule.

7. I write *provisionally* because the narrative will provide a continuing refinement of these matters as the history proceeds.

8. This is always the case in the relationship between the dominant narrator and the characters: how the narrator highlights dialogues through the use of direct, indirect, and other forms of reported speech is one of the chief indicators by which the reader is able to tease out the implied author's ideological perspectives.

9. I am using Alter's terminology here, *The Art of Biblical Narrative* (New York: Basic Books, 1981), pp. 63ff.

10. Contrast Deut. 17:18 where God himself is to do the choosing of the king.

11. McCarter, *1 Samuel*, pp. 161–62.

12. R. E. Clements, "The Deuteronomistic Interpretation of the Founding of the Monarchy in 1 Sam VIII," *Vetus Testamentum* 24 (1974), pp. 398–410, for example, recognizes that vv. 11–17 "leaves a very sharp tension within the chapter" (p. 401). "The Deuteronomists have here made use of a catalogue expressive of anti-monarchic feeling which is highly unusual in the context of the criticisms which they otherwise level against particular kings" (pp. 401–2). Clements interprets this passage by an appeal to literary history, "1 Sam viii is a Deuteronomistic composition and . . . its authors have made use of an already existing catalogue of royal oppressions in vv. 11–17" (pp. 408–9). What is missing in Clement's consideration here is any attempt to interpret this catalogue *as spoken by Samuel* in the context of the narrator's characterization of him in the story. (The same failure to interpret vv. 11–17 according to its voice structure is characteristic of M. Tsevat's discussion of the supposed intrusiveness of these verses: "If there is in the Old Testament one substantial addition to a literary unit that twists and thwarts its intent, it is these seven and a half verses, as Buber has conclusively shown. Not privileges but obligation and limitation are the substance of 'the rule of the king' or 'the rule of kingship' that is written down in a document and

deposited before God" [10:25] ["The Foundation of the Monarchy," p. 86]). Concerning the attitude of the Deuteronomists to monarchy as a whole, Clements believes that their position is explained by "the simple religious assumption that the question of Israel's kingship has been decided by Yahweh's election of David to the throne of Israel, and of his sons to succeed him in a dynastic succession" (p. 410).

As with most of the scholars who have written on 1 Samuel or portions thereof, Clements proceeds according to a genetic model that ignores essential features of the text like voice structure. That is to say, the catalogue of royal sins in 8:11–17 (18) is spoken by Samuel in the story for his own purposes and in accord with the History's characterization of him. What Samuel's purposes are, and what the Deuteronomists' characterization of him might be, are rarely discussed seriously in the secondary literature, and Clement's presentation of chap. 8 is no exception.

13. As Hertzberg has pointed out, *I and II Samuel* (Philadelphia: Westminister, 1964), p. 74.

14. See S. R. Driver's comments, *Notes on the Hebrew Text and the Topography of the Books of Samuel* (Oxford: Clarendon, 1913), p. 67.

15. B. Halpern, *The Constitution of the Monarchy in Israel* (Decatur, GA: Scholars Press, 1981), p. 224, has seen the necessity of this interpretive move but has not attempted to explain why Samuel in vv. 11–18 limits his speech to the restrictive aspects (from the people's viewpoint) of the monarchy. Halpern, so far as I am aware, does not deal with the narrative implications flowing from Samuel's speech as "meant to discourage the assembly from adopting monarchy" (p. 220).

16. B. Halpern, *Constitution of the Monarchy*, pp. 224ff., has nicely analyzed the range of biblical usages of this term and rightly focuses on its predominantly legal and decretal meanings, Nevertheless, his source-oriented perspective—I use Sternberg's terminology here, from *The Poetics of Biblical Narrative*, chap. 1—keeps him from seeing how *mišpat hammelek*, as Samuel describes it, precisely functions with respect to Samuel fulfilling or not God's injunction in v. 9. Why would God command him to detail *just* the king's powers without any of the corresponding restrictions or limitations? Or if God did not so limit Samuel, why then is Samuel's speech so limited? So far as I know, Halpern because of his historiographic emphases does not direct his attention to this discourse-oriented question.

17. In a study that is valuable in its efforts to take the final text of 1 Samuel–1 Kings 2 seriously, T. R. Preston, "The Heroism of Saul: Patterns of Meaning in the Narrative of the Early Kingship," *Journal for the Study of the Old Testament* 24 (1982), pp. 27–46, builds upon David Gunn's excellent study of Saul as a tragic hero (*The Fate of King Saul*) and shows in detail how 1 Samuel–1 Kings 2 exhibits "a unified structure in which the lives of Samuel, Saul and David are all intertwined in such a way that they follow the same basic pattern, foreshadowing and reflecting each other as the narrative progresses" (p. 28). Preston perceptively comments on how this pattern is foreshadowed in the Song of Hannah, wherein we find the "rise of the lowly, fall of the mighty" theme that will structure and books of Samuel. His suggestions of a self-serving Samuel who helps to bring about Saul's failure are in line with my own reading of the prophet. Preston's overall reading of the books of Samuel is generally insightful and persuasive, perhaps the best succinct statement of these books that I have so far encountered. Preston concludes that in contrast to David's house, which is under the curse of the sword, "Saul emerges as the narrator's hero—a hero who was also a failure, but a failure who is completing the 'rise of the lowly, fall of the mighty' pattern also died on the battlefield in defense of Israel, not in his bed with the moral fabric of Israel crumbling around him." (p. 44).

Like Gunn's depiction of the narrator's ideological perspective on Saul, Preston, in my opinion, here fails to balance his accurate picture of tragic elements in Saul's life with equally powerful features in the story that emphasize his culpability in spite of all that God and his human shadow, Samuel, had done to bring about Saul's failure. For example, with reference to his heroic depiction of Saul's death, Preston never considers the abhorrent view of suicide in Israelite ideology. (Even had he done so, I imagine that he would exculpate Saul's final act by again blaming "the evil spirit from the LORD.") My own position would be to affirm with Preston a contrast between Saul's and David's careers—after all, God's evil spirit is never present to help excuse David's despotic deeds—yet leave a significant portion of culpability at Saul's feet also.

While biblical narrative never dissolves the mystery inherent in the juxtaposition of divine omnipotence and human freedom, neither, I believe, does it wholly dissolve the latter, even in the case of Saul.

18. Apart from the work of scholars like Gunn, Preston, Jobling, Fokkelman, and Eslinger, recent studies do not take the final text of 1 Samuel seriously; they continue to resort simply to literary-historical explanations of what the book "means."

Bruce Birch, "The Development of the Tradition on the Anointing of Saul in 1 Sam 9:1–10:16," *Journal of Biblical Literature* 90 (1971), pp. 55–68, begins his discussion of this pericope with a literary-historical analysis and concludes "that the evidence shows that 9:1–10:16 cannot be considered to be a literary unity without some adequate explanation of the tensions within the section" (p. 57). Such tensions and inconsistencies as scholars have been accustomed to note within 9:1–10:16 call, therefore, for a "reconstruction of the growth of the section into its present form," which in turn "will first require a careful examination of the character and origin of the various materials in the section" (p. 57). Two things are clear from Birch's statement of the problem and the answers he gives for it. First, appearing only in 1971, the analysis he presents is understandably uninformed about matters such as characterization, point of view, voice structure, the function of repetition, and so forth—concerns necessarily involved in any discussion of "the literary unity of a text." Second, like most of the studies that will appear after it, and despite a small but influential number of biblical studies calling for a wider understanding of literary-critical issues than that previously fueling scholarly efforts, Birch's article equates the literary character of a biblical text with the origins of the material within it. In other words, one's discourse-oriented impressions about a text (does it appear to be a literary unity?) lead immediately to literary-historical considerations about such impressions. No other way to examine "the character of the various materials in the section" seems to be allowed. The literary-historical suggestions that Birch offers, therefore, are limited by his excessively narrow understanding of what is involved in a careful examination of the character, indeed the poetics, of biblical narrative. The particular source-oriented reconstruction this article presents is as thoroughly predictable and speculative as those studies with which it establishes a dialogue. (Birch's article is based upon his doctoral dissertation, which was later published: *The Rise of the Israelite Monarchy* [Decatur, GA: Scholars Press, 1976].)

J. Maxwell Miller, "Saul's Rise to Power: Some Observations concerning 1 Sam 9:1–10:16, 10:26–11:15 and 13:2–14:46," *Catholic Biblical Quarterly* 36 (1974), pp. 157–74, discusses chaps. 9 and 10 from a literary-historical perspective (pp. 157–61). The observations in this article are, from our discourse-oriented perspective, indistinguishable from those of the studies to which it refers. Once again, "evidences of literary unity" (p. 157) fuel Miller's discussion of literary origins, without his ever expressing a suspicion that the constituents of literary unity, as well as the means by which it is discovered or denied, might be a bit more sophisticated and complex than the usual commonsense articulation of "tensions and inconsistencies" found in the majority of contemporary biblical studies blissfully unaware of wider views of the matter that have been present in the humanities for many decades.

Joseph Blenkinsopp's "The Quest of the Historical Saul," in *No Famine in the Land*, ed. James W. Flanagan and Anita Weisbrod Robinson (Claremont: Scholars Press, 1975), pp. 75–99, is basically a historical reconstruction of Saul's history in 1 Samuel, a quest based upon literary-historical assumptions such as Noth's on the Deuteronomistic History and Blenkinsopp's frequently suggestive opinions. Blenkinsopp attempts to sift some "historically reliable information" (p. 81) from the extended narrative, but since the winning side has written the History (pro-Davidic Judahite traditions), Saul unavoidably gets short ideological shrift in it: "access to usable historical information has been rendered extraordinarily difficult by politically and theologically inspired polemic built into the primary sources" (p. 82). This article, despite the historical sensitivity of its author, reflects the methodological position of many other similar treatments of the material by basing a historical reconstruction upon narrow literary-critical assumptions that simply equate literary criticism with literary history. The resulting interpretation turns out to be literarily and historically shortsighted.

In a series of three studies on 1 Sam. 9–31 (I: *Journal for the Study of the Old Testament* 6 (1978), pp. 18–27; II: *JSOT* 18 (1980), pp. 74–90; and III: *JSOT* 22 (1982), pp.

95–117), W. L. Humphreys has "isolated an early narrative stratum in 1 Samuel 9–31" and sets out to "articulate important stages in the developmental history of 1 Samuel" (III, p. 96). For Humphreys, the brilliant depiction of the tragedy of King Saul is over-laid with two later stages in the literary history of the present text. A northern prophetic stage turns Saul from a tragic hero to a villain; and a southern Davidic stage turns him from elect to rejected. The heart of Humphrey's analysis is found in his second article, two features of which limit his analysis. First, after a promising and largely convincing first article, Humphreys seems to me finally to refuse to take the final step in approaching his material from a fresh new perspective. Everything Humphreys says about the characterization of Saul in his hypothesized pretext of an older layer of Saul material could just as aptly and accurately be said of Saul as characterized in the final text, the real text. Why then squander upon a pre-text such valuable insights as Humphreys presents to us, rather than show (as he does so admirably concerning the structure of chaps. 9–31 in his first article) how this subtle complexity is part of the real text? Why resort to literary history when poetics is what his interpretive thesis is all about?

Humphreys's second and third studies proceed in a spirit that appears greatly at odds with the holistic emphasis of his first article. In the final analysis, his final two articles explain the meaning of the real text totally by recourse to a reconstructed prehistory. The end result for Humphreys is a final story

offering perspectives and images of king, prophet, and deity that remain in tension with each other. No full or final resolution of that tension is possible. Nor is it necessary. 1 Samuel is a rich repository of varied expressions of distinct individuals and circles . . . (III, p. 111)

The conclusion of Humphreys's three-articled effort is that the final form of 1 Sam. 9–31 does not cohere very well artistically. His description of the process of composition ends up with a product that may be a work of art, but one that is simply " a rich repository of varied expression." How then did Humphreys get to the clear structure of the story that he "discovered" in the final form of the text? Is it possible that his "stages" might be contemporaneous perspectives woven into the text by a guiding intelligence? (Portions of Humphreys's three articles have been revised for inclusion in book form: *The Tragic Vision and the Hebrew Tradition* [Philadelphia: Fortress Press, 1985], chaps. 2 and 3.)

19. Of course, after recognizing the tensions and inconsistencies existing between chaps. 8 and chap. 9:1–10:16, as scholars have long been doing since Wellhausen's day, the search for further editorial activity continues. So Birch (see the preceding note), citing recent suggestions by Hertzberg and Seebass, will illustrate in detail how "a careful reading of the text discloses a number of tensions and inconsistencies in the pericope . . ." (p. 56) and argue that this pericope has a complicated literary history in which a final editor, imbued with prophetic traditions, took an old folktale, added an old etiological tradition (10:10–13), and combined these with other additions (9:15–17, 20–21, [25–26], 27–10:1 [LXX], 5–8, 16b) to produce our final text. The beat goes on.

20. Lyle Eslinger, *Kingship of God in Crisis*, pp. 291ff. nicely explores this aspect of the chapter.

21. Presumably, all the characters in the story know the name of the city.

22. Sternberg, *Poetics of Biblical Narrative*, p. 128.

23. Since Gressman, this anonymity is supposed to be indicative of the old folktale that is part of this pericope's complicated literary history. Thus B. Birch, "Anointing of Saul," *JBL* 90 (1971), pp. 58–60.

24. As we shall see, chap. 10 will greatly intensify this pattern with a whole series of miraculous predictions by Samuel to Saul of what would come to pass—"signs" (10:7) that Samuel speaks for God.

25. S. M. Paul, "1 Samuel 9, 7: An Interview Fee," *Biblica* 59 (1978), pp. 542–44, discusses the *hapax*, *t°šûrāh*, in 9:7 and suggests that a medieval exegete's insight (Menahem) has now been "substantiated by resort to Akkadian" (p. 543). For Menahem, followed by Rashi, *t°šûrāh* is "the fee of seeing [*šûr*, "to see"] which they bring to the seer." Paul concludes that Saul's reservation was that he had no "interview fee" to offer the seer.

26. This key word is certainly not exclusively prophetic, as even 2:16, 8:5; and 12:10 show, but it is a typical element of prophetic rhetoric, as commentators generally recognize.

27. *Hinnēh* serves many functions in narration. When spoken by the narrator, it can signal

a transition either from the narrator's to a character's point of view (for example, 9:14) or from narrated past to narrator's present (for example, Deut. 3:11); when spoken by a character, it points to something either present or made present by the character to his or her interlocutor. In this last characterological function its prophetic appropriateness is obvious. Few scholars discuss the poetics of *hinnēh*; A. Berlin is a welcome exception. See her excellent *Poetics and Interpretation of Biblical Narrative* (Sheffield; Almond Press, 1983), pp. 62–63, 67–69, and *passim*. See also Sternberg, *Poetics of Biblical Narrative*, p. 53.

28. On the other hand, as we shall later point out, there is also a facet of the author's ideological position that emphasizes the "perhaps" that is found even in authentic prophetic speech.

29. That *'îš* can be used not just to refer to a specific man (*lā'îš*) but (rarely) to a person generally speaking (*le''îš*—that is, "any man in general," or "some representative of mankind"—is seen from the statement of one of the Hebrews whom Moses had stopped from fighting with his fellow: "He answered, 'Who made you a prince and a judge over a man (*le'îš*)?' " (Exod. 2:14).

30. Shemuel Shaviv, "*Nābî'* and *nāgîd* in 1 Samuel IX 1–X 16," *Vetus Testamentum* 34 (1984), pp. 108–12, discusses the wordplay involving *nābî'* and *nāgîd* in this section of 1 Samuel as previously noted by Buber, J. V. Curtis, Vischer, and McCarter. Shaviv is concerned that proper credit for the "achievements of earlier scholars," that is, Buber and Vischer, be given them, noting, for example, that McCarter's is the only commentary he knows of that recognizes such wordplay, and even in this case McCarter "fails to indicate his source" (p. 112) for the *nābî'* wordplay. Shaviv's comments are a welcome broadening of the issues involved in such wordplay.

What is revealing about the *nābî'* wordplay is that source-oriented scholars tend not to recognize or discuss this feature of the story (McCarter is the exception, and even here Buber goes unnoticed), whereas discourse-oriented scholars usually pick it up, as noted in n. 1 above.

31. Alter, *Art of Biblical Narrative*, pp. 60–61.

32. Ibid., pp. 72ff.

33. Chap. 16 will further emphasize the groping of Samuel as he struggles to discover which one of Jesse's sons the LORD has chosen to replace Saul.

34. See especially Sternberg, *Poetics of Biblical Narrative*, pp. 94–96, on the ironic portrait of Samuel in chap. 9.

35. See *Moses and the Deuteronomist*, (New York: Srabury, 1980), chap. 2, for a detailed explanation of this phenomenon.

36. See on this point the brilliant analysis of Meir Sternberg in *Poetics of Biblical Narrative*, chap. 3. The application of these theoretical concepts to 1 Sam. 9 is fully my responsibility and not Sternberg's. It should be noted, however, that Sternberg at one point in his book refers to the unknown writers of biblical narrative as necessarily having "assumed a prophetic role in writing" (p. 94), so that, in this respect at least, our views are similar.

37. Ibid., p. 128.

38. As my review of representative secondary literature has been emphasizing ad nauseam (both my own and, I'm afraid, the reader's), the pattern within source-oriented studies of the History in general, as well as of this pericope in particular, is not even to recognize that features like perspective, voice structure, characterization, function of repetition, etc., have important implications for a superficial reading of the text, let alone for the construction of a detailed literary history.

39. In fact, as we shall shortly point out, all the characters speak mostly with imperfective verb forms, at least thirty-five of them, with the emphasis on the future.

40. I do not mean to imply that *higgîd* is necessarily a prophetic term, but simply that in the immediate context concerning the nature of kingship and prophecy the word serves a connective function in the narrator's choice of words, in accord with the LORD's injunction to Samuel in 8:9 to "declare" to the people the rights and duties of the king, the LORD's *nāgîd*. As already pointed out above, the *nāgîd*/*higgîd* wordplay in these chapters was emphasized already by M. Buber.

41. Recent studies on the relationship of the saying to its literary context are mostly source-oriented discussion. Thus, according to John Sturdy, "The Original Meaning of 'Is Saul Also Among the Prophets?' (1 Samuel XII, 12; XIX, 24)," *Vetus Testamentum*

20 (1970), pp. 206–13, both stories preceding the citation of the *mashal* were composed subsequently as etiological explanations for it, but both get its meaning wrong. Zeroing in on the *mashal* itself, Sturdy rejects "the *ha-* of surprise" in favor of "*ha-* expecting the answer 'no' " so that "the implication now is that it is a good thing to be a prophet, but Saul is not one, and he is valued negatively [*sic*] for this" (p. 211). The saying means something like "Saul's no prophet" and expresses hostility to Saul, holding it against him that in some sense he is not a prophet. Sturdy then looks for a setting in life that would explain the creation of the story and finds it in the tendencies of Davidic propaganda.

V. Eppstein, "Was Saul Among the Prophets?" *Zeitschrift für die Alttestamentliche Studien* 81 (1969), pp. 287–303, views the two stories as "an imaginative explanation of the well-known proverb presented, not without considerable artistry, as a conjectural event in the life of King Saul, but like many historical fictions anachronistic in conception" (p. 297). Eppstein also points to the probability of deliberate Davidic *tendenz* in the later understanding of the saying. Eppstein's discussion, like Sturdy's, is characterized by conjecture over the "possible origins of the stories associated with the saying" and speculation over the "original meaning of the saying" once they have relegated the stories that are its literary context to the ash heap of etiological explanation.

Simon Parker, in a comparative article, "Possession Trance and Prophecy in Pre-exilic Israel," *Vetus Testamentum* 28 (1978), pp. 271–85, resorts to field studies of religiously institutionalized altered states and distinguishes between "possession trances" and "visionary trances," the latter being "mediumistic," in contrast to the former. For Parker, possession was "*not* an element of Israelite prophecy" (p. 285).

42. Following Buber's insights, Eslinger, Miscall, McCarter, and others, as noted above in no. 1, have pointed out the paronomastic function of *higgîd* in 10:14–16.

43. David Gunn's failure to recognize this continuing feature of the stories that concern Saul explains why his interpretation of the fate of King Saul, while eminently perceptive, is incomplete, in my opinion. In David Jobling's discussion of chaps. 8–12 of 1 Samuel (*The Sense of Biblical Narrative II*, chap. 2), these negative features surrounding Saul and his kingship are similarly neglected.

44. Scholars such as Kyle McCarter (*1 Samuel*, pp. 195–96) and Peter Miscall (*1 Samuel*, pp. 64ff.) have perceptively pointed out the negative implications of choosing Saul here by the casting of lots, preceded as it is by a prophetic judgment oracle. Earlier studies have generally missed this point. Thus, Lindblom, "Lot Casting in the Old Testament," *Vetus Testamentum* 12 (1962), pp. 164–78, unaccountably overlooks the negative connotations with which the account has Saul, like Achan before and Jonathan after him, seized or "taken," (*nilkad*). Lindblom distinguishes between a "priestly" and a "civil" form and argues that both have coalesced in the present form of chap. 14 (the taking of Jonathan). Bertil Albrektson, "Some Observations on Two Oracular Passages in 1 Sam," *Annual of the Swedish Theological Institute* 11 (1977–78), pp. 1–10, believes that Lindblom's distinction between civil and cultic lot casting is not convincing. Neither scholar discusses this section from a discourse-oriented perspective.

45. Sternberg, *Poetics of Biblical Narrative*, p. 96.

46. McCarter (*1 Samuel*, pp. 198ff.) incorporates this additional material into 10:27 and integrates it well into his notes and comments. Although providing important background for the key events of the chapter, 4QSam^a adds little else to the esthetic and ideological dimensions of the story as found in the MT.

47. Lyle Eslinger, *Kingship of God in Crisis* (pp. 359–82), has done a nice job of collecting and discussing many of the more relevant attempts at interpretation of this chapter, especially those centered around the concluding events of vv. 12–15. To his list of readings of chap. 11 can be added a recent article by Diana Edelman, "Saul's Rescue of Jabesh-Gilead (I Sam 11:1–11): Sorting Story from History," *Zeitschrift für die Alttestamentliche Wissenschaft* 96 (1984), pp. 195–209. Edelman uses the "factual information" of 2 Sam. 2:4b–7 as a historical corrective to the details contained in chap. 11. Applying Baruch Halpern's suggestions of a widespread kingship ritual in Israel, Judah, and elsewhere in the ancient Near East to the subject matter of chap. 11, Edelman sees the middle element of the proposed ritual pattern (designation, battle, and confirmation) as the primary motivation whereby the writer of the story constructed what she characterizes as a "*šōpēt*-style tale." The narrative unit of 1 Sam.

1:1–11 thus appears to be an "artificially constructed tale of the so-called 'major' judges" (p. 207). From Edelman's perspective, therefore, as from that of most source-oriented scholars, the text essentially means that supposedly incoherent goal toward which its reconstructed literary history—usually a highly speculative affair—is supposed to tend.

48. McCarter, *1 Samuel*, p. 196.

49. Besides it occurrence here in 1 Sam. 11, the verb is found only in Is. 61:4; Pss. 51:12, 103:5, and 104:30; Lam. 5:21; Job 10:17; and 2 Chron. 15:18; 24:4, 12. Efforts to show how *hdš* could mean "to inaugurate" are unconvincing.

50. A common solution to the renewal question involves "surrendering v. 14 to the redactional scrap-heap," as Eslinger aptly characterizes it (*Kingship of God in Crisis*, p. 378). Convinced that such disposal is not necessary, Eslinger follows Buber here and describes the space between the end of chap. 10 and the beginning of chap. 11 as a period when Israel's kingship had become dormant, so that renewal became "absolutely necessary for the people to affirm their acceptance of and allegiance to the monarchy offered to them by Yahweh" (p. 379). Up to this point, Eslinger's explanation of the need for renewal is plausible. However, since he accepts the questioning or negative interpretation of the statement quoted and condemned by the people in v. 12, he is led to propose that v. 12 represents a hypocritical fabrication of these new monarchic converts who then go on to renew the kingship. This overall understanding of the chapter seems to me to wend almost as tortuous a path as the redactional interpretations Eslinger so justly rejects.

51. McCarter, *1 Samuel*, pp. 205–6.

52. If a literal renewal of the monarchy allows us to put the judicial picture of chap. 11 in proper perspective, it additionally offers one of the clearest illustrations I know of concerning the intimate connection between text criticism and the supposedly more subjective higher criticism that is in theory based upon it. Whether one points for justification to ancient translations like the Septuagint or modern interpreters like S. R. Driver (*Notes on the Hebrew Text*, p. 87), the MT in v. 12 ("Saul shall be king") has continued to be seen as "contradictory to the context" (McCarter, *1 Samuel*, p. 201), so that an actual or implied *not*, we are told, must be added to the verse. By *the context*, however, modern scholars mean something like "a narrative (supposedly from the Saul cycle of judge stories) rather artlessly incorporated into a monarchic context." In such an understanding, an artless redaction necessitates an artful emendation. Once again we might smugly believe that modern intelligence has discovered and corrected an ancient mistake based upon a scribal or redactional slip of the pen. However, perhaps it is our understanding of a vague or metaphorical renewal of the kingship and our belief in the necessity here for textual emendation that have missed the point. Whatever the case, we can comfort ourself with the knowledge that the Septuagint and other early translations began such ponderings very early indeed.

53. The *mošiaʿ* whom Jabesh-Gilead proposes to find in v. 3 turns out to be the LORD himself, according to Saul's words here in v. 13. John Sawyer's semantic study, "What Was a *mošiaʿ*?" *Vetus Testamentum* 15 (1965), pp. 475–86, tries to recover "the original meaning and *Sitz im Leben* of an important biblical word" (p. 476). He finds in it a possible forensic origin, suggesting a development from a definite office within a definite sphere of life (verbal defense) "to a title of God related to that same sphere of life, and from there to a title of God in any general context" (p. 485). Although I could not find its occurrence in 11:3 discussed by Sawyer, I would assume that its use there to refer to the military defender whom Jabesh-Gilead is seeking indicates for him a literary-historical point at which the original meaning of a verbal defender has already been extended to include a military defender.

54. A. Alt, *Essays on Old Testament History and Religion* (Garden City: Doubleday, 1968), p. 253.

55. Ibid., p. 251.

56. See, for example, McCarter's description in *1 Samuel*, p. 206.

57. For a suggestion of covenantal implications in these actions, see Polzin, "HWQY^c and Covenantal Institutions in Early Israel," *Harvard Theological Review* 62 (1969), pp. 227–40.

58. Elsewhere in the Bible the situation is similar: Hosea uses Gibeah's name as shorthand for sin and divine judgment in Hosea 5:8; 9:9; and 10:9.

59. Peter Miscall, *1 Samuel*, p. 66.

60. It is almost predictable that "and after Samuel" is usually seen as "redactional and secondary" (for example, McCarter, *1 Samuel*, p. 203).
61. Even if one were to accept the proposed emendation of 11:12 and thus implicate the people in a continuing insistence on kingship, Samuel's statement in 12:12 will still glaringly underplay his crucial intervention in commanding and carrying out the renewal of the kingdom in 11:14–15. In chap. 12 Samuel will try to put all the sin of kingship upon the people's shoulders, whereas by this point in the story he will have become kingship's greatest promotor.
62. M. Bakhtin, *The Dialogic Imagination: Four Essays*, ed. M. Holquist (Austin: Univ. of Texas Press, 1981), p. 305.
63. One is reminded here of how Josh. 13–20, in its listing of the many exceptions to Israel's occupation of the land, had similarly prepared for the unmasking, in ironic tones, of the sweeping judgments of authoritarian dogmatism in Josh. 21:43–45; see on this point R. Polzin, *Moses and the Deuteronomist*, pp. 128–34.
64. *Wattirû* (v. 12); *'im tîr'û* (v. 14); *ûr'û* (v. 16); *ûr'u* (v. 17); *wayyîra'* (v. 18); *'al tirā'û* (v. 20); *yir'û, r^e'û* (v. 24); and *hārē^ac tārē^eû* (v. 25).
65. I use *phraseological composition* in the sense proposed by B. Uspensky in *A Poetics of Composition* (Berkeley and Los Angeles: Univ. of Calif. Press, 1973).
66. "Behold the king whom you have chosen, for whom you have asked; behold the LORD has set a king over you" (v. 13)' "the king who reigns over you" (v. 14)' "your king" (v. 15)' and "in asking for yourselves a king" (v. 17).
67. For a survey of various interpretations of *fathers* in this verse, see L. Eslinger, *Kingship of God in Crisis*, pp. 485ff. Of the various emendations proposed for *fathers* here in v. 15, if one is indeed necessary, R. Weiss's suggestion of an original "against your houses," in "La Main du Seigneur sera contre vous et contre vos pères (I Samuel xii.15), *Revue Biblique* 83 (1976), pp. 51–54, is well argued for.
68. Of course, in theories like Cross's double-edition hypothesis, the ascription of v. 25 to Dtr² rescues Samuel, and thus Dtr¹, from preaching an utterly hopeless sermon here in chap. 12
69. L. Eslinger, *Kingship of God in Crisis*, pp. 408ff., cites some of the scholars who perceive similarities between these two chapters.
70. Deut. 18:15. See Polzin, *Moses and the Deuteronomist*, chap. 3, for an extended discussion concerning this identification.
71. When human and divine freedom come into conflict, as they so often do in the History, the Deuteronomist does not shrink from sometimes indicating how divine overwhelms human, as when Eli's sons do not listen to their father "because it was the will of the LORD to slay them" (2:25) or when an evil spirit from the LORD rushes upon Saul to torment him (16:14) and to instigate murderous actions against David (18:10). While such exceptional events as these might disquiet the reader, they nevertheless indicate, by their very nature as difficult exceptions to the normal presentation of man's freedom, how far removed the History is from that mechanical didacticism so often leveled against it by its more superficial readers.

Chapter 4: Saul Among The Baggage (13:1–15:35)

1. Besides the few works discussed in the endnotes of the last chapter, only two studies I know of discuss the narrative art of chaps. 13–15 with any king of discourse-oriented sophistication: David Jobling's *The Sense of Biblical Narrative I* (Sheffield: Almond Press, 1978; reprint, 1986) and J. P. Fokkelman's *Narrative Art and Poetry in the Books of Samuel, vol. 2, The Crossing Fates (I Sam 13–31 and II Sam 1)* (Assen: Van Gorcum, 1986). Both are distinctive in their use of a structuralist approach to literary analysis that is largely associated with the 1970s. Jobling in his most recent work indicates that his interests are now proceeding well beyond structuralism: *The Sense of Biblical Narrative II* (Sheffield: Almond Press, 1986), pp. 12ff.; Fokkelman, for his part, has not greatly altered his methodological orientation in vol. 2 of his voluminous study of the books of Samuel (a highly individualistic semiotic/structural approach to the text). I shall be discussing both scholars intermittently as I work my way through the rest of 1 Samuel, so I might as well clarify my own general attitude toward their work here at the outset.
   As my remarks in n. 1 of chap. 3 indicate, David Jobling's *The Sense of Biblical Narrative II* contains many insights into the structure and meaning of the History up

through 1 Sam. 12. Jobling takes the final form of the text very seriously indeed, and his description of the History's artful construction is a valuable contribution to our understanding of this section of the Bible. Although I differ with him with respect to describing the ideology of a number of crucial sections of the History and will continue to document these differences in endnotes, I nevertheless have learned a great deal from his discussions of the narrative.

As the rest of my book will reveal without my being able always to acknowledge it, J. P. Fokkelman's discussions of chap. 13–31 of 1 Samuel have increased my understanding of almost every one of these chapters of the History. I shall try to acknowledge those cases where our independently achieved interpretations are similar and will certainly indicate where we have a widely divergent understanding of a particular section. I have two general cautions about Fokkelman's massive two-volumed enterprise. First, his decision to treat the two parts of Samuel in reverse order—his vol. 1 dealing first with 2 Samuel and his vol. 2 then analyzing 1 Samuel—was, in my opinion, an unfortunate way to work through the artful construction of a text that is essentially narrative and where, therefore, sequentiality of reading is crucial to one's understanding of the story. Unless Fokkelman possesses a crystal ball, I cannot imagine his subsequent study of 1 Samuel not forcing him now to contemplate some massive revisions of his vol. 1, where he analyzed King David's career in 2 Samuel without benefit of the hard-earned insights into the career of Saul and his conflict with David, which form the subject matter of vol. 2. Second, I share Joel Rosenberg's impression that "Fokkelman, for one, seems to confuse 'a full interpretation' with belabored colon-by-colon and scene-by-scene analysis. It is not the totality of one's interpretation that matters, but the consequentiality" Rosenberg, *King and Kin: Political Allegory in the Hebrew Bible* (Bloomington: Indiana Univ. Press, 1986), p. 111. Moreover, as Rosenberg has pointed out in his own way (pp. 104–5), Fokkelman's overwhelmingly taxonomic emphases explain why his discussions often stop before form receives the enlivening breath of function within his interpretations.

2.	On the defective nature of 13:1, see the representative remarks of S. R. Driver, *Notes, on the Hebrew Text and the Topography of the Books of Samuel* (Oxford: Clarendon, 1913), pp. 96–97; K. McCarter, *1 Samuel*, vol. 8 of the Anchor Bible, (Garden City: Doubleday, 1980), pp. 222–23; and M. Sternberg, *The Poetics of Biblical Narrative* (Bloomington: Indiana Univ., 1985), p. 14.

3.	J. M. Miller, "Geba/Gibeah of Benjamin, *Vetus Testamentum* 25 (1975), pp. 145–66, presents a thorough discussion, with a source-oriented perspective, of the literary and archeological identification of Geba/Gibeah in 1 Sam. 13 and 14.

4.	For a discussion of *n'ṣîb* see Driver, *Notes on the Hebrew Text*, p. 80, and Fokkelman, *Narrative Art*, vol. 2, p. 28, both of whom prefer something like "prefect," "officer," or "governor." With respect to problematic details such as these (How old was Saul when he began to reign? Is it Geba or Gibeah, prefect or garrison?), my discourse-oriented emphases on how the text coheres and my constant jibes at source-oriented studies that ignore or deny such coherences should not be understood as a complete denial of those places in the narrative where text- or literary-historical explanations appear warranted. Thus, for example, 13:1 obviously needs text-critical reconstruction. Also, there seems to me no easy way to explain from a discourse-oriented perspective why Jonathan is first mentioned in the History (in 13:2) as one whose filial relationship to Saul needs no introduction, whereas the narrator later in the chapter (in v. 16) first brings up this relationship. Unlike the narrator's repeated references to "his father" and "his son" in 19:1–4, where Jobling is correct in suggesting ideological implications (*Sense of Biblical Narrative I*, p. 13), here at the very beginning of the story of Saul and Jonathan one would expect "his son" to be appropriately present in v. 2 and unremarkably absent in v. 16, but the opposite is the case. One might hope, therefore, that text history or literary history might provide a plausible solution to this minor kink in the text.

5.	In an early article on chap. 14, "Saul's Fall and Jonathan's Rise: Tradition and Redaction in 1 Sam 14:1–46," *Journal of Biblical Literature* 95 (1976), pp. 367–76, David Jobling seems to me to have made a false start in helping us understand what 1 Sam. 13–15 is all about. Jobling begins by assuming "that disparate traditions have gone into the formation of this section, but that they have been skillfully unified into the present form" (p. 367), He intends to "stay mainly with the MT and pay attention *only to the final literary form and context*" (ibid., emphasis mine) of chap. 14, a passage that "presents a skillful portrait of a rejected king, wholly coherent with the rejection oracles of chaps 13 and 15" (p. 368). Jobling explicitly rejects the view put forward by Conrad and Stoebe (and argued for in our own different ways by Fokkelman and myself) that there is a deliberate contrast in chap. 14 between two theologies, Saul's religious and Jonathan's more profane version: "But it is, in fact, hard to maintain, either in this chapter or in the larger narrative, a clear and consistent contrast between two theologies" (p. 370). As my own reading of the chapter in particular and the larger narrative in general suggests, the Deuteronomist consistently portrays Saul as tragically attracted to the divinatory aspects of acceptable Israelite ritual practices. Jobling, in my opinion, goes too far by starkly contending that "the contrast between Saul and Jonathan intends to show, not that the latter has a sounder theology, but that for the one out of divine favor all religious forms are useless, while everything tends to success for the one on whom Yhwh's favor rests" (p. 371).

The manner in which Jobling argues his case is revealing. To describe his position in some detail, Jobling appeals more to his literary-historical reconstructions of the text than to his avowed emphasis on "the final literary form and context" of the text, and he thereby supports his reading of the real text by appeal principally to his assumed pre-texts and their supposed incorporation into the final text. Thus, instead of basing his interpretation of the final text upon the internal relationship of features within the chapter, one to the other, and to external relations of this chapter to its literary context, Jobling, in apparent contrast to his later clarity on matters synchronic and diachronic, appears here to equate literary analysis with literary history: a textual unit, he seems to be arguing, primarily "means" what its supposed literary history tells us it means.

6. The common literary-historical "problem" of how one can go from a young, apparently sonless Saul in chap. 10 to a mature father of a grown Jonathan here in chap. 13 in only seven days seems to me an unnecessary complicating of the text. To believe, as McCarter, for example, does (*1 Samuel*, p. 228), that an older, unemended version of the story had the events of chaps. 13–14 happening long after Saul's search for his father's asses, that a later prophetic author understood only seven days to have passed from Saul's anointing to his sacrificing at Gilgal, and that the present text therefore is a redactional combination of the two accounts which is hopelessly incoherent from a chronological perspective is, once again, needlessly to deny the artful construction of the biblical text. Samuel's prediction (as well as apparent command) that Saul would (and should) go before him to Gilgal and wait seven days for him to come down and offer up sacrifice (10:8) never specifies when this predicted event will take place. In fact, this foreshadowing prediction is set off from all the other "signs" (10:7) that Samuel gave Saul the day of his anointing and that in fact "came to pass that day" (10:9), long before the events of chaps. 13–14. The common assumption that vv. 7b–15a represent the insertion of an account of Saul's indictment by Samuel into the older record is scarcely necessary.

7. See on this point Polzin, *Moses and the Deuteronomist* (New York: Seabury, 1980), pp. 91–110.

8. See Driver, *Notes on the Hebrew Text*, p. 101, for succinct syntactic remarks on this verse.

9. As indicated by McCarter, *1 Samuel*, p. 228.

10. See M. Weinfeld, *Deuteronomy and the Deuteronomic School* (New York: Oxford University Press, 1972), p. 336, for a convenient listing of such phraseology.

11. Fokkelman, *Narrative Art*, vol. 2, pp. 25–44, considers the account of the meeting of Samuel and Saul (13:8–15a) as occupying "a central position in I Sam." (p. 33). "We cannot avoid assessing this conflict in terms of power," but one's task is made especially difficult since "the narrator in no way indulges us by himself giving any value judgment or solution" (ibid.). Central to Fokkelman's position is his keeping open "the possibility here that the narrator was alive to some imperfection in Samuel and continued to maintain his own distance from this powerful figure" (p. 34). After alerting us to his desire for "phenomenological discipline," Fokkelman sometimes resorts to overpsychologizing Saul's situation, that is, to reconstructing for us, for example, what must have been Saul's inner thoughts as he waited for Samuel (pp. 36–37). Nevertheless, Fokkelman's instincts are often on the mark, as when he writes, "Samuel may think that Saul has failed the test, but the narrator betrays no trace of any attitude of judgment or cheap superiority over the doomed king" (p. 38). At this point in his reading, Fokkelman chooses to delay his evaluation of the dramatic conflict here

in chap. 13 until he has completed his analysis of chap. 15. So far in his interpretation, Fokkelman senses the narrator's sympathetic portrayal of Saul. Yet when the battle of Michmash Pass begins, Fokkelman presents us with his own picture of Saul that is merciless in its condemnation of him. And in spite of his opening caution about not idealizing Samuel, Fokkelman fails to pick up on any of the narrator's clear signals (especially in wordplay on *ṣiwwāh* in the confrontation) concerning Samuel's failure to keep the appointment as well as the ideological implications thereof.

12. The act itself of a king personally sacrificing could not be at issue in Samuel's condemnation of Saul: David (2 Sam. 6:17–18; 24:25), Solomon (1 Kings 3:15), and Ahaz (2 Kings 16:12) all offer sacrifices in circumstances that presume—even illustrate as in Solomon's case—the uprightness of their action. If we then consider the facility with which Samuel is shown to refer back to his prediction in 10:8 as both a command and an appointment of the LORD, Saul's guilt is still not established. That Samuel's words in 10:8 constituted a command is, at the most, only partially so. Like his series of verbal signs in 10:2–6 (thirteen imperfective verb forms), Samuel's words in v. 8 were predictive as well as imperative in meaning; only in v. 7 does Samuel issue Saul an unambiguous command: "When all these signs meet you, *do* what your hand finds to do"—a command that itself would encourage Saul's subsequent initiatives rather than condemn them. On the other hand, that Samuel's words in 10:8 constituted an appointment of some kind is certain, but this aspect of *miṣwat*, to which we will return below, simply highlights Samuel's failure to get to Gilgal on time. Apart from Samuel's questionable identification of the appointed time as a commandment of the LORD, nothing else in the story so far could possibly specify the *miṣwat* YHWH about which Samuel speaks. Samuel's presumed reference to 10:8 as God's command characterizes the prophet in chap. 13 as stretching a point in order to condemn Saul and highlights the prophet's failure to come, rather than Saul's failure to obey.

13. Later in the story, this self-serving attitude of Samuel toward Saul will best explain Samuel's angry crying all night when informed of God's rejection of Saul (15:11), his turning back after Saul even after God has rejected him (15:31), and God's subsequent dissatisfaction with his prophet: "Samuel grieved over Saul . . . And the LORD said to Samuel, 'How long will you grieve over Saul, seeing I have rejected him from being king over Israel?' " (15:35–16:1). Samuel continually prefers the royal devil he knows to the one he does not know. Samuel and Saul are bound together, therefore, as failed prophet to failed king. Even after his death Samuel will remain tied to Saul, who will succeed in bringing him up for a final dialogue. It is significant that on that occasion the resurrected Samuel will refer to Saul's disobedience of the LORD's voice with respect to Amelek but never mention his "disobedience" in not waiting for him at Gilgal. The reader must decide whether this neglect to mention the events of chapter 13 is the result of a redactor's blindness rather than the narrator's insight. Perhaps Samuel is more truthful after death than before it.

14. In spite of McCarter's plausible reconstruction of this verse, prompted by the LXX (*1 Samuel*, p. 227), I prefer to follow the MT here, to the obvious benefit of the negative characterization of Samuel I have been suggesting all along.

15. Joseph Blenkinsopp in an early article, "Jonathan's Sacrilege: I Sm 14, 1–46: A Study in Literary History," *Catholic Biblical Quarterly* 26 (1964), pp. 423–9, tries to show that chap. 14 is a particularly good example "of the narrative art of the early monarchy" lying midway—theologically and literarily—between an older poetic epic and an emerging "truly national historiography" (p. 449). Blenkinsopp wants to establish the original shape of chap. 14 as verse. He argues that "there is clear if intermittent evidence for rhythmic structure . . ." in chap. 14, which together with a whole variety of stylistic techniques "point straight back to oral composition" (p. 442). Such orally composed poems "betray their presence beneath the prose redaction of a later day" (p. 444).

In this article, Blenkinsopp tries to effect a more sophisticated literary analysis of biblical narrative than usually available in the scholarly literature of the time, yet he turns his perceptive instinct about the limitations of contemporary stylistic analysis primarily to applications of literary history.

16. For example, in Van Seters, *In Search of History* (New Haven and London: Yale University Press, 1983), discussed in the Introduction above.

17. In an original monograph, *The Just King: Monarchical Judicial Authority in Ancient Israel*

(Sheffield: Almond Press, 1979), pp. 71–89, Keith Whitelam devotes a chapter to "The Reign of Saul." Concerning chap. 14, Whitelam is concerned "with judicial implications of this narrative" (p. 73). Whitelam's approach, in this chapter as in the rest of his book, involves a welcome move away from central emphases on the literary history of passages. Although he frequently refers to literary-historical matters, he bases his conclusions about "the underlying forces that shaped the structure of society" more upon a wide sociological approach that is less dependent upon supposed written antecedents of the text than is the typical biblical study.

18. The statement in 13:21 ("the charge was a *pîm* [happᵉsîrāh pîm] for the plowshares and for the mattocks") is a good illustration of modern scholarship's growing awareness of the text's "factuality." Such references to the cost of living and other economic aspects in this expository section have turned out to be remarkably revealing. As late as 1913, S. R. Driver characterized *happᵉsîrāh pîm* as "hopelessly corrupt" (*Notes on the Hebrew Text*, p. 104). The very next year, Raffaeli discovered that *pîm* was the name of a weight for measuring silver. Years later Julius Bewer, "Notes on 1 Sam 13:21; 2 Sam 23:1; Psalm 48:8," *Journal of Biblical Literature* 61 (1942), pp. 45–46, could still lament the small recognition of Raffaeli's discovery in contemporary commentaries. By 1961, William Lane was able to cite the increasing number of references outside Palestine alluding to this weight, in "Newly Recognized Occurrences of the Weight-Name PYM," Bulletin of the American Schools for Oriental Research 164 (1961), pp. 21–23. Thus does source-oriented research truly advance our understanding of "hopelessly corrupt" texts. Such successes, unlike most of the mountains of theories within another branch of source-oriented studies, literary history, are based upon historical discoveries rather than upon speculation that is sometimes plausible (what Tigay calls "correct in general conception") and often groundless. For a discourse-oriented analysis of the expository information of 13:17–22, see Fokkelman, *Narrative Art*, vol. 2, pp. 44–46.

19. Concerning 13:23–14:23a, Fokkelman sometimes psychologizes his way toward an interpretation with little apparent connection to the extensive formal analyses that precede such inner psychological insights (*Narrative Art*, vol. 2, pp. 46–61). For example, commenting on Saul's reaction to Jonathan's initiatives, Fokkelman writes,

> What is going on in Saul's mind? My view is that Saul, robbed of his security by Samuel, is now hypersensitive to anything that he can interpret as insubordination. . . . Saul is now on edge. . . . What black thoughts and terrible feelings are now induced in the king? (pp. 59–60)

20. In an excellent study of the narrative role of Jonathan in chaps. 13–31, David Jobling remarks how Jonathan as a character is "flat, static and certainly opaque . . . , his attitudes and actions lacking any normal motivation" (*Sense of Biblical Narrative I*, p. 20). To explain such characterization, Jobling rejects any "psychologizing solutions" such as Hertzberg's and wonders "whether [Jonathan] is not a purely literary construction" created for the purpose of solving a theological problem: how can David succeed Saul? For Jobling, Jonathan's voluntary abdication is a narrative solution to a theological dilemma. There is much to commend in Jobling's explanation of how Jonathan's characterization functions within the larger story line. Among the many insights into the structure of that story line, Jobling picks up on the narrative similarity between "Jonathan's single combat (independent of Saul) against the Philistines [as] echoed in David's combat with Goliath" (p. 11). Moreover, the similarities between chaps. 14 and 19 are striking:

> In one case, Jonathan is under Saul's death sentence, in the other, David. Each is saved by an external mediation in which Saul acquiesces. Here, once more, David's experience recapitulates Jonathan's! (P. 13)

Along the way, Jobling also rightly criticizes J. Morgenstern, "David and Jonathan," *Journal of Biblical Literature* 78 (1959), pp. 322–25, for "finding the meaning of narrative rather from imported historical data than from implicit literary considerations" (p. 10).

21. For some helpful methodological considerations concerning editorial glosses in general and the supposedly spurious nature of 14:3a in particular, see M. Tsevat, "Studies in the Book of Samuel," *Hebrew Union College Annual* 32 (1961), pp. 209–16. Excursus I on 1 Sam. 14:3a, pp. 209–14.

254 **Samuel and the Deuteronomist**

22. Vv. 18, 23, 24, 31, 37; see 13:22.
23. Fokkelman, *Narrative Art*, vol. 2, pp. 46–83, also emphasizes the secular/sacred and active/passive contrasts in the chapter but draws interpretational conclusions about them that I cannot accept.
24. See my analyses in *Moses and the Deuteronomist*, chap. 4, *passim*.
25. I add a *perhaps* here because the narrator tells us that God did not answer Saul "that day." Thus it seems more likely that the events of vv. 36–46 are meant to be understood as taking place the next day, following the night of v. 34.
26. For a useful survey concerning Urim and Thummim, the ephod, and other methods for finding judgment in ancient Israel, see E. F. de Ward, "*Superstition and Judgment: Archaic Methods of Finding a Verdict*," *Zeitschrift für die Alttestamentliche Wissenschaft* 89 (1977), pp. 1–19. It is revealing how often a passage involving Saul's use of ritual practices is mentioned by de Ward.

On 14:41's reference to *'ûrîm and tummîm* in the Septuagint, see Driver, *Notes on the Hebrew Text*, pp. 117–118; Edward Robertson, "The *'urim* and *tummim;* What Were They?" *Vetus Testamentum* 14 (1964), 67–74; and A. Toeg, "A Textual Note on 1 Samuel XIV 41," *Vetus Testamentum* 19 (1969), pp. 493–98. Toeg believes that LXX of 14:41 is original and thus "sheds some light on one of the techniques of divination in ancient Israel" (p. 498).
27. Fokkelman contends that Saul's first oath in v. 24 should invoke the following "correct reaction" on the part of both reader and characters alike: "A general who withholds food from his army is not quite right in the head" (*Narrative Art*, vol. 2, p. 64). In writing about "Saul's pathology" (p. 68), Fokkelman characterizes Saul's second oath in the chapter (v. 39): "Even at this time, now that everyone feels in his heart that 'Saul has gone mad!'" (p. 74).
28. For C. E. Hauer, Jr., "The Shape of Saulide Strategy," *Catholic Biblical Quarterly* 31 (1969), pp. 153–67, chaps. 13 and 14 begin a recounting, throughout the rest of the book, of traditions substantiating Saul's strategically rational plans in securing Israel's defenses against its enemies. These traditions, Hauer believes, argue for a heightened respect for Saul, the military strategist, "tragic hero that he was" (p. 167).

Fokkelman's attempt to explain 14:47–52 as a "subversive dialectic" of writer or redactor, symbolic of the entire book of 1 Samuel, is, in my opinion, unconvincing (*Narrative Art*, vol. 2, pp. 82–83). By the end of his analysis of chaps. 13 and 14, Fokkelman offers a Greimasian model for synopsizing his interpretation: "The holy/profane contrast [discussed by Greimas in connection with a group of European folktales] can also be found in I Sam 13–14 as the contrast between true and false religion in the sense of deep internal conviction versus the superficiality of hollow ritualism' (p. 79). In Fokkelman's view, Samuel and Jonathan represent "true religion" and Saul "false religion." This overly stark and misleading presentation of the ideology of these chapters results, I believe, from Fokkelman's repeated practice of overpersonalizing or -psychologizing various aspects of the story, as well as from his penchant for imposing dramatic hyperbole and poetic symbolism upon the text—both tendencies in stark contrast to the cold and minute formal analyses that fill most of the pages of his book. As an example of the first tendency, Fokkelman writes, "And finally Saul pronounces the name of his son [in v. 44]. How much charged with fury, jealousy and other venom? and the reverse: how much absolute loneliness, despair and grief at being discarded fill Saul and keep him from his fellow men?" (pp. 74–75). And for sheer poetic symbolism, Fokkelman can achieve such homiletic heights as this:

> Just as the rocks [of 14:4] stand inaccessibly opposite one another, hard and sharp, and make any crossing a venture, so the antitheses created by Saul are rigid and implacable and the confrontation between father and son rock-hard and grim. Now we can understand the function of the detailed description of the landscape in 14:4–5: the columns of rock are the symbol of the conflicts and embody their qualities, rigidity, inaccessibility, the impossibility of unification. In order to respect their central place in the story and show their importance, the story also mentions their proper name—Only he who does not acquiesce in the duality and inaccessibility finds the reverse side of nature: sweetly flowing, energy-giving honey. Just when the energy is exhausted, creation shows Jonathan and the people its sweetness, nourishment and willingness. (p. 80)

It is almost as if Fokkelman strives by such rhetoric to offset the huge bulk of his formalistic analyses with intermittent bursts of personalized discourse to the reader, discourse whose accents remind us of the agonized questions found in the quasi-direct speech of Dostoevski's narrator.

29. On the confusing nature of Agag's last words in 15:32b, and the possible meanings of *mᵉdnt* preceding them, see the convincing suggestion of S. Talmon concerning conflated readings, "1 Sam. 15:32b–a Case of Conflated Readings," *Vetus Testamentum* 11 (1961), pp. 456–57.

30. 1 Sam. 15 has been well analyzed by Meir Sternberg in the concluding chapter to his *Poetics of Biblical Narrative*. Using Sternberg's insights as a starting point, I will at times build upon, at times depart from them.

31. Fokkelman, on the other hand, believes that Samuel's statement in v. 29 does not contradict v. 35, which is the narrator's word to the reader and not Samuel's to Saul. Once again Fokkelman offers psychologistic reasons. On one hand, "That message [that God *does* repent] would have the wrong effect on a despairing Saul" (p. 106), and on the other, "The current situation demands inexorability" (p. 107).

32. Samuel's argument probably intends to state that God will not repent, rather than that he, by divine nature, cannot do so.

33. On chap. 15 as representing either the voices of authoritarian dogmatism or critical traditionalism, see the slightly different view of P. Miscall, *1 Samuel*, pp. 98–114. My reading of chap. 15 suggests that the voice of critical traditionalism heard in the words and perspective of the narrator illustrates in this chapter how Samuel's initial position (God *must* punish) and his subsequent position as influenced by Saul's "return/repent with me" (God *will* forgive) both come dangerously close to a too rigid position that inappropriately pens God in. The Deuteronomist is here teaching that although God *can* repent of punishing Saul, he does not do so for his own mysterious reasons.

34. Fokkelman has a different picture of the prophet throughout the chapter: "Reviewing 15:1–33 now, there is only one party who can leave the stage with his head held high, Samuel" (*Narrative Art*, vol. 2, p. 110).

35. I have been influenced in these matters, as in many other theoretical points, by Mikhail Bakhtin. See, for example, *The Dialogic Imagination: Four Essays by M. M. Bakhtin*, ed. M. Holquist (Austin and London: Univ. of Texas, 1981), especially the first and last essays.

36. I am following here the suggestion of Talmon, "The 'Comparative Method' in Biblical Interpretation—Principles and Problems," *Supplements to Vetus Testamentum* 29 (Leiden: 1978), p. 355. This article contains valuable insights into these and related matters. In addition, Charles Conroy's "Hebrew Epic: Historical Notes and Critical Reflections," *Biblica* 61 (1980), pp. 1–31, is a helpful discussion of the applications of the term *epic* to biblical literature.

37. Whether the generic product we are about to describe should be termed "historiographic" is for critics more competent than myself to establish or deny. Also, it may be prudent for me to point out that my use of the terms *the History* or *the Deuteronomic History* to refer to the text I am reading is simply for purposes of pointing rather than defining.

38. Concerning all those students of the Bible who might rush to claim for, say, J, E, P, or the like some rights of generic paternity, the status of such "works" makes all the difference: I write to describe as novel a real text rather than an hypothesized pre-text.

39. Bakhtin, *Dialogic Imagination*, p. 342.

40. Ibid., especially pp. 338–55.

41. See ibid., pp. 20ff., for a helpful treatment of such aspects of generic differentiation.

Chapter 5: The Appearance of David (16:1–19:24)

1. Martin Kessler, "Narrative Technique in 1 Sm 16, 1–13," *Catholic Biblical Quarterly* 32 (1970), pp. 543–54, wrote an early article calling for greater scholarly attention to literary analysis of biblical narrative. Following the rhetorical lead of James Muilenburg, Kessler discusses a number of features in chap. 16 that are usually overlooked by source-oriented scholarship. Among the insights of this article, Kessler highlights *rā'ah* as a key word (following Buber), discusses narrative techniques of suspense and surprise, suggests that Saul's name (*šā'ûl* = "asked for") might have some connection with the people's demand for a king in chap. 8, notices the ideological tensions between God's word in 16:7 and the narrator's in 16:12, and generally provides a

convincing clarion call for greater scholarly interest in discourse-oriented study of the Bible. For a fuller, yet in my opinion less satisfying, treatment of this chapter, see Ashley S. Rose, "The 'Principles' of Divine Election: Wisdom in 1 Samuel 16," in *Rhetorical Criticism: Essays in Honor of James Muilenberg*, ed. J. J. Jackson and M. Kessler (Pittsburgh: Pickwick, 1974), pp. 43–67.

2. A number of authors may be mentioned who treat with seriousness the career of David as it develops in the final form of 1 Samuel. I will refer to David Gunn, *The Story of King David* (Sheffield: Almond Press, 1978) and J. P. Fokkelman, *Narrative Art and Poetry in the Books of Samuel*, 2 vols. (Assen: Van Gorcum, 1981, 1986), more than once in the following endnotes. I might also mention David Marcus, "David the Deceiver and David the Dupe," *Prooftexts* 6 (1986), pp. 163–71, who discusses two major trends discernible in David's career as described in the History:

> First, when David is commencing his career, both his attempts at initiating deception and countering deceptive acts against him are successful. It is only when he is at the peak of his power, and after the Bathsheba incident, that his fortunes in this area change. Second, many of these stories display a pattern of "measure for measure" [the deceiver himself gets duped]. Observing this pattern is especially helpful in the interpretation of Uriah's actions in the Bathsheba story, and in understanding the events described in 1 Kings 1 leading to the coronation of Solomon as successor to David." (P. 167)

Also, Kenneth R. R. Gros Lous, "King David of Israel," *Literary Interpretation of Biblical Narrative II*, ed. Kenneth R. R. Gros Louis with James S. Ackerman (Nashville: Abingdon, 1982), pp. 204–19, provides an excellent overview of the riches available to those who give serious attention to the final shape of the biblical account of David's career. Walter Brueggemann, *David's Truth in Israel's Imagination and Memory* (Philadelphia: Fortress Press, 1985), marries literary, sociological, and theological interests in his interpretation of David as seen in 1 Samuel (pp. 19–39 are primarily on chaps. 16, 17, and 24). Brueggemann is one of only a few modern scholars whose published work aims for some kind of interaction of new approaches either among themselves or in relation to older perspectives. Whereas many scholars promote their own perspectives and criticize others', Brueggemann in this rather popularized work tries to integrate insights based upon new currents of interest. Because it is a popular treatment, Brueggemann's book necessarily glosses over a number of crucial questions that face a literary or sociological reader of 1 Samuel: what, for example, is the meaning of 17:31–40, where David and Saul know one another, in relation to 17:55–58, where Saul does not seem to know who David is?

Among source-oriented treatments giving an overview of David's career as it is contained in 1 Samuel (and beyond), the following articles are representative. Niels Lemche, "David's Rise," *Journal for the Study of the Old Testament* 10 (1978), pp. 2–25, aims at reevaluating the early career of David as seen in 1 Sam. 16–2 Sam. 5, taking into account the pro-Davidic *Tendenz* of the narrative. Somehow or other, this source-oriented study is able to arrive at confident historical conclusions like "The anointing of David as described in 16,1–13 is totally unhistorical, as most scholars agree" (p. 4). How and why the author is able to conclude that "two narratives seem to contain some historical facts: Saul's attempt to murder David, ch. 19, and the narrative in ch. 20, the arrangement between David and Jonathan" is unclear to me. Often Lemche is sure that he knows "what really happened' in contrast to the biblical author's imaginative "talent for composition" (p. 8). Lemche believes that "the author of 'David's Rise' has thrown a veil over Saul's real motives by explaining Saul's hatred against David as something originating in Saul's insanity. *In reality* [emphasis mine], Saul's aversion to the up and coming man, David, has its reasons in the natural distrust an absolute ruler must always feel against subjects who are too successful" (p. 8). Besides Lemche's apparent assumption that literary criticism means nothing more than literary history, his ability to distinguish truth claim from truth value in the interpretation of ancient historiographic narratives like "David's Rise" is, in my opinion, questionable. Despite Lemche's constant disclaimers at key points in the article about caution in historical reconstruction, at too many places in his discussion he is overly confident that such reconstructions can be made. P. Kyle McCarter's "The Apology of David," *Journal of Biblical Literature* 99 (1980), pp. 489–504, is a comparative literary-historical exercise aimed at recovering "the presence of an underlying more or less unified composition [of 1 Sam. 16–2 Sam. 5] by an author with a clear point of view . . ." (p. 491). McCarter calls such a composition an "apology of David" and finds an analogue in the Hittite apology of Hattushilish. Whether such a biblical pre-text as the "Apology of David" ever existed, McCarter's "Thematic Analysis" (pp. 499–502) is a nicely framed summary of many of the apologetic aspects of the present text. Finally, John T. Willis, "The Function of Comprehensive Anticipatory Redactional Joints in 1 Samuel 16–18," *Zeitschrift für die Alttestamentliche Wissenschaft* 85 (1973), pp. 294–314, offers an explanation of the literary-historical development of the material in chaps. 16–18. "Redactional joints" are short summary statements added by a redactor to traditional materials being combined, which statements anticipate the redacted material that follows. The final redactor of this section of 1 Samuel, Willis proposes, found at hand essentially reliable traditions that already had redactional joints of their own, to which material he added 16:14–23 and 18:5 as redactional joints of his own. Willis's suggestions provide us with another highly speculative theory about the genetic composition of the text.

3. Fokkelman has nicely emphasized the double perspective of reader versus characters in this scene: "While Saul and his court think they are welcoming a musician, we realize that the Saulide monarchy is dragging in a Trojan Horse' (*Narrative Art*, vol. 2, p. 135). Fokkelman writes of the level of the narrator and reader as "level 2" while characters are on "level 1."

4. Fokkelmann has recognized that both *rā'āh* and *bâ'* are key words in this chapter (*Narrative Art*, vol. 2, pp. 114, 119, 121). When he comes to relate them in an interpretation (pp. 137ff.), he perceptively points out the pregnant uses of *rā'āh* (that is, "to select") in vv. 1 and 17, as well as a number of other striking parallels between the two sections of the chapter. On *rā'āh* in this chapter, see also R. Alter, *The Art of Biblical Narrative* (New York: Basic Books, 1981), pp. 148–149.

5. Fokkelman believes that God's correction of Samuel in v. 7 is directed at humanity in general and therefore is "less burdensome to Samuel than if God had criticized him personally as a prophet' (*Narrative Art*, vol. 2, p. 125). My reading is just the reverse: God's criticism is directed at Samuel personally, and the question is only whether it also has a deeper general significance for *all* prophets, insofar as their limited knowledge is in contrast to an omniscient God.

6. Fokkelman notices the similar language in 16:3 and 10:8 (*Narrative Art*, vol. 2, pp. 127ff.) but interprets the connection differently than I do.

7. The narrative contrast in chaps. 13 and 16 between prophetic and divine prediction is also highlighted through numeric detail. In chap. 13, seven days pass by and Samuel does not appear as he had promised, whereas in chap. 16 seven of Jesse's sons pass by and David appears: "This is the one" (v. 12), God points out as he had promised.

8. Of course, the text-critically based emendation of Agag's words supported by McCarter, *1 Samuel*, vol. 8 of the Anchor Bible (Garden City: Doubleday, 1980), p. 265, would preclude my reading here.

9. Fokkelman has also connected up the "rejection" and "tallness" of Eliab to make of him "a second Saul" (*Narrative Art*, vol. 2, p. 122).

10. Alter, *Art of Biblical Narrative*, p. 65.

11. S. R. Driver points out the frequentative force of the waw conversive form *ûbiʿʿatattû*, "and it would torment him," in v. 14, in conjunction with the participial form of the same verb at the end of v. 15, *mᵉbaʿittekā*, "is tormenting you" (*Notes on the Hebrew Text and the Topography of the Books of Samuel* [Oxford: Clarendon, 1913], p. 134). These two verb forms in vv. 14 and 15 illustrate respectively the expository and synchronic functions of imperfectives, and taken together they are an especially good example of dialogue-bound aspects so often found in the narrator's words, as R. Alter has emphasized. (Driver also points out the expository or summarizing function of the "series of perfects with *waw* conv. in v. 23," *Notes on the Hebrew Text*, p. 137.)

12. We ought to point out here that the young man's statement about David, "and the LORD is with him" (v. 18), not only refers back to v. 13, where God's spirit is said to come mightily upon David, but also carries with it wider narrative implications. For the Deuteronomic narrator at least, the phrase, when applied to individuals, refers solely to kings—David being the favorite referent—or to royal figures in the story like Samuel. Although the Chronicler uses the statement "the LORD (or God) was with him" to describe the Levite, Phinehas, son of Eleazar (1 Chron. 9:20), in all other cases, the biblical narrator refers only to royalty, either literally or metaphorically. Even

when the Deuteronomic narrator has *characters* state that God is with someone, this blessed individual turns out to be someone of the stature of Joshua, Gideon, Saul, David, or Jeroboam.

13. In biblical narrative, *rā'āh* is only rarely used in this providential sense. For example, "God will provide for himself a lamb" in the Akedah (Gen. 22:8) or God "has provided the best of the land for himself" (Deut. 33:21) or people are "to provide the best or fittest for Israel's throne" (2 Kings 10:3).

14. Uspensky, *A Poetics of Composition* (Berkeley and Los Angeles: Univ. of Calif. Press, 1973). pp. 83ff.

15. Notice how *to go* almost always expresses movement from the perspective of a point of departure, or at least of the moving object itself, whereas *to come* normally describes movement from the point of view of a destination and of the people there who view the movement from their own perspective. Notice further that even the moving object once arrived—here Samuel—can describe his own previous movement from the spatial point of view of those who saw him moving toward them: Samuel says, "*I have come* [to you] to sacrifice." Uspensky's *A Poetics of Composition* helpfully discusses these cross-cultural basics of how language represents perspective.

16. The narrative ambiguity surrounding David's "coming" into Saul's court reinforces what the reader already knows about David's anointing. This ambiguity is further reinforced by the phrase *la⁶ᵃmod lipnê* in vv. 21 and 22. In v. 21, after David comes, he "stands before [Saul]." Then in v. 22 Saul sends a request to Jesse to allow "David to enter my service." Hovering around this progressive strengthening of the phrase *la⁶ᵃmod lipnê* is a stronger meaning, one that typifies the heart of David's relationship to Saul in the story to come: David may stand before Saul, he may even enter into his service. Finally, however, *he will stand up against him.* Notice how the narrator has the elders of Samaria react to Jehu's demands in 2 Kings 10 to provide (*rā'āh* [!]) the best and fittest for the throne: "But they were exceedingly afraid, and said, 'Behold, the two kings could not withstand him (*la⁶ᵃmod lipnê*); how then can we stand?'" (v. 4).

17. See Sternberg's helpful analysis of general narrative strategies, *The Poetics of Biblical Narrative* (Bloomington: Indiana Univ., 1985), pp. 163ff.

18. For an excellent introduction to the military terms and background of this chapter, see McCarter's notes, *1 Samuel,* pp. 290–95, to whose bibliographic references one might add: Jack M. Sasson, "Reflections on an Unusual Practice Reported in ARM X:4," *Orientalia* 43 (1974), pp. 404–10, wherein he tangentially suggests that *mishāh* in v. 6 might be a euphemistic reference to something like "codpiece"; and A. Deem's short note in *Vetus Testamentum* 28 (1978), pp. 349–51, who also connects up the *mēṣaḥ* of v. 49 with *mishāh* of v. 6 so that Goliath was struck by David "at his greaves" (or alternately according to Sasson's suggestion, "at his codpiece"). For a representative source-oriented treatment of chap. 17, one can find an excellent illustration of how confidently some scholars have used form criticism to reconstruct the literary history of a pericope in Simon J. DeVries, "David's Victory over the Philistine as Saga and as Legend," *Journal of Biblical Literature* 92 (1973), pp. 23–36. DeVries not only thinks it "very probable that the Hebrew recension on which the Greek text [of 1 Sam. 17–18] is based was created in an effort to improve by omission a confused and conflate *Vorlage* that was substantially the same as our present Hebrew text" (p. 23), he also suggests that this conflate *Vorlage* had a complicated prehistory that itself went through at least four stages on its eventual journey toward the present MT.

For an example of how a noted folklorist would analyze chap. 17, see the interesting article by Heda Jason, "The Story of David and Goliath: A Folk Epic?" *Biblica* 60 (1979), pp. 36–70. Jason contends that the models of Propp and Skaftymov can help demonstrate that "our text . . . constitutes a complete literary work" and not one "that has been patched together mechanically from separate parts, each deriving from a different tradition" (p. 60). Jason's appendix on the shorter LXX version appears to me to be hampered by an insufficient understanding of the text-critical problems involved. Nevertheless, the article is an example of how modern approaches to ancient literature can illuminate old problems.

19. Fokkelman's remarks on the apparent incoherence between and within chaps. 16 and 17 are, in my opinion, unsatisfactory because they assert that *in this particular case* the Bible's "consistency requirements" are different from ours (*Narrative Art,* vol. 2, pp. 144ff.). There is no doubt that in many respects ancient and modern consistency

requirements are different; the question here, however, is whether the type of "inconsistency" represented, say, by the known-to-Saul David of chaps. 16:14–23 and 17:32–39 and the supposedly not-known-to-Saul David of 17:55—58 is an example of one of these differences. I maintain that such a supposed inconsistency as this would have been as obviously unacceptable to an ancient Israelite as it is to us.

Concerning Fokkelman's discussion of this chapter in general, the longer the pericope, the longer, unfortunately, Fokkelman's structural analysis: I wish that Fokkelman himself had left more of his "homework" (see p. 9 n. 9 of his book) out of the discussion. On the other hand, Fokkelman's detailed analyses usually make it clear to the reader how and why he gets to a particular interpretation; this is a characteristic worthy of emulation.

20. McCarter, *1 Samuel*, p. 298. McCarter follows a typical pattern here: one account is represented by 17:1–11, 32–40, 42–48a, 49, 51–54, and assumes that Saul already knows David according to 16:14–23; a second account is seen in 17:12–31, 41, 48b, 50, 55–58, and fits in with the secret anointing of David in 16:1–13, who only now at the end of chap. 17 is said to come to Saul's attention.

21. McCarter, *1 Samuel*, p. 306. It may be helpful here to describe my rationale for reading the MT of chaps. 17 and 18 without *trying* to answer any of the crucial text-critical and literary-historical problems raised by a significantly shorter Old Greek version of these chapters. The easiest way to proceed is to respond in some detail to a recent important study of these genetic questions.

Emanuel Tov has written a detailed article concerning the divergences between the "Old Greek" (OG is termed "LXX" in his study [p. 98 n. 1]) and the Masoretic Text of 1 Sam. 17–18: "The Composition of 1 Samuel 16–18 in the Light of the Septuagint Version," in *Empirical Models for Biblical Criticism*, ed. Jeffrey H. Tigay (Philadelphia: Univ. of Penn. Press, 1985), pp. 97–130. How does one explain, from text-critical and literary-historical perspectives, why the OG lacks the following verses of the Masoretic Text: 17:12–31, 41, 48b, 50, 55–58; 18:1–6a, 10–11, 12b, 17–19, 21b, 29b–30? On one hand, it is possible that the Greek translator worked from a Hebrew text of 1 Sam. 17–18 that was essentially like the longer Masoretic version of these chapters and then decided to abridge it for whatever reasons. On the other hand, it is also possible that the person or persons responsible for the Masoretic Text of chaps. 17 and 18 took a shorter version of the story, something like that represented by the OG of these chapters, and added large sections of a parallel account of these events (plus other details that are not parallel). The first part of Tov's article (pp. 98–118) presents a series of text-critical arguments for establishing his working hypothesis "that the short version of 1 Sam 17–18 reflected in the LXX was not an abridgment, either by the Greek translator or by a Hebrew scribe, of the long version found in the Masoretic Text. It is rather an independent and coherent version of the events" (p. 118). In this text-critical section of his study, Tov uses his considerable skills as a text critic to argue for a position that then becomes the basis for the literary-historical discussion forming the second part of his study (pp. 118–24).

Tov's text-critical reasons for seeing LXX *not* as an abridgment of the longer version found in MT but "as an independent and coherent version of the events" are persuasive, and they constitute an eminently plausible case *from an internal point of view*. By examining in great detail linguistic versus exegetical renderings, word order, quantitative representation, consistency, and Hebraisms in the LXX version, Tov is able to demonstrate that "the translation technique of 1 Samuel 17–18 may be described as relatively literal" (p. 113). If this be so, Tov further reasons, then "it is . . . not likely that he would have omitted 44 percent of the text. As in all arguments, this is subjective reasoning, but under the circumstances we consider this the most feasible argument, since it is based on the internal consistency of the translator's approach to his text. We therefore assume that the translator worked from a text which was much shorter than the Masoretic Text" (p. 115). Tov goes on to add some further arguments (pp. 115–118), but his analysis of translation techniques and the inferences he draws from it form the heart of his argument: a faithful and relatively literal translator would not have so severely abridged any supposedly longer Hebrew text here in chaps. 17 and 18.

The trouble with Tov's "working hypothesis" is its very plausibility, for what he argues with respect to his Greek translator could just as plausibly be argued for the

Hebrew "redactor" of the Masoretic version of chaps. 17 and 18. Since it is equally true, as Tov himself recognizes, "that the differences between the Masoretic Text and the reconstructed parent text of the LXX are larger in 1 Samuel 17–18 than in any other section of the book" (p. 116) and that "elsewhere in 1 Samuel the LXX lacks individual phrases or clauses, but nowhere does it lack so many as in chapters 17–18" (ibid.), it follows from these factors that Tov's "working hypothesis" also necessarily presumes a Hebrew copyist-turned-redactor (the one responsible for our present MT of chaps. 17–18) who, while everywhere else in the book (including the verses in chaps. 17 and 18 shared by LXX and MT) was relatively faithful to the presumed parent text underlying the LXX and MT, was, nevertheless, an egregious conflator in chaps. 17 and 18.

I am surprised that Tov did not recognize the self-defeating nature of his logical inference that a normally faithful translator would have remained faithful by not abridging chaps. 17 and 18. What is clear from Tov's exercise, it seems to me, is that no amount of internal text-critical evidence of the type Tov employs can render either alternative more likely than its opposite. Like Solomon with the feuding mothers, readers are confronted with two texts, one apparently mutilated and the other not. Tov wants to decide which *mater lectionis* did the mutilating, but, unlike Solomon's dilemma, our problem involves not being able to decide, through text-critical means, which baby has been harmed by its mother and what precisely is the nature of the mutilation: does one baby lack something or does the other baby have too much of something?

Since the second part of Tov's article is based upon the working hypothesis of the first part, his literary-historical discussion is also questionable. Tov assumes a "version 1" (represented by LXX) "to be more original than version 2 [especially represented, Tov believes, by those pluses in MT that parallel events or details in his version 1], since the latter has been added to it (or rather inserted in it)" (p. 120). (Tov makes no inferences about the authenticity of either version's *content*.) He concludes, "From the above discussion it is clear that the Masoretic version of 1 Samuel 16–18 was created by the juxtaposition of two separate accounts of the events, the complete version 1 and the partial (or partially preserved) version 2" (p. 121). The literary-historical result of Tov's reconstructions is an MT version that is largely but not completely incoherent and a LXX version that is largely but not completely coherent.

Tov's literary-historical argumentation is as self-defeating as his text-critical argumentation, and for similar reasons. Tov had earlier argued, "In sum, we cannot think of any motive which would convincingly explain an abridgement of the text" (p. 118). (Notice that this literary-historical question is discussed on pp. 116–18 as part of Tov's text-critical analysis and encountered just before he tells us that he is turning "from the realm of textual criticism to that of literary criticism and exegesis," p. 118.) But such a literary-historical position is similarly self-neutralizing. The literary-historical opponent of Tov can easily respond with a counter argument: is it any less likely that the Greek translator would abridge a longer incoherent text, and thus harmonize it, than that a Hebrew copyist would turn redactor and combine two originally semi-coherent versions of these events to produce a strongly incoherent conflate text? Once again there are, to say the very least, plausible literary-critical arguments for each side of the question. (For a text-critical view different from Tov's, see S. Pisano, *Additions or Omissions in the Books of Samuel* [Frieburg: Universitätsverlag, 194], pp. 78–86.)

In short, the genetic problems raised by the LXX and MT of chaps. 17 and 18 in their text-critical and literary-historical dimensions remain open to plausible solutions both for and against Tov's position as stated in this article. What is especially revealing about Tov's discussion is that the person "who combined versions 1 and 2" and "created a text displaying such inconsistencies" is called by Tov a "redactor" (p. 122). Once again, as we have seen throughout our review of scholarly research into the literary history of 1 Samuel, *redactor* is a code word for the producer of supposed literary incoherence.

Two minor comments. First, in Tov's appendix B (pp. 126–28), LXX's strange rendering of *midd°loq* as *ekklínontes ópisō* in 17:53 is not listed. On this crux going back to Wellhausen, see the suggestion of Msgr. Skehan, "Turning or Burning? 1 Sam 17:53 (LXX)," *Catholic Biblical Quarterly* 18 (1976), pp. 193–95. Second, Tov's article would have benefited from more accurate copyediting. It is understandable that multilingual studies are difficult to shepherd accurately into print, but in this case other reasons appear to be responsible for some errors. For example, the presentation of the text in English translation (pp. 102–6) is marred by 18:1–6a not being in italics, as it should be. Also, how many verses of the MT are lacking in the OG? Tov writes that the LXX is "lacking thirty-nine of the eighty-eight verses of these chapters" (p. 98). However, his editor, Jeffrey Tigay, writes about an "extra forty-nine verses found only in the Hebrew Text" (p. 97), An extra forty-nine verses in MT means that LXX lacks those forty-nine verses. So which number of verses does LXX lack, according to Tov and his "redactor": forty-nine or thirty-nine? (Following Tov's approach here, it may be conjectured that his redactor, Tigay, everywhere else so faithful to his Tovian source, had Tov's *thirty-nine* before his eyes but inadvertently substituted the number representing shared verses rather than LXX minuses.)

The present reading of chaps. 17 and 18, therefore, assumes that text criticism cannot offer a basis for the literary history of these chapters, and that literary-historical hypotheses about the relationships of LXX to MT here in chaps. 17 and 18 are unfounded when based on text-critical arguments such as we have been rehearsing. Moreover, my reading is a calculated response to literary-historical assumptions that the MT of chaps. 17–18 is a largely incoherent, conflate text composed of at least one and possibly two separate versions.

For students of the Hebrew Bible who would like to begin thinking about text-critical matters, an excellent little introduction is Kyle McCarter's *Textual Criticism: Recovering the Text of the Hebrew Bible* (Philadelphia: Fortress Press, 1986).

22. Under the usual assumption of narrative incoherence within and between chaps. 16 and 17, to call the supposed redactor of these chapters "heavy-handed," as McCarter does, is remarkably to understate the case. Such statements produce, in my opinion, a redactional picture as muddled as the text for which it is supposed to be the solution. This explanation suffers from a kind of literary schizophrenia: somehow or other, parts of the "redaction" cohere in the most artfully detailed way, even as other parts are supposed to involve glaringly basic narrative incoherences, such as Saul's apparent ignorance of David in vv. 55–58. This hodge-podge description of the real text's main characteristics gives us the profile of a redactor roughly analogous to a bumbling Shakespearean scholar who on the basis of extant manuscripts edits a remarkably erudite version of *Romeo and Juliet*—only, in the redacted version, Juliet falls in love with Romeo before ever she hears of him.

The kind of narrative incoherence assumed by most scholars here is totally different from that, say, caused by the notice of 13:1 in the MT, where Saul is said to be one year old when he began to reign. There, one needed only to suppose—quite plausibly— that the received text lacks a number that had somehow dropped out from the manuscript tradition. Here, however, as also in the varied perspectives between chaps. 8 and 9 on the figure of Samuel, the narrative "incoherences" are related intertextually in such a complicated way that scholars are forced to conclude that most artful features they might recognize to be present in the present text must preexist a redactor painfully insensitive to the artfulness of the traditions so often haphazardly conjoined.

23. Vv. 3 (twice), 11, 12, 23, 27, 30.

24. Vv. 10, 17 (twice), 18, 25, 26 (twice), 28, 32, 33, 36, 37, 39, 46 (twice), 47, 55, and 56.

25. Fokkelman's interpretation of Goliath, the ʾîš habbēnayîm of v. 4, as "the man of the space between" is consonant with the geographic/compositional comparisons I make in my reading of this chapter (*Narrative Art*, vol. 2, p. 147). This epithet of Goliath in v. 4 is interpreted by McCarter as "the man-in-between," that is, "an infantryman" (*1 Samuel*, pp. 290ff.).

26. See above, chapter 1, on 1 Sam. 1.

27. See Alter's *Art of Biblical Narrative*, p. 85.

28. See Alter's discussion of this general question in *Art of Biblical Narrative*, pp. 67ff.

29. Noted by Driver, *Notes on the Hebrew Text*, p. 145, as "remarkable."

30. This command uses the previous dialogue's key word, hālak, but in a profoundly disorienting manner. Except for God's command to Israel in Is. 55:3, no one, to the best of my knowledge, ever speaks about another "*going* to me," apparently because such a construction would involve contradictory perspectives. I suppose the construction could be used to mean "walk toward me," although I have not been able to find such a usage in biblical narrative.

31. See my *Moses and the Deuteronomist* (New York: Seabury, 1980), pp. 103–4.

32. There is no need here to psychologize the significant recurrence of this structure throughout chap. 17, as if to suggest that one has recovered some kind of deliberate plan an individual author was following in composing this story. The purpose of the preceding discussions on repetition is simply to suggest that the phenomenon of repetition is a two-edged sword for purposes of interpretation, and that the geneticist's confidence in it for literary-historical reconstruction is overblown. Our analysis of repetition suggests that the usual characterization of the present story as a crude redaction (primarily because of discrepancies presumed to exist in passages such as vv. 55–58) may ignore aspects of the text that make it anything but crude or incoherent. Whether we are reading here what may be called a thoroughgoing redaction or whether the story's esthetic dimensions are in large part the result of that kind of literary activity reserved for the word *authorial* is impossible to determine. Nevertheless, I am suggesting that the present text shows signs of being much more artfully constructed than usually allowed.

33. This theme of servitude to Saul, which will occupy the book until Saul's death, picks up on Samuel's depiction of, the "ways of the king" as involving enslavement of Israel (chap. 8) but in fact does not begin until the appearance of David upon the scene. It is no coincidence that from Saul's anointing in chap. 10 until David's introduction in chap. 16 the narrator never refers to *Saul's servants*. Only with 16:15, after the spirit of the LORD has departed from Saul (16:14) and as the matter of David is being brought up, do we hear of "Saul's servants." Thereafter in the book, the narrator, when speaking of a character's servants, will refer almost exclusively to Saul's: 16:17; 18:5, 22, 24, 26, 30; 19:1; 21:7; 22:6, 7, 9, 17; 28:7, (twice), 23, 25. Only in 21:12, 15 does he speak about Achish's servants and in 25:10, 40 about David's.

34. Jobling, *The Sense of Biblical Narrative I* (Sheffield: Almond Press, 1978), p. 13, has recognized a number of similar connections between chaps. 14 and 19, when Saul seeks David's life.

35. Chap. 18, in its somewhat jagged composition, does offer some narrative indication of redactional activity of a more haphazard nature than that usually suggested for chaps. 16–17. Nevertheless, literary-historical caution is still a salutary attitude even here in chap. 18. Notice, for example, that the utter transparency of the characterization of Saul in this chapter is conveyed by the narrator's inner psychological perspective in both the shorter Old Greek version (vv. 12, 21, 25, and 28) as well as the MT pluses (vv. 11, 17).

36. On the legal connections between this account of the marriage in chaps. 18 and its sequel in 2 Sam. 3:14–16, see Z. Ben-Barak, "The Legal Background to the Restoration of Michal to David," in *Studies in the Historical Books of the Old Testament,* ed. J. A. Emerton (Leiden: Brill, 1979), pp. 15–29.

37. The seminal study on the political implications of *'āhēb* in the book of Deuteronomy and its history is W. Moran, "The Ancient Near Eastern Background of the Love of God in Deuteronomy," *Catholic Biblical Quarterly* (1963), pp. 77–87. This study provided inspiration for brief notes on the political overtones in "the skillful unfolding of this complex political drama" (J. A. Thompson, "The Significance of the Verb LOVE in the David-Jonathan Narratives in 1 Samuel," *Vetus Testamentum* 24 [1974], pp. 334–80), which a subtle author or compiler skillfully bound together into a larger unity (Peter Ackroyd, "The Verb Love—*'ahēb* in the David-Jonathan Narratives. A Footnote," *Vetus Testamentum* 25 [1975], pp. 213–14).

38. The full range of biblical characterization (from Saul's transparency to David's opacity) is so well exemplified in this chapter that Robert Alter chose this pericope and its characteristics to begin his chapter on "Characterization and the Art of Reticence" (*Art of Biblical Narrative,* pp. 114–30). Alter provocatively suggests the possibility that the chapter presents Saul's deviousness as so transparent in order to convey his contemporaries' external as well as the narrator's internal views of him.

39. On this and other examples of self-abasement, and their relationship to insults in the Bible, see George Coats, "Self Abasement and Insult Formulas," *Journal of Biblical Literature* 89 (1970), pp. 14–26. Not recognizing these responses of David as matters of form, S. R. Driver, arguing for the lateness of the MT plus of v. 27, characterizes them as "difficult to understand" (*Notes on the Hebrew Text,* p. 155).

40. Saul's prophetic moves in chap. 10 are filled with negative overtones not only through the narrator's subsequent clarifications here in chap. 18 but also through his use

elsewhere of *hitnabbē*, "to prophesy," in predominantly unsavory contexts. In addition to 1 Kings 18:29, where heathen prophetic activity is referred to, and 1 Kings 22:8, 10, 18, where lying prophets are the issue, we will be confirmed in the negative implications of Saul's prophetic activity by the narrator's focusing on the issue even more pointedly in 1 Sam. 19. There, Saul and his royal court are even more drastically implicated in the evils associated with this kind of *tebel*, the unholy confusion of royal and prophetic offices.

41. David Jobling nicely emphasizes the strategic and structural importance of the language of these opening verses of chap. 19 (vv. 1–4), as well as of chap. 18 (vv. 1–5): *The Sense of Biblical Narrative I*, pp. 11–13. For his part, Fokkelman finds the first ten verses of chap. 19 as deliberately boring (*Narrative Art*, vol. 2, p. 259). Space prohibits me from noting every occurrence where Fokkelman has already singled out a textual feature that my own reading subsequently but independently discusses. My interpretations are usually so significantly different from his, I hope he will not underestimate how impressive I feel is his ability to zero in on key formal features of the text. Since there are few of the text's formal features that he does *not* comment on, I have felt some freedom in not having to cite all those instances where Fokkelman discusses a matter first.

Fokkelman's treatment of chaps. 18 and 19 (pp. 209–87) builds upon Saul's intermittent "psychotic attacks" (p. 222) and "the powder-keg of Saul's pathology" (p. 259), buttressed in the story by Saul's repeated prophesying, an activity of Saul's that "borders on madness" (p. 286 n. 72). Especially important in Fokkelman's treatment of chaps. 18 and 19 is his description of what he calls "the Michal scenes" (18:17–30 and 19:8–18) as having solid connections with Gen. 29 and 31 (pp. 274ff).

42. *Mût* in the *hifil* and *hofal:* vv. 1, 2, 5, 6, 11, (twice), 15,17.
43. *Nimlaṭ:* vv. 10, 11, 12, 17, 18.
44. This connection has already been pointed out by Fokkelman, *Narrative Art*, vol 2, p. 276.
45. In a similar manner later in the story, David will use the Ammonites to kill Uriah, his rival for the affections of Bathsheba.
46. Vv. 2, 3, 7, 11, 18, 19, 21.

Chapter 6: The King's Fugitive (20:1–23:28)

1. For Fokkelman, *Narrative Art and Poetry in the Books of Samuel*, vol. 2, *The Crossing Fates (I Sam 13–31 and II Sam 2)*, (Assen: Van Gorcum, 1986), narrative reasons rather than redactional assumptions explain why Saul in chaps. 20–23 continues to be "pitifully deranged" (p. 394), "in a paranoid state of mind" (p. 396), and "playing out a pathological program" (p. 405).
2. Even Fokkelman, who is a staunch and able defender of narrative art and the text's coherence, fails to address some important questions of coherence in chaps. 20, questions that his own interpretation would seem to require addressing. Literary-historical assumptions underlie most commentators' acceptance of incoherence, but what explain's Fokkelman's here?
3. See, for example, R. W. Klein, *1 Samuel* (Waco: Word Books, 1983), pp. 205ff., for the usual kinds of remarks on the incoherences of chap. 20 and the redactional assumptions such narrative inconsistencies provoke.
4. David Gunn, *The Fate of King Saul* (Sheffield: Almond Press, 1980), pp. 84–85, emphasizes Jonathan's naive comprehension, the basis of which, he believes, is "a simplistic view of good and evil."
5. Fokkelman has noted the irony present (in vv. 1–3) in David and Jonathan's respective relation to "knowing": "The knowing David uncovers what is kept concealed from the unknowing Jonathan" (*Narrative Art*, vol. 2, p. 298; see also pp. 306ff.).
6. David Gunn, *Fate of King Saul*, p. 85, refers back to 18:1–3 in setting up interesting ironies present in chap. 20; the connections are even tighter than Gunn suggests. Of course, literary-historical considerations will lead other scholars to suspect, for example, "that an editor or compiler may have added verse 3 [of chap. 8] . . . to provide a basis of 20:8 where the pact is presumed" (K. Sakenfeld, *The Meaning of Hesed in the Hebrew Bible: A New Inquiry* (Decatur, GA: Scholars Press, 1978], p. 83).
7. For example, 18:9, 12, 15, 17, 20, 21, 25, 29; 20:26.

8. 18:3, 16, 20, 30; 19:1; 20:17, 34, 39.
9. 18:26 is the closest we come to finding out anything about David's thoughts and feelings.
10. Vv. 3, 5, 6 (twice), 7, 9, 21.
11. "As the LORD lives!" (vv. 3, 21); LORD God of Israel!" (v. 12); "May the LORD do and continue to do!" (v. 13); "May the LORD be with you" (v. 13); "May the LORD protect David from his enemies" (v. 16); "The LORD is between you and me forever!" (v. 23).
12. "Far from it!" (*ḥālîlāh*, v. 2); "But truly (*wᵉûlām*) . . . as your soul lives!" (v. 3); "Far be it from you!" (v. 9); "Would I not (*wᵉlô*) tell you?" (v. 9); "Would I not then send and inform you?" (v. 12); "Would you not show me the loyal love of the LORD?" (v. 14); "Would you cut off your loyalty from my house?" (v. 15).
13. Vv. 2, 5, 12, 21, 22, 23.
14. *Šālaḥ*, "to send, send for, shoot (arrows)" in vv. 5, 12, 13, 16, 20, 21, 22, 29; *šulḥān*, "table," in vv. 29, 34. Also, the contrast between David's house and the king's table is emphasized by setting off David's town ("Send me [he said] to Bethlehem ['*ad bet-leḥem*]," vv. 27–28) and the king's table ("The son of Jesse did not come to the bread [*leḥem*]," v. 27; "He did not come to the table [*šulḥān*] of the king," v. 29). This wordplay between Bethlehem and the bread of the king's table is mentioned by Fokkelman, *Narrative Art*, vol. 2, p. 300.
15. There are three evenings ("the evening of the third day" v. 5), three days ("the third day" v. 12), three arrows (v. 20), and three bows to Jonathan (v. 41). G. R. Driver, "Old Problems Re-examined," *Zeitschrift für die Alttestamentliche Wissenschaft* 90 (1968), pp. 175–77, has attempted to work out the chronology involved in chap. 20 and is able to integrate many of the references to "three" or "third" into something like a coherent account. However, it may be that our defective knowledge of background information, complicated by the defective nature of the MT itself, will conspire to make such efforts at detailed intelligibility only partially successful. Most of the larger questions discussed in my reading remain unaffected by such obscurities. For example, whether Jonathan was standing (*wayyāqom*) or sitting opposite (*wayyᵉqaddēm*) Saul in v. 25 (a question investigated by B. A. Mastin, "Jonathan at the Feast," in *Studies in the Historical Books of the Old Testament*, ed. J. A. Emerton, (Leiden: Brill, 1979) pp. 113–24 affects our overall understanding of the episode hardly at all.
16. The way in which the central covenant between David and Jonathan is preceded and followed by their pacts involving, respectively, duplicitous and double-voiced language is a good indication of the ideological emphases of the chapter:

COVENANTS OF LOVE AND LANGUAGE

1. *David's Plan to Remove Jonathan's Ignorance* (Vv. 5–7)
   (v. 6) If your father misses me
   (*îm* plus inf. abs.
   const.)   then say. . .
   (v. 7) If (*îm*) he says . . . 'good'   then it will be well with me
   but if (*wᵉîm*) he is
   angry   then know . . .
2. *David and Jonathan's Covenant of Mutual Love* (Vv. 8–17)
   (v. 8) But if (*wᵉîm*) there is
   guilt in me . . .   then slay me yourself.
   (v. 9) But if I really knew . . .   then would I not tell you?
   (*îm* + inf. abs. const.)
   (v. 10) But if your father
   answers roughly   then who will tell me?
   (v. 12) But were I to find
   that . . .   would I not send and disclose
                                               it to you?
   (v. 13) But if it pleases my
   father   then the LORD do to
                                               Jonathan

(v. 14) If (*îm*) I am still
    alive   then show me . . .
3. *Jonathan's Plan to Tell David That He Now Knows* (Vv. 18–23)
   (v. 21) If I say, 'The arrows
      are on this side,'
      (*îm* + inf. abs.)   then it is safe for you.
   (v. 22) But if I say, 'The
      arrows are beyond
      you,'   then go . . .

17. Emunah Finkelstein, "An Ignored Haplography in Samuel," *Journal of Semitic Studies* 4 (1959), pp. 35–57), suggests that the present MT of 20:23, 42 is the result of a haplography: an original *ʿēd ʿad ʿôlām* ("the LORD . . . is between you and me, a witness forever"). While there undoubtedly is merit in this suggestion, the probability of haplography is lessened, I believe, by the missing *ʿēd* having to have been lost twice (in vv. 23 and 42). Does one assume that the same mistake was made twice, or rather that *ʿēd* dropped out by accident in one of the verses, and then was removed in a leveling process in the other verse?
18. Apparently David, more than Jonathan, recognizes this (see 23:17).
19. Fokkelman, *Narrative Art*, vol. 2, pp. 346 ff., has recognized that the "lad versus David and Jonathan" configuration in v. 39 functions, at a deeper level, to describe the narrator's and reader's privileged situation versus the lad's unknowing one. Moreover, for Fokkelman, the arrow ritual sets up a symbolic similarity between the lad and David.
20. On the many problems of grammar and syntax in chaps. 20 and 21, see Fokkelman, *Narrative Art*, vol. 2, pp. 356ff., and especially, S. R. Driver, *Notes on the Hebrew Text and the Topography Books of Samuel* (Oxford: Clarendon, 1913), pp. 160–78.
21. We postpone until chaps. 23 a discussion of how Ahimelech's unwitting action in *giving* questionable food to David suggests Jonathan's unwitting action in *eating* such food.
22. David Gunn, *Fate of King Saul*, p. 87, has already seen that there are intertextual connections between the episode of the priest's massacre and those involving Saul's rejection. The massacre "parodies the scenes of Saul's rejection" and "presents Saul in . . . a terrible reversal of role."
23. Solomon, too, will pray in similar fashion at a similarly central point in his story (1 King 8:23); it is significant that these formulations of David and Solomon are found in speeches that Noth considered structurally and ideologically central to the Deuteronomist's own composition.
24. Alter, *The Art of Biblical Narrative* (New York: Basic Books, 1981), p. 66.
25. Kyle McCarter, *1 Samuel*, vol. 9 of the Anchor Bible (Garden City: Doubleday, 1980), p. 358, would call such an interpretation as this "uncritical," and I suppose it can easily be seen as such from a literary-historical viewpoint. Still, from a compositional perspective, the structural oscillations in the present weaving together of the stories seems remarkably sophisticated.
26. For a discussion of the missing inquiry of David at Nob, see Fokkelman, *Narrative Art*, vol. 2, pp. 389ff., and Miscall, *1 Samuel: A Literary Reading* (Bloomington: Indiana Univ. Press, 1986), pp. 134–35.
27. The word used, *ʿam*, may very well mean "army" here.
28. The usual understanding of Saul's slaughter of the priests of Nob as a fulfillment of the oracle of 2:27–36, and of Abiathar and Zadok as the priests prophesied in 2:33 and 2:35, respectively, is well anchored in the text, especially in the narrator's reference to Abiathar in 1 King 2:27. Nevertheless, such comforting clarities should not cause us to ignore the multivoiced nature of the prophecy in chap. 2 and of that particular stage in its fulfillment recounted here in chap. 22. Just as the oracle itself referred all at once to royal, priestly, and judicial succession, so also does the prophesied event here in chap. 22 have a number of facets that ought not to be neglected in too narrow a historicist interpretation. Abiathar escapes the wrath of Saul in chap. 22 (according to 2:33), but so does David in chap. 21 (according to 2:35). Fate of priest and king is as intertwined in fulfillment as in oracle. And indeed, the fate of the faithful (*neʾᵉmān*) priest with the sure (*neʾᵉmān*) house (2:35) is intimately bound up

with that of David himself ("And who is so faithful [*ne'ĕmān*] among all your servants as David?" [22:14]) and his "sure house (*bayit ne'ĕmān*)" reiterated in 1 Sam. 25:28 and I King 11:38. The oracle can also be seen from the vantage point of the exile; here finally, it apparently looks to a postexilic succession from royal back to a kind of judicial/priestly rule, as idealized in 1 Sam. 7, and perhaps realized in the person of Ezra, who, it turns out, is a descendant of Zadok (Ezra 7:2).

29. McCarter, *1 Samuel*, p. 367; see also Fokkelman, *Narrative Art*, vol. 2, p. 430.

30. There are sixty-one occurrences of words based upon *YD'* in 1 Samuel, and twenty-two of these instances are in chaps. 20–23, mostly in chap. 20: 1 Sam. 1:19; 2:3, 12; 3:7, 13, 20; 4:6; 6:2, 3, 9; 10:8, 11; 12:17; 14:3, 12, 38; 16:3, 16, 18; 17:28, 46, 47, 55; 18:28; 20:2, 3 (three times), 7, 9 (twice), 27, 30, 33, 39 (twice); 21:2, 3 (twice); 22:3, 6, 15, 17, 22; 23:9, 17; 24:12, 21; 25:11, 17; 26:4, 12; 28:1 (twice), 2, 3, 9 (twice), 14, 15; 29:9. By itself, this enumeration means little, but seen against the background of the thematic concerns everywhere evident in chaps. 20–23 as well as in chap. 28, such concentrations of occurrences do not seem haphazard. D. Winton Thomas, "Notes and Studies," *Journal of Theological Studies* 21 (1970), pp. 401–2, suggests that *yóda'tî* (21:3) and *nóda'* (22:6) are not related to I *YD'*, "to know," but to II *YD'*, which is presumed to mean in the *Hifil* something like "to say farewell, take leave of."

31. See McCarter, *1 Samuel*, pp. 368–72, for a plausible explanation of the awkward construction of v. 6 and for a suggestion about the genesis of vv. 1–13.

32. As Alter points out with respect to 2 Sam. 2:1—a similar case of oracular communication even though neither priest nor ephod is explicitly mentioned—the narrator transforms an oracular signal into intelligible speech by taking a yes/no response and verbalizing it for purposes of the story and according to the bias toward dialogue of biblical narrative (*Art of Biblical Narrative*, p. 69).

33. Indirect discourse, as Voloshinov has shown, in *Marxism and the Philosophy of Language* (Cambridge, MA: Harvard Univ. Press, 1986), pp. 128ff., tends to remove the expressive features of a message and to concentrate on a condensed, reprocessed, more analyzed formulation of a message's content, and it may be that the narrator's atypical use of indirect speech, especially unusual here with the verb of declaring (*higgîd*, 22:21; 23:7, 13), is meant to emphasize the impersonal, bureaucratic, or repetitive nature of such communications, even as the frequent use of imperfective verb forms conveys their timely function. Fokkelman, *Narrative Art*, vol. 2, p. 341, has noted how rare is the author's use of a *kî* clause to give explanation.

Chapter 7: Providential Delays (24:1–26:25)

1. Kyle McCarter, *1 Samuel*, vol. 8 of the Anchor Bible (Garden City: Doubleday, 1980), p. 400.

2. Klaus Koch, *The Growth of the Biblical Tradition* (New York: Scribners, 1969), pp. 132–48.

3. How the characterization of David in chaps. 24–26 fits in with an overall view of his life and career depends upon whether this or that commentator recognizes a darker side to David in the early stage of his career. While much indeed is ambiguous in many biblical texts, one thing is at least clear from recent treatments of David: the History's characterization of him is much more complex than many earlier commentators' idealized or sanitized versions of it would suggest.

   Kyle McCarter has written a clear defense of the view that the final form of 1 Sam. 16–2 Sam. 5 reflects an original narrative whose main purpose was to establish David's lawful accession to the throne of Israel: "The Apology of David," *Journal of Biblical Literature* 99 (1980), pp. 489–504. Keith Whitelam, "The Defense of David," *Journal for the Study of the Old Testament* 29 (1984), pp. 61–87, has widened the scope of discussions about a supposed "apology of David" by using a sociological approach to understand 1 Sam. 9–1 Kings 2. Whitelam discusses the functions and proposed audiences of propaganda and defines effective propaganda as that which answers "the conscious or articulated and particularly the unconscious or unarticulated needs of the audience" (p. 67). (Whitelam's proposal to analyze the propaganda of the biblical defense of David in this way reminds me of Klyde Kluckhohn's approach to the study of myth and ritual in "Myth and Rituals: a General Theory," *Harvard Theological Review* 35

[1942], pp. 45–79.) Central to Whitelam's analysis is his identification of the intended audience of this pro-Davidic propaganda, the urban elite in preexilic Israel (p. 65). Whitelam also writes under the assumption that the "realistic' picture of David achieved by the inclusion in the story of his failings and sins "is due not to the objective standpoint of the author(s), but rather the defensive nature of court apologetic" (p. 70). The resulting picture of a largely idealized David is produced, according to Whitelam, by "a technique employed by the davidic bureaucracy to allay suspicions and protect the image of the king and his successors" (p. 78). While Whitelam is clearly one of the best practitioners of the emerging sociological approach to biblical material, and while his sensitivity to the literary dimension of the text is better than most of his sociological colleagues, the idealized portrait of David that he finds in 1 Sam. 9–1 King 2 is highly problematic, as the studies I will shortly cite would all suggest. Whatever may have been the bureaucracy's propagandistic intentions for Davidic material as it may have existed from the tenth century to the exile, if one were to suppose that the History itself (more or less what we have in the final form of the text) was composed *after 587*, then the use of all this "highly defensive davidic material" may have had a much different purpose, and certainly a much different kind of audience, than earlier. This new audience could see all of David's warts—as all of Saul's sins—as a condemnation of kingship itself, including that of David's house. Whitelam's analysis may be perceptive when applied to the hypothesized pre-text written about, say, by McCarter, but what would Whitelam's valuable approach produce were he to leave aside his preexilic concerns and proceed upon an analysis of 1 Sam. 9–1 Kings 2 as an *exilic* piece of propaganda? My reading of the History tries to provide a number of literary answers that have implications congenial to Whitelam's sociological perspective.

In basic opposition to such views as McCarter's and Whitelam's, a number of scholars have recently argued for a less idealized portrait of David in the History. Jack Cargill, "David in History: a Secular Approach," *Judaism* 35 (1986), pp. 211–22, has written a persuasive article describing how "the picture of David that emerges from a more critical approach is that of an opportunist of great talent, ambition and pretensions, whose personal relations were manipulative, but also often passionate or excessively indulgent' (p. 212). Cargill believes that "preserved information which *contradicts* the source's apparent purpose or bias [that is, to provide an apology for David] is more likely to be true than information which is consistent with it" (ibid.), and therefore that the highly unfavorable aspects of David's character rooted in many biblical passages carry a far greater historicity than those favoring him. I take a slightly different tack in my reading when I suggest a similarly duplicitous characterization of David almost from the outset of his career. Read within their literary context and under the assumption that an exilic perspective undergirds them, the various episodes involving David and Saul in 1 Sam. 16ff., even those most obviously laudatory of David, succeed in burying him as much as praising him. David Marcus's splendid article, "David the Deceiver and David the Dupe," *Prooftexts* 6 (1986), pp. 163–83, ably suggests an entirely credible narrative strategy that integrates the earlier and later phases of David's biblical career: David the successful deceiver goes on to become David the consistently duped, in a measure-for-measure fashion. Both Cargill and Marcus cite the short but suggestive article on overall narrative strategy in the life and career of David by Morton Smith, "The So-called 'Biography of David' in the Books of Samuel and Kings," *Harvard Theological Review* 44 (1951), pp. 167–69.

Leo Perdue has also written an important article ' "Is there Anyone Left of the House of Saul . . .?' Ambiguity and the Characterization of David in the Succession Narrative," *Journal for the Study of the Old Testament* 30 (1984), pp. 67–84. Working from suggestive treatments by Kenneth Gros Louis, "The Difficulty of Ruling Well: King David of Israel," *Semeia* 8 (1977), pp. 15–33, and David Gunn, *The Story of King David* (Sheffield: Almond Press, 1978), Perdue amplifies the biblical narrator's intentionally ambiguous technique in characterizing David in the succession narrative: "The storyteller's design is to demonstrate the complexity of David" (p. 71). Perdue is wonderfully perceptive in his contrasting of various interpretations of David either as a "dynamic character" who alternates between deception and faithfulness according to the vicissitudes of time and circumstances, or as a "static character" who is "consistently deceitful, ruthless and treacherous, with self-interest the driving force behind his speeches and actions" (p 79). Confining his discussion to episodes from the succession narrative, Perdue asks whether one can choose between these dynamic and static portraits of David, and he answers himself with a concluding question: "Is it not possible that the double portrait of David reflects the ambiguity many Israelites held about the institution of monarchy in general, an ambiguity reflected in many biblical texts?" (p. 80). James Vanderkam's "Davidic Complicity in the Deaths of Abner and Eshbaal," *Journal of Biblical Literature* 99 (1980), pp. 521–39, is a redactional and historical study suggesting that the Court History candidly portrays David as implicated in the murder of Abner and Eshbaal, events that pave his way to the throne. As I mentioned earlier (in my Introduction), this thorny presence of the Court History, with its profoundly negative view of David, is so bothersome to John Van Seters that he removes it *in toto* from the Deuteronomist's brilliant history. Walter Brueggemann's recent book, *David's Truth in Israel's Imagination and Memory* (Philadelphia: Fortress Press, 1985), explores the polyvalent and highly complex portraits of David that cohere only with great difficulty in the biblical narratives about him. In general Brueggemann follows a "from good to bad" movement in the History's presentation of David. Finally, as noted in a previous chapter, Thomas R. Preston's "The Heroism of Saul: Patterns of Meaning in the Narrative of the Early Kingship," *Journal for the Study of the Old Testament* 24 (1982), pp. 27–46, is for me one of the best concise formulations of arguments for a more negative characterization of David and a more humane and sympathetic portrait of Saul in 1 Sam.–1 Kings 2, while David Gunn's *The Fate of King Saul* (Sheffield: Almond Press, 1980), remains the most persuasive book-length treatment of the subject.

4. Leaving aside chap. 25 for the moment, Saul is the one who seeks in 19:2, 10; 20:1; 22:23 (twice); 23:10, 14, 15, 25; 24:3; 26:2, 20; 27:1, 4; 28:7; David *denies* he is seeking Saul's life in 24:10; and what God seeks in 20:16 is not clear.

5. See David Gunn, *Fate of King Saul*, p. 96: "Are we then to see Nabal as another Saul?" Gunn shows clearly that Nabal is a Saul figure in the story and concludes that "one of the important functions of Abigail's speech, in the context of the story as a whole, is to foreshadow Saul's death" (p. 100). See also Whitelam, "Defense of David," p. 76. We might also point out that the placement of the reference to *Samuel's* death at the beginning of chap. 25 (v. 1) is also a narrative foreshadowing of Saul's death. As we have been suggesting, their character zones are so closely united in the narrative that reference to the death of the one brings with it an intimation of the death of the other. Chap. 28 will further expand on this connection.

6. 2:30; 6:7; 8:9; 9:13; 10:19; 12:2, 7, 10, 13; 13:14; 15:1, 25; 18:22; 19:2; 20:29, 31; 21:4; 23:20; 24:21, 22; 25:7, 17, 26 (twice), 27; 26:8, 11, 16, 19, 20; 28:22; 29:7, 10; that is, chaps. 24–26 contain twelve of thirty-three occurrences.

7. 24:2, 5 (twice), 10, 11, 21; 25:14, 19, 20, 36, 41; 26:7, 21, 22, 24.

8. Besides the instances of virtual questions in these chapters (24:20; 25:11), there are formally marked questions in 24:10, 15 (twice), 17; 25:10 (twice), 11; 26:1, 6, 9, 14 (twice), 15 (three times), 17, 18 (three times).

9. As we shall see below, Saul's questions in 24:12 and 26:17 indicate an ideological dimension to these episodes.

10. The story of Abigail is often recognized as highly artificial. Adele Berlin writes, "The plot, as well as the characters, is unrealistic" (*Poetics and Interpretation of Biblical Narrative* [Sheffield: Almond Press, 1983], p. 31). Berlin calls chaps. 25 an exemplum, and both Gunn and Levenson discuss many of its allegorical features. I am surprised that the contrived and artificial plot and characterization of chaps. 24 and 26 are not more widely emphasized in the literature that I read while preparing this book. Fokkelman, for example, is ecstatic over the art of these chapters, but in my opinion he neglects their artifice; he continues to interpret the words and actions of its characters with as much realistically psychological shading as his minute structural analyses can support. On the other hand, chapter 6 of David Gunn's book on King Saul mentioned in note 3 above, while recognizing that "it is tempting to see this chapter [chap. 24] (and to some extent the two that follow) as somewhat flabby, overburdened by a preponderance of rhetoric in the form of set speeches" (p. 91), still shows many instances of the story's significance that disprove any seriously damaging suggestions of didacticism or overburdened rhetoric.

11. As, for example, K. McCarter, "The Apology of David," *Journal of Biblical Literature* 99 (1980), pp. 489–504.

12. As noted by Gunn, *Fate of King Saul*, p. 95; see also Miscall, *1 Samuel: A Literary Reading* (Bloomington: Indiana Univ. Press, 1986), pp. 148ff., and Fokkelmann, *Narrative Art and Poetry in the Books of Samuel*, vol. 2, *The Crossing Fates (I Sam 13–31 and II Sam 1* (Assen: Van Gorcum, 1986), pp. 458ff.

13. That David's decision is divinely inspired is only implicit in chap. 24; in 25:26, 34, David is said to have been restrained by God from killing or harming the Saul figure, Nabal, and his household.

14. This self-interested aspect of David's repeated appeal to "Yahweh's anointed" is discussed by Whitelam, "Defense of David," p. 73.

15. Jon D. Levenson's "1 Samuel 25 as Literature and History," in *Literary Interpretations of Biblical Narratives*, vol. 2, ed. K. R. R. Gros Louis (Nashville: Abingdon, 1982), pp. 220–42, is a fine discussion of the Abigail story in its literary and historical context. Levenson highlights many instances of paronomasia, the varied means of covert characterization, and the structured rhetoric of its characters, all features that underscore the "subtle, consummate artistry"of this episode (p. 238). Levenson goes on to suggest that 1 Sam. 25 is a proleptic glimpse of the Uriah episode and of David's fall from grace. Yet all of this literary analysis is for Levenson simply a preparation for the really serious business of biblical scholarship. "The fact is . . . that for the biblical scholar, a point arrives at which the artistry ceases to be the goal of our endeavor and becomes an obstacle in the way of our recovery of the historical meaning of the passage" (ibid). There is good reason for those who desire it, assuredly, to get on with the task of historical reconstruction, which is never achieved through purely esthetic contemplation. Indeed, Levenson goes on to make some highly plausible historical comments concerning David's rise to the throne through strategic marriages.

There is a missing link, however, in Levenson's discussion, whereby he may give a false impression about biblical scholarship. As he points out at the beginning of his article, "the categories of literary artistry and historiography are not so independent as many a scholar of the Bible may think" (p. 220). One aspect of this connection is well made in the article, using a subtle understanding of the text to reconstruct something of the events recounted therein (perhaps some four hundred years earlier!). Another aspect of this connection between the literary and historical dimensions of the text is missing from Levenson's discussion: what does the final form of the text, that is, 1 Sam. 25 in its literary context within, say, Deut.–2 Kings, tell us, through the very artistry that Levenson is so adept at describing, about the historical period in which it reached its final form? Here, I submit, the text's artistry is in no way an obstacle to historical reconstruction but rather a necessary, perhaps even primary means of producing it; and what goes for the exilic reconstruction goes for the Davidic period as well.

16. On this allusion to Goliath's death in the fate of those who pursue David and in Nabal's heart of stone, see also Fokkelman, *Narrative Art*, vol. 2, pp. 508, 520.

17. See my discussion in chap. 4 of *Moses and the Deuteronomist* (New York: Seabury, 1980), pp. 146–204.

18. One has only to think of the false start and providential delay themes of Gen. 2–3 ("On the day you eat of it, you shall surely die," God says to Adam in 2:17, yet this does not happen) or of the flood story (wherein God repented of having made humankind, yet it will survive even to the writing of the History) to realize that these ideologically charged concepts pervade much of biblical narrative and help to unify the perspective of so many different stories from such different epochs in Israel's history.

Chapter 8: Saul and His Sons: The End (27:1–31:13)

1. *Sāpāh* is an important word in 1 Samuel. David escapes to the land of the Philistines to avoid being swept away *(essāpeh)* by Saul's hand (27:1). The use of *sāpāh* in 1 Samuel indicates a close connection between the fates of king and people. In chap. 26 David foreshadowed the fate of Saul: "or he shall go down into battle and be swept away *(w'nispāh)*" (v. 10). Chap. 28 will have Samuel prophesy Saul's death by bracketing it with references to the LORD giving Israel into the hand of the Philistines (28:19). This bonding of the fates of king and people harks back to Samuel's sweeping prediction in

12:25: "But if you [O Israel] still do wickedly, you shall be swept away (*tissāpû*), both you and your king." Now, the narrator's first clear indication of the inner thoughts and feelings of David (27:1) reveals to us someone whose striving to avoid the fate of Saul and Israel turns out to be prophetically accurate on the personal level but ominously mistaken according to the wider vision of the History. In David Gunn's general reflections at the end of his book, *The Fate of King Saul* (Sheffield: Almond Press, 1980), he emphasizes an important preliminary contrast between the characterizations of Saul and David in 1 Samuel: "David is a *favourite* of Yahweh. Saul, on the other hand, appears as a victim. For David, Yahweh is "Providence"; for Saul, Yahweh, is 'Fate' (pp. 115–16). At the same time, as my reading suggests, there is more to these characterizations than a contrast of individuals. The story emphasizes in many different ways how differences between God's favorites and his victims ultimately dissolve before larger mysteries of human experience. David may be God's favorite king—as Israel is his favorite people—yet such favoritism means very much less in the story when Moses' words in Deut. 8:20 and Samuel's in 12:25 are understood to play such a central role in the History. In the exile (as in the holocaust) God's "favorite" dissolved into God's "victim," so that seeing David or Saul as simply God's favorite or victim turns out to be only part of the picture. My comments here are not meant to disregard the many aspects of the Saul story that Gunn discusses so profitably: Gunn is never simplistic in his approach to the text. In my opinion, Gunn's view, for example, that "Saul, therefore, is kingship's scapegoat" (p. 125) goes a long way toward helping one see how the "fate of Saul/fate of Israel" union is forged in the History.

2. Fokkelman points out the wordplay of *pšt* (27:8) and *mišpat* (27:11), with its ironic overtones about David's practices, in *Narrative Art and Poetry in the Books of Samuel*, vol. 2, *The Crossing Fates I Sam 13–31 and II Sam 1* (Assen: Van Gorcum, 1986), p. 562.

3. It seems that the narrative strategy signaled by that modern turn of phrase, "Meanwhile, back at the ranch . . .," has an ancient counterpart that was as effective then as now: by means of such strategies, the ancient reader managed to roll the scroll with as much suspense as we moderns continue to turn the page.

4. If we combine the information of 28:6 with our analysis of David's inquiring of God in chaps. 22–23, where we found three modes of David's inquiry of God (by prophet, 22:3–5; by ephod, 23:6–12; and indeterminate, 23:1–5, the fully articulated form of God's answers to David in 23:1–5 might be seen as implying divine communication by dream, just as this mode is explicitly mentioned in 1 Kings 3, at the beginning of Solomon's rule. In connection with Saul's attempts to inquire of God by Urim, it may be significant that he does not mention this mode when complaining to Samuel's shade (28:15); perhaps he intends to hide from Samuel his slaughter of the priests of Nob and his loss thereby of the priestly ephod.

5. J. Lust, "On Wizards and Prophets," in *Studies on Prophecy*, ed. Daniel Lys, et al. Leiden: Brill, 1974, pp. 133–42, compares consultations with diviners and with prophets and finds some difficulties in H. A. Hoffner's reconstruction of the *modus operandi* in consultations with *'obôt*, "necromancers." (See Hoffner's article in *Theological Dictionary of the Old Testament*, vol. 1, pp. 130–34, on *'ôb*.) Lust derives *'ôb* from *'ab*, "father," and suggests, "The *'ôbôt* designated originally the spirits of the deceased fathers living in the Netherworld" (p. 139). Lust makes the interesting observation that the priestly casting of lots, using the technical term *šā'al*, comes to an end with Saul's death and occurs in none of the biblical books after 1 Samuel. Subsequently, foreign practices of divination forbidden to Israelites had a Yahwistic counterpart in the consultation of Yahweh through the prophets.

6. W. A. M. Beuken, "I Samuel 28: The Prophet as 'Hammer of Witches,' " *Journal for the Study of the Old Testament* 6 (1978), pp. 3–17, argues for the incident in chap. 28 as portraying "a true prophetic oracle" (p. 6) and discusses how Saul's consultation has troubled commentators down through the ages. K. A. D. Smelik has provided a useful survey of precritical interpretations of chap. 28 in "The Witch of Endor: I Samuel 28 in Rabbinic and Christian Exegesis till 800 AD," *Vigiliae Christianae* 33 (1977), pp. 160–79.

7. Besides these larger issues which make of chap. 28 a fitting climax for what has preceded, two minor details are echoes of elements from previous events. First, as pointed out with reference to chap. 19, when the woman of Endor asks Saul, "Why have you deceived me? You are Saul" (28:12), we are reminded of Saul's accusation of

his daughter: "Why have you deceived me thus, and let my enemy go?" (19:17). Michal used David's clothes to disguise his absence; Saul puts on "other garments" (28:18) to deceive the woman of Endor. In both cases, clothing (*BGD* = "to deal treacherously with," and *beged* = "clothing") functions as disguise and treachery at the same time. Second, Samuel's apparition from the underworld is related to David's appearance out of the cave in chap. 24 through the reactions of David and Saul to these meetings:

24:9:   *wayyiqqod (dāvid) 'appayim 'arṣāh wayyištaḥû*
          "David bowed with his face to the earth and did obeisance."
28:14:   *Wayyiqqod [Šā'ûl] 'appayim 'arṣāh wayyištaḥû*
          "[Saul] bowed with his face to the earth and did obeisance."

It would appear that as David bowed down before Saul, the one who by now ought to be dead, so Saul now bows down before Samuel, the one who is really dead.

8. Although in chap. 28 Saul's death is mentioned, while in chaps. 2–3 Eli's death is never brought up, still both occur in conjunction with serious defeats of Israel by the Philistines in which all five sons are slain in battle (4:11; 31:2). But the fathers die in separate fashion: Eli falls and breaks his neck when informed of the bad news, and Sauls falls upon his sword to avoid disgrace at the hands of the Philistines.

9. There is no need to remark here on the ancient unity of 1 and 2 Samuel: I refer to "the end of the book" only in a descriptive way, to indicate a certain part of the text. Needless to say, the death of Saul provides a natural break in the story and helps to explain why later hands separated the longer text at this point.

10. There are some additional contrasts in the way food functions at the beginning and end of the book. When Hannah-Israel could not yet have a child (that is, a king), "she would not eat" (1:17); when Saul finds out that he and his sons would die (that is, the end of a dynastic house), "he refused and said, 'I will not eat'" (28:23). And the "morsel of bread" that Eli's survivors implore from his successors (2:36) contrasts notably with the morsel of bread Saul refuses from the woman of Endor.

11. On the distinction between being taken captive, *nišbāh*, and going into exile, *gālah*, see S. R. Driver, *Notes on the Hebrew Text and Topography of the Books of Samuel* (Oxford: Clarendon, 1913), pp. 221–22, who points out, "Though they may be often applied to the same transaction, they denote different aspects of it" (p. 221).

12. The reader will remember that in chap. 15 God intended to punish Amalek for opposing Israel when it came up out of Egypt. Here in chap. 30, a young Egyptian is the ironic cause of Amalek's further defeat by Israel. David Gunn perceptively points out how David's confrontation with the Amalekites in chap. 30 contains a number of pointed contrasts to Saul's disastrous experience in chap. 15, *Fate of King Saul*, pp. 110–11. On this point see also Fokkelman, *Narrative Art*, vol. 1, p. 589.

13. S. R. Driver points out that *yārad* in v. 4 signifies the Israelite point of view even though Achish is the one speaking; in v. 6 it is Achish the Philistine who also swears by the LORD in v. 6. In v. 9, with *ya'aleh*, "the Philistines speak from the point of view which would be natural to them, when they were invading the high central ground of Canaan" (*Notes on the Hebrew Text*, pp. 219–20).

14. Notice that the reference in 31:7, "on the other side of the Jordan," is to be taken quite literally (so S. R. Driver, *Notes on the Hebrew Text*, p. 229) and indicates how thoroughgoing the Philistine victory was. Such details help to show how appropriately this event can foreshadow the end of the history even as it centers on the death of Saul.

15. Jobling, *The Sense of Biblical Narrative*, vol. 2 (Sheffield: Almond Press, 1986), pp. 44–87. As I mentioned in a previous chapter, my view differs from Jobling's in that the foreshadowing account and the account foreshadowed are, in my opinion, *both* profoundly condemnatory of kingship's evils.

16. Fokkelman writes, "The narrator has given his character Saul a dignified and even heroic death by this text 1 Sam 31 . . . [Saul] did not shrink from killing himself" (*Narrative Art*, vol. 2, p. 630). I wonder whether suicide would have been considered "heroic" to an Israelite reader. Suicide appears such an abhorrent practice, I suggest, that it approaches the unthinkable in Israelite ideology. How else, for example, can one explain the complete absence of this practice from discussion in the long speeches of Job and his four friends? Whether good or bad in varying circumstances, why is it *unsayable* in Job's?

Subject Index

(Hebrew words beginning with 'aleph and 'ayin appear at the beginning of the index.)

Scripture Index

ROBERT POLZIN is Director, School of Comparative Literary Studies and Professor of Religion at Carleton University. He is the author of *David and the Deuteronomist* and *Moses and the Deuteronomist,* both volumes in his series on the Deuteronomic History, as well as *Late Biblical Hebrew.* With Herbert Marks, Polzin is the general editor of the series Indiana Studies in Biblical Literature.